Reading
the Family Dance

Reading
the Family Dance

Family Systems Therapy
and Literary Study

Edited by

John V. Knapp and
Kenneth Womack

DELAWARE

Newark: University of Delaware Press
London: Associated University Presses

Associated University Presses
2010 Eastpark Boulevard
Cranbury, NJ 08512

Associated University Presses
Unit 304
The Chandlery
50 Westminster Bridge Road
London SE1 7Q4, England

Associated University Presses
P.O. Box 338, Port Credit
Mississauga, Ontario
Canada L5G 4L8

The paper used in this publication meets the requirements of the American National Standard for Permanence of Paper for Printed Library Materials Z39.48-1984.

Library of Congress Cataloging-in-Publication Data

Reading the family dance : family systems therapy and literary study / edited by John V. Knapp and Kenneth Womack.
    p. cm.
    Includes bibliographical references and index.
    ISBN 0-87413-823-X (alk. paper)
    1. Family in literature. 2. Literature, Modern—20th century—History and criticism. 3. American literature—20th century—History and criticism. 4. English literature—20th century—History and criticism. 5. Systemic therapy (Family therapy) 1. Knapp, John V., 1940– II. Womack, Kenneth.
  PN56.F3 R43 2003
  809′.93355—dc21
                                         2002152984

PRINTED IN THE UNITED STATES OF AMERICA

John V. Knapp would like to dedicate his work
on *Reading the Family Dance*
to his wife Joan
and his daughters Margaret, Lara, Joanna, and Jennifer.

Kenneth Womack would like to dedicate his work
on this volume
to the people who have taught him the meaning
and value of "family":
his father Fred, his brother Andrew, and his wife Andrea.

Contents

Part III: The World: Reading Family Systems in extremis

Acknowledgments

JOHN V. KNAPP AND KEN WOMACK WOULD LIKE TO THANK DONALD C. Mell, Christine A. Retz, Karen G. Druliner, and the anonymous reviewers from the University of Delaware Press for their sage advice. The editors would also like to thank their friends and colleagues at Northern Illinois University and Penn State Altoona, respectively, for their support.

John V. Knapp would like to thank his co-editor, Ken Womack, who has been a pleasure to work with, and to the many contributors to this volume, each of whom brings an interesting and fresh perspective to the texts examined. John V. Knapp would also like to acknowledge the love and support of his entire family, including his wife and companion, Joan Schwarz; his four beautiful daughters—Margaret A. Knapp, Lara M. Cantuti (son-in-law, Eric), Joanna Haskin, Jennifer Schmeiser (son-in-law, Brian, and the most recent family addition: Abigail Joy Schmeiser)—his sisters, Shirley Carroll and Janet Discenza, and their families; his late in-laws, Ed and Ida Schwarz; and the founders of his own family-of-origin, his late parents, Victor and Anna Knapp.

Ken Womack would like to acknowledge the many people who worked behind the scenes to see this volume through its production, including Carole Bookhamer, Todd Davis, James Decker, Lee Ann De Reus, Matt Masucci, and Michael Wolfe.

Reading
the Family Dance

Family Systems Therapy and Literary Study: An Introduction

John V. Knapp

As fast as thou shalt wane, so fast thou grow'st,
In one of thine, from that which thou departest,
And that fresh blood which youngly thou bestow'st
Thou mayst call thine, when thou from youth convertest.
Herein lives wisdom, beauty, and increase,
Without this, folly, age, and cold decay.

—Shakespeare, Sonnet 11

This could be the start of something big!

—Steve Allen

I

IN APRIL OF 1998, KENNETH WOMACK AND I EDITED A SPECIAL ISSUE OF *Style* (31.2) entitled "Family Systems Psychotherapy and Literature/Literary Criticism." Although several individuals had published essays or book chapters developed, more or less, from what we now call a family systems therapy (or FST) perspective, this issue of *Style* was the first attempt at consolidating a number of divergent FST-oriented critical essays in a single volume.[1] Perhaps more importantly, this issue demonstrated exactly how wide ranging the several FST models could be for literary study.

Our hope then was that the *Style* volume would tempt the critical appetites of other literary scholars into sampling the fascinating wares inside. The response has been gratifying. Many individuals—literary academics, critics, students of literature, and family therapists—have composed a variety of practical analyses of literary works from this social-psychological perspective. As the new kid on the literary criticism block, FST has also generated much interest, theoretically, in those scholars employing psychological literary theory—as may be seen in the diver-

13

sity of contributors to this volume—as well as with practicing therapists.

Hence, this book is our collective answer to the many literary critics seeking a volume that demonstrates the breadth of FST's theoretical possibilities. Indeed, at least one school of criticism, evolutionary psychology, contends that "the absence of a theory of human nature in literary criticism is one of its major weaknesses."[2] Steven Ozment's controversial and well-known theories of childhood and family life in earlier centuries suggest that literatures past and present can be usefully reexamined from a perspective other than psychoanalytically based modes of description.[3] While FST does not intend to recommend itself as a totalistic pan-theory, it does offer an alternative view of the human condition, one that many critics continue to find productive and revelatory. At the conclusion of this introduction, I will briefly detail each author's specific contribution. Before doing that, however, it would be helpful to explain to those unfamiliar with family systems therapy the basic concepts and working assumptions that comprise this social-psychological therapy, one that clearly has emerged as a useful tool for reading works of literature.

II

Those of you who belong to literature departments may have asked yourselves, as I have asked myself, why is it that the construction of an argument in our discipline so often relies on using "naïve realism" as a negative or scapegoat that a given author, text, period, or genre can be shown to rise sophisticatedly and self-consciously above. . . . Realism is not any old subject for criticism; it's what we have told ourselves we exist by not being. . . . Every time a text is triumphantly shown to transcend realism, therefore, the demonstration is only partly about the text; it is also a pious exercise in disciplinary self-corroboration, a demonstration that the discipline of literary criticism is justified in its distinctness and autonomy. [Yet the] issue is not between representation and nonrepresentation . . . but between differing representations. . . . If the project of realism can be conceived as . . . community building in this shared but unequally shared space, then there's still plenty for it to do.[4]

Family as Matrix of Identity

From the point of view of family systems psychotherapy, the family system becomes the source of the matrix of identity, rather than only the individual character.[5] Thus, the "causes" of a given problem in growing up (and beyond) in fictional and real families is much less the person construct or single event, and more the emotional process that links people and events.[6] The whole is greater than the sum of its parts (the principle of *emergence*),[7] so that to understand a member(s) of a fictional family, one needs to understand the family system—the "biological" family or step-family.[8] In actual therapeutic (and presumably, literary critical) practice, one always notes an unresolvable and fluctuating tension between the representations of the individual (biological) self ("hard reality") and the living system to which that self belongs, the family network ("soft or cultural reality"). It is important, therefore, when looking at an *emergent* family system not to fall into the other extremity, "holistic reductionism," which leaves the represented person (and his/her ethical responsibilities) out of the system.[9]

Family as Coevolutionary Ecosystem

Secondly, families are said to represent a *coevolutionary ecosystem*.[10] Within the family system, each member is said to help determine the conditions for the development of all the other family members. For the family as a unit, the surrounding sociocultural system forms the coevolutionary ecosystem. 1) Individual, 2) family, and 3) social environment (work, church, school, clubs, etc.) represent a complex, close-knit, three-tiered feedback system with each of its units belonging to a different "logical" type (i.e., a unit of a lower order is an element of a unit of a higher order.[11]

Shlomo Ariel has noted the difficulties of generalizing from a given family to its surrounding culture and vice versa since "culture is notoriously difficult to define." He suggests that the best way to proceed is to define the cultural world surrounding a specific family "as a system possessing the same properties and obeying the same laws as the family system." Furthermore, he suggests that the "coping mechanisms employed by families are at least partly dictated by the specific cultures to which they belong."[12] Of course, in literature (and film), among the more interesting situations readers respond to are those times when fictional families feel the tugs and stresses of two juxtaposed cultural systems, particularly when intergenerational or intrafamilial conflict arises from their differing cultural codes. As Ariel observes:

In immigration countries such as Israel and the United States, there are many intermarriages in which the wife comes from an individualistic cultural community and the husband from a traditional collectivist cultural community. Such marriages are often characterized by a coalition of the parents and their son against the wife and blurred boundaries between the husband and his family of origin . . . [a situation thought] dysfunctional . . . in the theory of structural family therapy [but] normative in the husband's culture.[13]

Whatever the cultural ratios, one of the most significant familial tasks is to provide support for both the person's *integration* into a solid family unit and his/her *differentiation* into relatively independent selves—to think, act, and feel for oneself.[14] This mutual process is life-long, as members of one's primary group change from family-of-origin to one's created (married, cohabitating, close-knit intimates) family. Such development is somewhat different for males and females,[15] and often widely divergent in different cultures.[16] In functional families, each member develops a *solid self*, able to act, think, and feel so that the inside and outside of the self are usually congruent.[17] In dysfunctional families, fear and anxiety usually force members to create a *pseudo-self*, so that one's inner feelings and outer behavior are often *not congruent*. Hence, Virginia Satir believes, in contrast with Freudian thinking, that sex is *not* the basic drive of man; rather, "the sex drive is continually subordinated to and used for the purpose of enhancing self-esteem and defending against threats of self-esteem."[18]

Family Hierarchy

All families have *subsystems*: a) spouse-spouse (at the top of the *hierarchy*); b) parent-child; c) sibling-sibling.[19] Maintenance of *boundaries* between various subsystems may range from rigid to diffuse, although the parent's boundary from children is clearly separated by sexuality and responsibility.[20] The original pair-bond (spouse-spouse) forms a *dyad*; dyads are thought to be inherently unstable as each member of the pair-bond seeks to develop a new self who is now part of a larger entity. During the inevitable pushes and pulls to establish a balance between intimacy and self-independence, the pair-bond can become unstable, calling in a third entity (child, parent, friend, lover, career, etc.) in order to reduce the tension and establish an equilibrium, even though this is often done at the considerable personal expense of the third party. The "Milan School" has developed a systematic "paradox and counter paradox" approach to help resolve family difficulties when the third entity is one of the family's children. As Mara Selvini Palazzoli, et al. has theorized, "this implies relationally redefining the symptoms in terms of a protective-sacrificial conduct the patient is said to be enacting for the benefit of someone else in the family."[21]

With this third entity the pair then form a *triangle*, and the original relationship is thus said to be *triangulated*, where one or the other spouse may be *enmeshed* (overly involved) with, say, the child while the other is *disengaged* or uninvolved.[22] *Parentification* may occur when a child assumes or is assigned a parental role (e.g., primary emotional bonding or primary breadwinner tasks.[23] Usually, this third element reduces intimacy even though both of the original partners yearn for their former mutual intimacy—but each on his/her own terms. Not only are there problems, therefore, between spouses when the third element is a child, but among siblings as well.[24]

Family Niches

According to Frank J. Sulloway, brothers and sisters vie with one another to establish what he calls a favorable "*family niche.*" Sulloway claims that the "longer siblings live with one another, the more different they become," and that such differences exemplify what Darwin referred to as the "principle of divergence. Throughout organic nature, *diversity* is a useful strategy that allows species to compete for scare resources."[25] In addition, sexual reproduction not only "halves the genetic contribution of each parent" to a given child, but it also "rearranges the sequence of genes through a process called *recombination.* . . . For this reason, many genetic influences are unique to the individual and cannot be passed on through inheritance. Such traits are said to be *emergent.*"[26] Consequently, as children grow up,

> they undergo *adaptive radiation* ("multiple forms that diverge in character") in their effort to establish their own *individual niches* within the family. By pursuing disparate interests and abilities, siblings minimize direct competition. . . . From a Darwinian point of view, personality is the repertoire of strategies that each individual develops to survive childhood. The bulk of these strategies are *sibling* strategies . . . [seeking] to maximize parental investment.[27]

Because siblings "are so different, they engage in frequent social comparisons. . . . Younger siblings are especially sensitive to adverse comparisons with their older siblings" and so are "drawn to interests and activities that older siblings have not already cultivated." As a consequence, "dramatic differences" among siblings "are commonplace. They arise because siblings cultivate distinct *niches* within the family."[28] Niche creation may, however, be conflicted and could give rise to rebellion and secrets to cover it.

Family Secrets

The effects of secrets on the family system is often devastating because it introduces distortion at the fact-gathering level (Imber-Black). For example: A tells B something about C; B's feelings, thoughts, behavior, theoretizing about C are all based on information obtained about C but B is asked to keep it a secret. When this information is incorrect or a lie, and B is bound to secrecy, B cannot check out information about C. Secrets help maintain illusions and prevent evidence contrary to one's fixed perception. B cannot do anything to change relationship with C.

Homeostatic Balance vs. Morphogenesis in the Family Life Cycle

In the vocabulary of early cybernetic theory, families are said to maintain homeostatic balance through *constancy loops*. Family change occurs through variety loops. *Homeostatic* balance is the equilibrium in the system. The family is an *open system* and yet has limitations on its openness.[29] *Morphogenesis* is a deviation from the usual balance in all relationships in the system.[30] Life events in families, such as the children growing up and, at least initially, rejecting some or all parental values introduces change in habitual family expectations. Not all unsettling changes, however, are ultimately negative. Indeed, in a dysfunctional family, *morphogenesis* is the risk families must take: change or die (divorce) because *homeostasis* is far stronger in families than morphogenesis. Once a pattern (e.g., a triangle) is set in motion, it may last the lifetime of the members involved.[31]

Any change in the system affects all members. Families (as well as individuals) undergo a *life cycle* (courtship, marriage, first child, subsequent children, career moves [choices], illnesses, leaving the nest, aging, and death of spouse, sibling), and families are said to have *developmental tasks* appropriate to a given stage in the life cycle as they evolve over time.[32] For example, with the birth of the first child, the dyad (spouse-spouse) must overnight become a triad; each parent must now relate to the child both separately and as a pair-bond, and must as well adjust to the inclusion of the child's needs into the spouse's availability and interest in the other spouse. Carl Whitaker thinks of marriages with words like "engagement," "involvement," and "locked in together." He says that it "is ordinarily a lessening of 'engagement' in a marriage that leads to a *provocative* act by one partner or the other."[33]

Transactional Conversation Rules

All family interaction is governed by *transactional rules*; if A does X, B will counter with X2 or Y; A then responds to B's response, and vice versa. Thus, family behavior is an adjustive process where cues are given and individual members respond to those stimuli. These rules are largely unspoken, circular, and oftentimes, endless. Understanding events in a family is best understood by a cyclical model of causality (A>B>C>A>, . . .). *Punctuation* is an attempt by individuals to divide cyclic processes into beginnings, middles, and ends (e.g., Mom to squabbling children: "Who started it?" Children: "He did it! She did it!"—with everyone pointing to one another like Haldeman, Erlichman, Mitchell, and Dean of Watergate fame).

Ultimate cues for action are understood through *metacommunication*, which serves to mark the *context* of a communications act. Metacommunication could be called communication or information about the act of communication itself, and may take almost any communicative and sometimes nonverbal form: eyerolling, shrugs, tonal qualities, and facial gestures. The "simultaneous transmission of mutually exclusive messages and behavioral imperatives on the level of communication and metacommunication" is called the *"double bind."*[34] Schizophrenic children of parents who simultaneously hugged them and pushed them away to keep from getting too close were victims, in Bateson's view, of the double bind. Much of Bateson's work was, however, built on early theories of schizophrenia, before the mental disorder's genetic and biochemical origins were better understood.[35]

Family Themes and Myths

Families and individual family members are influenced by *themes* that are present in the preceding generation and are transmitted from one generation to the next through narratives, family stories, assumptions of "correct" behavior, etc. (e.g., we are survivors; or in our family, we never fight; therefore, we better not talk about the problem). William Randall suggests that the family is a "collection of stories—however differently compiled and told by different family members—through which each of us sees ourselves, interprets others, and makes sense of our world. It is a repertoire of 'forms of self-telling' by which we each transform our existence into experience."[36]

Another view sees some themes as becoming family myths. According to one FST theorist, family myths may be categorized as follows: 1) *myths of harmony* (rosy pictures of a family's past and present life); 2) *myths of forgiveness and atonement* (often one family member is made solely responsible for the family's predicament; scapegoat); 3) *rescue myths* ([subset of number 2] a person outside the family is attributed magical powers and regarded as the savior and benefactor, or one person is expected to achieve life goals not possible for grandparents, parents, or siblings).[37]

The interactive and circular quality of family behavior has led FST theorists to posit the principle of *equifinality* (many "causes" can result in the same "effect"; the same "cause" can result in different "effects"). Equifinality applies to development within family processes since it is impossible to make deterministic predictions about family or human development. This element of the general FST theory has been under attack by many, including some feminist theorists, because it appears to do away with the issues of time, history, and responsibility. By focusing on the "here and now," some FST practitioners have tended to minimize family history and individual responsibility from the past.[38] More recently, many FST practitioners have tried to integrate knowledge of previous actions within the family and plans for solving contemporary familial issues. Indeed, James Framo contends that "hidden transgenerational forces exercise critical influence on current intimate relationships."[39]

III

Today, individuals from many disciplines practice family therapy and thus continue to debate theory, the definition of marriage and family therapy, and who represents the field professionally.[40]

The four essays in part I of this volume, "The Self: Family Systems Therapy and the Quest for Identity," each look at select characters' searches for identity while still enmeshed in family life. Although FST is concerned primarily with an individual's evolution in a group structure—particularly the person in the family—it suggests that the individual's life-long identity development begins with twin motives: a departure from family-of-origin values and assumptions, as well as a grounding in, and often uneasy allegiance to, those same qualities. Consequently, mimetic characters (and persons) individuate as they emerge over time while, simultaneously, both retaining and developing intimate connections. Recent clinical and historical work (see Ariel; Kegan; O'Day; Ozment) suggests that the twin needs of most human beings—the need for agency and self-direction and the need for affliation and connectedness—are not mutually exclusive by any means, in spite of a Western (read American) cultural tradition that often forces its heroes and heroines to conclude that they are. The essays here suggest otherwise.

In that regard, Kenneth Womack's essay, "Lucy Honeychurch's Rage for Selfhood: Family Systems Therapy, Ethics, and E. M. Foster's *A Room with a View*," shows us a heroine who rejects such forced binary choices and opts instead for personalized growth through a ratio of evolving balances. Womack demonstrates the ways in which Lucy remains unable to evolve fully as an individual, remaining too dependent on others for life choices that must ultimately be hers. Rosemary Babcock's "The Enigmatic Jane Eyre: A Differentiation Story without Family in Charlotte Brontë's *Jane Eyre*," moves the reader into considering the fourth wave of feminist criticism regarding this novel. Babcock demonstrates how Jane and Rochester reject the earlier Gilbert and Gubar marriage plot requiring the couple to take on the roles of oppressed/oppressor or dominant/submissive. Rather, Babcock's Jane marries Rochester because she (and he) can retain both their independence and their connectedness to the ones they love. Gary Storhoff's "Even Now China Wraps Double Binds around My Feet: Family Communication in *The Woman Warrior* and *Dim Sum*" demonstrates the difficulty that people have in negotiating these balances when individual and family interact with both the ancient traditions of the Chinese home country and the promises and conflicts of their emergence into the new Chinese-American culture. Lee Ann De Reus's reading of Barbara Kingsolver's *Animal Dreams* identifies the processes by which Codi Noline—one of the children of an emotionally absent father and a mother who dies when Codi is three—begins, as an adult, to establish a mature sense of self. Drawing upon the identity theories of Erik Erikson and James Marcia, De Reus illuminates Codi's emotional evolution over the course of the novel.

In part II, the essayists examine characters whose ability to define the self is circumscribed by family life that does not so much nurture their growth as place obstacles to it for the sake of the whole. These roadblocks are often (and tragically) set as much out of love and family protectiveness as for negative reasons. In Joan I. Schwarz's "Family Dynamics and Property Acquisitions in *Clarissa*," the much-discussed heroine is victimized more by her own family's desire to defend family values and to expand the family estate as by the bounder, Lovelace. Schwarz's extensive understanding of eighteenth-century British inheritance law combines with family systems to move the center of critical discussion away from the outside abductor of the young Clarissa and back toward the internal workings of her family life. Steven Snyder's "Circular Ties: A Family Systems Reading of A. S. Byatt's *The Game*" focuses on the tragedy of sibling rivalry as each sister tries but fails to understand the other's needs for an appropriate balance of family love and independence. Snyder then discusses the siblings' mimetic conflicts with Byatt's interest in the romantic aesthetics of circular fictional design and structure. In "The Family Dynamics of Toni Morrison's *The Bluest Eye*," Jerome Bump looks at Morrison's African-American families and their growing awareness of what is problematic in both judging and being judged by physical appearances. Sara Cooper's "Forging a Family Discourse in Marilene Felinto's *The Women of Tijucopapo*" takes the average North American and European reader into the relatively unfamiliar world of Latin American (in this case, Brazilian) women writers. Cooper explores the growth of Felinto's character Risa, a child of the slums, who finds a "family" among the independent "women of Tijucopapo," or in Portuguese, the *Mulheres de Tijucopapo*. Cooper skillfully discusses how FST can be applied even to a novel dominated by a first-person narrative voice. Finally, in my own "Family Games and Imbroglio in *Hamlet*," I use game theory from the Milan School of FST to reconsider several characterological issues in literature's best known dysfunctional family, where sibling rivalry, parent-child coalitions, and spousal betrayal point to why Shakespeare thought that something really was rotten in Denmark.

The four essays in part III examine the family *in extremis.* Todd Davis's "Crusading for the Family: Kurt Vonnegut's Ethics of Familial Community" explores the relationships between the author's own family history and the fictions that Vonnegut has created. James M. Decker's "Hollywood Exiles: Nathanael West's *The Day of the Locust* and Family Systems Therapy" tries to understand the possibility of family life in perhaps one of the most unusual communities on earth—Hollywood, California. Marco Malaspina's "Are Happy Families All Alike: The Strange Case of Dr. Petruchio and Ms. Katherine" argues that, contrasted to the protagonist's unhappy experiences with her family-of-origin, Kate finds in Petruchio both emotional acceptance and an unusual means of retaining her feisty independence. Finally, Denis Jonnes combines the cultural and political history of America in the 1950s with family systems in order to provide new readings of the major short stories of Flannery O'Connor. Jonnes focuses on paradigmatic O'Connor narratives as he explores the intersections between apparently unusual family dynamics and O'Connor's vision of the postwar American South.

NOTES

1. See Bump, "Family Dynamics of the Reception of Art;" Cohen, *Daughter's Dilemma,* Jonnes, *Matrix of Narrative,* Knapp, *Literary Character* and *Striking at the Joints;* and Womack, "Only Connecting," "Passage to Italy," and "Unmasking Another Villain."

2. See Jobling, "Personal Justice and Homicide in Scott's *Ivanhoe*: An Evolutionary Psychological Perspective," *Interdisciplinary Literary Studies* 2.2 (2001): 29–43.

3. See Ozment, *Ancestors.* See also Aries, *Centuries of Childhood;* Stone, *Family, Sex and Marriage in England;* and DeMause, *History of Childhood.*

4. Robbins, "Modernism and Literary Realism."

5. Since character constructs in literature are based, whole or in part, on representations of living systems, authors may be said to reproduce the only evidence possible in their fictions: aesthetic reconstructions, rearranged in part or whole, of lived (or living) people. Of course, as constructs, literary characters may be deployed for many other reasons as well, aesthetic, generic, and political; the most widely discussed works of literature emphasize the tensions and interactions among these and representational demands. From an FST perspective, representations of family in the lives of human beings are the prism through which critics focus in literary analysis.

Put a bit differently, the family as well as the individual, is a living system, and, according to Palazzoli, Boscolo, Cecchin, and Prata's *Paradox and Counterparadox,* every living system "has three fundamental characteristics: 1) *totality* (the system is largely independent of the elements which make it up"; hence the family *emerges* out of the collection of individuals comprising its system); "2) *autocorrective capacity*, and therefore the tendency toward homeostasis; families are self-regulating systems possessing the critical property of *negative entropy*: i.e., families can acquire energy from their environment to organize and maintain functioning; 3) *capacity for transformation*" (56).

In more abstract and mathematical terms, Ludwig von Bertalanffy's *General Systems Theory* defines a system as "a set of differential equations with the property that information about the state of the system influence(s) the system's rate of change." Applying human applications to von Bertalanffy's ideas, Jeffery Vancouver's "Living Systems Theory" has discussed what he calls Living Systems Theory (LST). LST is a paradigm in organizational science that 1) "provides a framework for describing the micro (i.e., human), macro (social organizations), and meso (interaction between the two) levels of the field without relying on reductionism or reification. The more parsimoniously it can do this, the better"; 2) "provide(s) a model of the major processes of dynamic interaction between individuals, situations, and behavior to address the major phenomenon of the field like behavior, cognition, and affect"; and 3) provide(s) researchers with [interesting] research ideas" (165).

6. Minuchin and Nichols, *Family Healing*, 112.

7. *Emergence*: In *Growth of Biological Thought* the evolutionary biologist Ernst Mayr points out that both living and nonliving systems "almost always have the property that the characteristics of the whole cannot (not even in theory) be deduced from the most complete knowledge of the components, taken separately or in other partial combination." This appearance of novel properties in whole systems "has often been evoked to explain such difficult biological realities as mind, consciousness, and even life itself. . . . Perhaps the two most interesting characteristics of new wholes are that 1) they, in turn, can be become parts of still higher-level systems; and 2) that wholes can affect properties of components at lower levels." This latter phenomenon is sometimes referred to as 'downward causation' and is particularly useful in understanding family systems. However, for Mayr, explanatory *reduction* alone is simply incomplete, "since new and previously unpredictable characters emerge at higher levels of complexity in hierarchal systems" (65). Obviously, this is one of the fundamental guiding principles of FST; in *Dancing with the Family* Whitaker and Bumberry observe that the self "emerges" into a family, and the family and the selves making up that family possess properties no one individual alone can contain (60).

A simple demonstration about *emergence*: take a fertilized human egg, cut it in half, and what do you get after nine months? Normally, twins! Take these same twins, cut one of them in half, and what do you get? Arrested for murder! Left alive, these twins remain separate but genetically very similar living systems inside another living system called their family. Conversely, no practitioner of FST forgets that the family is also made up of independent (but simultaneously interdependent) selves and that the therapist must sometimes *reduce* his/her attention to one or more of those individuals. Most FST practitioners thus move up and down what I have elsewhere called the "snakes and ladders of abstraction," switching between emergence and reduction as the therapeutic need arises. Hence, reduction—in therapy, literary criticism, and in psychological research—is a necessary *complement* to emergence.

8. Minuchin and Nichols, *Family Healing*, 63; Visher and Visher, *Therapy with Stepfamilies*, 34–39. Obviously, there will be certain cultural differences in the structure and dynamics of families across the world. As the internet and

satellite TV make once-exotic family constellations more familiar, so then must FST-oriented literary criticism expand to include what was once the other. In this volume, we have acknowledged some of these differences by looking at Asian-American (Storhoff), African-American (Bump), and South American (Cooper) representations of family life as well as North American and Western European family structures. Even among the latter, there are often major differences; see, for example, the contrasts in families between those of the North and South of France. See Todd, *Making of Modern France*, 10–26.

9. See Dell and Goolishian, "Order Through Fluctuation;" and Palazzoli, Cirillo, Selvini, and Sorrentino, *Family Games*, 260, 289.

10. See Churchman, *Systems Approach;* and Bateson, *Steps Toward an Ecology of Mind.*

11. See Mayr, *Growth of Biological Thought.*

12. Ariel, *Culturally Competent Family Therapy*, 8–9.

13. Ibid., 13.

14. See Bowen, *Family Therapy in Clinical Practice;* Kegan, *Evolving Self* and *In Over Our Heads;* and Ozment, 73.

15. See Ben-Amos, "Gifts and Favors" and "Reciprocal Bonding, see also Haley, *Uncommon Therapy,* 40.

16. Ariel, *Culturally Competent Family Therapy*, 61; 158–61.

17. Clearly, the debts owed to psychoanalytic thinkers like D. W. Winnicott in such works as *The Maturational Process and the Facilitating Environment* is here apparent. His distinction between "true" and "false" selves has its echo in Bowen's *Family Therapy in Clinical Practice* as "solid" vs. "pseudo-selves." One of the major differences between FST and psychoanalysis (read psychoanalytic literary criticism) is that the former clearly acknowledges its roots in early psychoanalytic practice (after all, FST grew out of dissatisfaction with individual psychoanalytic therapy) and, not surprisingly, has come to use some of its vocabulary, albeit for its own differing reasons.

18. Satir, *Conjoint Family Therapy*, 55.

19. Simon, Stierlin, and Wynne, *Language of Family Therapy*, 183–85.

20. Minuchin, Lee, and Simon, *Mastering Family Therapy*, 226–27. Minuchin, et al. suggest that cultural differences play an important part in deciding where such boundaries form. For example, in working with African-American families, the therapist "may need to explore the extended family. The importance of the kin network may stretch all the way back to African roots as well as laterally into the contemporary necessity of coping with poverty and racism. But a Black family that has attained middle-class status may be facing a stressful choice between helping the extended family or disconnecting [in that way] from them" (24). Ariel also suggests that boundaries are more subjective, and are often related to "the question to what extent the family tolerates individual pecularity and deviance and [even] whether it sees individuation as legitimate"—a concept "difficult to convey in Japanese culture," for example (*Culturally Competent Family Therapy*, 60).

21. Palazzoli, Boscolo, Cecchin, and Prata, *Paradox and Counterparadox*, 7.

22. Imber-Black, *Secrets in Families and Family Therapy*, 64–66. Palazzoli, Boscolo, Cecchin, and Prata, *Paradox and Counterparadox*, 143–48.

23. Boszormenyi-Nagy and Framo, *Intensive Family Therapy*, 143–212.

24. Demo and Cox, "Families with Young Children," 884–85.

25. Sulloway, *Born to Rebel*, 83, 85.

26. Ibid., 87.

27. Ibid., 85–86.

28. Ibid., 93, 95.

29. Simon, Stierlin, and Wynne, *Language of Family Therapy*, 81–82.

30. In more technical terms, according to William T. Powers's *Behavior, morphogenesis* is the positive feedback loop. *Positive feedback*: a feedback situation in which a disturbance acting on any variable in a feedback loop gives rise to an effect at the point of disturbance that aids the effect of the disturbance. *Homeostasis* or *negative feedback*: in this situation, a disturbance acting on any variable in the feedback loop gives rise to an effect at the point of disturbance which opposes the effect of the disturbance (285–86).

31. See Minuchin, *Families and Family Therapy*, and Bowen, *Family Therapy in Clinical Practice*.

32. See Boscolo and Bertrando, "Reflexive Loop of Past, Present, and Future;" see also Kegan, *Evolving Self*.

33. Whitaker and Bumberry, *Dancing with the Family*, 197.

34. See Bateson, *Toward an Ecology of Mind*; and Simon, Stierlin, and Wynne, *Language of Family Therapy*, 223.

35. See Goodwin and Jamison, *Manic-Depressive Illness*, 96–123; Salzinger, "Road from Vulnerability to Episode," and Subotnick and Nuechterlein, "Prodromal Signs and Symptoms of Schizophrenia Relapse.'

36. Randall, *Stories We Are*, 196.

37. Simon, Stierlin, and Wynne, *Language of Family Therapy*, 133.

38. Palazzoli, Cirillo, Selvini, and Sorrentino, *Family Games*, 159–60.

39. Framo, "Personal Retrospective," 299.

40. Fred P. Piercy, Douglas H. Sprenkle, Joseph L. Wetchler, and Associates. *Family Therapy Sourcebook*.

Part I
The Self: Family Systems Therapy and the Quest for Identity

Lucy Honeychurch's Rage for Selfhood: Family Systems Therapy, Ethics, and E. M. Forster's *A Room with a View*

Kenneth Womack

"Why will men have theories about women? I haven't any about men."
—Lucy Honeychurch

As an exemplar of the female *BILDUNGSROMAN*, E. M. FORSTER'S *A Room with a View* (1908) traces Lucy Honeychurch's social and intellectual development from her experiences as a young woman in the throes of late adolescence who merely encounters life to her transformation into adulthood when she finally hungers for all of the meaningful artistic and interpersonal possibilities that living entails. The terminology of family systems therapy offers a particularly useful means for explicating Forster's illustrations of the novel's ethical and developmental implications. The family systems paradigm also provides a powerful interdisciplinary mechanism with which to examine Forster's philosophical debt in *A Room with a View* to *Principia Ethica* (1902), G. E. Moore's Bloomsbury-era manifesto on the social and ethical rewards of friendship and aesthetic experience. Lucy's belated recognition of the values inherent in life's interpersonal and artistic possibilities illustrates her passage from late adolescence into a fully realized sense of selfhood.

Yet in dramatic contrast with such classic female *Bildungsromane* as Charlotte Brontë's *Jane Eyre* (1847), George Eliot's *The Mill on the Floss* (1860), Kate Chopin's *The Awakening* (1899), and Sylvia Plath's *The Bell Jar* (1963) in which young women discover new senses of self beyond the familial and other social systems in which they were reared, Lucy's interpersonal growth and self-development only come to fruition when she is acted upon by a host of other, largely male and matronly female characters who exert their wills and whims upon her emerging psyche. Perhaps even more significantly, Forster's coterie of characters often function as the de facto interpreters of Lucy's life experiences, as the people to whom she goes for counsel about the specific nature of her transformation from late adolescence into incipient adulthood. Quite obviously, *A Room with a View* hardly merits consideration, then, with the classic, more liberating *Bildungsromanae* by Brontë, Eliot, Chopin, Plath, and a host of other writers whose female protagonists discover greater senses of selfhood through their own unmediated experiences and, more importantly, on their own terms. Remarkably—and despite a host of critical examinations of *A Room with a View* as a model of the female *Bildungsroman*—scholars have neglected to consider Forster's decidedly *non*-feminist rendering of Lucy's progress toward adulthood and self-liberation.[1]

Lucy's principal dilemma, her inability to achieve selfhood on her own terms, is certainly not a new problem within the culture of young womanhood. As a number of contemporary family theorists including Monica McGoldrick, Carol Gilligan, and Jane Kroger have demonstrated, young women of the approximate age of Lucy—a largely reticent and endlessly deferring late teenager—are typically expected to differentiate themselves among confining and increasingly narrow spaces of social decorum and acceptability. In her insightful essay, "Women through the Family Life Cycle," Monica McGoldrick observes that "only very recently has female development been considered at all."[2] Developmentally, McGoldrick adds, "women have been expected from the point of early adulthood to 'stand behind their men,' to support and nurture their children, and paradoxically, to be able to live without affirmation and support themselves." In many instances, McGoldrick concludes, "the pressure on women not to take full advantage of independent living may be intense."[3] In short, many young women begin to lose interest in intellectual and artistic pursuits and find themselves forced to choose between being shunned for staying true to themselves or struggling to exist within society's—Forster's Edwardian society, as well as our own, ostensibly more enlightened one's—narrow definitions of femaleness. Carol Gilligan's *In a Different Voice* (1982) suggests an even more dangerous aspect regarding the onset and establishment of female selfhood. Our culture often understands and nurtures women, she argues, in terms of their places in the life cycles of their masculine others. Young women rarely experience genuine individuation themselves, Gilligan writes, because they tend to sacrifice personal autonomy in order to defer to male interpersonal needs. According to Gilligan, "The elusive mystery of women's development lies in its recognition of the continuing importance of attachment in the human life cycle. Woman's place in man's life cycle," she adds, "is to protect this recognition while the developmental litany intones the celebration of separation, autonomy, individuation, and natural rights."[4] As this essay will demonstrate, Lucy's Edwardian-era experiences are no different. Her moments of self-discovery occur almost entirely at the bidding of Forster's male characters, who explicate, and hence define, the nature and degree of her transformation into adulthood. Lucy's adult persona, then, results from the efforts of others to shape her identity, as opposed to originating from her own attempts at self-actualization. *Bildungsromane*, in the genre's most explicit definition, may be novels about growing up, but in many ways, *A Room with a View* is a novel about Lucy growing up at the cultural and institutional will of a patriarchal society that evinces little regard for her own notions of self-discovery and identity creation.

There is little question that *A Room with a View*—as with Forster's other novels, including most notably *Where Angels Fear to Tread* (1905) and *Howards End* (1910)—functions as the author's rather explicit attempt to adopt an ethical stance in terms of interpersonal relationships and the intellectual and artistic life of the mind. Scholars have clearly demonstrated Forster's appropriation of Moore's ethical sensibilities in his other fictions. *A Room with a View*, with its depiction of Lucy's transformation into adulthood in a world that valorizes the ethical properties of friendship and aesthetic experiences, is no different. In *Principia Ethica*, Moore's moral philosophy argues for the recognition of a variety of ideal states of human existence, especially regarding the quality of the interpersonal connection that human beings share. "The best ideal we can construct will be that state of things which contains the greatest number of things having positive value, and which contains nothing evil or indifferent," Moore writes, "*provided* that the presence of none of these goods, or the absence of things evil or indifferent, seems to diminish the value of the whole."[5] For Moore, this "value of the whole" concerns the nature of our relationships within the greater human communities in which we live. In terms of family systems psychotherapy, this state of affairs refers initially to the family, that human community with which we all begin our interpersonal lives, then the world outside of one's parents and siblings, the larger family dynamic that we encounter beyond our original family systems as we create our own lives. In addition to celebrating the virtues of courage and compassion in human interaction, Moore remarks that "by far the most valuable things, which we know or can imagine, are certain states of consciousness, which may be roughly described as the pleasures of human intercourse and the enjoyment of beautiful objects."[6] In this way, Moore's ethical schema underscores the significance of friendship and aesthetic experience as profound avenues toward the consummation of the "value of the whole."

When considered in terms of the tenets of family systems psychotherapy, Moore's moral philosophy offers a useful means for interpreting the construction of Lucy's personal identity in *A Room with a View*. Lucy clearly establishes her adult persona among a valued assemblage of friends and relations, and her well-developed esteem for art, literature, and music exists as a central aspect of her being. Yet Lucy's transformation into adulthood comes at a significant interpersonal cost that goes entirely unnoticed in Forster's novel. Her progress from adolescence to young womanhood occurs with all of the attendant difficulties and confusion that invariably accompany such transformative moments. For Lucy, though, such instances of interpersonal change and individuation are channeled through a host of other characters who act upon her, interpret her every experience, and thus shape her self-construction.[7] As Jane Kroger notes in *Identity in Adolescence: The Balance between Self and Other* (1996), these very same, often masculinized filters have always impinged upon the creation of female selfhood. Young women, simply put, often establish senses of self in relation to their male others, who act as the interpersonal mirrors via which they evaluate their appearances, their opinions, and the quality of the public manifestations of their selves. Kroger usefully refers to this latter moment in the female developmental cycle as the construction of a young woman's institutional self. "Transition to a new form of independence from the interpersonal is the hallmark of late adolescent and young adult identity. During such transformation," Kroger writes, "the individual must once again undergo the loss of an old balance; this time, it is one's relationships that become object to the new self, now embedded in its institutional or ideological formations."[8]

For Lucy, this transformative moment proves to be fraught with difficulty, confusion, and, at times, interpersonal trauma. This period of her transition from late adolescence into adulthood—the very same period that accounts for the entirety of *A*

Room with a View's narrative—depicts Forster's protagonist in the act of testing her ideas about life against the opinions of her (largely older, male) companions, as well as making very few genuine choices of her own. The choices that she does make herself invariably prove to be the incorrect ones—at least in terms of the opinions of her friends and relatives. Not surprisingly, her inability to assert her own sense of self—indeed, her inability to make her own mistakes from which to learn and grow—results in her near-epic series of lies that accounts for the final third of the novel. A systemic reading of her experiences in the novel—and, in particular, her various attempts at asserting herself both within and against the purview of her society—reveals the many ways in which the self that emerges at the conclusion of *A Room with a View* exists as the product of the institutional, cultural, and sociological forces that characterize her world. These various forces ultimately construct a version of "Lucy" that satisfies her cohort's vision of what her adult self *should* look like, as opposed to the individuated self that might result from Lucy's own—and in some instances, vastly different—needs and desires.

Lucy's progress toward adulthood begins, rather fortuitously, in Florence, which Forster's young protagonist visits in the stifling company of her cousin and chaperone, the inimitable Charlotte Bartlett. Given Forster's well-known penchant for the ethical philosophy inherent in Moore's elevation of friendship and aesthetic experience, Florence's magisterial environs would *seem* to be the consummate proving grounds for Lucy's locus of self-discovery. In *Where Angels Fear to Tread*, Forster underscores the Italian culture's valuation of community, art, and beauty as inalienable properties of human goodness. In many ways, *A Room with a View* is no different. Its Florentine setting depicts aesthetic beauty at nearly every turn—from the frescoes and old-world sensibilities of Santa Croce to the splendid natural ambiance of the Italian countryside. The novel similarly reveals the passionate nature of the Italian cultural persona, as evinced by the sudden eruption of a street fight in Florence to a carriage driver's unrestrained passion for his beloved. Yet Lucy can only experience these moments of aesthetic and interpersonal exhilaration through the filter of her traveling companions' rather narrow and exacting Edwardian sensibilities. Even Lucy's spirited approach to her piano playing—a repertoire that includes crashing musical waves of Schumann and Beethoven—falls under the critical gaze of her cohorts, many of whom clearly pine for her to adopt the more delicate melodies of Chopin that seem more befitting of proper English womanhood.

Lucy experiences Italy almost entirely from within a cocoon—an Edwardian social microcosm, if you will—that consists of her English companions, including the aforementioned cousin Charlotte, the spinsterly Misses Alan, the kindly Reverend Arthur Beebe, the conceited resident English chaplain Cuthbert Eager, the flamboyant novelist Eleanor Lavish, and the socially liberated Emersons—the father and son whose views serve to shape and reshape Lucy's persona throughout the novel. A number of critics have already noted Forster's fairly explicit ethical identification of those characters who can appreciate precisely what "a room with a view" entails and their counterparts for whom aesthetic experience has little, if any, residual value. In a similar fashion, readers can easily identify the ethical proclivities of Forster's characters by observing those travelers who require the exacting counsel of their *Baedeker* guidebooks at all times and those characters who prefer to experience foreign travel unburdened by a text that approaches Italy with all of the cultural baggage inherent in Western expectations and social propriety.[9] Clearly, such a schema affords us with a valuable means for differentiating between the characters who evince the potential for shaping Lucy's ethical sensibilities and those individuals who can only serve to undermine her personal growth because of their inability to appreciate the uplifting ethical power of aesthetic experience and human community. Quite obviously, Mr. Beebe and Mr. Emerson possess the capacity, at least in Forster's ethical schema, for positively shaping Lucy's adult persona, while Reverend Eager, with his calculated, passionless approach to art and humanity alike, would seem to be an unwelcome influence. For Reverend Eager, life exists entirely on an intellectual plane. Even his Italian pronunciation reveals his inability to shed his Edwardian sensibilities in favor of the more liberating mindset that Forster's Italy seems to offer: "Italian in the mouths of Italians is a deep-voiced stream, with unexpected cataracts and boulders to preserve it from monotony," Forster writes. "In Mr. Eager's mouth it resembled nothing so much as an acid whistling fountain which played ever higher and higher, and quicker and quicker, and more and more shrilly, till abruptly it was turned off with a click."[10]

Conversely, Mr. Beebe and Mr. Emerson appear to provide Lucy with the kind of ethical and more socially liberating counsel of which Forster implicitly seems to approve. Mr. Beebe, for example, knowingly recognizes Lucy's potential for living on a more aesthetic and spiritually rewarding plane of being. "If Miss Honeychurch ever takes to live as she plays," he predicts, "it will be very exciting—both for us and for her."[11] Despite his apparent regard for her potential for self-actualization, Mr. Beebe cannot help but later attribute Lucy's desire to go out alone among the Italians to "too much Beethoven."[12] Lucy also absorbs repeated counsel from Mr. Emerson—whose own Emersonian qualities appear to draw upon his well-known, albeit American, name-sake's valorization of self-reliance. As with Mr. Beebe and in sharp contrast with Reverend Eager, Mr. Emerson clearly enjoys Forster's authorial blessing because of his own appreciation for the transformative possibilities inherent in aesthetic and interpersonal experience. "Let yourself go," he implores Lucy. "Pull out from the depths those thoughts that you do not understand, and spread them out in the sunlight and know the meaning of them." Yet Mr. Emerson's invitation to Lucy to discover herself on her own terms ultimately finds its origins in her ability to do so through the filter of his son's personality. "By understanding George you may learn to understand yourself," he adds. "It will be good for both of you." In addition to quoting passages from the quasi-existential verse of A. E. Housman, Mr. Emerson entreats Lucy to "make my boy think like us. Make him realize that by the side of the everlasting Why there is a Yes—a transitory Yes if you like, but a Yes."[13]

Significantly, Lucy responds to Mr. Emerson's unwanted counsel by rebuffing his advice and eschewing what he intimates to be her responsibility for sharing in George's own process of self-discovery and progress toward adulthood: "You'll think me unfeeling," she answers, "but your son wants employment. Has he no particularly hobby? Why, I myself have worries, but I can generally forget them at the piano; and collecting stamps did no end of good for my brother. Perhaps Italy bores him," she adds. "You ought to try the Alps or the Lakes."[14] Clearly, Lucy makes a conscious choice to view the world through her own, well-considered lens. Mr. Emerson's philosophy of living may indeed provide her with exactly the kind of counsel that will enhance her own process of self-transformation. Yet, as the novel demonstrates, her repeated attempts at making her own decisions and at following her own courses of action collide, time after time, with resistance in the form of what others have in mind for her. When Lucy tries to find her own voice among the world of adults, that same, ostensibly more knowledgeable world exerts its will upon her and silences her efforts to follow her own pathways to self-discovery; even if those very same pathways lead her to make mistakes during her ensuing voyage toward adulthood, at least they will have been her own mistakes, and hence, genuine moments of learning and self-knowledge.

Family theorists identify such a period of identity exploration as the "moratorium" phase of psychological development. During moratorium, young women such as Lucy attempt to forge a sense of identity from among the interpersonal, occupational, and ideological possibilities that present themselves at various junctures. Characterized by moments of identity exploration, the examination of various potential life decisions, and a growing interest in commitment to a more fully realized sense of personal identity, moratorium is a signal moment in any young person's progress toward maturity and the achievement of genuine adulthood.[15] Clearly, Forster depicts Lucy in the throes of her own moratorium stage, only to be thwarted by the needs and desires of the masculine others who opt to interpret Lucy's experiences for her after she suspends her own wishes in favor of their age, gender, and perceived wisdom. McGoldrick attributes the deferral that many young women such as Lucy exhibit to an enduring psychosocial need to "define their development in terms of their ability to attract a male." Such tendencies, according to McGoldrick, "are bound to be detrimental to their self-esteem, fearing to appear smart, tall, assertive, or competent, worrying about losing their chances of finding an intimate relationship with a male. It is in keeping with social norms that during the adolescent years girls often confuse identity with intimacy by defining themselves through relationships with others."[16]

The many ways in which others interpret the quality of Lucy's experiences for her characterize the duration of her stay in Italy. Moments after musing, rather ironically, that "nothing ever happens to me," Lucy witnesses a sudden and very violent street fight in the Piazza Signoria that leaves an Italian mortally wounded and dying at her feet. Almost predictably, Lucy faints at the sight of blood and violence, only to be rescued by George, who had been observing her from across the square. After recovering, she tells her rescuer that "now I am well. I can go alone, thank you."[17] When his gentlemanly virtue renders it impossible for her to return to her hotel alone, she acquiesces to his desires for socially and culturally engendered propriety. Not surprisingly, he later disposes of her souvenir photographs after he realizes that they were covered with blood during the melee in the square. "Thank you so much," she tells him, quickly resuming her own gendered place in the Edwardian social schema. "How quickly these accidents do happen, and then one returns to the old life!" As with his father, though, George assumes the mantle of masculinity and opts to interpret Lucy's experience for her. "Something tremendous has happened," he tells her. "It isn't exactly that a man has died."[18]

We soon discover that what has in fact happened to Lucy—and at the bidding of her unsolicited social interpreter, George, no less—involves, yet again, the kind of self-knowledge that Lucy can only gain in *A Room with a View* via the well-honed filter of a masculine point of view. During a day trip to the Italian countryside in which Lucy's companion preps himself for romance by chanting "courage and love," George finds himself so moved by the splendor of the countryside and by Lucy's own beauty that he cannot help but take advantage, rather triumphantly, of the nexus of aesthetic beauty and Lucy's emergence on the hillside before him. "For a moment he contemplated her," Forster writes, "as one who had fallen out of heaven. He saw radiant joy in her face, he saw the flowers beat against her dress in blue waves. The bushes above them closed. He stepped quickly forward and kissed her."[19] Reveling in the moment, an exuberant George walks all the way back to Florence in a driving rain, leaving Lucy to be simultaneously admonished and consoled for *his* impertinence by her cousin.

Once back at the hotel, Charlotte takes charge of matters—despite Lucy begging to handle her own affairs and to at last "understand" herself—and chastises George and obtains his vow of secrecy while a perplexed Lucy waits alone in her room. In both instances, Lucy is acted upon by supposedly more knowledgeable others; on the hillside, George interprets the moment for her, opting in the end to surprise her with an unbidden kiss. In the hotel, Charlotte trumps Lucy's quest for acting in an adult manner and handles the situation with George herself. "You are so young and inexperienced, you have lived among such nice people," Charlotte tells Lucy, "that you cannot realize what men can be."[20]

Remarkably, Lucy's season of personal transformation becomes even more complicated when she returns to England and her mother's home in Surrey. Once again, she makes a personal choice—albeit a terrifically bad one—only to be thwarted in her attempt at self-liberation by her friends and relations. When Lucy accepts the conceited and socially arrogant Cecil Vyse's proposal of marriage, she does so of her own volition. She may very well be, in Mr. Emerson's words, in the confusing malaise of yet another "muddle," but she makes a choice nevertheless. Her family and friends' unhappy response—while warranted, given Cecil's smug disposition—denies her the opportunity to learn from her own mistakes, to engage in the kind of trial-and-error process through which we often, and frequently all-too painfully, derive true self-knowledge. From her brother Freddy's outward disgust for her fiancé to Mr. Beebe's reluctant acceptance of her relationship with the contemptuous Cecil, Lucy's engagement meets with both derision and sadness among her community. Rather than opting to question Lucy about her reasons for accepting Cecil's proposal, they choose to interpret her decision, to malign it as an unfortunate reality in their lives.

Conversely, Cecil and his equally snobbish mother interpret the engagement as a triumph of social design. They consider Lucy, moreover, to be "a work of art" of sorts to be molded in their more opulent, socially redeeming image. "Make Lucy one of us," Mrs. Vyse implores her son. "Lucy is *becoming* wonderful—wonderful."[21] Agreeing with his mother's assessment of Lucy's pliable and still diffuse identity, Cecil remarks that "I shall have our children educated just like Lucy. Bring them up among honest country folks for freshness, send them to Italy for subtlety, and then—not till then—let them come to London. I don't believe in those London educations," he adds. "At all events, not for women." While Cecil and his mother unashamedly interpret Lucy's persona for their own, socially driven purposes, Mrs. Honeychurch likewise critiques Cecil's unseemly nature for her daughter, who can only defend her betrothed and look beyond his all-too apparent faults. "Since Cecil came back from London," Mrs. Honeychurch tells Lucy, "nothing appears to please him. Whenever I speak he winces," she adds. "I see him, Lucy; it is useless to contradict me. No doubt I am neither artistic nor literary nor intellectual nor musical."[22] Despite her obvious concern for her daughter's future, Mrs. Honeychurch can do no more than offer an appraisal of Cecil's character, stopping short, as with Lucy's other mentors, of providing genuine counsel that she can make do with as she pleases.

Amazingly, Cecil succeeds in accomplishing his own undoing with Lucy when he arranges for the Emersons to find lodging, rather predictably, in Surrey. Once back in Lucy's orbit, George never thinks of asking Lucy about her own wishes, opting instead to speak in great platitudes about providence: "It is Fate," he observes. "Everything is Fate. We are flung together by Fate—flung together, drawn apart."[23] Later, he even resorts to reciting his father's quasi-Moorean philosophy about the necessity of finding the perfect "view." According to Mr. Emerson, George says, "views are really crowds—crowds of trees and houses and hills—and are bound to resemble each other, like human crowds—and that the power they have over us is sometimes supernatural, for the same reason."[24] Rather than outwardly questioning her about her engagement with Cecil, George chooses to speak obliquely about fate and the perfect view; in so doing, he clearly assumes a position of intellectual superiority—hoping, as he surely does, that Lucy will eventually come around and realize the error of her ways. When Cecil reads a risqué passage from Eleanor Lavish's latest novel that turns out to be a thinly veiled retelling of Lucy's encounter with George on the hillside—apparently, Charlotte's purported vow of silence about the events in Italy did not apply to her—an inspired George takes advantage of the moment and kisses Lucy yet again. The second kiss resembles the circumstances of the first because it occurs at George's bidding. Perhaps more significantly, though, it demonstrates both Cecil *and* George acting upon Lucy, rather than at her behest.

In Cecil's case, he reads the passage from Lavish's blue novel for comic purposes only—to make fun of the writer's purple prose. In so doing, though, he actually succeeds in interpreting the events of Lucy's life for her once more. When read aloud from the pages of Lavish's novel, the events on the Italian hillside only serve to embarrass her. When George kisses an unsuspecting Lucy for the second time during their brief and, perhaps more importantly, almost entirely wordless relationship, he wrests the power of decision from her; in short, he opts to choose himself for Lucy despite her imminent betrothal to Cecil. At this juncture in the novel, Forster pointedly reports to the reader that "Lucy had developed since the spring. That is to say, she was now better able to stifle the emotions of which the conventions and the world disapprove."[25] The exact nature of Lucy's "development," though, should clearly be debated. Rather than developing into a fully realized human being who can rely on her self-sufficiency and aplomb to see her through life's difficulties, Lucy has become a decidedly different, unindividuated person who relies upon silence and deflection in order to navigate the dilemmas inherent in life. When she attempts to rebuke George for his actions, she barely utters a word before he launches into a lengthy

dissertation in which he explicates Lucy's dysfunctional relationship with Cecil for her: "He's the type who's kept Europe back
for a thousand years," George remarks. "Every moment of his
life he's forming you, telling you what's charming or amusing or
ladylike, telling you what a man thinks womanly; and you, you of
all women, listen to his voice instead of your own."[26]

George is absolutely correct, of course, in his assessment of
Lucy's fiancé. Cecil evinces little regard for Lucy's emotions or
for her own wishes about her destiny. But despite his implicit
protests to the contrary, neither does George. As with his rival,
George merely acts upon Lucy, attempting to reshape her into
something that he can understand, something that makes sense
in his gendered Edwardian world. The most interesting aspect of
Lucy's lack of interpersonal development in the novel reveals itself when she responds, both internally and externally, to her resulting "muddle" with George. Simply put, she responds to her
greatest moment of personal crisis by lying—and in truly epic
fashion, no less, to almost everyone she knows. Faced with a situation for which she can hardly begin to imagine a solution, Lucy
resorts to equivocation to resolve her dilemma. When she be-
rates George for kissing her the second time in Surrey, she lies
to him about her true feelings. Hence, he interprets the nature of
her situation for her. When she cancels her engagement with
Cecil, she finds herself unable to explicate her own reasons for
terminating their relationship and in desperation simply repeats
George's earlier comments about Cecil's social ineffectuality.

Amazingly, her lies, or at least the power and conviction with
which she delivers them, actually prompt Cecil to recognize, in
awe and for the first time, that she is a "new person" with a "new
voice."[27] It is truly ironic that Lucy must lie—and lie ram-
pantly—in order to effect a genuinely adult voice of her own. Remarkably, it is only during the throes of lying to her mother that
she finally concocts a plan for pursuing adulthood beyond the
safety of her family system. "I shall want to be away in the future
more than I have been," she tells her mother. "I have seen so
little of life; one ought to come up to London more—not a cheap
ticket like to-day but to stop. I might even share a flat for a little
with some girl," she adds. "I want more independence."[28] The
ways in which Lucy's developmental evolution ebbs and flows
at various instances throughout *A Room with a View* underscore Robert Kegan's theories about human development as a
"meaning-constitutive activity." As Kegan observes in *The Evolving Self: Problem and Process in Human Development* (1982),

moments such as Lucy's drive for independence from the comforting environs of her family system find their origins in the subject's desire to merge with "life itself." Simply put, Lucy wishes to validate herself by indulging in a "personal, independent achievement" beyond the Honeychurch ménage.[29]

Only scant moments after declaring her independence from her mother and life in Surrey—and, quite obviously, in the throes of lying to nearly everyone whom she encounters—Lucy comes into the orbit of Mr. Emerson, who interprets her emotional state for her and, rather amazingly, even attempts to explain to Lucy the nature and cause of her self-deception. "It seems to me," he tells her, "that you are in a muddle."[30] When Mr. Emerson attributes Lucy's dismay to her predicament with his son, she attempts to reproach him for his assumption. "How dare you?" she remarks. "Oh, how like a man!—I mean, to suppose that a woman is always thinking about a man." Once again, Forster depicts Lucy in the act of attempting to establish her own voice when confronted by the needs and desires of her emotional interpreters. Undaunted, Mr. Emerson ascribes Lucy's emotional state—correctly, it turns out, given the narrative imperatives of Forster's novel—to a kind of "shock": "You're shocked, but I mean to shock you," says Mr. Emerson. "It's the only hope at times. I can reach you no other way. . . . George will work in your thoughts till you die. It isn't possible to love and to part," he adds. "You can transmute love, ignore it, muddle it, but you can never pull it out of you."[31]

Despite her efforts to find her own voice in the world of adults, Lucy rather docilely accepts Mr. Emerson's version of her emotional condition. Deferring yet again to the wisdom of her male others, a much-relieved Lucy finds that Mr. Emerson "gave her a sense of deities reconciled, a feeling that, in gaining the man she loved, she would gain something for the whole world." Years later, Forster writes, Lucy "never exactly understood . . . how he managed to strengthen her. It was as if he had made her see the whole of everything at once."[32] After having acquired the ostensible (and unchallenged) wisdom inherent in Mr. Emerson's words, Lucy discovers that suddenly and rather magically her muddle is gone. In contrast with her earlier drive for independence from her family-of-origin, Lucy eschews personal liberation in favor of Mr. Emerson's counsel. Lucy's quiet acceptance of the elder Emerson's advice signals both the deferential nature of her socially inscribed female psyche, as well as the process of "rebalancing" that Kegan describes in *The Evolving Self*. "Every new balance," Kegan writes, "represents a capacity to listen to what before one could only hear irritably, and the capacity to hear irritably what before one could hear not at all."[33]

While Lucy spends much of her "courtship," for lack of a better word, with George in a state of utter confusion, George, as with his father, evinces little doubt about the nature of his feelings for Lucy—or, more importantly, *her* feelings for him: "I acted the truth—the only thing I did do—and you came back to me."[34] It is interesting that George, as a man, reveals absolutely no confusion about his emotional connection with Lucy, nor about the nature of their shared destiny. The politics of gender identity, however, encode Lucy's persona in substantially divergent ways from her male counterparts. As Ruthellen Josselson observes in *Finding Herself: Pathways to Identity Development in Women* (1987), "Women differ in how much they are willing or able to explore possibilities within themselves, how much they realize their individuality and uniqueness, and how much they allow themselves to be defined by others."[35] By deferring to the Emersons' version of her persona, Lucy permits them to define her on their own terms and in regard to their masculinized worldview. Her protracted bout of lying merely represented a belated attempt to eschew external points of view and thus to assert herself in a world of largely male, more strident, and more persistent personalities.

This should hardly be surprising, as David R. Matteson has demonstrated in his recent study of gender differences, given the very different ways in which men and women continue to be socialized in this very late, and very post-Edwardian era. According to Matteson's research, the highest levels of self-esteem continue to be found in masculine subjects, while many women evidence lower levels of self-esteem and often remain undifferentiated altogether.[36] Matteson's research reveals that the decision-making process, which obviously confronted Lucy with substantial difficulties throughout *A Room with a View*, "appears to be related to greater personality differentiation, to increased cognitive and moral complexity."[37] Yet Lucy—despite her own best efforts—remains undifferentiated in Forster's narrative and unable to establish her own voice in an adult world that can only comprehend her persona in terms of a committed romantic union.[38] Clearly, Mr. Emerson's pointed attempts to develop Lucy's interest in a relationship with his son underscore one of Matteson's principal hypotheses about women and identity development: "that if a woman had not reached an achieved identity early enough, there was social pressure to divert her energy from identity search to development of intimacy."[39]

The real tragedy of Lucy's story lies in the fact that she will, in all probability, never achieve genuine differentiation from the family and extrafamilial systems in which she was reared. The artistic and social promise that Mr. Beebe observed in Lucy's persona early in the novel, moreover, likely will never come to fruition as she continues to sublimate her own desires to the whimsy of her community. As McGoldrick notes, young women such as Lucy invariably defer their own dreams and interpersonal expectations in an effort to secure and sustain the "approval" of others.[40] Obviously lacking in her own socially inscribed strength and in meaningful avenues for interpersonal development at the conclusion of *A Room with a View*, Lucy is left to ponder the nature of youth, passion, and a forebodingly "mysterious" form of "love attained" about which she is barely "conscious."[41] Lucy's uncertain identity and her female status—particularly during an Edwardian era that impels her to defer her own emotions and desires in favor of the needs of her male counterparts—only serve to problematize her capacity for growing up in a functional and psychologically healthy manner.[42] Perhaps even more alarmingly, Lucy's already difficult passage into adulthood—despite her obvious affinity for the touchstones of friendship and aesthetic experience that characterize the ethical life both in *Principia Ethica* and in Forster's fictions—will surely detract from her ability to participate fully in Moore's socially invigorating concept of the "value of the whole" that Forster celebrates in *A Room with a View*.

NOTES

1. For a valuable study of Forster's feminist imperatives, see Finkelstein, *Forster's Women*.

2. In "Women through the Family Life Cycle," Monica McGoldrick notes that, generally, "male theories have failed to describe the progression of relationships toward a maturity of interdependence" in women. In McGoldrick's estimation, most male theoreticians tend to "ignore female development" altogether, opting instead to examine human development without regard for significant gender differences in the progression of the human life cycle (202–3).

3. McGoldrick, "Women through the Family Life Cycle," 202, 204, 208.

4. Gilligan, *In a Different Voice*, 23.

5. Moore, *Principia Ethica*, 185.

6. Ibid., 188.

7. Individuation, or the process of establishing a sense of autonomous iden-

tity, becomes increasingly more difficult as women advance further into adulthood. As Ruthellen Josselson observes in *Revising Herself*, women engage in a life-long process of subordinating their own interests in favor of the needs of others. For this reason, female identity often consists of an endless process of revision. "Like slowly turning kaleidoscopes," Josselson writes, "the shifts in a woman's identity involve rearrangement of pieces, now accenting one aspect and muting another, now altering the arrangement once more" (243).

8. Kroger, *Identity in Adolescence*, 158.

9. See Sullivan, "Forster's Symbolism," see also Rahman, "Double-Plot in E. M. Forster's *A Room with a View*."

10. Forster, *A Room with a View*, 50.

11. Ibid., 24.

12. Ibid., 30.

13. Ibid., 21–22.

14. Ibid., 22.

15. See Patterson, Sochting, and Marcia, "Inner Space and Beyond," for further discussion regarding the four stages of identity formation, which include identity diffusion, identity foreclosure, moratorium, and identity achievement (11–12).

16. McGoldrick, "Women through the Family Life Cycle," 215.

17. Forster, *A Room with a View*, 32–33.

18. Ibid., 34–35.

19. Ibid., 55.

20. Ibid., 60.

21. Ibid., 99; italics added.

22. Ibid., 110.

23. Ibid., 104.

24. Ibid., 129.

25. Ibid., 132.

26. Ibid., 136.

27. Ibid., 142.

28. Ibid., 159.

29. Kegan, *Evolving Self*, 193.

30. Forster, *A Room with a View*, 165.

31. Ibid., 166.

32. Ibid., 168.

33. Kegan, *Evolving Self*, 105.

34. Forster, *A Room with a View*, 171.

35. Josselson, *Finding Herself*, 7.

36. Matteson, "Differences Within and Between Genders," 93.

37. Ibid., 96.

38. In this instance, differentiation refers to a person's capacity for separating their notion of themselves in relation to others. In *Theory and Technique of Family Therapy* Barnard and Corrales define "differentiated" selves as functional family members who possess the transgenerational capacity for producing yet other selves with full senses of identity (36–37).

39. Ibid., 99.

40. McGoldrick, "Women through the Family Life Cycle," 215.

41. Forster, *A Room with a View*, 172.

42. It is clearly possible to suggest that the novel concludes with Lucy enjoying some semblance of personal individuation. In one rather veiled instance,

Forster writes that George "had helped himself, it is true, but how stupidly! All the fighting that mattered had been done by others—by Italy, by his father, by his wife" (170). Yet, once again, Lucy's self-emergence is read through the masculine lens of another. Rather than explicitly depicting Lucy in the act of establishing some form of emotional and interpersonal evolution, Forster opts to narrate the conclusion of *her* story—of her *Bildungsroman*—as a virtual afterthought in his discussion of another character's psychological fate.

The Enigmatic Jane Eyre: A Differentiation Story without Family in Charlotte Brontë's *Jane Eyre*

Rosemary D. Babcock

WHEN JANE EYRE UTTERS THE WORDS, "READER, I MARRIED HIM," AT the conclusion of her retrospective narrative, she and Rochester have been married for ten years. The four-word statement is resolute; it connotes both contentment and self-assuredness. And, when we have reached this part in the narrative, we, as readers, know what Jane has had to overcome as a marginalized member of society—a governess who falls in love with her boss, or "master" (as Brontë's nineteenth-century narrative would have it). Her words reflect an accepted resolution to the blanket nineteenth-century commentary on the plight of women without patrimony—those women who, by marrying, are saved either from a life of spinsterhood in which they are dependent on relatives for food and shelter, or, as in Jane's case, saved from a life in the service of others, living with a family but never a part of the family. We can, then, read Jane's statement as a thematic assessment of nineteenth-century English literature when marriage was the quest for every young girl, particularly one such as Jane.

Following this thematic reading as a basis for discussion, however, would lead me to join the community of contemporary critics, among them Sandra Gilbert and Sally Shuttleworth, who embrace Jane primarily as a character of thematic representativeness and, in some respects, see her as selling out to the conventionalized marriage trap. In her essay "Plain Jane's Progress," Gilbert, for example, recognizes that the dilemma for women in the nineteenth century is to be both independent and married. She presents Jane as victor and victim of such expectations. In marrying the "maimed and blinded" Rochester who is newly humbled by his circumstances, Jane achieves her goal of selfhood and marriage on her own terms.[1] Paradoxically, how-

46

ever, Gilbert argues that the marriage forces Jane to "withdraw" into the remote forest of Ferndean where both she and Rochester are socially and spiritually isolated.[2] Similarly, in *Charlotte Brontë and Victorian Psychology,* Shuttleworth states that Brontë, by constructing parallel histories of Jane and Bertha, struggles to present a model of womanhood and femininity in *Jane Eyre* that would not negate the image of "female empowerment and control."[3] Shuttleworth concludes, however, that the "harmony and stasis" of the conventional ending in marriage suggests a "form of self-annihilation."[4] In contrast, then, to the traditional nineteenth-century thematic reading that sees Jane happy and content through matrimony, Gilbert's and Shuttleworth's arguments represent critics who ultimately view Jane's solution as a thematic representation of loss via marriage and reinforcement of patriarchal order—her narrative a negative one of dismay, disillusionment, or self destruction.

Both the nineteenth-century assessment and contemporary criticism tend to focus on Jane largely as a thematic character and, in doing so, tend to neglect a more mimetic understanding of her. In *Reading People, Reading Plots: Character, Progression, and the Interpretation of Narration,* James Phelan points out that while it is not unusual for critics to privilege the thematic dimension over the mimetic, it is frequently seen as a "reductive" practice that typically "moves" readers away from the "richness of response that authors and texts invite their audiences to have." The assumption that literary characters are not really characters but rather some abstract idea such as jealousy, honor, or ambition is challenged as an arbitrary premise by Phelan who believes that literary characters cannot be "adequately summed up" by their thematic representativeness alone.[5]

I share Phelan's opinion. While I do not discount examining Jane's thematic qualities, a significant part of my experience of Jane's character remains chiefly in the mimetic sphere; she may be a vehicle for carrying ideas, but Jane is also a plausible mimetic character, a possible person who exhibits the characteristics of an individual who participates in the interactional world of her various family groups. By focusing on Jane as a construct clearly representative of both an autonomous and interactional human being, I can avoid the generalizations that plague a thematic analysis of character and engage in an even richer response to Brontë's narrative than it already commands.

I will argue that Jane's self-assured statement of her achieved reality as a married woman is not the statement of someone who has sold out to nineteenth-century patriarchal expectations for women. Rather, it is a significant and powerful statement of an independent woman who seems secure in the intimacy and companionship that her choice affords her. Jane's statement serves, too, as a testament to the created family that is formed when she and Rochester marry—the realization of the goal of family that has eluded her from childhood until young womanhood. It is this reading that, I believe, has been neglected during the last two or three decades of critical discussion, one that helps to explain why the novel has remained popular since it was published over 150 years ago. By using the language of family systems psychotherapy as a tool of literary analysis and adding to it data from Robert Kegan's constructive-developmental study of an individual's process of evolution that he outlines in *The Evolving Self: Problem and Process in Human Development*, I will examine Jane's emotional development—an evolution in which she reconciles her lack of family of origin to achieve both connection with others and a heightened sense of self. Thus, I will focus on Jane Eyre as a character who functions primarily in the mimetic sphere.

Although there are literary critics who have explored Jane's mimetic qualities, they tend to analyze her through the glasses of Freudian-based psychoanalysis that—as an intrapsychic study of character—often neglect to give significance to Jane's interpersonal relationships.[6] In *Striking at the Joints: Contemporary Psychology and Literary Criticism*, John V. Knapp takes issue with such psychoanalytic views. He questions how Freudian concepts such as "drive reduction and primary process," concepts that are no longer accepted in contemporary psychology of how the mind and brain function, can be taken as explanatory evidence useful to literary criticism.[7] Knapp suggests that the "limitations" of an intrapsychic psychology like Freud's—and more recently, Lacan's—have kept literary critics from a thorough analysis of the "*inter*personal difficulties" that many literary characters experience.[8] By privileging the intrapsychic dynamic in *Jane Eyre*, for example, psychoanalytic critics neglect much of the significance of the complex interrelationship between Jane and her relatives (both the Reeds and the Rivers), her interaction with various mother figures such as Bessie and Miss Temple, and her intriguing relationship with Rochester.

Jane's interaction with these characters is crucial to her psychological development and ultimately guides her to achieve differentiation of self and to establish a solid family unit of her own. Family systems psychotherapy, an interpersonal system in which the family becomes the source of the matrix of identity rather than the individual character, provides a useful critical eye with which to examine the text for transactions that contribute to Jane's experiences of integration, differentiation, and development of a solid self.[9] In casting off the *intra*psychic glasses, then, one can look at Jane from a family systems perspective to determine the nature and extent of her *inter*personal connections. Because Kegan's theory demonstrates the development of meaning-construction in the context of the interactions between organism and environment (or social being and society) rather than the internal process of maturation alone, it is an appropriate adjunct to family systems psychotherapy. By relating Jane's growth to Kegan's system of balances—a system that recognizes the "assimilation of new experience to the old [conversational] 'grammar'" of the self—I can discuss Jane's emotional development within her family matrix and identify her further as a representational human being who undergoes the complex evolution of personality development.[10] The combination of these two systems provides alternative insights, critically, into Jane's mimetic traits that previous thematic and psychological criticisms do not and thus establishes her as a faithful representation of a constantly evolving individual within a familial matrix.

In family systems therapy, the transactions that take place within families are considered key to understanding the family dynamic. In *Mastering Family Therapy: Journeys of Growth and Transformation,* Salvador Minuchin discusses the various patterns of interaction and their importance.[11] The level of proximity and intimacy, who is responsible for whom as well as who is "excluded, scapegoated, and abused," are among the interactions that can take place within a family unit. "How nurturing, support, and power [are] played out" in such transactions become, according to Minuchin, the "parameters" that define the family structure as family members "construct each other."[12] Brontë's narrative provides evidence of just such transactions taking place between Jane and members of her nontraditional family system. Keeping in mind Jane's marginalized situation as an orphan, I look for patterns of interactions between her and the Reeds. I look, too, for a voice or voices who speak for her not only in her infancy and in her early adolescence while at Gateshead but also during her years spent at Lowood as she grows from child to young adult. An examination of Jane's verbal and nonverbal transactions with Rochester also contributes usefully to my study of her interpersonal connections. What emerges in the narrative is a portrait of Jane transcending nineteenth-century strictures, learning to love and to connect with others by extracting the best standards and models of integrity from sources outside the traditional family matrix.

Jane's victory is hard-won. During her ten years of residence with the Reed family, she has neither the security of a family system nor, it would seem, role models upon which to pattern her behavior. The family dynamic at the Reed household had developed a pattern of ugly negative transactions in which Jane is either engaged in a fracas with John Reed, scapegoated in the nursery, or banned from the Reed family matrix until she can acquire a "more sociable and childlike disposition."[13] Rather than succumb to the emotional and physical rebuffs made to her by the Reed household and integrate into the family system on their terms, Jane exercises what little independence is open to her to deal with their rejection. To "endure," Jane physically removes herself from the volatile family system by hiding in the window seat—ostensibly to seek solace in her books.[14] Her distancing, however, is in itself a type of metacommunication by which Jane attempts to be heard and/or to be recognized when it would seem that all avenues of expression are closed to her.[15]

Recalling in later years these early experiences at Gateshead, Jane states her position as an outsider in the Reed family: "I was a discord in Gateshead Hall; I was like nobody there; . . . a heterogenous thing . . . a useless thing . . . a noxious thing."[16] From a family systems perspective, Jane upsets the equilibrium within the Reed family system when she arrives at Gateshead as an infant. She not only unwittingly triangulates the Reed spousal dyad by stealing her uncle's affection from his wife, but also she usurps the place of his own children in his loyalty and affection. When Jane's uncle dies, Aunt Reed and the children drive Jane out of the family unit. In retrospect, Jane identifies her earlier sense of alienation by referring to herself as an "interloper" in that family system, aware that she no longer was connected to the Reed family by any tie after her uncle's death.[17]

While the negative treatment Jane received at the hands of the Reeds and the subsequent alienation she felt represent the plight of the orphan in the nineteenth century, such behaviors serve at the same time as agents for her mimetic representativeness.[18] Jane's rebellious independent actions and reactions to the Reeds when she was part of their family unit indicate her awareness that she is the victim of grave injustices to both body and spirit. By acting and reacting, Jane exercises her need for self-preservation. At the same time, she begins the process of creating a new concept of self. When speaking out against being labeled deceitful in front of Mr. Brocklehurst, for example, Jane admits to feeling "freedom, . . . triumph . . . unhoped-for liberty." Moreover, in the aftermath of her outburst—although feeling remorse at speaking back to her elders—she recognizes the encounter with her aunt to be "the hardest battle [she] had fought, and the first victory [she] had gained."[19] Thus, Jane achieves the first in a series of personal victories in which she asserts herself to preserve her spirit.

Jane's ready assimilation of victorious experience to the old conversational "grammar" of her oppressed self and the accommodation of this old "grammar" of her selfhood at the Reeds to new experience represents the tension between self-preservation and self-transformation that, according to the process of evolution outlined by Kegan in his study, is at the heart of all living things.[20] When Jane retreated to the window seat to escape John Reed's blows or her aunt's chastising, for example, she was operating in a pattern typical of Kegan's third stage of development in which the individual is unable to express anger but instead feels "sad, wounded, or incomplete."[21] In the act of defending herself against the charges leveled against her, Jane exercises not only her capacity for independence but also makes a major step in her emotional development. No longer embedded in the interpersonal "shared context" of the third balance, Jane moves into the fourth balance of Kegan's five-step evolutionary standard. This evolutionary balance, whose strength lies in the person's "new capacity for independence," does not leave the person robbed of interpersonal relationships but rather appropriates them to a new place in the maintenance of a personal self-system.[22]

It would seem that Jane's ability to evolve emotionally would be seriously impeded in the Reed household, a family system lacking the positive interpersonal influence necessary for an individual to differentiate. There is, however, textual evidence that Uncle Reed provided an immutable source of interactive support for Jane when he—in loyalty to his dead sister—brought her as an orphaned "infant" into his home.[23] While Jane admits no memory of her uncle who died when she was about one year old, the thought that, if he were alive, he would have "treated [her] kindly" comforts and sustains her during her terror in the red room.[24] Further evidence that uncle and niece formed a strong emotional bond during their brief time together—a bond that

spans and endures over the years—is further confirmed when
Jane is privy to Mrs. Reed's deathbed musings nine years after
her departure from Gateshead. Mrs. Reed reveals that her husband's devotion and attention to Jane was extraordinary: "Reed
pitied it [the infant who wailed in its cradle all night]," Mrs. Reed
recalls. "He used to nurse it," she continues, "and notice it as if
it had been his own; more, indeed, than he ever noticed his own
at that age. . . . In his last illness, he had it brought continually to
his bedside."[25] It seems clear from Mrs. Reed's account and
Jane's recollection that, despite the tension it caused within his
family, Uncle Reed was a key initial source of social contact for
Jane as she engaged his attention during her early phases of development.

Kegan's explanation of relationship dynamics provides insight
into the significance of the uncle/niece attachment to Jane's
overall emotional development. His study illuminates both the
importance of infant activity in initiating life themes that inaugurate an individual "towards the activity of evolution" and of an
early consistent presence in an infant's life.[26] Kegan emphasizes
the significance of this last point, stating that "who comes into a
person's life may be the single greatest factor of influence to
what that life becomes."[27] Moreover, Kegan says, there is a reciprocal exchange between infant and a consistent presence—none
of which is more "powerful than the glance, the interplay of
eyes"—and the infant's survival and development depends on
this reciprocal exchange or "capacity to recruit the invested attention of others."[28] As development continues, the infant, instead of being fused with the primary caretaker, is able to relate
to him or her. Thus, by creating an "object world" or "other
world," the infant "begins the history of successively joining the
world rather than incorporating it."[29] As Kegan points out, "evolutionary activity involves the very creating of the object (a process of differentiation) as well as our relating to it (a process of
integration)."[30] Mrs. Reed's account of the interaction taking
place between Uncle Reed and the infant Jane fits the consistent
presence and reciprocal exchange pattern deemed by Kegan as
necessary to the process of differentiation and integration.

New research done on the behavior of babies in their cribs and
in the nursery supports and extends Kegan's view and thus provides even greater insight into the drama going on between Jane
and her uncle as he responded to her cries in the night and had
her with him during the day. In *Scientist in the Crib: Minds,
Brains, and How Children Learn*, for example, Alison Gopnik,

Andrew N. Meltzoff, and Patricia K. Kuhl discuss the newborn's ability to sharpen his or her focus up to about a foot away and conclude that not only do babies seem "designed to see people who love them more clearly than anything else," but also they are "connected to people in a special way."[31] As Kegan emphasizes the importance of a baby's ability to recruit the invested interest of others, Gopnik, et al. report that babies as young as one month "flirt" by spontaneously timing and coordinating their own expressions, gestures, and voices with those of another.[32] Through this close-up and personal action, babies form attachments by developing " 'internalized working models' that are systematic pictures of how people relate to one another—[or] theories of love."[33] Kegan's study and this recent research help to explain the interaction that must have taken place between uncle and niece. Jane's ability to experience feelings of comfort emanating from thoughts of her uncle during her red room confinement nine years after his death indicate that their early interactions enabled her, indeed, to connect to him in a "special way."

Jane's contact with her uncle came at a most critical time in her development. Kegan, for example, believes the early months in a child's growth to be age-specific windows of opportunity that aid the child in the making of meaning and, therefore, are crucial to an individual's becoming autonomous. Gopnik, et al. acknowledge that there are some researchers who subscribe to the thought that a baby's brain is open to "experience of a particular kind only during narrow periods of opportunity," but, they state, all agree that the "neural sculpting that goes on during the early phases of development is unique and deeply influences the rest of development."[34] The early months of Jane's development when Uncle Reed was a consistent presence—and she was in what Kegan terms the infant's most *social* period—were, as these studies indicate, the most advantageous time for her to benefit from her uncle's love and nurture, to develop her own internal working model of how people relate and learn to love.[35]

While Brontë's text does not identify those who may have nurtured Jane during the nine years she spends at Gateshead after Uncle Reed's death, Bessie stands out as her helpmate.[36] Sometimes portrayed by Jane as possessing a "capricious and hasty temper and indifferent ideas of principle or justice," Bessie, nevertheless, lends Jane emotional and physical support—support that translates into a sustained pattern of nurture seemingly not provided by anyone else at Gateshead.[37] Bessie, for example, had a knack for telling fairy tales and making tea parties special occasions. And, when the rest of the household shuns Jane, Bessie engages her in small tasks, provides her with holiday treats, and tucks her into bed. In addition, Bessie recognizes Jane's vulnerable position in the Reed family matrix. Believing that Jane is treated too harshly by Mrs. Reed, she advises her to be "bolder."[38] Further, Bessie is Jane's only source for information about the world outside of Gateshead. The little Jane knows about school comes from Bessie's limited knowledge of both the wonders of the curriculum and the realities of the discipline. And, it is Bessie who walks Jane from the "hostile roof" of Gateshead to the coach bound for Lowood, kisses and embraces her, and urges the guard to "be sure and take good care" of her as she embarks alone on her journey.[39] In spite of her somewhat volatile temperament, the narrative shows Bessie to be a balanced combination of gentleness and discipline, consistent and unselfish in her sensitivity to Jane's needs.

When Jane is summoned to her ill aunt's side, the significance of Bessie's kind acts and the impact she had on Jane during those crucial early years of her development is reinforced. Received by Bessie at the gate house, Jane observes "old times crowded fast back" with Bessie "bustling" around her.[40] With characteristic aggressiveness Bessie commands Jane to sit still by the fire. And with equally characteristic "youthful lightness of heart," she lends special touches to the daily tea ritual she prepares for Jane. Fondly savoring Bessie's little attentions to her, Jane, in turn, entertains Bessie with stories of Thornfield and the "gay company" that visits there, knowing that such details were "precisely of the kind [Bessie] relished."[41]

This exchange between the two women seems to be just a pleasant interlude in the narrative. But when viewed in terms of family systems and of Kegan's model, the exchange takes on greater significance and forms another link in determining Jane's emotional growth. Jane's recognition of Bessie's attentions and her reciprocal response to Bessie's needs add to the scope of her mimetic representativeness. Moreover, the transaction mimics the earlier interactions between the two, establishing Bessie as a positive role model and confirming the long-term effect she had on Jane's move toward autonomy. Bessie's early attentions to Jane fit a classic pattern of nurture set forth by Susan Mackey in her essay, "Nurturance: A Neglected Dimension in Family Therapy with Adolescents," in which she defines nurturant acts as "behaviors directed toward another individual with the intent of providing physical or psychological nourishment." When the nurturer "accurately assesses and responds to the emotions and needs of the other individual" (as we see Bessie doing in her interactions with Jane), an important dimension of a successful nurturant act occurs.[42] Moreover, the one on one dyad—that so marks Jane's and Bessie's initial interaction at Gateshead and is reenacted during their brief reunion years later—is important to the development of behavioral tasks and rituals that are, according to Mackey, "designed to increase connection [and/or] nurturance."[43] The significance of Bessie's brand of nurture is further reinforced by the Gopnik study which states that if an infant or young child has even a relatively brief experience with a person "who doesn't turn away" that experience can provide the child with an alternative picture of "how love can work."[44] Uncle Reed did not turn away from Jane, nor did Bessie. Present at crucial times in her development, Bessie, too, initiates patterns of love and attachment into Jane's life that are central to understanding her capacity to differentiate and to integrate into society.

Just as interactions with her uncle and Bessie provide Jane with a history that helps to establish her as a mimetically developing character, so, too, does her pattern of interaction with Miss Temple. On Jane's first day at Lowood, Miss Temple begins her nurture by advising Jane on how she can best earn the regard of others and by setting into motion the process that clears her of the charges of liar leveled by Mrs. Reed and repeated to the student body by Mr. Brocklehurst. With Bessie no longer available to tend to her, Jane comes to rely heavily on the physical and psychological nourishment of her mentor, who fills the roles of "mother, governess, and . . . companion" to her during her critical adolescent and early teen years.[45] When Miss Temple leaves Lowood to be married, she severs the dyad that the two have formed during their eight-year association. Moreover, the homeostatic balance that Jane had come to enjoy within the larger family system at Lowood is disrupted. Jane's narrative affirms that she feels unease in this major transition in her differentiation process:

From the day [Miss Temple] left, I was no longer the same: with her was gone every settled feeling, every association that had made Lowood in some degree a home to me. I had imbibed from her something of her nature and much of her habits: more harmonious thoughts: what seemed better-regulated feelings had become the inmates of my mind. I had given in allegiance to duty and order; I was quiet; I believed I was content: to the eyes of others, usually even to my own, I appeared a disciplined and subdued character.[46]

Deprived of her emotional anchor and the "serene atmosphere" that she felt in her presence, Jane is left in her "natural element and beginning to feel the stirring of old emotions"—the emotions of anger and alienation that marked her earlier years at Gateshead. As this compelling passage in the narrative continues, Jane reaches a breakthrough in her differentiation process: she "remembered" that the world is "wide"; "hopes and fears, [and] sensations and excitements awaited those who had the courage to go forth." Her language is marked by words that denote change: "I altered"; "I had undergone a transforming process," Jane writes. As part of her transformation process, Jane recognizes a need to go forward into the "real world" and to "seek knowledge of life amidst its perils."[47]

As Jane acts upon her awakened sensibilities to go forward and "seek knowledge" of life, her confidence in her own ability to reason and to find solutions is extraordinary. Entertaining the idea of leaving Lowood, she formulates her plan for action step by step. A newly confident Jane asks herself exactly what it is she wants and, then, arrives at a way to achieve her goals. When stymied on how to go about seeking a new position, for example, Jane orders her brain to "find a response, and quickly." As she organizes her thoughts, Jane initiates a mental self-litany that is an all-encompassing plan for change. Her eye traces the white road that winds around the base of a mountain—and she longs to "follow it further!" She gasps for "liberty"—but her prayer seems "scattered on the wind"; she petitions for change and stimulus—but these prayers, too, seemed "swept off into space." Moreover, when Jane realizes her thoughts are too impractical and abstract, she narrows her desires. By virtue of her decision to seek "new servitude," and thus use the talents she has developed at Lowood, Jane settles on a practical solution to her restlessness and need for change.[48] In her decision-making process, Jane displays an independence of spirit that, while exemplifying a central thematic idea in the narrative, also demonstrates her mimetic capabilities. Jane's capacity to be practical and to have pride in her ability to arrive at a solution to her problem is confirmation of her continuing personal evolution and the result, at least in part, of the nurturing environment provided by Mr. Reed, Bessie, and Miss Temple.

How Jane integrates her developing awareness into interactional patterns with others is evident in distinct instances in the narrative. By examining them, it is possible to measure the blossoming of her mimetic traits. When Jane interacts with her students at Morton School, for example, she demonstrates her ability to experience the example of others and then to use that experience in a positive way. By replicating the kindnesses shown to her by Miss Temple when she was a student, Jane fills her students with confidence. She elevates them in their own eyes and they, in turn, seek to excel in order to "merit" the deferential treatment she gives them.[49] Jane's interpersonal sensitivity enables her to recognize the gifts of character not only in her students but also in her recollections of her uncle, her observations of Bessie, and later in her relationship with Rochester. Thus, Jane displays a consistent pattern of evolution as a mimetic character, one whose humanness we can recognize even to the point of likening her to someone that we may know or that we may wish to emulate.

Evidence of Jane's increasing individuation of self appears prior to these patterns of interaction with her students at Morton School. When she returns to Gateshead for her obligatory visit with Mrs. Reed, for example, the narrative shows that time has quelled Jane's "longings of vengeance" and hushed the "promptings of rage and aversion" that marked her feelings of bitterness and hate for her aunt when she departed for Lowood.[50] Although Jane admits that she still "felt as a wanderer on the face of the earth," her narrative offers evidence that she has gained a heightened sense of self. Feeling a "firmer trust" in herself and her powers, and a "less withering dread of oppression," she acknowledges that the "gaping wound" of the wrongs she endured were "healed," the "flame of resentment extinguished."[51] The knowledge that their nine-year estrangement has not softened the elder woman's opinion of her (her aunt is resolved to think her "bad" to the last) brings tears to Jane's eyes.[52] But they are tears of painful acceptance rather than of anger; Jane is empathetic with her aunt and realizes how it must have been "most irksome to find herself bound by a hard-wrung pledge to stand in the stead of a parent to a strange child she could not love, and to see an uncongenial alien permanently intruded on her own family group."[53] Because of her positive experiences at Lowood, Jane is able to cast off the identity imposed upon her by circumstances at Gateshead. By expressing a willingness to "forget and forgive" all injuries she suffered there, Jane demonstrates an ability to remain both compassionate with her aunt and cognizant of her own shortcomings, thus continuing her movement toward differentiation of self.[54]

Jane's interactions with her aunt at Gateshead and with her students at the Morton School take place during and after her months at Thornfield where her developing autonomy is both challenged and strengthened by her relationship with Rochester. As she interacts with Rochester prior to their engagement and again at Ferndean, the dialogue between them often represents transactions that are both characteristic of family dynamics and well explained by the family systems process. Transactions, Minuchin states, can manifest themselves in hundreds of small ways that are generally the "essence of minutiae." He emphasizes the significance of the seemingly mundane "minutiae" to the interpersonal dynamic, stating that the transactions—in which nurture, support, and power can be played out—become the "cement" that solidifies relationships.[55] A sampling of the dialogue between Jane and Rochester shows it to be typical of the exchanges Minuchin describes—made up of seemingly small and unimportant details that when examined reveal the attempts of both to assert power in the relationship. Soon, however, it becomes apparent that Jane exercises and maintains substantial command over Rochester beginning in the days that follow their first meeting and continuing at Ferndean, where Jane reaches a level of intimacy with him that does not compromise her autonomy.

A few days after Jane meets Rochester for the first time, for example, they engage in a tête-à-tête in the dining room at Thornfield, initiated when Rochester catches Jane gazing at him: "You examine me, Miss Eyre . . . do you think me handsome?" Rochester's direct question makes Jane uncomfortable, and feeling flustered, she slips and remarks, "No, sir," when, in fact, she believes that if she had time to deliberate she would have replied with "something conventionally vague and polite."[56] Rochester's brazen attitude is noticeable in his undercutting of her responses throughout the conversation. He calls Jane a "little nonnette; quaint, quiet, grave, and simple," remarking that she is "not pretty" any more than he is handsome.[57] By claiming his age and experience have earned him the right to be a "little masterful, abrupt," Rochester attempts to excuse his "superiority."[58] His intent to exert verbal control over his new governess is evident.

Jane, however, does not succumb to these initial pressures. Although Gilbert portrays Jane as dominated by Rochester, his "sexual knowledge" posing a "barrier" to their equality, this early exchange demonstrates that Rochester rarely dominates Jane.[59] Moreover, further textual evidence indicates that Jane usually develops the banter between the two and engages in nonverbal transactions that shape their exchanges as well. For example, after her initial apologies and concessions to Rochester's statements—"Allow me to disown my first answer. I intended no point of repartee: it was only a blunder"—Jane holds her ground.[60] When pressured to speak, Jane assumes a calculated silence. Her method of metacommunication—"Instead of speaking, I smiled, and not a very complacent or submissive smile either"—prompts Rochester to command her to speak. Her rather indifferent and unyielding manner forces Rochester to compromise, leaving the choice of subject and the "manner of treating it" entirely to her. Continuing the standoff, Jane sits and says nothing, silently thinking: "If he expects me to talk for the mere sake of talking and showing off, he will find he has addressed himself to the wrong person."[61] Throughout this transaction, Jane shapes and directs their discourse, successfully subverting Rochester's attempts to exert his master status over her. By refusing to heed his commands, Jane demonstrates that she has, in her process of differentiation, learned to value and to assert her independence.

Jane's behavior in this initial transactional exchange closely parallels the behavioral patterns outlined in the fourth balance of Kegan's developmental model of personality in which self-government and the "capacity for independence"—to own one's self—is the central concern of the individual.[62] Maintenance of self-government becomes an end in itself; therefore, individuals in this balance feel that no one has the right to control them. Although Jane acknowledges Rochester's higher status as her employer, she remains unintimidated by his attempts to control her, preserving both her self-government and her sense of independence. For example, further along in the conversation, Rochester attempts repeatedly to exercise his authority; Jane continues to combat it. In response to Jane's commentary on the difference between insolence and informality, Rochester remarks that "not three in three thousand raw school girl governesses would have answered me as you have just done." To further assert his authority over her, he impudently says, "I don't mean to flatter you: if you are cast in a different mould to the majority it is no merit of yours: Nature did it . . . for what I yet know, you may be no better than the rest; you may have intolerable defects to counter-balance your few good points."[63]

Despite such humiliating remarks, Jane does not so much as wince at Rochester's attempt to degrade her; she does not retaliate audaciously; she does not leave the room in tears.[64] Instead, she firmly stands her ground, looks up at Rochester until their eyes meet, and, without saying a word, she thinks to herself that he also is no better than the others. Her facial expressions are telling enough for Rochester to respond promptly: "Yes, yes, you are right . . . I have plenty of faults of my own."[65] As in the earlier part of this exchange, even Jane's nonverbal cues reflect her strong will. As she develops the course of their dialogue, Rochester is forced to concede to her, reluctantly modifying his conversation as an appropriate response for further conversations. Jane's command of both the verbal and nonverbal transactions continues, and she delivers a more direct message in the final moments of this exchange. Tiring of Rochester's speech, Jane gets up to put Adele to bed. When Rochester remarks that she is leaving because she is afraid of him, she promptly explains: "Your language is enigmatical, sir: but though I am bewildered, I am certainly not afraid. . . . I have no wish to talk nonsense."[66] Jane not only combats Rochester's verbal dominance, but she effectively develops responses that allow her to maintain command throughout the transaction.

To Rochester's surprise, Jane is indeed well-versed in the art of verbal sparring. She has already experienced the injustices of such hierarchical relationships with males in her interactions with the abusive John Reed and the pompous Mr. Brocklehurst who have served, ironically, as valuable negative models for her. From them, Jane has learned strategies to combat domineering men. As she has throughout her continuing development, Jane draws on past experience, adapting what she has learned to a new but somewhat similar situation. From the outset of her relationship with Rochester, Jane assumes an active role in their transactions, thereby preserving her independence. Thus, it is not only the intrapsychic but also the interrelational analysis of Jane that helps us to understand the complexity and breadth of her character.

As with the earlier part of this exchange, the dynamics of this later transaction accurately delineates the dynamics of an interaction between two people mediating in Kegan's fourth or *institutional* phase. At this stage in their relationship, Rochester and Jane react defensively to one another, illustrating behavior that is typical of people who view the other as a threat to their individual independence. Because Rochester's participation in the bantering scene is crucial to understanding transactional processes as illuminated by family systems therapy, it is important to briefly examine his family-of-origin and development.[67] Like Jane, Rochester has been triangulated out of his family system—in his case by his father and his brother. As the second son, Rochester is a victim of the laws of primogeniture and therefore is excluded from inheriting the family property and wealth.[68] His father arranges for his ill-fated marriage to Bertha, the daughter of a West-Indian land owner—a position that would allow Rochester to gain control over her wealth. Because the mental history of Bertha's family is not taken into consideration when the marriage agreement is entered into, Rochester believes his father has failed him. Both Rochester and Jane see themselves as isolated in society—their places as problematic. Kegan posits that the danger in this fourth balance is excessive control. Although Rochester strives to control their conversations, Jane maintains control of their transactional exchanges, further demonstrating the complexity and the trajectory of her development. Thus, Phelan's argument that characters cannot be "adequately summed up" with a simple and neat thematic summary seems increasingly relevant to Jane's character.[69]

The complex nature of Jane's differentiation process is further evidenced when Jane and Rochester are reunited at Ferndean. At that time, Jane declares to Rochester that he would benefit from having her as neighbor, nurse, housekeeper, and companion. In *Unbecoming Women: British Women Writers in the Novel of Development*, Susan Fraiman interprets this final scene as a regression for Jane who had left Thornfield to maintain her individuality. She believes Ferndean may be nothing more than a "still newer servitude" for Jane and the narrative one that urges readers to "turn away from individualism."[70] By becoming her husband's "eyes and hand," Jane, in Fraiman's opinion, assumes an ambiguous position: on the one hand, Rochester's crippling gives her a "physical advantage and the importance of being relied upon"; on the other, it puts her in the role as "interminable caretaker."[71] But by analyzing this exchange between Jane and Rochester in terms of family systems and measuring it in relationship to Kegan's stages of growth, a quite different interpretation emerges.

From the moment Jane walks into the parlor at Ferndean, it appears that the level of banter between the two merely picks up where it left off months earlier. "I have found you out—I am come back to you," Jane announces. Rochester hesitates, calling himself a "sightless block" not worthy to have anything but fatherly feelings for her.[72] Jane is momentarily put off. But quickly she intuits his real feelings of vulnerability. Admitting to herself "no difficulty" with his impairment, Jane finds fresh courage to resume her "livelier vein" of conversation. "It is time some one undertook to rehumanise you," she teases.[73] When Rochester directs her attention further to his disheveled appearance, asking her if he is hideous, Jane playfully replies, "Very, sir: you always were, you know," aware that all she said or did seemed to "either console or revive him." Rochester replies with a witty comeback of his own: "Humph! The wickedness has not been taken out of you, whereever you have sojourned."[74] Making a hasty escape from this exchange in a much different manner than months before when she did so because she had "no wish to talk nonsense," Jane leaves Rochester to wonder about the rest of her story and herself gleefully to reflect that she has the means of "fretting him out of his melancholy for some time to come."[75] It is apparent that Jane has become even more adept at dictating the direction of their discourse, diffusing conflict, consoling and reviving the brooding Rochester. Her avowal that "in his presence I thoroughly lived; and he lived in mine" contradicts most emphatically the notion that she plans to settle for the role of caretaker for Rochester and be subject to him as her master as Fraiman suggests.[76]

More memorable is their conversation the following day. When she is prodded by the jealous Rochester, Jane playfully paints a portrait of St. John Rivers as a Greek god and leads Rochester to believe that she has been intimate with him. Jane's information puts Rochester in the submissive role, forcing him to respond irritably, "Damn him! . . . Did you like him, Jane?"[77] Rochester, however, realizes that Jane is teasing him and participates in the banter by reacting playfully. In fact, he acknowledges this verbal dance a few moments later by countering the validity of Jane's statement that St. John had proposed marriage to her by replying: "That is a fiction—an impudent invention to vex me."[78] By implementing and recognizing such nuances in their own discourse Jane and Rochester reveal the complex nature of their relationship.

The subtle differences marking this series of conversations reflect the level of intimacy reached between the two since their first encounter at Thornfield. As noted, their early repartee reflects both operating from the balance in which maintaining self-government (nobody controls me!) is the ultimate goal. In the early stage of their relationship, then, it is inevitable that their egos clash; both seek to control their own *self* and do not allow the other to mediate for them. This mindset, in fact, was the source of Jane's flight from Thornfield when she discovers on her wedding day that Rochester has been deceitful. For Jane, Rochester's pleas for her to remain with him produce an anxiety that results from her recognition that she is about to lose her self-governing rights. Instead of staying at Thornfield to work out a solution to remain with a man she loves dearly, she flees to preserve her individuality. When Jane says, "I care for myself. The more solitary, the more friendless, the more unsustained I am, the more I will respect myself," she declares emphatically her increasing autonomy.[79]

By the time Jane returns to Rochester, however, she has gone beyond this balance in her evolution. She realizes that an increased sense of autonomy—the "sense of self, self-dependence, self ownership" that Kegan identifies as the hallmark of the fourth balance—by itself has its shortcomings.[80] Profiting from the life-altering experiences that prompted her to leave Thornfield as well as those while she was away at Marsh End, Jane reaches a degree of evolution that can be measured in terms of Kegan's fifth or final balance.[81] In this balance the "self" is now separate from the institution; the self "runs the organization, where before there was a self who was the organization."[82] The individual has a capacity for intimacy that was not possible in the fourth equilibrium because one now has a "self," both for one's self and to share. For Jane (as it is for Rochester), it is no longer her ultimate concern to preserve the practices of self-government.[83] Jane has a different objective. Although inheriting her uncle John Eyre's wealth leaves Jane economically independent with the right to claim the family home at Marsh End as her own, she chooses to seek out Rochester. To secure a relationship that will allow her to maintain a balance between both real intimacy and relative independence is her goal.

In the final transaction in the narrative, Jane maintains a balance between her desire for independence and her desire to obtain intimacy in the relationship with a "new form of openness" that marks Kegan's fifth balance.[84] A close analysis of the dialogue shows that Jane, as she does in their earlier encounters, shapes and directs much of the conversation and thus determines the course of their relationship. But, instead of practicing the defensive and egotistic behavior that was visible in their transaction at Thornfield, Jane, taking her cue from the positive influences that she has known, assesses and responds to Rochester's emotional and physical needs. Ultimately, it is her determination to be Rochester's wife and her belief that he would "claim [her] at once as his own" that gives her encouragement to seek such intimacy.[85] She no longer resists the romantic advances previously shunned. "Why should I," she states, "when both he and I were happier near than apart?" She caresses Rochester and smoothes his hair; she softens the details of her wandering and starvation rather than "inflict unnecessary pain."[86] When urged by Rochester to divulge information on her whereabouts since she left Thornfield and of her relationship with St. John, Jane calmly replies, "You shall not get it out of me to-night, sir; you must wait till to-morrow." Jane's reply provokes Rochester into calling her a "mocking changeling"; the entire transaction marks her as a savvy strategist and conversationalist.[87]

Although critics have marginalized Jane's heroic flight to Ferndean, her return to Rochester was a deliberate choice on her part. As she cajoles Rochester out of his melancholy, Jane exhibits an authority over their exchanges and thus an authority over their relationship that provides powerful evidence to counter not only Fraiman's claim that Jane devalues or sacrifices her individuality to become a mere caretaker for a diminished Rochester, but also those claims of Gilbert and Shuttleworth who contend that Jane sells out to the uncontrollable power of the patriarchy—able only to cope with a weakened and crippled Rochester.[88] Once reunited with him, Jane does not devalue or sacrifice her individuality. Instead, she determines that Rochester is the right husband for her—fulfilling a goal of family that has eluded her throughout her life. When Rochester questions her sincerity in wanting to marry him, Jane's response validates this agency: "Sacrifice! What do I sacrifice? Famine for food, expectation for content. To be privileged to put my arms round what I value—to press my lips to what I love—to repose on what I trust: is that to make a sacrifice? If so, then certainly I delight in sacrifice."[89] The fervor of Jane's response is not that of a woman who has no other choices but to marry a debilitated man. Rather, her response indicates self-assurance in her decision to make this important life choice.

When Jane Eyre, then, utters, "Reader, I married him," her rhetorical statement is dramatic in its simplicity and powerful in its insinuation. Just as Brontë's novel, *Jane Eyre,* is recognized as an enigma in nineteenth-century literary terms, Jane Eyre, herself, is an enigma, confounding the paradigm of the nineteenth-century woman who must forego independence and succumb to the era's sociological expectations.[90] It is true that Jane's options are dictated by her station in life and the era in which she lives. Thus, they are always limited. But Jane makes choices when it would seem she has none to make. As she moves through each step of her emotional development, she defines her world and achieves her struggle for independence on terms that are available to her. In each step of her evolvement, Jane arrives at a place compatible with her sense of independence, her traits of resourcefulness and resiliency marking her as representative of a plausible person. Initially, Jane makes the decision to walk away from Rochester because to stay would compromise her integrity. She preserves her integrity again when she walks away from St. John. Jane's acceptance of his proposal would force her to eschew romantic passion for religious fervor—a fervor she does not share with Rivers. Upon her arrival at Ferndean, Jane feels a sense of completeness within herself: "I am an independent woman now," she proudly proclaims.[91] Her decision to marry Rochester is one of choice rather than one of yielding to nineteenth-century patriarchal standards and expectations. With him, the balance of intimacy, companionship, and independence that Jane seeks is hers.

By novel's end, Jane has achieved a "rebalancing" or "new locating" of the self, an evolvement that is consistent with Kegan's fifth balance.[92] In her, Brontë has created an intricately complex character who undergoes a process of evolution that mirrors the evolvement of a real and plausible person, one who extracts and assimilates the best standards and models of integrity from sources outside the traditional family matrix, learning to preserve and transform her self, to love and connect with others. By using the language of family systems psychotherapy to open up the nature and extent of Jane's interpersonal connections and Kegan's system of balances to measure the complexity of adult experience that Jane recovers from her early attachments and connections, a new dimension of Jane's character is revealed—a richer reading of her character experienced than a thematic or intrapsychic reading can uncover. Although Jane may be identified with the social issues that she foregrounds as a thematic character, she need not be dismissed simply as a thematic representation of nineteenth-century social issues and the ideology that defines it. Rather, Jane can be described most aptly in Kegan's terms as a "value-originating, system-generating, history-making" individual.[93] As such, her status as a character who functions primarily in the mimetic sphere is firmly established.

NOTES

This essay began as a seminar joint project with John Kim, graduate student at Northern Illinois University and teacher at Adlai Stevenson High School in Lincolnshire, Illinois. While more recent drafts and authorship have been mine, including presentation of a condensed version of this essay at the Midwestern Conference on Film, Language, and Literature in March 1999, I wish to thank John for his initial input—particularly his coordination of the bantering scenes from the text. I also wish to thank John V. Knapp, who has been generous with both his knowledge and his time in reading and responding to my conference presentation as well as to subsequent drafts of this essay.

1. Gilbert, "Plain Jane's Progress," 498. In her edition of Brontë's *Jane Eyre*, Beth Newman observes that Richard Chase, drawing on psychoanalytic concepts, was the first critic to suggest what has become commonplace; once Rochester is blinded and maimed he loses some of the dangerous sexual power he holds over Jane, and she is transformed into the "Victorian domestic angel" or the "Victorian status quo" (453–54). See Chase, "Brontës."

2. Gilbert, "Plain Jane's Progress," 500.

3. Shuttleworth, *Charlotte Brontë and Victorian Psychology*, 151.

4. Ibid., 182.

5. Phelan, *Reading People, Reading Plots*, 27. See Phelan for his definitions and discussion of the three components that make up a character construct, especially 3–27. See also his essay, "Character, Progression, and the Mimetic-Didactic Distinction," for additional discussion of character constructs.

6. Shuttleworth's study is Freudian based. See also Sadoff, "Father, Castration, and Female Fantasy in *Jane Eyre*," which focuses on Jane's internal, intrapsychic conflicts.

7. Knapp, *Striking at the Joints*, 37.

8. Ibid., 195. In *Introductory Lectures in Psychoanalysis*, Sigmund Freud explicitly warned against involving family members in his clients' therapy. Likening therapy to the surgical field, he questioned the success rate of operations "if they had to take place in the presence of all the members of the patient's family, who would stick their noses into the field of the operation and exclaim aloud at every incision" (459).

9. For an overview of family systems history and terminology, see Knapp, "Family Systems Psychotherapy."

10. Kegan, *Evolving Self*, 44. Kegan, who borrows many of his evolutionary metaphors from Swiss psychologist, Jean Piaget, has developed a five-step system of balances, with each new balance forming what he calls an "evolutionary truce." Each of these truces "strikes a subject-object balance and thus becomes a way of knowing the world" (44). Briefly, these steps are as follows: first equilibrium (Impulsive Balance): authority is all-powerful; second equilibrium (Imperial Balance): one can only see through one's own needs; third equilibrium (Interpersonal Balance): self is no longer its own needs; rather it has

them; fourth equilibrium (Institutional Balance): movement from "I am my relationships" to "I have relationships"; fifth equilibrium (Interindividual Balance): one now has a self, both for one's self and to share. For an in-depth chart and discussion of balances, see 85–110. See also Knapp, *Striking at the Joints*, 168–76.

11. Minuchin, Lee, and Simon, *Mastering Family Therapy*, defines family as "a group of people, connected emotionally and/or by blood, who have lived together long enough to have developed patterns of interaction and stories that justify and explain these patterns of interaction" (29).

12. Minuchin, Lee, and Simon, *Mastering Family Therapy*, 29–30.

13. Brontë, *Jane Eyre*, 5.

14. Ibid., 8.

15. Metacommunication, Virginia Satir states in *Conjoint Family Therapy*, is a "message *about* a message." Humans cannot communicate without simultaneously metacommunicating by gestures, facial expression, body posture and movement, tone of voice, and mode of dress (76). When, where, with whom, under what circumstances, and what is the contract between the persons carrying on the interchange are, Satir states, all factors in the verbal and nonverbal process of communication (75). Considered "reliable indicators of interpersonal functioning," metacommunication techniques, then, are useful aids to family systems therapy (63).

16. Brontë, *Jane Eyre*, 12. Jane knew that her uncle had taken her as "parentless infant to his house" and in his last moments he had required a promise of Mrs. Reed to rear and maintain her "as one of her own children" (13). In *Daily Life In Victorian England*, Sally Mitchell discusses the laws that were in place that governed the status of orphans in Victorian England, any one of which may apply to Jane's own history. For example, "fathers were legally, in all circumstances, the guardians of their children." If a father died before the child turned twenty-one, it was necessary for his will to name a substitute guardian who then had the same rights over the child (now called a "ward") in all matters just as the father would have (106). Although English law had no provision for "legal" adoption until the 1920s, orphaned children were informally adopted by a friend or relative who simply took them in to "raise as their own" (106). The children were often sent to training schools or charitable institutions that would prepare them for a career or, like Jane, were educated at special boarding schools in order to learn to support themselves as governesses. See also Mitchell's discussion of Victorian family life in middle class homes (141–49).

17. Brontë, *Jane Eyre*, 13.

18. Ample textual evidence demonstrates the troubled Reed family system. The pattern of dysfunction that marked their treatment of Jane followed them into their adult years.

19. Brontë, *Jane Eyre*, 31–32.

20. Kegan, *Evolving Self*, 43–44.

21. Ibid., 97.

22. Ibid., 101.

23. Brontë, *Jane Eyre*, 13. Jane is first made aware of her heritage and the transgenerational conflict her parents' marriage generated when she overhears the servants relate her parents' history (21).

24. Ibid., 11, 13.

25. Ibid., 203–4.

26. Kegan, *Evolving Self*, 77.

27. Ibid., 19.

28. Ibid., 17–18. Kegan explains: "The consequence of this beguiling, the infant's relationship with her primary caretaker, like that of her relationship with physical objects is her further development, a new kind of consciousness, a qualitative growth in her making of meaning" (18).

29. Ibid., 18. See also Kegan's discussion of an infant's ability to orient to an object even if it is absent from view (80–81). See also Winnicott, "Transitional Objects and Transitional Phenomena" in *Playing and Reality*, 1–25; and Woodward, "Infants Selectively Encode the Goal Object of an Actor's Reach." Although Winnicott is a neo-Freudian psychologist and Woodward a cognitive psychologist, both have conducted clinical studies in object-relations with babies and young children to determine how children reason and initiate their relationships with people.

30. Kegan, *Evolving Self*, 77.

31. Gopnik, Meltzoff, and Kuhl, *Scientist in the Crib*, 29, 31.

32. Ibid., 30.

33. Ibid., 49.

34. Ibid., 189–90. Although Daniel N. Stern's *Interpersonal World of the Infant* discusses age-specific phases of infant behavior, Stern believes that the infant's first order of business in creating an interpersonal world is to "form the sense of a core self and core others," a task largely accomplished during the period between "two and seven months"of age (70). Gopnik, Meltzoff, and Kuhl, *Scientist in the Crib*, published in 1999, supercedes Stern's study. Their findings reveal that within just a few days after babies are born they "recognize familiar faces, voices, . . . smells" and, at birth, their "mother's voice" (27). The authors state that new developmental research indicates that an "innately determined foundation, powerful learning abilities, and implicit tuition from other people," allow babies to "spontaneously revise, reshape, and restructure their knowledge" (7, 53). Within the first nine months, infants can tell the difference between expressions of happiness and sadness (28). And the "basic groundwork" or a human's ability to "understand thoughts and beliefs, . . . perceptions, emotions, desires, and feelings" is, the authors state, "in place after only a few years" (52–53). The authors pay tribute to Jean Piaget's early studies (studies that influenced Kegan) in observing the working of a child's mind (14–16).

35. Kegan, *Evolving Self*, 18.

36. Mr. Lloyd, the apothecary, and Helen Burns befriend Jane. In a brief appearance in the narrative at a pivotal time for Jane, Lloyd, for example, recommends she be sent away to school. Jane states that she felt "sheltered and befriended . . . raised and upheld" by his kindness (Brontë, *Jane Eyre*, 15).

37. Ibid., 24.

38. Ibid., 33.

39. Ibid., 35, 200.

40. Ibid., 199.

41. Ibid., 33, 199.

42. Mackey, "Nurturance," 489.

43. Ibid., 504–5.

44. Gopnik, Meltzoff, and Kuhl, *Scientist in the Crib*, 49.

45. Brontë, *Jane Eyre*, 73.

46. Ibid., 73.

47. Ibid., 73, 74.

48. Ibid., 74, 75.
49. Ibid., 322.
50. Ibid., 202.
51. Ibid., 200.
52. Ibid., 203.
53. Ibid., 13.
54. Ibid., 202.
55. Minuchin, Lee, and Simon, *Mastering Family Therapy*, 30.
56. Brontë, *Jane Eyre*, 115.
57. Ibid., 115–16.
58. Ibid., 117.
59. Gilbert, "Plain Jane's Progress," 488. Shuttleworth argues that Brontë's text "offers a fierce critique of the perverted, self-destructive forces of Rochester's sexual tyranny" with both Jane and Rochester treating their association as "fierce battle for the preservation of autonomy" (*Charlotte Brontë and Victorian Psychology*, 169–70).
60. Brontë, *Jane Eyre*, 115.
61. Ibid., 117.
62. Kegan, *Evolving Self*, 101.
63. Brontë, *Jane Eyre*, 118.
64. Rochester's attempt to degrade Jane seems to be a practice in flirtation; he makes such impudent statements because he is attracted to her. Such schizophrenic-like communication is called the "double-bind," or a meta-message that is at odds with the verbalized message. Gregory Bateson, a founder of Strategic Family Therapy—a family systems school of intervention—first identified the patterns derived from the "double-bind." See Knapp, "Family Systems Psychotheraphy," 237.
65. Brontë, *Jane Eyre*, 119.
66. Ibid., 122.
67. Rochester's mimetic development is important to the family systems analysis process, but I wish to focus primarily on Jane's evolvement in this essay.
68. In *Introduction to English Legal History*, J. H. Baker states that "these rules of inheritance lasted, with few alterations, until 1926" (307).
69. Phelan, *Reading People, Reading Plots*, 27.
70. Fraiman, *Unbecoming Women*, 117, 120.
71. Ibid., 118.
72. Brontë, *Jane Eyre*, 382, 383.
73. Ibid., 384.
74. Ibid., 385.
75. Ibid., 386.
76. Ibid., 384.
77. Ibid., 388.
78. Ibid., 390.
79. Ibid., 279.
80. Kegan, *Evolving Self*, 100.
81. It should be noted that an in-depth analysis of Rochester's development would show that he has also reached this fifth balance in Kegan's model. At this point in the narrative, he no longer obsesses over maintaining self-government. Rather, as his declaration "Ah! Jane. But I want a wife" demonstrates, he wants a companion with whom to share his life (Brontë, *Jane Eyre*, 391).

82. Kegan, *Evolving Self*, 103.

83. St. John is partially responsible for aiding Jane's evolvement to the fifth equilibrium. While his tyrannical presence over her is difficult for her to over-come, ultimately she realizes that to marry him would have been "an error of judgement" (Brontë, *Jane Eyre*, 368). More important, the lack of emotion and love from St. John is the catalyst for Jane's understanding that, although she has individuated and met her goals to maintain her independence, her needs will be fulfilled only when she finds someone who will love her as she loves him.

84. Kegan, *Evolving Self*, 108.

85. Brontë, *Jane Eyre*, 383.

86. Ibid., 387.

87. Ibid., 386.

88. Sightless and maimed though Rochester may be, Jane describes him as quite the opposite from being diminished. Coming upon him at Ferndean, unob-served, she sees the same "strong and stalwart" figure with "raven-black" hair and unaltered features that she remembers. "Not in one year's space, by any sorrow, could his athletic strength be quelled, or his vigorous prime blighted," she notes (Ibid., 379).

89. Brontë, *Jane Eyre*, 392.

90. Brontë incorporates elements of romance with the Gothic tradition while weaving social issues into her narrative that involves, in particular, the limited options open to women and to men without patrimony in the nineteenth cen-tury. Thus, she separates herself from the rising tradition of realism in the novel that reflects the age.

91. Brontë, *Jane Eyre*, 382.

92. Kegan, *Evolving Self*, 103, 105.

93. Ibid., 104.

"Even Now China Wraps Double Binds around My Feet": Family Communication in *The Woman Warrior* and *Dim Sum*

Gary Storhoff

ONE OF THE MOST PROMISING DEVELOPMENTS IN THE INTERDISCI-plinary study of literature and psychology has emerged from the practice of critics who explore how literary texts chart family roles and systems. Central to this interrogation is family systems theory. Literary critics who employ family systems theory nec-essarily look beyond the psychoanalytic assumptions of the indi-vidual as an "autonomous psychological entity" and of "the family only as a collection of relatively autonomous people, each motivated by his or her own particular psychological mecha-nisms and conflicts."[1] Instead, the critic discovers the sources of an individual's behavior within a much larger *inter*personal dys-function in the family as a whole. As John V. Knapp writes, "The combination of critical skill and psychological understanding can enrich one's reading of [a] novel more interestingly in a way dif-ficult for anyone viewing the text through eyes seeing only intra-personal psychology."[2] This kind of investigation increases our understanding of an author, expands our understanding of the possibilities of character constructs, and adds another dimen-sion to the view that literature expresses fundamental ideas about how we live.

To apply a Western psychological theory to an Asian-American text, however, is problematic, since the author's work may often be twisted to become a general statement about Asian Ameri-cans. Sau-ling Cynthia Wong, for example, writes, "At stake is not only the existence of the minority writer's voice but the possible perversion of that voice to satisfy the white reader's appetite for exoticism."[3] Wong cautions against reading Maxine Hong Kings-ton's *The Woman Warrior* in particular as a "guided Chinatown tour."[4] Kingston echoes Wong's admonition in her interviews, where she defends herself against the charge that she "exotic-izes" Asian Americans to increase her literary reputation; Kingston explains that she is not speaking for the entire Chinese-American community but is expressing her own subjective vision of her ancestral heritage as an American in her novel: "The myths I write are new, American."[5] The critic must necessarily be cautious in interpreting an ethnic text.

It is possible, however, to be too cautious, and out of an exaggerated wish to preserve the sanctity of an ethnic group's "Otherness," overlook the specific disharmonies or dysfunctions in an ethnic family that may be partially a consequence of their immersion in an alien culture, but that may also be shared by other, so-called "mainstream" families. As psychologist Shlomo Ariel writes, "A description of a family system . . . is incomplete if it fails to include certain identifying cultural features."[6] Nonetheless, "incomplete" does not mean "impossible," and this essay seeks to discover human similarities, however different we may be in local habits and customs. Kingston's novel is especially read as an interrogation of common problems of a nuclear family. Kingston herself insists that her own work crosses racial and ethnic boundaries in her dramatization of family issues. She explains that her literary purpose is to problematize the concept of "family" beyond restrictive racial boundaries; to analyze "universal" family conflicts, promoting healing within the family unit: "[The Woman Warrior] is about building a human psyche and how to get straight with parents and ancestors and then become able to intuit, to realize yourself as a human being."[7] Both Kingston and similar Chinese-American works, such as the film Dim Sum: A Little Bit of Heart (1987; dir. Wayne Wang), explore those intimate struggles that everyone experiences within the family: battles over power and roles, grief over individuation, attempts to tolerate fragmentation and discontinuity within the family, and the hoped-for reconciliation between the generations. These fundamental familial struggles antedate whatever difficulties Kingston (and similar authors) may have experienced as women or as ethnic writers in America.[8]

The debate over the "universality" as opposed to the "cultural localism" of a multicultural text, especially The Woman Warrior, has been predictably contentious.[9] This essay departs from the familiar debate—is the text ethnic or "universal"?—by focusing on typical dysfunctions in family communications. Family systems theory provides this unique perspective on ethnic works by introducing the concept of "the double bind," defined by Gregory

Bateson in *Steps to an Ecology of Mind* as "a situation in which no matter what a person does, [he or she] 'can't win.'"[10] In a double-bind communication, a parent sends two different messages, one explicit, literal message that is immediately contradicted or qualified by a second, more abstract "metacommentary" that contradicts the literal message.[11] A parent's demand for affection from a child, for example, may be contradicted by the parent's stiffening body when the child touches him or her. Bateson argues that the victim of chronic double binding will eventually become unable to distinguish between logical levels of a message. To such an individual, even a parent's simple question—"How can I help you?"—is problematic. Is the question a friendly offer? A threat? A cruel joke? A family systems approach to *The Woman Warrior* and *Dim Sum* would shift attention from the individual characters (Maxine and Geraldine) to the individual in the family's communicational context.

As far as I know, my argument about double-binding communications within the families of *The Woman Warrior* and *Dim Sum* has not been discussed by previous critics.[12] I would in no way imply that double-bind patterns of communication afflict all Chinese-Americans, since, as therapists Insoo Kim Berg and Ajakai Jaya write, "there is no 'typical' Asian-American family."[13] On the contrary, family systems theorists recognize that double-bind communications transcend race and ethnicity, and can be discovered in many (most?) families. In fact, therapists Carlos Sluzki and Eliseo Veron regard the double bind "as a universal pathogenic situation."[14]

Maxine suffers in a "double bind," forged in China but continuously imposed in America.[15] Maxine is aware of the double bind, of the paradox of desiring liberation and restriction simultaneously: "Then [as a liberated woman] I get bitter: no one supports me; I am not loved enough to be supported. That I am not a burden has to compensate for the sad envy when I look at women loved enough to be supported. Even now China wraps double binds around my feet."[16] Her sense of paradoxical desires derive from a childhood of double-bind messages from her family, especially her mother. Maxine must contend not only with her mother's criticism, but also with Brave Orchid's extraordinary accomplishments: her survival under harsh circumstances and her assertion of her own selfhood as a Chinese physician. Brave Orchid's communications to Maxine are experienced as paradox: as a girl, she should be a slave, a "maggot in the rice"; but she should also prevail against the world as a Woman Warrior. Her escape from her family's double bind is the plot's organizing principle.

Geraldine Tam, the adult protagonist of the film *Dim Sum,* suffers a similar situation as Maxine, as her mother demands that she simultaneously accomplish antithetical goals. Geraldine (Laureen Chew) is an accomplished, mature Chinese-American woman who has achieved a degree of responsibility and authority; yet like Maxine, Geraldine is engaged in a mother-daughter nexus that often renders her powerless. Geraldine is preparing for her Ph.D. orals while also trying to care for her mother, Mrs. Tam (Kim Chew), who, she constantly reminds Geraldine, would like to see her daughter married—supposedly Mrs. Tam's duty as a Chinese mother. Geraldine is considering marriage to her boyfriend Richard (John Nishio), but her marriage would necessitate leaving her mother in San Francisco for Richard's home in Los Angeles, where Richard practices medicine. Obviously, Mrs. Tam has mixed feelings about Geraldine's future departure, but she never reveals these feelings to her daughter—or overtly, at least, to the viewer. Only from Mrs. Tam's facial expressions, gestures, and apparently unmotivated actions and remarks does the viewer infer her reluctance to see her daughter become independent. Mrs. Tam's ambivalence over Geraldine's future choices is concealed as she herself attempts to play the role of the proper Chinese mother, preparing her daughter for a conventional marriage.

Geraldine's plight is complicated by Mrs. Tam's conviction that death is near. Mrs. Tam believes she will die soon because of a prediction made long ago, when she was a child, by a fortune-teller she visited when she lived in China. By carefully setting out her burial clothes at the film's beginning, Mrs. Tam wordlessly communicates to Geraldine the precarious nature of their life together. Geraldine's "abandonment" of her mother for Richard would understandably precipitate Geraldine's considerable guilt and self-recrimination—though of course Geraldine does not believe in prophecies, as her mother does. How Geraldine attempts but ultimately fails to resolve her double bind is at the center of the film's plot. Geraldine's story, unlike Maxine's, ends with failure because Geraldine cannot in good conscience act upon her own initiative. While Maxine discovers creative ways through art to transcend her double bind, Geraldine remains trapped in hers at the film's conclusion.

In each narrative, a first-generation Chinese-American daughter struggles to form her adult identity amid the confusion of paradoxical messages from her mother, and the tension of trying to individuate from her family while simultaneously being a dutiful daughter. The two mothers' overt and direct communications are, however, generally revised or reversed by subtle communications that the daughters only occasionally recognize. The daughter must decode messages from a confusing array of the parent's actions, gestures, rituals, and conflictual—even contradictory—spoken words within contexts that may qualify or even contradict the surface meanings of those words. The mothers in *The Woman Warrior* and *Dim Sum* convey significant cues for their daughters' choices and actions, as if to direct them unilaterally, but because these cues are often embedded in paradoxical communications, the daughters are uncertain how to respond. In essence, both Geraldine and Maxine are initially placed in situations where they "can't win." Their mothers are Chinese-born and have deliberately resisted assimilation, although the mother in *Dim Sum* takes pride in the fact that she becomes an American citizen during the film's narrative. Both Brave Orchid and Mrs. Tam speak Cantonese, and both retain their cultural habits, rituals, and beliefs. Neither mother ventures far out into her urban environment, but instead they send their daughters to act as their representatives. Nevertheless, they are very different in their personalities and their surface communicational style.[17]

In *The Woman Warrior*, Brave Orchid, the survivor of a subsistence-level life in China, is well aware of the dangers for the family that result from an individual's excessive or extravagant behavior, and she has witnessed the calamities that are reserved especially for a woman who disregards or ignores conventionalities and the "necessities" of life. As Sau-ling Cynthia Wong has observed, Brave Orchid's world is grimly circumscribed by the perceived antithesis of "necessity" and "extravagance." All activity is evaluated by Brave Orchid from a narrowly utilitarian criterion; the code of necessity dictates intrinsic value, while "extravagant" behavior—action that has no direct material or utilitarian benefit to the family or the community—is strongly discouraged. From her deprived youth in China, Brave Orchid learned too well the lessons that food may run out, that a child's play is wasteful and divisive, that boys are more useful and desirable than girls, and that the persistent need for simple necessities of life must dominate every life-choice, not only for herself but for her family.[18] To emphasize to Maxine the importance of persistent, vigilant self-denial, she fills her daughter's childhood with "talk-stories" of life in the old China, her China. Maxine is engrossed by these imaginative, rich stories, yet there is a greater purpose than to evoke Maxine's enchantment. These talk-stories are moral exempla, but they also convey criticism, admonitions, and put-downs of Maxine's accomplishments, especially in the only area that Maxine as a child can shine: her schoolwork. School has no immediately utility for Brave Orchid's family. Thus, Brave Orchid—herself a successful student of medicine in China—warns Maxine, "You can't eat straight A's."[19] It is no wonder, then, that Maxine as a child laments, "My American life has been such a disappointment."[20] It is Maxine's task within her family to affirm her own identity, separate from her family's view of what she should be, while at the same time maintaining her close tie to her mother—obviously her more significant parent in her life in this text.

Brave Orchid in *The Woman Warrior* and Mrs. Tam in *Dim Sum* present a study in contrasting parental methods, a consequence of their differences in both background and character. Mrs. Tam seems a much "nicer" mother than the grim Brave Orchid. In contrast to Brave Orchid, Mrs. Tam is a woman of very few words, and is seemingly childlike and passive in her interactions with her daughter, Geraldine. Mrs. Tam is from Hong Kong, and therefore she shows no concern about Chinese communism, the possibility of her original family's starvation, their political oppression, or potential losses of family property. On the contrary, for much of the film, she happily plans to visit her family in Hong Kong. She is clearly from a higher class and a more affluent background than the tough, resourceful Brave Orchid, who is from the peasantry on the rural mainland. In contrast to Mrs. Tam, Brave Orchid is anxious about the family members who must survive the precarious politics of the People's Republic of China, and she continually sends money to support them, depleting their meager family resources. Mrs. Tam eagerly plans throughout the film to go to Hong Kong to visit her family, but Brave Orchid sadly says, "We have no more China to go home to."[21] As a mother, Brave Orchid often seems harsh and domineering, to Maxine's understandable resentment, since she seems to have absorbed her mother's indomitable spirit and feels compelled to resist her domination.

Brave Orchid is especially anxious about Maxine's sexuality. As criticism has amply noted, *The Woman Warrior*'s opening story "No Name Woman" is a covert admonition against Maxine having premarital sex. The shamed "No Name Woman," who has been deprived even of her identity by her brother, Maxine's father, got pregnant, brought humiliation to her family, and eventually committed suicide by throwing herself and her baby into a well. She both destroys herself and her child, as well as polluting her neighbor's water source, thus gaining a small measure of revenge. This lost aunt, Brave Orchid implies, made a wrong choice and was punished accordingly; the story of the aunt is intended to represent the peril of sexual self-indulgence and the inevitability of the family's punishment. The No Name Woman made a tragic mistake, from Brave Orchid's perspective, opting for "extravagance" even in the face of her family's humiliation and the village's terrible retribution.

But the talk-story also implies a judgment against Maxine for having any desire whatsoever. As Paul Outka suggests, in the story "the savage punishment [is] meted out upon the female body for expressing physical desire of any kind, a punishment that economically and brutally reduces the aunt to a set of perpetually unfulfilled desires."[22] Maxine, then, must continuously struggle for individuation from her mother, and as a narrator, she inspires the reader's trust that she will successfully achieve individuation. Accordingly, she narrates the novel from the point of view of a middle-aged woman who has finally come to terms with her upbringing and her mother.[23] Maxine depicts her past self as a defiant, often peculiar child, who thwarts her mother's iron control with her own rebellious behavior—she refuses to untangle her hair, she effects a limp, and she feigns illness for an entire year, for example. This conflict is especially pronounced concerning Maxine's own sexuality, as she attempts to make herself attractive to "the Caucasian, Negro, and Japanese boys," rather than only to the Chinese boys whom Brave Orchid prefers.

In contrast to Brave Orchid and her firm ideas of right and wrong, Mrs. Tam seems unusually open-minded, unbiased, flexible, and generous with her children and their choices. The contrast between the two mothers is especially manifest in their very different responses to their children's sexuality. Compared to Brave Orchid's emphasis on chastity for the sake of survival (the ostensible moral of "No Name Woman"), Mrs. Tam appears untroubled and unconcerned about her daughters' active sexual lives. In fact, Mrs. Tam seems to be a paradigm of the noncontrolling, unprejudiced, and tolerant mother. Unlike Brave Orchid, who insists that Maxine consider only Chinese-American boys as possible suitors (even the unsavory Chinese-American boy who collects pornography and who seems to stalk Maxine at their laundry), Mrs. Tam seems quite comfortable in a multicultural world and is unconcerned about her possible son-in-law's race or ethnic background.

One scene from the film especially seems designed to make the point of Mrs. Tam's tolerance. During a Chinese New Year celebration at her home, Mrs. Tam is shown sitting in the middle of her family of three generations. The viewer is led to infer the significance of the family gathering, and the camera pans across all the family members' faces, although no introduction to any particular person is given. The director makes very clear, however, that Mrs. Tam enthusiastically welcomes Amy, her unmarried daughter, and Amy's son, who is the child of Amy's relationship with an African-American. Later in the scene, she plays with her African/Chinese-American grandson and takes obvious pride in his enjoyment of her cooking—to him, and to Amy, she offers "a little bit of heart," both literally and figuratively. Her warmth and generosity is mirrored by the other family members, who seem equally unprejudiced and accepting. This is an unusually "open" family system, we are led to believe.

Admirably, Mrs. Tam extends this same tolerance and acceptance to her daughter Geraldine. The film underscores Mrs. Tam's generous spirit and relaxed attitude when she appears to accept with equanimity the fact that the unmarried Geraldine and Richard are sleeping together in her house. While Geraldine and Richard are embarrassed at Mrs. Tam's unexpectedly finding them together in bed—"She should have knocked," says Richard—Mrs. Tam never mentions the matter to them throughout the film, and seems to enjoy the company of her prospective son-in-law without moral judgment.

Surprisingly, Geraldine, the daughter of softhearted, generous, and tolerant Mrs. Tam, seems the exact opposite of Maxine. Paradoxically, Mrs. Tam's weakness is her greatest strength in controlling Geraldine; Mrs. Tam's silence, a powerful voice that overwhelms Geraldine's sense of independence. Geraldine cannot seem to escape the control of her soft-spoken, gentle, ostensibly passive mother, and although she is a Ph.D. candidate, she seems baffled by the subtleties of their relationship. Though exceptionally intelligent and accomplished, presumably on her way to a successful professional life beyond graduate school, Geraldine nevertheless seems perpetually her mother's child—the dutiful, good Chinese daughter, still living with her mother and willingly providing for her every need.[24] At the center of the film's plot is Geraldine's need to decide the direction of her life. She struggles over whether to stay with her apparently fragile and innocent mother, marry her Chinese boyfriend Richard (which *seems* to be what Mrs. Tam wants her to do), or leave home and explore other, not yet imagined possibilities.

Ironically, these two very different mothers both place their very different daughters in double-bind situations. So different in temperament and style, Mrs. Tam and Brave Orchid create double-bind situations with their communications to control their daughters, so that neither daughter can immediately respond to their situations with rationality or independent judgment. Yet Brave Orchid's double-binding communications offer a reprieve, a way to escape, for embedded in the double messages she sends her daughter, Brave Orchid interweaves positive alternatives with oppressive commands, liberating choices with restrictive orders. As she admits to Maxine, "That's what Chinese say. We like to say the opposite."[25] If Brave Orchid oppresses Maxine, she also encourages Maxine's liberation, for her talk-stories "make [the] mind large, as the universe is large, so that there is room for paradoxes."[26] The key complication of the double-bind message for Maxine is that Brave Orchid teaches both by direct precept ("girls are geese in the corn") and by her talk-stories of her own accomplishments and ability to work hard.

Brave Orchid's communications promote independence, even while they overtly seem to restrict and deprive Maxine. Brave Orchid, for example, tells story after story which seem to affirm women's subservient role in traditional patriarchal structures, but at the same time she subverts that message with her own example, and those of others, who choose to defy patriarchal restrictions. The shameful story of the No Name Woman, then, is clearly a parable about a woman's need to be virtuous and chaste in a male-dominated society marked by scarcity, yet Brave Orchid also reveals that her husband has forbidden her to tell the story. In the telling, Brave Orchid defies and honors her husband simultaneously. The story both warns against violating social and moral norms that her husband and she herself endorse, but she also covertly encourages Maxine to "tell"—to violate the code of silence the patriarchy enforces. As Thomas J. Ferraro writes, "Brave Orchid's apparent ultimatum against communal trespass can now be seen to have sown the seeds of its own destruction ... suggesting that beneath their contract of silence lies an unspoken sanction of countercultural voice."[27] Obviously, Brave Orchid has discovered through her talk-stories a transcendence of her own double bind. Furthermore, Maxine's fugal elaboration of No Name Woman's story becomes, in Wong's words, "a parable of heroic resistance, however, modest in scope and fatal in form, to the dictates of Necessity."[28] Maxine's childhood oscillates between the restrictiveness enforced by her parents on the surface and the liberation hinted at beneath the obvious "morals" of her mother's talk-stories.

Seen in this paradoxical context of family communications, Brave Orchid's talk-story of her own medical training in China is also a double-bind message that may either liberate or imprison, depending upon Maxine's interpretive choice. As an esteemed village physician in China, Brave Orchid purchased a female slave, and her strong implication to Maxine is that Maxine should beware—she could be sold as a slave if she does not behave. One meaning of the story, then, is that Brave Orchid is strong but Maxine is terribly vulnerable. Yet this talk-story too is double-edged: Brave Orchid later tells Maxine: "Who said we could sell you? We can't sell people. Can't you take a joke? You can't even tell a joke from real life?"[29] Brave Orchid's slavery story is her means of parental control, not to be interpreted on an entirely literal level; she, it is made clear, is confused about how to exert power and control over her daughter in an alien environment.

Threatened by Brave Orchid's disabling message, Maxine can also act upon her mother's enabling example. In Brave Orchid's talk-story describing her leaving her village, studying medicine at school, fighting with the Sitting Ghost, and her subsequent medical practice, she subtly conveys to Maxine the injunction to be practical and obedient to a social order, and that the utility of her actions is to be emulated. But she also inspires Maxine herself to become independent and self-resourceful, a meaning that Maxine has intuitively understood in her proud description of her mother: "My mother may have been afraid, but she would be a dragoness ('my totem, your totem'). She could make herself not weak."[30] While in medical school, Brave Orchid had to confront the "Sitting Ghost" that terrorized her fellow students, and she spends the night with the Ghost and mocks it: "You have no power over a strong woman," Brave Orchid tells it, "You are no more dangerous than a nesting cat."[31] With great pride, Maxine tells how her mother defeats the Sitting Ghost with her perseverance and courage; and the implication on the talk-story is that Maxine too can achieve transcendence, through full acceptance of Brave Orchid's moral: "Good people do not lose to ghosts."[32]

Mrs. Tam operates differently with her daughter Geraldine, telling her no talk-stories but behaving as if she were the "perfect mother"—docile, accepting, quiet, smiling. But she, like Brave

Orchid, also creates a double bind for her daughter. She feigns helplessness and naïveté to tie Geraldine to her. Unlike Brave Orchid, who takes pride in her ruthless commitment to the world of "Necessity," Mrs. Tam seems to be the child of her own daughter, with Geraldine playing the role of her mother's caretaker: Geraldine gently brushes her mother's hair (a motif in the film), does the grocery shopping for her mother, and otherwise acts in the world as a parentified child of the widowed Mrs. Tam. Meanwhile, Mrs. Tam seems timid and confined, seldom venturing beyond her small apartment; her conversations with her Chinese friends, spoken almost entirely in Cantonese, revolve primarily around the need to get Geraldine married. The friends all agree that Mrs. Tam's obligation as a Chinese mother is to promote— perhaps even coerce—her daughter's marriage. Mrs. Tam, unlike Brave Orchid, seldom speaks at length, yet with her passive, dependent behavior, she manages to convey a confusing array of mixed messages. Is Geraldine supposed to marry her boyfriend Richard, move to Los Angeles, and leave her mother alone? Several times in the film, Mrs. Tam tells Geraldine that this is her definite will and desire. The viewer's confidence that Mrs. Tam actually wishes marriage for Geraldine is increased by the film's scenes of Mrs. Tam's conversations with neighbors and friends, beyond Geraldine's hearing. Mrs. Tam constantly professes her wish that Geraldine marry soon, and her incomprehension that Geraldine's marriage has not yet occurred.

Mrs. Tam even creates a scene with her friends that humiliates Geraldine into admitting that she probably would like to marry soon—as, Mrs. Tam says, all good Chinese mothers supposedly wish for their single daughters. Geraldine is asked by Mrs. Tam to carry in a cake to her visiting mahjong players. But Geraldine resists her mother's request, since she knows that Mrs. Tam's friends will ask her about the possibility of her own marriage, and this question, understandably, seems too intimate for Geraldine to discuss. Yet Mrs. Tam insists that Geraldine confront the friends with the symbolic cake; and rather than politely refuse her mother and leave the apartment, Geraldine surprisingly obeys, with the predictable result. Geraldine carries in the cake, and the friends immediately ask Geraldine when she will be married. Embarrassed, Geraldine gives an equivocal answer and leaves the room, receiving the message that in not marrying, she is disappointing her mother, a message that the neighborhood women confirm, once again outside of Geraldine's hearing—but obvious enough to her.

It would seem, then, that in her reluctance to marry, Geraldine is disappointing her mother. But this primary message is contradicted by Mrs. Tam's subtle, often nonverbal metacommentary, which occurs outside of her friends' perspective. The viewer infers, in scene after scene, that Mrs. Tam fears Geraldine's marriage and departure, even though she promotes this supposedly wished-for event. At the beginning of the film, Mrs. Tam makes it clear to Geraldine that her death is imminent. Mrs. Tam's fear of death exposes her profound insecurity as an immigrant, and her terror of facing America without her daughter. She is psychologically dependent on Geraldine. Even though she has lived in America for over forty years, she has made little progress in becoming assimilated. She speaks primarily Cantonese, and the comic scene when she prepares for her citizenship test with Geraldine—she misses Geraldine's question about who was America's first president—seemingly indicates that her life would be limited indeed if she were to live alone.

Mrs. Tam seems to feel that she lacks the resources to live alone. Yet many objective facts established throughout the film's narrative contradict this dismal assessment: Mrs. Tam has established a strong network of friends (each of whom apparently lives alone); she has a strong and supportive family that lives within a reasonable proximity, a fact implied in the family's visit to Mr. Tam's grave; and despite minor disagreements with her brother-in-law, Uncle Tam, she is capable of assisting him in organizing and running a business establishment. Nevertheless, family rituals—requiring Geraldine to persistently brush her hair, for instance—communicate to Geraldine that Mrs. Tam's life depends upon Geraldine's staying in San Francisco. Geraldine's presumptive marriage, supposedly ardently desired by Mrs. Tam, would on this level of abstraction constitute Geraldine's (literally) fatal betrayal of her mother.

Geraldine's third alternative, one that is only implied by Geraldine's gestures and facial expressions throughout the film, is to follow her instincts, leave both her mother *and* Richard, and test herself alone, outside of her narrow and confined world. This possibility of complete liberation from familial, gender, and racial boundaries is lived out by Geraldine's friend, who lives alone, works as a successful professional woman, refuses even to date Chinese-American men, and only occasionally visits her mother (in Hong Kong).[33] But this third alternative is not even acknowledged as a possibility by Mrs. Tam—or by Geraldine herself.

Geraldine is not entirely oblivious to her mother's ploys, but she is unable to escape her double bind. She tells Uncle Tam (Victor Wong) that she understands that her mother is pushing her to marry Richard, but that "she doesn't care how I feel." The uncle, the only one in the film who is truly looking out for Geraldine's best interests, tries to solve Geraldine's dilemma by offering to marry Mrs. Tam himself. On the face of it, this possible marriage between Uncle Tam and Mrs. Tam does not seem absurd, since not only do they work extremely well together in his tavern (he manages the business and she does the books), but they also share a warm and mutually supportive friendship. However, such a marriage would violate Mrs. Tam's secret, psychological need: to be cared for as if she were a child. When she refuses Uncle Tam's marriage proposal with laughter, he tells her, "You have an inconsistent attitude toward [Geraldine]. You want her to marry yet you don't want her to leave." Mrs. Tam replies, "But I am only being a mother."

Geraldine's departure, then, represents this family's battlefield of the double bind. It is not coincidental that Geraldine's decision to live on her own for a short time precipitates a critically revealing moment of family dynamics in the film's narrative. Geraldine plans to spend some time with her close friend, and she packs her bags and wishes her mother well, telling her that she will be back on the weekend to help with grocery shopping. But immediately after Geraldine leaves, Mrs. Tam becomes "critically ill" and lands in the hospital, forcing Geraldine to return home out of guilt and worry. Yet the film humorously reassures the viewer that there is no cause for alarm in the following scene in which the Uncle Tam laments Mrs. Tam's condition: as she lies in the hospital, he laconically bemoans not her anticipated death, but his anguish at the forfeiture of Dim Sum—all that good Chinese food that would be lost with Mrs. Tam's death.

Hence, a double-bind message is also communicated nonverbally in both texts, primarily through the use of food and cooking.[34] In both the film and the novel, meals are simultaneously signs of love and affection, and weapons of aggression and control. The various characters' attitudes toward food often mask unexpressed emotions, and mealtimes are often the arenas for subtle mother-daughter conflicts. Further, the preparation and serving of food seems to be another way in which the mothers convey indirect messages to their daughters. For Mrs. Tam, the preparation of a good Chinese meal (like Dim Sum) can be a way to express love for Geraldine, a statement that she finds emotionally difficult to express in words. Certainly, this is one meaning of the New Year's banquet, discussed earlier. But food can also be used as a strategy of pressuring Geraldine to follow Mrs. Tam's wishes (as in the incident with the cake), or of undermining Geraldine's confidence. Mrs. Tam serves Dim Sum ("a little bit of heart") to Richard and Geraldine as a hint that they should soon marry, especially since Mrs. Tam realizes that they are now sleeping together. And when Geraldine attempts to cook anything, her mother discredits her: "It doesn't smell right," she comments about the soup that Geraldine has specially prepared for her homecoming from the hospital.

In *The Woman Warrior*, food is also used with a double meaning: to convey essential ideas about survival, but also to create conflict in an attempt at parental control. Brave Orchid cooks food that reminds the family of the harsh subsistence of life in China, served to the children to teach them to be tough. Brave Orchid's purpose is salutary, since Maxine learns that her mother "won in ghost battle because she can eat anything . . . all heroes are bold toward food."[35] Thus, there are no extravagant delicacies served in Maxine's household; besides four- and five-day leftovers of squid eye, "My mother has cooked for us: raccoons, skunks, hawks . . . snakes, garden snails," Maxine says.[36]

As a result of these often tension-filled dinner table experiences, both Maxine and Geraldine develop an aversion to food and cooking. "I would live on plastic," Maxine declares.[37] She often burns the food when she cooks; she refuses to prepare food for other people, and she lets the dirty dishes stand until the scraps rot. Like Maxine, Geraldine is no cook. Geraldine prefers to live on Cheez Wiz and vitamin pills when not served her meals by her mother. When she and her uncle attempt to prepare a Chinese meal during Mrs. Tam's hospitalization, the result is a culinary disaster, so they cheerfully eat hamburgers and fries at McDonald's instead. In her insecurity, Geraldine admits that she often deliberately refused to learn how to prepare certain dishes so that her mother would have to do it. Then, she surmised, Mrs. Tam would choose not to die. For Geraldine and Maxine both, emotional control has become a bilateral issue between daughter and parent, frequently revolving around the dinner table. Eventually, both Maxine and Geraldine must attempt to resolve the double bind that their mothers have created and that they have acceded to. Within the cultural range possible for them, they must differentiate from their families and choose their own adult identities, while simultaneously remaining connected. But the two texts reveal divergent destinies for the two daughters.

In *The Woman Warrior*, Kingston deliberately disrupts the novel's chronology in order to dramatize Maxine's escape from the double binding she has experienced in her family. At the novel's end, Maxine as the college-age adolescent ultimately is driven to confront her mother about her mother's strange and confusing messages, and in a lengthy outburst she attacks her mother—the imperfect parent—for all the confusion she has experienced in her lifetime. Maxine writes, "I told the hardest ten or twelve things on my list all in one outburst." She rages back at Brave Orchid, screaming her complaints and wrongs, and vows to become independent: "I don't want to listen to any more of your stories; they have no logic. They scramble me up. You lie with stories. You won't tell me a story and then say, 'This is a true story,' or, 'This is just a story.' I can't tell the difference."[38] Although blaming, rage-filled, and uncontrolled, her diatribe against her mother is therapeutic for Maxine. Her repudiation of her mother's talk-stories marks own independence: she leaves the Chinese world of her parents, refuses to marry, vows to become an engineer rather than a doctor as her mother wishes, and adopts a liberal political philosophy. To Maxine's intemperate attack, Brave Orchid, the "champion talker," can only respond, "I knew you were going to turn out bad."[39]

Yet this angry outburst is not the conclusion, but only the beginning of Maxine's gradual and ongoing individuation from her family of origin. Maxine's success at arriving at her adult identity does not occur without cost to her relationship with her mother.[40] From a family systems view, a nodal point in the mother-daughter relationship is dramatized in a chronological disruption of the narrative line. In "Shaman," approximately midway through the book and presumably several years after her angry "break" with her mother, Maxine as an adult achieves a sad resolution in a deeply moving scene with Brave Orchid. Now elderly, Brave Orchid tells Maxine that "there's only one thing that I want anymore"—she wants Maxine living with her, "not wandering like a ghost from Romany."[41] Immediately, Maxine senses Brave Orchid's past dominance and her own automatic resistance: "She pries open my head and my fists and crams into them responsibility for time, responsibility for intervening oceans."[42] Rejecting her mother's final effort to control her, she tells Brave Orchid that she needs to live far from her mother and can visit only infrequently, since coming home causes old anxieties, anger, and guilt to return—manifesting themselves in Maxine's psychosomatic illnesses (colds, headaches, asthma, and undiagnosed chest pains) and anxiety attacks.

Brave Orchid, now lonely and yearning for her six grown children to be home with her, painfully listens to Maxine explain why she must keep her life separate and her contact with home and family at a minimum. For once, Brave Orchid's reply is straightforward, not meant to control or confuse, but to console, since (the reader infers) the mother understands her daughter's desperate need to be independent: "It's better, then, for you to stay away. The weather in California must not agree with you. You can come for visits. . . . Of course, you must go, Little Dog."[43] Maxine feels released from her guilt and her acutely felt weight of responsibility as Brave Orchid's daughter: "The world is somehow lighter," she explains. "She has not called me that endearment for years—a name to fool the gods"[44] In her independence, Maxine also extends to her mother a generous spirit of forgiveness and acceptance, and in so doing, feels almost weightless: "A weight lifted from me. The quilts must be filling with air. The world is somehow lighter."[45]

This generosity and sense of reconciliation is sustained at the novel's end, when Kingston's resumes her linear, autobiographical chronology by telling a final talk-story, one told by both Brave Orchid and Maxine in the final pages. Kingston writes, "The beginning is hers, the ending, mine."[46] Understandably, most critics have ignored Brave Orchid's story and focused on the mother/daughter's talk-story's "ending," Maxine's story of T'sai Yen, the poet who "sang about China and her family."[47] Maxine's story, it is argued, represents Maxine's resolution to become an artist, and her reconciliation with the dominant, English-speaking culture.[48] As Cheung writes, "Kingston's version [of the legend of Ts'ai Yen] dramatizes the interethnic harmony through the integration of disparate art forms."[49] Simmons also discovers in Ts'ai Yen a symbol of reconciliation: Ts'ai Yen is "a woman who knows her sorrow and her loss, but who can still see the reality of the world in which she finds herself and the humanity of those who inhabit it."[50]

Yet Brave Orchid's story about her own mother is just as important as Maxine's story that expresses her reconciliation and professional resolution. Brave Orchid's portion of the mutually created talk-story demonstrates through artistic representation how individual character is at least partly a product of family experience. Brave Orchid's story—unlike Maxine's much more individualistic creation—explicitly expresses the mother's acceptance of her daughter, of their shared love of art, and of their intrafamilial connectedness. Brave Orchid conveys through her talk-story the importance of art as a means of detachment from the family, while simultaneously affirming art as a feature of this family's centrality and emotional unity. In her portion, Brave Orchid tells of how her own mother brings her entire family to the theater, which she loved, despite the threat of an imminent attack by bandits, who "followed the actors." The grandmother, whose wish to visit the theater is resisted by her family (and perhaps by Brave Orchid herself), says, "I don't want to watch that play by myself. How can I laugh all by myself? You want me to clap alone, is that it? I want everybody there. Babies, everybody." When the bandits attack, the family rushes from the theatre and arrives home safely. Their survival is attributed to the power of the theater—"proof to my grandmother that our family was immune to harm as long as they went to plays. They went to many plays after that."[51] The grandmother's didactic "moral"—theater-going defeats ill-fortune—humorously conveys the old family's superstition, which literalism Maxine (of course) rejects.

But on a deeper level, Maxine and her desire to tell stories are affirmed by Brave Orchid's story about her theatre-loving mother. Brave Orchid tells the story because it illustrates for her how art can rescue the individual within the family, and how literature (talk-stories) can provide emotional strength and wisdom within a group. "I want everybody there," the grandmother says; through connection with the family, one can truly appreciate life and discover a kind of protection from the struggles of the world. Maxine's grandmother emphasized the family's solidarity as a way to take pleasure in art, but also as a way to resist the fragmentation that would have proved fatal against the bandits. The life-threatening bandits are the novel's imagined surrogates for all those hostile, life-denying elements of American culture that Maxine has confronted throughout the novel: viciously racist employers, sexist colleagues, condescending teachers, unpleasant boyfriends, even the threat of madness and total loss of control—in short, all those enemies whom the Woman Warrior must combat. But Brave Orchid's story assures Maxine that she does not have to be isolated. "Everybody is there" for the grandmother—and for Maxine too, even as she strikes out from her family, achieving differentiation, to create her own talk-stories.

This confident sense of resolution and reconciliation effected in the novel is apparently mirrored in Kingston's personal life. In response to an interviewer's question, Kingston says that she feels relieved of the double binding she describes in *The Woman Warrior*: "I no longer feel double binds around my feet. I feel like a very peaceful, healthy person and I don't know why."[52] Surely a part of her sense of harmony and peace derives from her renewed connection to her family.

Dim Sum does not end with *The Woman Warrior*'s sense of promise and potentiality, but with the family's double bind undissolved and continued, since Geraldine and Mrs. Tam never unscramble their mixed messages, never achieve the difficult, painful, but essential resolution that Brave Orchid and Maxine attain. As a result, Geraldine is unable to achieve a genuine selfhood at the film's end. Just returned from her long-awaited visit to China, Mrs. Tam sits with Geraldine on the bed and they talk, just as Brave Orchid and Maxine talk in *The Woman Warrior*. "Richard and I made some decisions," Geraldine begins the conversation with her mother. But Mrs. Tam is much more interested in the toys she has brought back from China than in what Geraldine has to say—the decisions that Geraldine has made about herself, Richard, and her mother. Mrs. Tam refuses to listen to Geraldine's painfully thought-out resolutions about her own future, resolutions that have also been withheld from the viewer.

Before Geraldine can reveal her decisions, Mrs. Tam giddily explains that another Chinese fortuneteller has told her she is not going to die soon after all. Her premonition of death has all been a foolish mistake, Mrs. Tam tells Geraldine, a comical result of the first fortune-teller's mathematical error. So Mrs. Tam assures her daughter that she will likely live many more years after all. Geraldine does not have to get married for a long, long time, Mrs. Tam tells her, but can stay with her, taking care of her as usual. Then, Mrs. Tam turns from Geraldine and laughingly plays with the childish trinkets and toys she has brought back from China, as if to emphasize that the role-reversal the film has constantly hinted at, has now been fully accomplished: Mrs. Tam has become the child, utterly dependent; Geraldine, the fully parentified and highly responsible mother-daughter. The film ends with a closeup of Geraldine's half-smiling but tearful, pained face, as she presumably accepts the personal cost of what she has just been told. She has failed to make her mother hear her own message, but at the same time she herself has failed to decode her mother's double-binding communication. By choosing not to confront her mother, as Maxine finally does, Geraldine has tied herself more securely to her. Unlike Brave Orchid, Mrs. Tam unwittingly refuses to release her daughter; unlike Maxine, Geraldine appears caught in her mother's confusing world, trapped permanently in her mother's double bind.

In his discussion of the double-binding communication, Gregory Bateson argues that although double binds are by no means rare in human systems, they are often a source of an individual's creativity. Double binds are not simply "crazy-making": "It seems that both those whose life is enriched by transcontextual gifts and those who are impoverished by transcontextual confusions are alike in one respect: for them there is always or often a 'double take.'"[53] That is, for a person caught in a double bind, sometimes creative acts and new sequences of behavior are the individual's responses rather than paralysis or a sense of hopelessness. The individual (like Maxine) transforms what could be seen as a handicap into an advantage, integrating limitations and restrictions into her own enterprise for liberty. In a recent book on the double bind, internationally known therapist Mony Elkaim agrees that the double bind can be recognized as a common ground of our humanity: the double bind adumbrates "the central place of paradox in the human condition and the personal creativity we need to summon up, as members of a system, in order to enlarge our field of possibilities."[54] Unlike Geraldine, Maxine succeeds in "enlarging [her] field of possibilities," and in so doing, makes "[her] mind large, as the universe is large, so that there is room for paradoxes."[55]

NOTES

1. Kerr, "Chronic Anxiety and Defining a Self," 35.
2. Knapp, *Striking at the Joints*, 69.
3. Sau-Ling Cynthia Wong, "Autobiography as Guided Chinatown Tour?" 261.
4. Ibid., 248.
5. Kingston, "Personal Statement," 24.
6. Ariel, *Culturally Competent Family Therapy*, 15.
7. See Skenazy and Martin, *Conversations with Maxine Hong Kingston*, 110.
8. Wang, Wayne, *Dim Sum: A Little Bit of Heart* has been recommended as a complement to *The Woman Warrior* in the classroom in Lim, *Approaches to Teaching Kingston's "The Woman Warrior*, 41–42, 65, 72.
9. See Frank Chin, "Most Popular Book in China;" Dasenbrock, "Intelligibility and Meaningfulness in Multicultural Literature;" Holaday, "From Ezra Pound to Maxine Hong Kingston;" Lee, "*Woman Warrior* as Intervention; Li,

"Naming of a Chinese American 'I';" VanSpanckeren, "Asian Literary Background of *The Woman Warrior*;" and Wong, *Reading Asian American Literature.*

10. Bateson, *Steps to an Ecology of Mind*, 201.

11. Ibid., 203.

12. In Chan and Harris, "Listen, Mom, I'm a Banana," Chan and Harris do not use the term "double-bind," but they describe a cultural double-bind for Asian-Americans learning English: "on the one hand the children have to learn to communicate with Americans . . . on the other hand, they have to find means to communicate with their parents, whose ways eventually become more foreign to them than those of the foreigners" (76). Similarly, King-Kok Cheung sees Maxine's problem in wholly ethnic terms: "Trying to conform to both the feminine and the masculine ideals of her society, Maxine as warrior is caught in a double bind." See Cheung, "Don't Tell," 166.

13. Berg and Jaya, "Different and Same," 31.

14. Sluzki and Veron, "Double Bind as a Universal Pathogenic Situation," 251–62. Significantly, family system theorists are extremely concerned about the difficult cultural issues that arise when a therapist, especially an American, attempts to assist a Chinese family. See Linda Wang, "Marriage and Family Therapy with People from China;" Hong, "Application of Cultural and Environmental Issues in Family Therapy;" and Berg and Jaya, "Different and Same."

15. As Kingston says, the narrator of *The Woman Warrior* "doesn't have a name. Her name isn't Maxine; that's my name. I see this as a literary text that's very separate from myself. Throughout, nobody calls her anything. The point is that she is still in search of her name." See Skenazy, "Kingston at the University," 133. Respecting Kingston's point, I will nevertheless refer to the novel's protagonist and narrator as "Maxine," and to Kingston the author as "Kingston" to minimize the inevitable confusion my reader may experience with names.

16. Kingston, *Woman Warrior*, 48.

17. Regarding her negative view of Chinese family life and her criticism of Chinese patriarchy, Kingston's work in particular has been vehemently attacked for portraying a "fake," stereotypical Chinese culture. See, in particular, Chin, "Most Popular Book in China." Kingston also has vigorous defenders. See especially Schueller, "Questioning Race and Gender Definitions;" TuSmith, "Literary Tricksterism;" and Wong, *Reading Asian American Literature*, 272.

18. Wong, *Reading Asian American Literature*, 191–211.

19. Kingston, *Woman Warrior*, 46.

20. Ibid., 45.

21. Ibid., 106.

22. Outka, "Publish or Perish," 453.

23. Too often, narrational point of view is misinterpreted because critics feel that Kingston is not allowing Maxine her own individual voice, due partly to feminist concerns that Maxine is oppressed by her patriarchal culture. Other critics see Maxine struggling with internal, psychic conflicts. In "Kingston's *The Woman Warrior*," Elise Miller, for example, uses object relations theory to show how Maxine "[reenacts] infantile modes of being in and relating to the world" (138). For Miller, Kingston writes in the first-person only after the Moon Orchid incident (149).

24. Critics often exaggerate the cultural determination of Maxine's and Geraldine's commitments to their families (see, for example, VanSpanckeren,

"Asian Literary Background of *The Woman Warrior*"). Yet despite the obvious cultural conditioning of their Chinese background, the two daughters, as I shall argue, are forced to deal with very diverse demands—"filial obligation" takes radically different forms in the two texts. Thus, Geraldine feels not only a cultural injunction to care for her mother, but an intensely individual one as well because of her mother's communication system.

25. Kingston, *Woman Warrior*, 203.

26. Ibid., 29.

27. Ferraro, *Ethnic Passages*, 164.

28. Wong, *Reading Asian American Literature*, 192.

29. Kingston, *Woman Warrior*, 202.

30. Ibid., 67.

31. Ibid., 70.

32. Ibid., 73. As Wong argues in *Reading Asian American Literature*, Brave Orchid may be at least partially resentful of her own subordination in a patriarchal world when she abandons her medical career and comes to America, even as she defends and supports that world (200).

33. As Geraldine's foil, this friend seems to enjoy an imagined ideal life outside of Geraldine's realm of choices, since she seems to control her own destiny and regards Geraldine's conflicts with a degree of amusement. Yet the film makes a judgment about the friend as well, one that mirrors the painfulness of Geraldine's dilemma. The friend prepares to visit her mother in Hong Kong, and when she returns from the visit, she tearfully tells of how her mother unexpectedly died shortly after the long-awaited visit from all her children, who are living all over the globe. We discover in her revelation that she had concealed her sense of guilt and responsibility to her mother; clearly, the friend's freedom is purchased at great emotional price.

34. Although Outka's concerns in "Publish or Perish" are different from mine, his article on the pervasive food and hunger imagery in *The Woman Warrior* resembles my argument that Maxine moves toward individuation. In his judgment, the trope of food ineluctably leads Maxine to realize that she must "learn to care for herself, because no one else is going to take care of her. Taking care of herself means both eating and talking" (479). In contrast, critics sometimes overemphasize the issue of ethnicity and minimize the necessity of separation within the individual's first social unit, the family. See Fong, "Maxine Hong Kingston's Autobiographical Strategy in *The Woman Warrior*," see also Hunsaker, "Nation, Family, and Language." For a therapist's discussion of the difficulties faced by Asian-American children gaining independence within the family, see Berg and Jaya, "Different and Same."

35. Kingston, *Woman Warrior*, 88.

36. Ibid., 90.

37. Ibid., 92.

38. Ibid., 202.

39. Ibid., 202, 204.

40. Maxine's confrontation with Brave Orchid has been variously interpreted—some critics see the verbal battle as inevitable but tragic, while others insist that the final struggle with her mother is in reality very benign, even salutary for Brave Orchid and Maxine. See Joan Lidoff, "Autobiography in a Different Voice." On the other hand, critics sometimes overstate Maxine's degree of resistance to her mother and thereby oversimplify the separation from her mother that Maxine effects. See Helen Buss, "Memoir with an Attitude;"

see also Chan and Harris, "Listen, Mom, I'm a Banana." Perhaps Kingston in an interview has offered the most balanced view of her relationship with her mother, in showing that she has absorbed some qualities from her parent but rejected others: "If you just look at her from a kind of side view, she is very eccentric. . . . I've fought hard not to be eccentric like my mother. I am nevertheless most eccentric." See Jody Hoy, "To Be Able to See the Tao," 56.

41. Kingston, *Woman Warrior*, 107.

42. Ibid., 108.

43. Ibid.

44. Ibid., 108–9.

45. Ibid., 108.

46. Ibid., 206.

47. Ibid., 243.

48. See Ferraro, *Ethnic Passages*, 189–90; Outka, "Publish or Perish," 479–80; Cheung, "Don't Tell," 171–72; Fong, "Maxine Hong Kingston's Autobiographical Strategy in *The Woman Warrior*," 121–23; and Simmons, *Maxine Hong Kingston*, 102–6.

49. Cheung, "Don't Tell," 171.

50. Simmons, *Maxine Hong Kingston*, 105–6.

51. Kingston, *Woman Warrior*, 207.

52. Kay Bonetti, "Interview with Maxine Hong Kingston," 35.

53. Bateson, *Steps to an Ecology of Mind*, 272.

54. Elkaim, *If You Love Me, Don't Love Me*, 20.

55. Kingston, *Woman Warrior*, 29.

Exploring the Matrix of Identity in Barbara Kingsolver's *Animal Dreams*

Lee Ann De Reus

> Strange that some of us, with quick alternative vision, see beyond our infatuations, and even while we rave on the heights, behold the wide plain where our persistent self pauses and awaits us.
>
> —George Eliot, *Middlemarch*

IN BARBARA KINGSOLVER'S CRITICALLY ACCLAIMED NOVEL *ANIMAL Dreams* (1990), we accompany the protagonist, Codi Noline, in her quest for acceptance, love, and identity as she journeys home to Grace, Arizona, to confront her past and her dying, distant father. Weaving Native American folklore, flashbacks, and dreams, Kingsolver tells the tale of a young woman's search for meaning in life. It is this quest for a renewed sense of self that lends itself well to the study of identity development in Kingsolver's novel.

While Kingsolver's fiction has enjoyed high praise—including numerous literary awards, such as the 1990 Edward Abbey Award for Ecofiction and the 1991 PEN Center USA West Literary Award for Fiction—there is a paucity of Kingsolver criticism, including only one book-length, academic literary analysis in existence to date, Mary Jean DeMarr's *Barbara Kingsolver: A Critical Companion* (1999), which offers merely a rudimentary introduction to Kingsolver's works. Further, attention by critics has focused primarily on her themes of ecology, feminism, political activism, and concern for Native American and African peoples and culture. Although all of her novels contain strong female characters, the specific examination of an individual female's identity development in conjunction with a family systems analysis is absent in the criticism devoted to Kingsolver. In a 1994 interview with Jennifer Fleischner, author of *A Reader's Guide to the Fiction of Barbara Kingsolver*, Kingsolver states that *Ani-*

mal Dreams was predicated on the following questions, "Why do some people engage with the world and its problems, while others turn their backs on it?" and "Why is it that these two sorts of people often occur even in the same family?"[1] By their very construction, Kingsolver's questions implore us to consider the nature of individual identity development in the context of family relationships.

In this essay, I will identify the process by which Codi begins to establish her sense of self in the world. Drawing on the intellectual traditions of several eminent scholars as well as their critics, this paper will utilize Erik Erikson's theory of psychosocial development, James Marcia's identity statuses, and Family Systems Therapy as a means for illuminating and marking Codi's level of identity development. To better understand the complexities of the identity formation process, however, consideration will also be given to identity researcher Sally Archer's feminist criticisms of Erikson and Marcia, as well as to several individual cognitive and sociocontextual factors, such as the family, which are known to influence the creation of self.

No single individual has influenced our understanding of identity development more than Erik Erikson. Considered the premiere theorist of identity, he is credited for bringing this vital element of our existence to the forefront of popular and scientific attention.[2] While multiple frameworks for understanding identity exist, Erikson's understanding of identity is embedded in an eight-stage psychosocial theory of development from infancy to old age.[3] This life-span developmental approach is a particular strength of this model, as it provides an understanding of development over time. Unlike any other identity theory, Erikson's model also integrates the historical, biological, psychological, and sociocultural forces that shape individual development. As Erikson himself observes, "The whole interplay between the psychosocial and the social, the developmental and the historical, for which identity formation is of prototypal significance, could be conceptualized only as a kind of psychosocial relativity."[4] So influential is Erikson's work that traces of this theory are found in most, if not all, other stage theories of adulthood and identity theory.[5] For example, Erikson's key identity concepts of identity crisis, foreclosure, and moratorium are virtually inherent in all discussions of adolescent development and for the purposes of this paper, lend themselves well to an analysis of Kingsolver's *Animal Dreams*. Until a new grand theory is tested and established, Erikson's theory will maintain its central position and value for understanding identity formation.[6]

According to Erikson's eight-stage life cycle scheme of development, identity formation is the primary task of adolescence. Labeled as Identity versus Role Confusion, this fifth developmental stage builds on the resolution of preceding stages and serves as a foundation for adulthood.[7] The outcome of Identity versus Role Confusion sets the stage for the subsequent psychosocial stages of Intimacy versus Isolation, Generativity versus Stagnation, and Integrity versus Despair to be found during the years of young, middle, and later adulthood, respectively.[8] A positive resolution of this identity crisis prepares the adolescent for adulthood while irresolution of this stage results in a sense of confusion about one's identity or role in life. Further, the sense of identity established during late adolescence determines to a great degree an individual's success in intimate relationships. Similarly, whether or not an individual experiences positive or negative resolution of the Identity versus Role Confusion stage is associated with one's ability to be generative or make a meaningful contribution to one's children or community. Finally, identity outcomes have bearing on one's last psychosocial task of finding meaning in life before it ends.[9]

It must be noted, however, that Erikson's theory is not without limitations. Identity researchers fault this model for its lack of attention to intrapsychic developmental structures.[10] While structural stage models such as those proposed by Jane Loevinger and Robert Kegan attend specifically to the intrapsychically defined stages of meaning construction, they do so at the expense of contextual factors influencing development. Psychosocial models such as Erikson's, however, are thought to reflect an intermediate position between structural stage and sociocultural approaches, viewing identity in terms of the interaction between internal structural characteristics and social tasks demanded by a particular society or social reference group.[11] Thus, due to the historical significance, timelessness, and comprehensiveness of Erikson's psychosocial theory of identity development as well as its ease of "fit" with the storyline, his model will serve as the framework for the present analysis of Codi's experiences in *Animal Dreams*.

Other critics of Erikson's work include feminists who have negatively judged his theories for portraying a primarily Eurocentric male model of normality with an emphasis on the stereotypical male characteristics of will, autonomy, competence, industry, initiative, personal agency, and individuation.[12] Based on this reading of Erikson, it has been argued that this theory reflects the values of a capitalistic, patriarchal society as opposed to recognizing the importance of attachments, intimacy, and relationships in people's, especially women's, lives.[13] Further, Erikson has been criticized for viewing women's reproductive and mothering capabilities as the single most important determinants of her adult identity while men can achieve identity through intellectual, occupational, and other public endeavors.[14] The unfortunate consequence of this conceptualization, according to Archer, is an artificially constructed dichotomy that portrays identity in narrow terms.[15] Historically, identity researchers have perpetuated this dichotomy by analyzing the intrapersonal identity variables of vocation, religious, and political ideologies for men while women's identity was determined by interpersonal variables related to sexuality and family roles (as though males are not sexual, or husbands or fathers). By dichotomizing identity versus intimacy, one set of characteristics precludes the expression of the other.[16] In response, identity researcher Sally Archer calls for a feminist approach to identity that is orthogonal in nature and therefore recognizes androgynous characteristics of both males and females. The dichotomy of identity versus intimacy, according to Archer, "prevents us from getting on with an understanding of human development. Very few people live without community, and very few people are comfortable having no inner sense of self."[17]

So why use Erikson? As Archer notes, "It is a subjective preference to choose to either ignore Erikson's theory or select components of it as a foundation or as a framework for one's understanding of the concept." However, she continues, "Rather than expend energy arguing over whose position is most true . . . it would appear far more fruitful to draw upon this bounty and enthusiastically embrace learning about identity formation from multiple perspectives."[18] For the purposes of this essay, Erikson's psychosocial theory of development provides a framework for analysis that, when combined with various feminist critiques, creates a particularly resonant and revelatory tool for a largely inaugural reading of Kingsolver's *Animal Dreams*.

Identity is often characterized as "a consistent definition of one's self as a unique individual, in terms of roles, attitudes, beliefs, and aspirations."[19] As the key developmental task of adolescence, identity formation is best understood as an evolutionary "process." The complexities of this process involve the interaction of an individual's biology, psychology, and societal contexts which result in themes of stability and change, psychological autonomy and connection, and intrapsychic and contextual components across adulthood.[20] James Marcia, a seminal scholar in this area, describes the identity formation process as involving "a synthesis of childhood skills, beliefs, and identifications into a more or less coherent, unique whole that provides the young adult with both a sense of continuity with the past and a direction for the future."[21] Identity formation, then, creates a paradox of separating oneself from one's past and environment while finding new connections to the separated self.[22] It is this simultaneous experience of both belongingness and separateness, according to Kegan, that is necessary for the continued development of the individual.[23] Optimal identity development, according to Erikson, is the discovery and establishment of one's niche or place in the larger community. However, it is important to note that once discovered, an individual's identity does not remain fixed but is dynamic as shifting needs and circumstances necessitate change in an individual's sense of self.[24] From the Family Systems Therapy perspective, according to John V. Knapp, "one of the biggest jobs for the family is to provide support both for integration into a solid and enduring family unit and differentiation into relatively separate selves—being able to think, act, and feel for one's self."[25]

Building on Erikson's identity work, James Marcia has moved the empirical research in this area forward with his creation of four distinct identity statuses into which persons can be categorized. According to Marcia, these statuses are the outcomes of an identity formation process that can be divided into two discrete steps of exploration (questioning, experimentation) and commitment (resolving questions, deciding on a role or niche). These statuses, which range from lower to higher levels of ego maturity, include diffusion, foreclosure, moratorium, and identity achievement. A diffused individual exhibits no signs of exploration, nor does he or she endeavor to make occupational or ideological commitments. An individual who is foreclosed in identity has foregone exploration and accepted parental values and advice without question or the examination of alternatives. An individual is considered to be in a state of moratorium if he or she is actively searching for an identity, while an identity achieved person has made self-defined occupational and ideological commitments following a period of questioning and searching.

Similar to her criticisms of Erikson, Archer has taken Marcia to task for the reductive methodology imposed by his four identity statuses. It is her contention that such taxonomies inadvertently discount the context and motivations surrounding identity development. Thus, Archer proposes that "social facts" such as teenage pregnancy, sexual abuse, and the feminization of poverty, for example, must be considered as determinants of female identity formation given that "the identity process for the female adolescent can easily be described as potentially confusing and complex."[26]

Like Archer, Carol Markstrom-Adams has also given consideration to intervening factors thought to influence adolescent identity formation. From her synthesis of a broad body of theoretical and empirical literature, much of which is embedded in Marcia's identity status model, several social-contextual and individual cognitive factors were ascertained as pertinent to the creation of a sense of self. For the purposes of this essay, the contextual factors of family relationships and ethnic and racial group membership, the cognitive factors of assimilation and accommodation, differentiation and integration, and continuity of self, as well as relevant social facts, will be discussed.

In *Animal Dreams*, Codi Noline is in the developmental period of early adulthood (twenty-three to thirty-nine years of age)—which is characterized by Erikson's psychosocial crisis of Intimacy versus Isolation and Generativity versus Stagnation—at the time of her move back to her hometown of Grace, Arizona, to care for her ailing father. However, Codi appears to be rather delayed in her development as her struggles in the novel revolve around her search for an identity. With no sense of purpose in life, she moves from job to job, lover to lover, unable to make commitments: "I tended to drift, like a well-meaning visitor to this planet awaiting instructions."[27] And upon arriving in Grace, Codi says that "I was *here*, after all, with no more mission in life than I'd been born with years ago."[28]

The untimely death of Codi's mother at the tender age of three, her emotionally unavailable father, and her own miscarriage at the age of fifteen culminate in a lost young woman in her early thirties with little sense of identity. At this point in the novel, Codi exhibits a diffuse identity status (the least developmentally advanced) by her lack of commitment to values or goals, lack of identity exploration, and expressed feelings of dissatisfaction and emptiness: "I spent my whole childhood as an outsider to Grace. . . . I'd sell my soul and all my travelling shoes to *belong* some place."[29]

As stated previously, identity formation does not occur in a vacuum and must be understood in context as social facts and the social environment exert great influence on all developmental processes. The social facts that transpire upon her return to Grace and prove consequential to Codi's identity development include her position as a biology teacher at the local high school, her reconnection with Loyd Peregrina, the father of her miscarried baby, the environmental catastrophe about to befall Grace, and the kidnapping and murder of her younger sister Hallie by Nicaraguan rebels. The social-contextual factors identified in relation to identity and to be discussed here in conjunction with these social facts include family relationships and ethnic and racial group membership.

Creating a sense of self is clearly linked with particular styles of family interaction and communication. A family system that balances closeness with encouragement toward autonomy and individuation is considered an optimal family environment for facilitation of identity development. Research has shown that adolescents in these families engage in more identity exploration and make more stable identity commitments. Conversely, families characterized by little parent-child closeness and connectedness have been associated repeatedly with difficulties in resolving the adolescent identity crisis with diffused youth reporting the least emotional attachments to parents.[30] Further, diffusion is related to adolescent perceptions of maternal and paternal rejection coupled with a perceived affection-lacking relationship with the mother. Thus, it is not surprising that diffusion is associated with strained and distant relationships between adolescents and their parents.[31] According to Knapp, "fear and anxiety usually force members to create a pseudo-self, so that one's inner feelings and outer behavior are not congruent, since one's thoughts must be carefully monitored to avoid intensifying anxiety and fear through exposure to others of whom one is afraid."[32]

The death of Codi's mother, due to complications following the birth of Hallie, was for Codi a vague memory that resulted in the negative resolution of the first developmental crisis, trust versus mistrust. Feeling abandoned and relegated to the negligent care of their father, Codi and her sister were subjected to the desperate, awkward attempts of Doc Homer to raise daughters acceptable to a community that had previously rejected him. For example, Doc Homer's insistence that the girls wear specially ordered orthopedic shoes to prevent irreparable harm to their bodies created by impractical footwear was the cause of much humiliation inflicted by their peers during their school years. Although conceived out of love for his daughters, many of Doc Homer's parenting techniques were interpreted by the girls as uncaring, strict codes of conduct whose violation met with harsh punishments. Codi's resulting relationship with Doc Homer is quite characteristic of the distant parent-child relationship associated with diffused adolescents. This is evident when she described her father as "being like no one else, being alone, was the central ethic of his life."[33] As Codi contemplates this remoteness, she recalls that "from Doc Homer you didn't expect hugs and kisses. He was legendary in this regard. Hallie and I used to play a game we called 'orphans' when we were with him in a crowd: 'Who in this room is our true father or mother? Which is the one grownup here that loves us.'" Waiting for a sign of affection or recognition from any adult in the room, Codi learns at a young age that "that person would never be Doc Homer," validating her perception that her father did not love her or Hallie.[34] This acuity of a distant father persisted into adulthood when upon her return to Grace Codi lamented that conversing with her father while he developed pictures in his darkroom "was the nearest I'd ever come to feeling like I had a dad."[35] The emotional unavailability of Doc Homer, combined with the distressing loss of Codi's mother at age three, leaves her without the loving, supportive attachments and the nurturant socialization characteristic of most parent/child relationships, contributing to her diffuse identity formation. Says Codi, "Nobody, not my father, *no one* had jumped in to help when I was a child getting whacked by life."[36] Without a secure family base, Codi has no solid foundation from which to conduct her identity exploration.

Codi's isolation while "getting whacked by life" is nowhere more apparent in the novel than when she endures a tragic miscarriage at the age of fifteen. Too ashamed and fearful to confide in Hallie, Doc Homer, or Loyd Peregrina, the baby's father, Codi miscarries the six-month-old fetus at home and buries it immediately in the backyard. Doc Homer, who is quite aware of Codi's pregnancy, observes the burial and later protects and marks the grave with stones; yet ironically, the only parental comfort he can muster is to offer her medication to alleviate the post-delivery symptoms. As Doc Homer laments, "This is the full measure of love he is qualified to dispense."[37] For Codi, the miscarriage is a turning point in her life, which she describes as dividing her from the people she knows:

As Hallie had bluntly pointed out in her letter, I'd marked myself early on as a bad risk, undeserving of love and incapable of benevolence. It wasn't because of a bad grade on a report card, as she'd supposed. It ran deeper than that. I'd lost what there was to lose: first my mother and then my baby. Nothing you love will stay. Hallie could call that attitude a crutch, but she didn't know, she hadn't loved and lost so deeply . . . she'd never been born—not into life as I knew it. Hallie could still risk everything.[38]

Unable to trust others and take risks, Codi copes with her painful past and negotiates her teen years by repressing her childhood memories and creating obdurate boundaries between herself and life. As Codi keenly surmises about herself from this point forward: "I wasn't keeping to any road, I was running, forgetting what lay behind and always looking ahead for the perfect home, where trains never wrecked and hearts never broke, where no one you loved ever died."[39] The combined social facts and context of the death of Codi's mother, Doc Homer's conflicted parenting, and Codi's miscarriage at age fifteen propel her identity on a developmental trajectory toward diffusion.[40]

Another social-contextual factor related to identity formation is that of ethnic and racial group membership. At issue is the necessity for racial and ethnic minorities to reconcile the cultural values of their own minority group with those of the mainstream culture. Further, ethnic and racial prejudice may limit opportunities for identity exploration.[41] For Codi, however, the intervening factor is not her particular membership in a racial group, but rather her *lack* of identification with any ethnicity. Out of shame for his family history and heritage in Grace, Doc Homer has not provided his daughters with a complete family record, exacerbating Codi's uninformed sense of self. Underpinning her deficient knowledge of family history, Kingsolver artfully contrasts Codi's misinformation with Loyd's keen sense of his own Native American heritage. In one poignant scene when Loyd inquires about Codi's ethnicity by asking, "What are you?" Codi replies, "I have no idea. My mother came from someplace in Illinois, and Doc Homer won't own up to being from anywhere. I can't remember half of what happened to me before I was fifteen. I guess I'm nothing. The Nothing Tribe."[42] A paucity of information regarding family history proves to be another barrier to Codi's self-discovery.

The second category of intervening factors related to identity formation includes individual cognitive aspects such as cognitive assimilation and accommodation, cognitive complexity, and the ability to conceptualize continuity of self.[43] Cognitive or identity assimilation gives the individual positive information about the self, even if this information is inaccurate. Forms of identity assimilation include self-justification, identity projection, defensive rigidity, and lack of insight. If not in balance with accommodation, individuals may resist change and have limited self-awareness, possibly resulting in a foreclosed identity. In comparison, identity accommodation is the creation of a realistic appraisal of the self in relation to experiences, which may result in the change of identity. Positive changes in identity, self-doubts, considering alternatives, and responding to external influences are all mechanisms of identity accommodation. In extreme cases, individuals may have an underdefined identity and a reliance on external factors as opposed to individual factors in decision-making, possibly resulting in identity diffusion or a prolonged moratoria.[44]

Codi utilizes negative assimilation and accommodation strategies early in the novel as methods for protecting herself against positive self-attributions and for avoiding the difficult process of self-discovery and creation. Negative assimilation is accomplished by Codi's subconscious suppression of all memories prior to the age of fifteen. Without the knowledge and life meaning of several significant events such as the death of her mother and the details surrounding her miscarriage, Codi is left with an identity void that only the interpretation of these events could fill. Negative accommodation is evidenced initially by Codi's reliance on external factors to determine her life course. "I was suddenly disgusted with what I was doing. I'd go anywhere Carlo wanted, I'd be a sport for my students in Grace, I'd even tried to be a doctor for Doc Homer. . . . If I kept trying to be what everybody wanted, I'd soon be insipid enough to fit in everywhere."[45] Further, in order to avoid resolving her own identity crisis, Codi chooses to live vicariously through, and in the shadow of, her younger sister Hallie, whom she idolizes. In reference to Hallie, she remarks, "Every man I'd ever loved had loved Hallie best and settled for me. It didn't bother me as much as you might think; I could understand it. I loved her too."[46] This judgement of herself as inferior to Hallie provides Codi with a convenient excuse for life's failures and for self-sabotaging her own identity resolution.

Cognitive complexity, or the ability to use more sophisticated and efficient modes of cognitive functioning, is characterized by differentiation and integration. Differentiation requires the adolescent to examine various complexities of the personality and psyche as a means for determining likes and dislikes, interests, values, motives, and so on. The inability to introspect to this degree may result in a premature foreclosure of identity or an opting out of the identity search process altogether as in the case of diffusion. An inability to integrate the complexities of personality and psyche may result in ongoing states of moratoria where the individual is able to differentiate but not integrate by making a commitment to an identity.[47] Initially, Codi is unable to differentiate as she lives her life according to those around her.

This is evident in her choice to attend medical school, not for herself, but rather to garner approval from her father who was also a physician: "It's true that I tried myself to go into medicine, which is considered a helping profession, but I did it for the lowest of motives. I did it to win love, and to prove myself capable."[48] Codi's desire to win her father's love and overcome the space between them is predictable behavior from a diffused adolescent who perceives parental rejection.

Codi's lack of differentiation, however, is most discernible in her dependent relationship with her sister Hallie. Codi describes her attachment to Hallie as being "like keenly mismatched Siamese twins conjoined at the back of the mind."[49] For Codi, Hallie represents all things virtuous: stability, autonomy, a sense of direction and purpose, optimism, strength, and hope. She is Codi's anchor and a shield against her own insecurities. Thus, with Hallie in her life, Codi is able to substitute dependency for the difficult process of self-creation.

The first turning point for Codi in her identity development is when she—literally and figuratively—returns to Grace. With Hallie's departure to fight for peasant farmers in Nicaragua, Codi is slowly weaned of her codependence and pushed toward autonomy. Previously diffused in her identity, Codi shifts to the status of moratorium and begins to forge a new identity after this relocation and her ensuing life experiences. It is during Hallie's absence that Codi reconnects with long-lost friends, her father, and Loyd Peregrina. As a result, Codi begins to explore her occupational, interpersonal, and ideological options and begins to move beyond the psychosocial stage of Identity versus Role Confusion to Intimacy versus Isolation and Generativity versus Stagnation. Codi is unwittingly engaged, for example, in a process of introspection and self-definition due to an environmental crisis that occurs in Grace. As Codi's biology expertise is called upon by the townspeople to avert ecological disaster created by a local mining company, she begins to feel needed and discovers in herself a degree of passion about the environment that rivals her sister's enthusiasm—an aspect of Hallie's persona that Codi envies. Unable to contain her newly developed desire for environmental justice, Codi carries her activism into the classroom, where she delivers a fervent plea to the students to be responsible stewards of the world around them. Of her classroom rant, she says, "I felt strangely high. Furious and articulate."[50] From this experience, Codi is drawn closer to her authentic self as she experiences brief glimpses of what life could be like for her in the future.

As Codi's work roles and ideological commitments become defined, her relationship with Loyd evolves simultaneously. The combination of his patience and loving support for Codi foster her ability to accept his wise counsel that "for everybody that's gone away, there's somebody that's come to you." Hence, "You can trust that you're not going to run out of people to love."[51] This line of reasoning represents a major paradigm shift for a woman whose entire life was previously predicated on a personal philosophy of scarcity and fear. Codi's acceptance of Loyd's advice likewise serves as the catalyst for her resolution of Intimacy versus Isolation.

The validation that Codi receives from her successful leadership of the local community against the Black Mountain Mining Company and her award as teacher of the year empower her to confront Doc Homer at last about her dearth of family history. Doc Homer's worsening dementia impedes this process, however, preventing absolute resolution of the relationship for either the father or daughter. As Codi observes, "We were comically out of synchrony—a family vaudeville routine. Whatever one of us found, the other lost."[52] Yet with a new-found determination, Codi is not deterred from piecing together her past. Information from women in the community and family relics in the attic provide Codi with the necessary clues to discover her family's historical connection to Grace. In addition, these revelations afford Codi with new insights about her father: "He was doing exactly the opposite of setting himself apart. He was proving we belonged here, were as pure as anybody in Grace."[53] The orthopedic shoes and the strict parenting methods were his loving attempts to prove that his daughters *belonged* in the community of Grace, despite his own previous rejection. Realizing that she had misjudged his actions, Codi is able to forgive Doc Homer and let go of her previous perception of paternal rejection.

From this point in the novel, Codi's identity formation process is catapulted forward from moratorium to identity achievement due to Hallie's untimely death. This event forces Codi to at last differentiate from her sister and reconcile her past with her present and her future, the result of which is the conceptualization of the continuity of self—the third and final intervening factor in identity formation. This important component of identity formation is the ability to conceptualize the self as the product of existence over time. This process provides an integration and understanding of the continuities between the self in the past, present, and the person whom one will become in the future.[54] Failure to do so may result in feelings of aimlessness and meaninglessness, the likely causes of a diffuse identity.[55] As Codi's past is unveiled, negative assimilation is overcome and meaning is created out of her assorted life events. Codi's realizations are exemplified when she says, "I was getting a dim comprehension of the difference between Hallie and me. It wasn't a matter of courage or dreams, but something a whole lot simpler. A pilot would call it ground orientation. I'd spent a long time circling above the clouds, looking for life, while Hallie was living it."[56] No longer afraid of love or dependent on Hallie to protect her from confronting her self, Codi finally achieves her own "ground orientation."

In *Animal Dreams*, Kingsolver provides us with the portrayal of a woman's life that goes beyond the archetypal tale of a woman's courtship leading to marriage. Unlike *Cinderella* or *Anna Karenina*, Codi discovers the empowering possibilities of self-determination—not through a man or suicide, but via an empowerment that is derived en route to her own identity.[57] In Codi, Kingsolver successfully achieves Archer's androgynous female who exhibits the stereotypical male attributes of will, autonomy, competence, industry, initiative, personal agency, and individuation *in the context* of her intimate relationships, thereby defying the traditional and limiting dichotomy of inter- *and* intrapersonal characteristics of identity. In the end, with her current and past psychosocial crises resolved and her present sense of identity achieved, Codi emerges as a self-possessed young woman capable of genuine commitments both to herself and to others.

NOTES

1. See Fleischner, *Reader's Guide to the Fiction of Barbara Kingsolver*.

2. See Josselson, *Revising Herself*, 6, 27; see also Kroger, *Identity Development*, 8.

3. See Kroger, *Identity Development*, for a summary of five different theoretical approaches to identity. Identity is currently studied among social scientists via one of five general theoretical frameworks. In brief, these frameworks can be described as follows: 1) the historical approach addresses conditions that precede the contemporary concern with identity; 2) the structural stage approach examines the changing internal structures of ego development through which an individual gives meaning to life experiences; 3) the sociological approach focuses on the role society plays in influencing identity development over time; 4) the narrative approach uses people's stories about their lives in an attempt to assemble many varied life factors into an integrated whole that reflects some sense of sameness or continuity to these experiences; 5) the psychosocial approach which attempts to integrate the roles played by society and individual's psychology and biology in developing an identity. See xi.

4. Erikson, *Childhood and Society*, 23.

5. See Kroger, *Identity Development*, 14; see also Bee, *Journey of Adulthood*, 35.

6. Berger, *Developing Person Through the Lifespan*, 65.

7. In infancy, the central issue of development is trust versus mistrust. Positive resolution of this stage will result in feelings of trust from environmental support while a negative resolution is equated with a fear of others. This stage is followed by autonomy versus shame and doubt in early childhood during which time a toddler will develop a sense of self-sufficiency if exploration is encouraged. If discouraged, the child will develop self-doubts and dependence. During the play years, the developmental issue is initiative versus guilt. If resolved positively, the young child will discover self-initiative and ways to manipulate his or her environment as opposed to guilt imposed by adults due to the child's actions or thoughts. The final stage of childhood occurring during the school age years is industry versus inferiority. At this time, children will develop a sense of competence if successful at their endeavors such as schoolwork or sports. Conversely, feelings of inferiority will ensue if the child experiences no sense of mastery. See Berger, *Developing Person Through the Lifespan*, 40; see also Kroger, *Identity Development*, 10–11.

8. Kroger, *Identity Development*, 10.

9. Ibid., 11.

10. Ibid., 26.

11. Ibid., 15.

12. Knowledge about women's development in general is minimal. Many scholars of adult development in particular agree that the empirical study of development is devoid of women's experiences. See Archer, "Feminist's Approach to Identity Research," 29; Baber and Allen, *Women and Families*, 18; Franz and Stewart, *Women Creating Lives*, 5; Gergen, "Finished at 40," 472; Josselson, *Revising Herself*, 9; Lytle, Bakken, and Romig, "Adolescent Female Identity Development," 175; Patterson, Sochting, and Marcia, "Inner Space and Beyond," 12. Most of what is known about adult development has been formulated on studies of men and used for the interpretation of women's lives. In addition to Erikson, prominent theorists such as Levinson, Vaillant, and Kohlberg have also been criticized by feminist scholars for their male conceptualizations of adult development. As Gergen observes, "To judge from the major studies of life-span development at middle adulthood, one would think only men survived the third decade of life" ("Finished at 40," 475).

It should be noted, however, that in later life, even Erikson himself questioned the usefulness of his theory for women and reconsidered its implications. See Ryff and Migdal, "Intimacy and Generativity," 471. For example, Erikson noted that his theory did not yet take into account the many changes that have occurred in society; see Hall, "Conversation with Erik Erikson," 24. Rapid social change with respect to women's roles during Erikson's life is not doubt one of the reasons for contemporary feminists' dissatisfaction with the accuracy of his theory for women's lives.

13. Berzoff, "From Separation to Connection," 51.

14. Gergen, "Finished at 40," 476. In Erikson's defense, he was the first social scientist to advocate a human development model that included an ethic of "care" as the hallmark of midlife See Snarey, *How Fathers Care for the Next Generation*, 16. Further, the model includes issues of trust, intimacy, and generativity which are typically associated with women's, not men's lives.

15. Archer, "Feminist's Approach to Identity Research," 27.

16. Ibid., 43.

17. Ibid., 30. Archer's own research in this area has demonstrated that "females have approached identity formation either comparable to or in a more sophisticated manner than that of males" (43). In the intrapersonal male domains of identity, females and males approach the task of identity formation similarly. With respect to the interpersonal female domains of connection, females have exhibited either comparable or more sophisticated processes of identity development. In addition to Archer's findings, minimal sex differences have been documented in numerous other studies (e.g., Lytle, Bakken, and Romig, "Adolescent Female Identity Development," 182; Kroger, *Identity Development*, 106), yet these findings are rarely included in textbooks, perpetuating the belief that the sense of self and the desire for connection are incompatible as opposed to intertwined.

18. Ibid., 31.

19. Kroger, *Identity Development*, 3.

20. Ibid., 9.

21. Marcia, "Ego Identity Status Approach to Ego Identity," 3.

22. McAdams, *Intimacy, and the Life Story*, 29.

23. See Kegan, *Evolving Self*, 81–85; see also Kegan, *In Over Our Heads*, 340–41.

24. Kroger, *Identity Development*, 12.

25. Knapp, *Striking at the Joints*, 65.

26. Archer, "Feminist's Approach to Identity Research," 45.

27. Kingsolver, *Animal Dreams*, 10.

28. Ibid., 28.

29. Ibid., 30.

30. Fullinwider-Bush and Jacobvitz, "Transition to Young Adulthood," 88; Kroger, *Identity Development*, 108.

31. Markstrom-Adams, "Consideration of Intervening Factors in Adolescent Identity Formation," 175.

32. Knapp, *Striking at the Joints*, 65.

33. Kingsolver, *Animal Dreams*, 69.

34. Ibid., 72.

35. Ibid., 73.

36. Ibid., 15.

37. Ibid., 142.

38. Ibid., 233.

39. Ibid., 236.

40. Ruth Ellen Josselson, another noteworthy identity researcher, suggests that a third dimension of connectedness be added to the dimensions of exploration and commitment when determining identity status for women. In particular, women in diffusion not only lack commitments and directed exploration but are also isolated. Distant from their parents, they have not found a long-term, stable, healthy relationship to function in their stead. Their position in relation to their parents can be characterized as "I don't know where I stand, but you stand far away from me." For most of the novel, this is particularly true for Codi's relationship with her father. Women in foreclosure sustain strong commitments to their parents: "Here I stand, loyally at your side." In moratorium, women are caught in the struggle between autonomy and loyalty to their parents: "If I stand here, will you still be there for me?" In Codi's case, there is some resolution of the distant relationship with Doc Homer; however, confronted with the reality of his progressive decline in health, Codi must face her father's continued emotional absence. In identity achievement, women state, "Here I stand," because they posses a secure family base from which to conduct their explorations. In the absence of her parents, Codi has recognized and accepted Loyd and the doting women of Grace, whom she affectionately refers to as her "fifty mothers," as her family by the end of the novel.

41. Markstrom-Adams, "Consideration of Intervening Factors in Adolescent Identity Formation," 176.

42. Kingsolver, *Animal Dreams*, 213.

43. Markstrom-Adams, "Consideration of Intervening Factors in Adolescent Identity Formation," 179.

44. Kroger, *Identity Development*, 65; Whitbourne, *The Me I Know*, 34.

45. Kingsolver, *Animal Dreams*, 201.

46. Ibid., 10.

47. Markstrom-Adams, "Consideration of Intervening Factors in Adolescent Identity Formation," 185.

48. Kingsolver, *Animal Dreams*, 36.

49. Ibid., 8.

50. Ibid., 255.

51. Ibid., 297.

52. Ibid., 289.

53. Ibid., 284.

54. Akhtar, "Syndrome of Identity Diffusion," 1382; Baumeister, *Identity, 12;* Erikson, *Childhood and Society*, 22.

55. Markstrom-Adams, "Consideration of Intervening Factors in Adolescent Identity Formation," 186.

56. Kingsolver, *Animal Dreams*, 225.

57. Josselson, *Revising Herself*, 7.

Part II
The Family: Family Systems Therapy and the Discourse of Community

Family Dynamics and Property Acquisitions in *Clarissa*

Joan I. Schwarz

ONE OF SAMUEL RICHARDSON'S KEY THEMES IN THE FIRST EDITION OF *Clarissa* (1747–48) concerns the early relationships among family dynamics and British eighteenth-century values regarding money, land, and acquisition. Each aspect of acquisition is a transaction reinforced by early eighteenth-century law: Clarissa's inheritance from her grandfather, her possible inheritances from her uncles, her portion from her father from his marriage settlement realizable at the time of a future marriage, and the potential merger of the Solmes' estate with her grandfather's estate. Of these transactions, the most important is Clarissa's inheritance from her grandfather because it is the motivating event in the novel, illuminating both the familial dynamics of power and control and its relationship to wider cultural and legal matters. In this essay, therefore, I will discuss how the external legal structure which shapes this prototypical eighteenth-century hierarchical family provides an understanding of how disruptions in the traditional legal transactions produces significant subsequent emotional strains on the internal structures and dynamics of the Harlowe family.

Had Richardson created Clarissa as merely a resource of her father, a daughter whom he could legally control, Richardson would have had neither plot nor novel. Clarissa's place in the family changes dramatically with her inheritance and instead of being an "excess child," a term reserved for younger sons and daughters not in line for the family inheritance, she has become a propertied eighteenth-century *feme sole*. Her financial leverage thus introduces what family systems (FST) critics call morphogenesis into the Harlowe family dynamic and helps to change it in significant ways. Clarissa is now a single propertied female, able to own property and chattels which she could bequeath by will, make contracts, sue and be sued.[1] Despite having given over the management rights to her father to appease the family's anger, Clarissa is a feme sole with an estate which she will manage in her own right once her trustee, Cousin Morden, arrives from Italy. With her estate, her "niche" in the family hierarchy changes dramatically.[2] With this behest, she now has legal rights and power comparable to the eldest Harlowe son, her brother, James Jr. Indeed, Clarissa is more powerful than most single women in the eighteenth century, a position which prominently distinguishes her from women's traditional financial status.

The world of *Clarissa* scholarship, as discussed below, has speculated on several related matters: why James Jr. has so much more power within the family, how he use inheritance law to his advantage, why the Harlowe family does not stop James Jr. when his "plan" forbids Clarissa from returning home, and why the Harlowe parents, especially the mother, do not step in and contravene James Jr.'s decisions that weigh so severely against Clarissa. I will argue that the Harlowe family's traditional homeostatic balance is severely taxed when the external legal rules of partial settlement law are disrupted by the grandfather's devise to an "excess" granddaughter; further, that the internal dynamic of the family is inverted by Clarissa's new-found power, which disarms her parents and enrages her brother, with all of them fearing a loss in familial property acquisition and authority. An analysis of the external legal rule structure which govern the Harlowe family dynamic, namely, partial settlement law, sheds light on the Harlowe's quarrel and on James Jr.'s control over the disruptive situation that ends with Clarissa's death. This analysis will also help frame the major disruption in the Harlowe family's transactional balance as we employ family systems theory (FST) to examine the novel.[3]

The key issues involve the Harlowe's collective anxiety about whether or not they can control Clarissa now that she is propertied, whether they can protect their family legacy with some of the grandfather's land being denied James Jr., and whether or not their traditional patriarchal familial unity can be preserved. Since familial presumptions about boundaries are thrown into doubt with her inheritance, the morphogenetic influence of the grandfather's bequest must, at all costs, be thwarted and family equilibrium restored. Hence, for the Harlowes, a return to the original familial homeostasis means reverting the Harlowe financial hierarchy to its original status prior to the grandfather's bequest. Since James Jr. has the most to lose as a result of his grandfather's devise, he is unofficially designated as the one to reestablish the homestatic balance in the family system.[4] From these assumptions, I will answer the following questions: in his unofficial position, how does James Jr. plan to keep Clarissa from returning home; how does he convince his hitherto doting parents to cooperate with his efforts to ostracize her from the family; and finally, how does he employ marriage settlement law to his own advantage? Learning how intertwined both the legal and family dynamics are, we can then understand the harshness of the Harlowes' rules designed to drag a rebellious Clarissa back into its system.

As I have argued elsewhere, Richardson was knowledgeable of marriage settlement law and how these laws affected the family dynamic as well as the pressures that were created when a daughter was to marry.[5] We know he was knowledgable both of general law and specifically of settlement law because he drafted marriage articles for his own daughter Mary (one of four daughters) in preparation for her marriage to Phillip Dichter, a Bath surgeon.[6] In contrast to Richardson, a concerned father who did not want his three younger daughters to have insufficient portions, Harlowe Sr. [hereinafter referred to as the father] is not dedicated to protecting his younger "excess" daughters, Arabella and Clarissa. Rather, as family patriarch, this fictional father believes his eldest son the rightful one to receive not only the bulk of the Harlowe marriage settlement, but all the inheritances in the family as well. Hence, this family's homestatic balance is externally framed, in part, by eighteenth-century British property rules which dictated how family wealth was to be gained and distributed from generation to generation. For the Harlowes then, the destabilization of what they perceive to be family cohesiveness begins with decisions about distribution of family wealth after their death, the problems of inheritance, and the equity of the distributions to the younger daughters. Mara Selvini Palazzoli describes some typical sibling "moves" during what she has called "wars of succession" in some European families.[7]

Partial settlement law was so-called because it did not settle all aspects of the estate for the excess children at the time the parents were married. Because portions for all sons, except for the eldest, and for all daughters were discretionary and set later as the children aged, unscrupulous eldest sons could and often did successfully exploit the law, depleting portions set aside for the excess children primarily because no trust was in place to protect these assets. The eldest could simply alienate property at will and thereby diminish the value of the estate. Later in the century, this legal loophole was closed with a strict settlement statue; in the new law, a settled estate (cash and/or land) was bound by a chain of settlement established at the time of the parents' marriage. Portions were then designated for excess children and placed in a trust, unable to be touched by an eldest son. Furthermore, a process called resettlement was also established wherein each son was limited in his power of alienation of land, thereby protecting succeeding generations.[8] James Jr. [hereinafter referred to as the son] was not subject to strict settlement laws during the time frame of the novel (c. 1701), and was therefore in a legal position to control all discretionary portion allotments, even canceling such portions if he felt it necessary to garner all the inheritances for his future peerage.

Richardson's assumed "authorial audience," that is, the specific contemporary readers he had in mind who would read this novel, would have understood the estate problems in the novel, just as twenty-first-century readers tacitly understand references to real estate and inheritance issues in such contemporary fiction as, say, Richard Ford's *Independence Day* (1995).[9] Despite excellent scholarship on *Clarissa*, criticism thus far has not provided readers with *both* an understanding of the larger partial settlement legal issue *and* an explanation of how these legal issues help define this propertied family's dynamic.

Three recent works on law, literature, and *Clarissa*, while helpful in their own right, are each limited in their providing the contextualization necessary for connections between eighteenth-century marriage settlement law and legal evidence on the one hand, and applications of this understanding to family dynamics in the novel on the other. The most well-known of these, Susan Staves's *Married Women's Separate Property in England, 1660–1833* (1990), discusses how property disbursements affected the family, especially women trying to protect the property they believed rightfully theirs. Staves discusses numerous cases regarding strict settlement, but, unless one is very well acquainted with eighteenth-century law, the task of making connections without knowing the relationship between the framework and the legal evidence is virtually impossible for a nonlawyer. Thus, making the connections between the law Staves explicates and the legal "moves" portrayed in eighteenth-century novels is again problematic. Hence, while Staves's book is complex and includes much case law, the limitations for the literary scholar not legally trained are serious. One still wants to know how this legal evidence explains the fictional particularities in *Clarissa*, or for that matter, in any other eighteenth-century fiction.

Conversely, in *Family and the Law in Eighteenth-Century Fiction* (1993), John Zomchik does analyze *Clarissa* specifically, explaining how Clarissa exemplifies the newly emerging juridical subject. He provides neither the legal framework nor the case law to explain the complexity of eighteenth-century property disputes, nor does he explain how the law could inform a fictional family dynamic like the Harlowe's. After surveying the ideological function of law and family in the eighteenth-century's developing market economy, he analyzes how individuals in fiction, but not whole families, are identified with the principles and aims of the law. Again, while insightful, his discussions tend toward broad generalizations rather than detailed connections between marriage settlement law and its operation in the Harlowe family.

A third scholar who addresses legal matters in *Clarissa* is Thomas Beebee in *Clarissa on the Continent* (1990). Beebee not only claims that the legal specifics of the Solmes deal "remain somewhat unclear and preposterous," but he also posits that this "lack of clarity only reinforces the mythic patriarchial image of James Jr., Solmes, Mr. Harlowe, and Uncle Anthony freely sharing land among themselves because they are male."[10] While Beebee correctly assesses the legalities involved in the Solmes deal and the complexities of marriage settlement law consuming the Harlowes, his conclusions that such transactions were "preposterous" are, I would argue, erroneous; hence his misunderstanding of this legal transaction undermines the significance of Richardson's complex legal foundation, the very matrix of the novel itself. Thus, while these three works are effective in their own way, each is limited in coordinating the connections among family dynamic, legal history, and the several character's motivations, connections that I believe are needed for an insightful reading of the complexities of *Clarissa*.

THE EXTERNAL LEGAL STRUCTURE SHAPING THE HARLOWE FAMILY: PROPERTY LAW AND *CLARISSA*

While the Harlowes proceed as if they can control Clarissa's life and finances, Richardson shows that they have no real legal power over her without her consent to their authority.[11] To combat her independence, the Harlowes immediately argue that they will attack the legality of the grandfather's will, an act all too familiar to us as readers. While the grandfather himself thinks the will might be flawed and that his"bequests and dispositions" for Clarissa may not be "strictly conformable to law," no tangible evidence in the novel suggests that the will is legally unsound.[12] This "fact" leads us to an interesting question: if the will is in fact legal, why then would Richardson have the Harlowes argue illegality, and would such illegality affect Clarissa's feme sole position?

A review of the actual history of legal restraints on wills between the 1720s and 1740s reveals no legal problems with the grandfather's will.[13] Parliamentary concerns with will making dealt with the attestation process regarding legatees and creditors who were also witnesses to the will and restraints regarding the testator's devise of his property by will. Because Richardson does not mention problems with any of these legal flaws, and given these assurances from history that these were the main parliamentary concerns about wills, we can thus assume that the grandfather had legally and rightfully willed his lands to Clarissa. After all, since there is no will contest from the Harlowe family, we can presume that Richardson framed the family legal struggle for a different reason.

Given the Harlowes' inability to overturn the grandfather's will, James Jr., the son, employs other strategies to further his plans to recapture the grandfather's estate. The son soon learns that the family is not only without legal means to control Clarissa's financially, but that her new-found independence has emboldened her in other areas of her life as well. Indeed, they are incapable of commanding her on such matters as her correspondence with Lovelace, her rejection of Solmes, and her refusal to return home.[14] Clarissa's recalcitrance flies in the face of the family's traditional hierarchy of authority. Without her cooperation and ultimate consent in each of these situations, the Harlowe family is thwarted and short of a forced marriage, they cannot legally demand that she cooperate with anything they require of her. Clearly, Clarissa is a free agent, and much to their dismay, the usual remedies available to them by means of partial settlement law ironically provide them with little leverage to control her or her acts. In order to understand how Clarissa's inheritance really did frustrate the family's propertied status, a look at the family's financial arrangements is in order.

THE GRANDFATHER'S PRESUMED MARRIAGE SETTLEMENT: ARTICLES ON THE FATHER (JAMES SR.)

The father is the second son of Clarissa's grandfather. Assuming that the setting of the novel takes place some time between mid-1720s and mid-1740s, we also can assume that at the time of the grandfather's marriage, perhaps in the early restoration period, he may have provided for Clarissa's father (his son) by means of the partial marriage settlement. When his son later married, the grandfather was not legally required to settle anything on a second son since he would have been an "excess" child. However, from textual evidence, we can infer some tentative conclusions about what the grandfather left James Sr. by looking at the opening lines of the will's preamble where we learn how the estate was divided up. We learn that the estate the grandfather left Clarissa was "principally of his own raising," but it was not even half of the real estate he owned.[15] We also know, not only from Clarissa's mother's behavior but also from the grandfather's will, that Clarissa's father married the daughter of a viscount.[16] Hence, clearly cognizant of his own son's wealth, acquired in the various ways he has listed, the grandfather decided to skip leaving a large part of his estate to any of his sons (Harlowe Sr; or to John and Anthony, Clarissa's two uncles) and instead left it to Clarissa.

How the father became wealthy, despite his status as a second son, is best understood in light of the law of dowry in the eighteenth century. Generally, the ratio between the size of the woman's dowry, the portion that the parents bestowed on their daughters, and the size of the jointure, which was the amount the husband settled upon his wife as the annual provision paid to a widow, was standardized. Essentially, the size of the provision which a man made for his wife's possible widowhood was naturally dependent on the amount of money she brought into the family.[17] The common formula at the end of the seventeenth century for the relation of portion and jointure was £1,000 of portion for every pound of jointure.[18]

In the Harlowe family, we can reasonably assume that the father must have received a substantial settlement from his father, even as a second son, because he would have needed a jointure for his wife. appropriate to her "very large portion" and her status as a "worthy daughter by both sides of very honourable famiies."[19] We also know from the mother herself, in a conversation with Clarissa, that she brought "a still larger fortune into the family than you will carry to Mr. Solmes."[20] In addition, several large estates "unexpectedly [fell] in to him [the father] on the deaths of several relations of his present wife.[21] Hence, either with his settlement, or with his wife's fortune, the father was able to purchase the Harlowe estate, which was then to descend to his eldest son.

In theory at least, marriage to a daughter with a large portion, such as the mother's, normally resulted in an accession of land which descended to the eldest son and then remained permanently in the family.[22] Essentially, the bride was required to make a contribution toward enlarging her prospective husband's estate with either land or cash. Portions which were intended to provide an income to contribute toward the maintenance of the wife were usually fixed with reference to the annual income they would yield.[23] If the daughter's portion were in cash, the marriage settlement often required purchase of estates that were to descend with the patrimony. The net effect became cumulative, with a successful match in one generation enhancing the family's bargaining position in the next generation. Such marriage settlements consolidated and preserved each family's acquisitions.[24]

The Father's Presumed Marital Settlement

Given the novel's sketchy details, the kind of marriage settlement Clarissa's parents established upon their marriage also is similarly open to interpretation. Clarissa's father and mother probably married sometime in the last decade of the seventeenth century or early in the eighteenth century when strict settlement was still not fully instituted. Accordingly, the parents' marriage settlement, like that of the grandfather, did not necessarily provide portions for either Arabella or Clarissa as excess children. We know from the text, however, that the father did, in fact, provide unspecified portions for them. Clarissa tells Anna of a discussion her family apparently had in happier times regarding marriage. She speaks of their ambition of "raising a family," however much already elevated, so that they gain "rank and title":

> My uncles had once extended this view to each of us three children, urging that as they themselves intended not to marry, we each of us might be so portioned. . . . While my brother, as the only son, thought

the two girls might be very well provided for by ten or fifteen thousand pounds apiece.[25]

This passage is important for understanding the son's "plan." We can tell from the reference to "portions" of "ten or fifteen thousand pounds" that the father had apparently provided these portions for his two daughters, but had not specified exactly how much they were to receive, in what form (cash or possibly, rents), or when. Such ambiguity was the result of partial settlement law. In the early stages of marriage settlement law (prior to strict settlement), the exact amount of the portion, either in cash or land, and the date of allocation was not set, according to Lloyd Bonfield, until the daughter was scheduled to marry; to have allocated the amount any earlier would have made her "dangerously" independent.[26] Conversely, if the Harlowes' marriage settlement had been a strict settlement, the exact amounts to Arabella and Clarissa, the form of the portions, and their distribution would have been specified; furthermore, these portions would have been contingent remainders protected by a trustee.[27] Since we are not told these specifics, we can infer that the Harlowes' marriage settlement was in fact a partial settlement in which the entail in remainder would go to James Jr. as the eldest son. Unfortunately, the portions for Clarissa and Arabella, since they were not placed in a trust, would be vulnerable to James Jr.'s usurpations. Because of such ambiguity in distribution of family assets, these partial settlements often caused serious difficulties for the well-being of any family's excess children. Jane Cox says that, prior to strict settlement, wills and inheritance law generally were part of a "lax system which enabled even overheard death-bed utterances to be sanctioned as legal bequests without much difficulty."[28] The Harlowe family indeed reflects most of these problems.

First of all, the amount of portion varied widely among the younger sons and the daughters, according to parental affection and the circumstances of the family. The decision regarding the appropriate amount of provision was left to the discretion of the parent at the appropriate time, either upon a daughter's marriage or a son's majority. When the amount of the portion, or its form, was not determined at the time of the parents' marriage, a favored child could often receive more than the other excess children, causing sibling hostility within a family.[29] This favoritism worked in reverse as well. Even if a daughter (or younger son) were granted a portion, it was still subject to parental control because if the daughter eloped or otherwise married without parental approval, she married without the provision that could keep her property from going entirely to her husband as common law dictated.[30] Restricted by the precedence of partial settlement, all families, including the Harlowes, could vary the amount of portions according to their prejudices for their children. Only by means of strict settlement law did equity and equality of distribution of family wealth provide security for the excess children in a family.

Hence, the partial settlement law was clear in establishing the hierarchical family organization in the early eighteenth century. Inside this hierarchical system, the legal rules were clear for each family member: an eldest son, whether favored or not by his parents, would receive the family's property in order to preserve the family's landed position; the daughters, no matter how favored, and any younger sons, would receive discretionary portions, sufficient to marry them to an appropriately propertied spouse, but not so large as to diminish the distribution of family wealth from generation to generation. When this legal dynamic is upset by one family member, especially one who is not supposed to have power or leverage in the family system, as is the case with Clarissa as an excess daughter, the family's hierarchical organization is loosened and such morphogenesis produces significant subsequent emotional strains on the entire system. The alliances are disturbed and the members of the system pressure the one who has allegedly disrupted the intrafamily alliance. Indeed, as Luigi Boscolo points out:

> When one family member accepts the negative position in the system, all the others become healthier, they become united, they are all angels. . . . Everyone unites to attack one member [in this instance, Clarissa] who agrees to take all the sins on her shoulders.[31]

While it is the grandfather who initially upsets the hierarchical distribution pattern, he is a generation removed from the Harlowe family system, while Clarissa is an "excess child" firmly within it. In family systems language, she clearly becomes the identified patient (IP), or the one who needs to realign herself with the rules of the family. All future dynamics in the system therefore operate to force her back into the hierarchical family organization. Hence, from a systemic perspective, the real threat to the Harlowe family, as I have argued elsewhere, is not Lovelace, the character usually perceived as the "villain" of the novel.[32] Rather, the real threat to the Harlowe family system is Clarissa herself, for she must, according to the parents and James Jr., return to her original powerless position in order to restore the family's original homeostatic balance. Thus, even her loving mother sees such an equilibrium as crucial to the family's reputed existence. In a letter to Mrs. Judith Norton, Mrs. Harlowe expresses her horror at her daughter's throwing away all that the mother fervently believes valuable:

> Our other children had reason, good children as they always were, to think themselves neglected. But they were likewise so sensible of their sister's superiority and of the honor she reflected upon the whole family, that they confessed themselves eclipsed without envying the eclipser.... The dear creature ... gave an eminence to us all. And now that she has left us, so disgracefully left us! we are stripped of our ornament, and are but a common family![33]

Yet, with her inheritance in hand, the status quo cannot be restored, even though Clarissa attempts to return her family life back to what it was before her grandfather's devise. Why she is unsuccessful in restoring the family system is the focus of the following.

THE INTERNAL DYNAMIC OF THE HARLOWE FAMILY SYSTEM

Under the eighteenth-century partial settlement system, Arabella and Clarissa necessarily have not been guaranteed equity and equality. The grandfather's will even states that James Sr. can "bestow his favours accordingly, and in greater proportion, upon Miss Arabella and Master James," as he saw fit, implying that the amounts of the settlement for James Jr. and of the portions for Clarissa and Arabella were not fixed at the time of their parents' marriage.[34] Because of the discretionary nature of the portions to the daughters, John Jr., as the eldest son, could not be certain of the amount of his settlement. In other words, the amounts when determined for Clarissa and Arabella would necessarily reduce the amount James Jr. would inherit; any favoritism to a daughter could and often did enter into the parents' determination of portions for daughters.

Such a conflicted dynamic existed in the Harlowe family. Recall how honestly Mrs. Harlowe speaks of her favoritism for Clarissa, angrily lamenting that with her gone, the Harlowes are "but a common family," while at the same time boasting that "there was not anybody equal with her, in their own opinions, as to envy what all aspired to emulate."[35] For her part, Clarissa is desperate, early on, not to alienate her mother, whom she loves dearly even in the context of her outward rebellion: "My uncles may be hard-hearted—my papa may be immoveable—I may suffer from my brother's ambition and from my sister's envy—but let me not lose my Mama's love; at least her pity."[36] Although Clarissa's view of the family dynamic is more accurate than her mother's, she still misjudges her Mama's ultimate allegiences. Mama insists, albeit gently, that her daughter must adhere to the family's party line because *Clarissa* is the one who has sinned, not her father, brother, sister, or uncles: "You have my love! You have my pity! But oh my dearest girl—I have not yours." As their conversation continues, Mrs. Harlowe resorts to the time-honored use of tears as she reveals that the family equilibrium is ultimately more important to her than even the love of her favorite child: "So, Clery, you are already at defiance with your papa. I have had too much cause before to apprehend as much—What will this come to? . . . You forget that I must separate myself from you, if you will not comply. . . . Will you choose to break with us all?"[37]

Her male sibling feels no such compunctions. As eldest son, James Jr. believes he needs to stop Clarissa—at any expense—from garnering parts of the estate that he asserts are rightfully his. Perhaps James Jr. did not envy Clarissa enough to harm her when she was the family favorite but still merely an excess daughter; it was another matter, however, when that favoritism with the grandfather triggered an inheritance which James Jr. believes was rightfully his. If favoritism for Clarissa could diminish one inheritance, there was always the possibility that the two uncles, who also favored Clarrisa, could leave their property to her as well.

The second problem with the partial settlement is also evident in the Harlowe family system. Because the specific amounts of the portions were often left to the discretion of the eldest male child, many of them resented allocating portions to their sisters and younger brothers.[38] If the eldest male chose to be parsimonious, all the "excess children" in the family, whether sisters or younger brothers, suffered. As one sixteenth-century commentator, Thomas Wilson, stated:

> The elder brother must have all, and all the rest that which the cat left on the malt heap, perhaps some small annuity during his life or

what please our elder brother's worship to bestow upon us if we please him, and my mistress his wife.[39]

Similar commentary appeared in contemporary periodicals, one referring to the settling of one's estate on the eldest son as a "scandalous practice" and remonstrating: "I know nothing more monstrous than for Parents to talk of natural Affection towards their Progeny, and yet leave all their younger Children Beggars, to enrich, very probably, a prodigal extravagant Heir."[40]

James Jr. represents this "scandalous practice." Clarissa repeats one of James Jr.'s numerous complaints to Anna regarding daughters who encumber the family estate and rich older relatives who are merely his stewards:

> "That a man who has sons brings up chickens for his own table . . . whereas daughters are chickens brought up for the tables of other men." This, accompanied with the equally polite reflection, "that, to induce people to take them off their hands, the family stock must be impaired into the bargain."[41]

This unfortunate metaphor has echoes of the Chinese Baron in Maxine Hong Kingston's *The Woman Warrior* (1989) who speaks of girl children as "maggots in the rice."[42] Because partial settlement law did not provide that the male heir would necessarily provide the allocated portions to the excess children of a marriage, the eldest son was not restrained from alienating (selling) the land he had inherited from his father. Rather, upon his father's death, the eldest son came into possession as the tenant in tail with full powers of disposition (ownership in fee simple), and as such, no trust was in place to protect any contingent remainders for the excess children. With this kind of marriage settlement, the father's control over his eldest son ended with the father's death. Only with the implementation of the strict settlement was the eldest son restrained because the strict settlement required first, that he receive a life estate which restrained his power of alienation for one generation, and second, that a trust be put into place prior to his possession so as to protect the excess children's portions.

A third complicating and perhaps more disturbing matter with the partial settlement was the diminished power the father had over his eldest son even while still alive, an often unsettling change in the heretofore traditional family dynamic. No less a luminary than Sir Francis Bacon argued that entailing eldest sons bred sons who were "disobedient, negligent and wasteful, often marrying without the Father's consent and growing insolent in vice knowing that there could be no check of disinheriting him."[43] Restraint on the eldest son was possible only if the father and son joined in what was called "resettlement." A resettlement could occur only before the death of the life tenant and in practice occurred upon the marriage of the eldest son. The father and son would join in a settlement in which the son relinquished his entail in remainder, which he could have alienated once in possession of it, and instead accepted a life estate to commence upon the determination of his father's life interest. In order to prompt his son to make such a sacrifice, the father settled some form of present income upon the son to support his household until he came into possession of the estate. The existing settlement was then broken, and replaced with one which spanned a further generation.

In the Harlowe household, James Jr. probably would not enter into a resettlement agreement, even if asked by his father, because James Jr. does not need to make such a sacrifice. He has plenty of income to support his household until he receives his father's estate after receiving a considerable estate from his godmother, as well as another estate in Yorkshire.[45] Furthermore, he has paid off the mortgage on the Hervey's property, thereby making them financially indebted to him as well.[46] Consequently, since James Jr. received his father's estate as a tenant in tail, he could alienate it and refuse the portions for Arabella and Clarissa with impunity.

Because of the leverage an eldest son had in the early stages of marriage settlement law, James Jr. could therefore effectively manipulate Clarissa by threatening to control or eliminate her portion *and*, as a means of legal harassment, sue her in an attempt to invalidate the grandfather's will, thus leaving her completely without resources. Tightening his control over Clarissa was necessary for James Jr. because, as he tells his uncles, he was greatly apprehensive that this "little siren is in a fair way to out-uncle as well as out-grandfather us both."[47] Clarissa aptly sums up James Jr.'s power when she writes to him near her death that "an only son [is] more worth in the family account than several daughters."[48]

James Sr. had long acquiesced to his only son, "whose violent temper made himself both feared and courted by the entire family." The father rationalized his abnegation of parental authority by claiming that James Jr. was the only one in the family "who was to build up the name and augment the honour of it"; hence, James Jr. has assumed full power over his parent's family.[49] He has them bind themselves by a signed paper in support of James Sr's ostensible paternal authority "against Lovelace, as a libertine and an enemy to the family."[50] James Jr. tells Clarissa that her mortification will be great "so long as you prefer that villainous Lovelace, who is justly hated by all the family. . . . But the stronger you hold, the greater must be the force."[51]

Not convinced that this family pact was sufficient to turn the uncles against Clarissa, James Jr. works up another means of acquisition to further the Harlowe—that is, his own—estate and honor. He concocts a plan "which will very probably prevent [Clarissa's] grandfather's estate going out of the family and may be a means to bring a still greater into it."[52] After all, James Jr. knows his goal to become a peer can only be fulfilled with sufficient property interests.[53] He gets Solmes to agree that he will settle all he is worth on Clarissa, by promising that if they married and she should die without children and he has none by any other marriage, he will grant all reversionary interests to the Harlowes.[54]

This plan, while excessively contingent in nature, is apparently sufficiently probable for James Jr.: upon marriage to Solmes, the estate from Clarissa's grandfather, which is geographically contiguous to Solmes's estate, would merge with Solmes's and "double the value of a considerable part of his own."[55] If no children were born to Solmes in his marriage with Clarissa or anyone else, and upon Clarissa's death, he would allow the two estates to revert to the Harlowes.[56] Solmes also promises James Jr. that he "will make exchanges of estates, or at least that he will purchase the northern one." Solmes tells Clarissa that he agrees with James Jr.'s plan because "it must be entirely consistent with the family views that we increase our interest in this country . . . and provides a very great probability of being on a footing with the principal in the kingdom."[57]

Clarissa is amazed at the family's acceptance of this plan, commenting that "such an accession to the family as may happen from marrying Mr. Solmes . . . since now a possibility is discovered . . . that my grandfather's estate will revert to it, with a much more considerable one of the man's own."[58] She is upset to know that Solmes would agree to allow for a reversionary interest of this sort because it would "rob [his family] of their just expectations" and "their natural rights and reversionary prospects." With this offer, he negates what would have been the normal lines of inheritance: if Solmes ultimately left no legitimate issue, his estate would revert to his relations—brothers and sisters, if he had had any; and if his brothers and sisters had predeceased their children, to his nieces and nephews, if he had any. Clarissa declares the plan as being "equally against law and equity."[59] Her statement, however, is more of a moral than legal assessment of the situation, for the arrangement was legal.

In fact, this legal descent of property would have been similar to that of the uncles' estates going first to their brother, James Sr., because they had no children, and then ultimately to their nephew and nieces: James Jr., Clarissa, and Arabella.[60] The difference was that, as a business arrangement, Solmes would have forced this line of descent as a condition of his marriage to Clarissa, thereby denying his family-of-origin their right of consanguinity to his property. He coldly used his estate as a bargaining tool, in contrast with the grandfather who willed some of his lands to Clarissa, whom he took "pleasure of considering her as [his] own peculiar child," as a legacy of love.[61]

Anna tells Clarissa that the plan is so well established that she cannot prevail, that "everyone seems apprized of your brother's and sister's motives . . . and enjoy their successful malice."[62] Anna also informs Clarissa that they are so adamant that they "will never hearken to any accommodation, or terms" and that they "will not let them [the Harlowe relations] cool—at least til their uncles have made such dispositions, and your father too perhaps, as they would have them make."[63]

So closely does James Jr. monitor all events that he enlists even those relatives in the extended family system and even upbraids his uncles when they decide to "alter and new-settle their wills." Further, James Jr. confronts Uncle John and asks whether Clarissa has made any new application to him to be reinstated into his favor. Uncle John, while avoiding a direct answer, hopes that Clarissa is to be married and that a general reconciliation will occur. Furious, James Jr. reminds his uncle that he cannot be reconciled to her "but by general consent."[64] James Jr.'s plan is put into effect, requiring all family members to agree that Clarissa not be allowed to return home until she consents to marry Solmes.[65] The family system has been so disrupted—the hierarchical system so threatened—that Clarissa's promises to leave Lovelace, will her estate back to her family, and remain single, are insufficient. Given all the complex scheming to aggrandize the family wealth, James Jr. simply cannot afford to have Clarissa return to the family under her own terms. Clarissa correctly speculates to Anna that perhaps her promise to remain single and have no heirs but her brother and sister are insufficient financial inducement because "it may be, my brother is insisting upon equivalents for his reversion in the estate."[66] James Jr.'s plan is so rigidly defined that even the remote probability of Solmes's reversionary interests accruing to the Harlowes is preferable to Clarissa's promise of remaining single and having her interests revert to the family. Anna comments on James Jr.'s recalcitrance:

> If you were never to marry, the estate they are so loath should go out of their name, would in time I suppose revert to your brother; and *he* or *his* would have it, perhaps much more certainly this way, than by the precarious reversions Solmes makes them hope for.[67]

Clarissa again correctly assesses the skillful manipulation by which James Jr. has established his plan when she tells Anna: "Now [that] my brother has engaged my father, his fine scheme will walk alone without needing his leading strings; and it is become my father's will that I oppose, not my brother's grasping views."[68] Not even Lovelace detects the viciousness of the plan when he first attests that James Jr. and Arabella "at first intended no more by the confederacy they formed against this their angel sister, than to disgrace and keep her down."[69] The plan, however, then takes on a deadly life of its own. As Clarissa observes, the "battle lines are drawn with high stakes" when James Jr. threatens "to abandon Harlowe Place, never to see it more—So they are to lose a son, or to conquer a daughter."[70] And certainly in losing a son, they will lose the possibility of James Jr.'s title and its significance for their family.

James Jr.'s revenge against Clarissa is equal in intensity to his revenge against Lovelace. Clearly aware of the depth of James Jr.'s hatred, Clarissa sums up her brother when she declares to Anna: "My brother!—But possessing everything, he has the vice of age mingled with the ambition of youth, and enjoys nothing—but his own haughtiness, and ill-temper."[71] She even tells her mother, "I am grieved at heart to be obliged to lay so great blame at my brother's door, although my reputation and my liberty are both to be sacrificed to his resentment and ambition."[72] Cousin Morden characterizes most accurately the destruction for which James Jr. is responsible; he is that "hot-headed man (who, as far as I know) has done more to ruin his sister than Lovelace himself, and this with the approbation of you all that I will not again enter into your doors or theirs.[73]

Underlying all this anxiety about the family's loss of the grandfather's estate and the actual and potential diminution of the Harlowe estate lies the unacceptable threat and near-reality of Clarissa's choice to be independent of her father's authority and his management of her estate, and independent of James Jr.'s control. Her defiance, as they characterize it, seems to threaten their plans for the future. Given that children's marriage patterns tended to accelerate the growth of great estates, Clarissa's assertion of independence actually *is* a major threat to the Harlowes' accumulation of wealth, power, and hope for a peerage in the family. After all, marriage contributions through portions did the most to increase the size of estates. In 1701, Sir William Temple made this observation about the business of family wealth and accumulation:

> These contracts would never be made, but by men's avarice, and greediness of portions with the people they marry, which is grown among us to that degree, as to surmount and extinguish all other regards or desires: so that our marriages are made, just like other common bargains and sales, by the mere consideration of interest or gain, without any of love or esteem, of birth or of beauty itself, which ought to be the true ingredients of all happy compositions of this kind, and of all generous productions. Yet this custom is of no ancient date in England.[74]

By rejecting that "marriages are made . . . by the mere consideration of interest or gain"—a refusal to subordinate marriage to wealth and family aggrandizement, as was the norm—Clarissa upsets the Harlowe family dynamic as much as her grandfather had done with his will. In effect, Clarissa is in spirit rightfully her grandfather's kin because, like him, she follows her own dictates rather than honor the requirements of family lineage and wealth accumulation. The Harlowes, or any comparable family, believed that they could not afford to suffer lightly such an affront to its authority. Her father, believing himself a "justly incensed Father" upbraids her as a "perverse girl" who has defied his authority and reviled her brother and is therefore deserving of his "utmost resentment."[75] Because she is so valuable a commodity to the family, the Harlowes cannot bring themselves to grant her the simple right of a "consenting negative"—*not* to marry someone unacceptable to her.[76]

Helping to fuel the family's perception of her as "perverse," Clarissa outspokenly asks Uncle Antony "if then such narrow motives [as James Jr.'s] have so little weight with me for my *own* benefit, shall the remote and uncertain view of family-aggrandizement, and that in the person of my brother and his descendants, be thought sufficient to influence me?"[77] Her haughty insistence to Solmes that "I am independent of you, sir" certainly was inflammatory behavior for an eighteen-year old female, even though legally true.[78] As a feme sole with an estate, Clarissa possessed the same legal rights of property alienation and will devise as propertied males and was capable of living financially independent of male support, including even her father's portion. She writes to Anna that "my father himself could not bear that I should be made sole as I may call it, and independent, for such the will as to that estate and the powers it gave (unaccountably, as they all said), made me."[79] Because of her power and her rights equal to her brother's, Clarissa has inverted the family power distribution so much so that her family sees no other solution than to unite against their formerly beloved and favorite daughter to restore the family power and authority, but now with James Jr. as its leader.[80]

As Richardson's audience would have known, Clarissa would give up these rights only by marrying and becoming a *feme covert*. Then she would lose her financial strategies and her power, and would have to relate to her husband as a child to her parents, unable to exercise the rights and responsibilities that accompanied a full legal existence. Hence, she would be relegated to second-class citizenship in the realm of private law and lose her right to her grandfather's estate. Too fully aware of how she will be stripped of the rights and responsibilities should she be married, Clarissa describes marriage with a certain dread:

> To be given up to a strange man; to be engrafted into a strange family; to give up her very name, as a mark of her becoming his absolute and dependent property: to be obliged to prefer this strange man to father, mother—to everybody; and his humours to all her own—Or to contend, perhaps, in breach of a vowed duty for every innocent instance of free will: to go no-whither: to make acquaintance: to give up acquaintance—to renounce even the strictest friendships perhaps; all at his pleasure, whether she think it reasonable to do so or not, Surely, sir, a young creature ought not to be obliged to make all these sacrifices but for such a man as she can approve.[81]

Clearly, Clarissa is fully aware of the powerful differences between a feme sole and a feme covert. For all her naivete about the legalities of her grandfather's will, she is aware of the power the estate has given her as a single woman. In discussing Solmes's settlements with her Uncle Anthony, Clarissa pridefully and perhaps somewhat condescendingly tells him:

> Dear, dear sir, what are settlements to one who has as much of her own as she wishes for?—who has more in her own power, as a single person, than it is probable she would be permitted to have at her disposal as a wife![82]

Threatened by her power and perceived disobedience, the Harlowes denounce the legitimacy of her position, negating it at every turn, despite her repeated assurances that she does not want to manage her own estate and would even return it if she could return home. These assurances aside, the Harlowes and Clarissa know that when her Cousin Morden arrives from Italy, they lose all possibility of controlling her. Since he is trustee, he can remove the estate from her father's management and place in in her own hands.[83] While their threats to litigate are merely pretense, Colonel Morden's actual removal of the estate from her father's management is de facto legal control, which effectively eliminates any leverage they would possess. Given these impending pressures, James Jr. expedites his plan, driven on at a "violent rate" so as simultaneously to recapture the grandfather's estate and to gain Solmes's potential reversionary interests at the same time.[84]

With this intensive assault on Clarissa, we see the avarice and self-serving nature of the Harlowes. While Lovelace's abduction and rape are grievous faults against Clarissa, her own family, especially James Jr., are the chief catalysts for her departure from home and chief reasons for her inability to return. Hence, the reader can now see clearly many transactions within the household: first of all, James's legal position is supported by law and he is well within his right to usurp his father's authority. Second, his betrayal of Clarissa by keeping her out of the family is consonant with the scandalous practice of eldest sons in the eighteenth century. Third, the Harlowes (Sr. and wife) are powerless against James because a resettlement has not taken place and James Jr. has been handed control of the Harlowe estate. He can, if he chooses, appropriate both Arabella and Clarissa's portions.

Yet for all this legalistic leverage, James Jr. fails to control Clarissa.[85] Instead, James Jr., with the entire family joining him, fail because Clarissa continues to make choices that thwart their moves. As the novel soberly displays, Clarissa continues to exercise her "consenting negative" against society's demands and, in freeing herself from all family and legal restraints, is able finally to control her own life, albeit only, and tragically, through death.

NOTES

1. Samuel Richardson, *Clarissa*, L:457, L:1191.
2. See Sulloway, *Born to Rebel.*
3. See Knapp, *Striking at the Joints,* see also Kenneth Womack, "Unmasking Another Villain in Conrad Aiken's Autobiographical Dream," *Biography* 19.2 (1996), 137–57.
4. See Boscolo, Cecchin, Hoffman, and Penn, *Milan Systemic Family Therapy,* see also Wetchler and Piercy, "Transgenerational Family Therapies," 34.
5. Schwarz, "Eighteenth-Century Abduction Law and *Clarissa,*" 299–300. Many of the legal issues debated in Parliament during the early 1720s, such as clandestine marriages, frivolous arrests, disorderly houses, attestation of wills, and attestation of devises of real estate were all social issues with which Richardson dealt in *Clarissa.* Richardson did not only print these debates but listened to them as well. In his correspondence with Lady Bradshaigh, written in late November or early December 1749, Richardson told her that he had been afflicted with a nervous malady and had "been forced to deny I had at pleasure, from one branch of my business, to hear the debates of both houses of Parliament." See Carroll, *Selected Letters,* 134.
6. See Schwarz, "Clarissa and the Law."
7. Palazzoli, Cirillo, Selvini, and Sorrentino, *Family Games,* 84–88.
8. See Bonfield, *Marriage Settlements,* 46–81; Schwarz, "Clarissa and the Law," 434; and Spring, "Strict Settlement Law."
9. See Rabinowitz, *Before Reading.*
10. Beebee, *Clarissa on the Continent,* 105.
11. Samuel Richardson, *Clarissa*, L:36.
12. Ibid., L:53.
13. A brief history of legal restraints on wills which existed between 1720 and 1740 reveals issues that need consideration in determining the validity of the will. See Schwarz, "Clarissa and the Law," 430–33. Since the conquest in England, no fee simple or fee tail could be disposed of by testament, except in Kent and some ancient boroughs and a few particular manors where Saxon immunities subsisted by special indulgence. Only estates for a term of years could be disposed of by testament. This feudal restraint on alienations by deed vanished early in English history on all property with the exception of that devised by wills; the restraint remained on wills for centuries after it was removed from all other alienations because of fear that the testator was either infirm or that he was perceived to be infirm and that his devise would be suspicious. See Blackstone, *Commentaries on the Laws of England,* 2:375. Furthermore, the public policy theory between 1300 and the early eighteenth century also dictated that restraints should remain on devises because they were not subject to public scrutiny in the same way as wills were. That is, by their very nature, devises did not make public a person's successor, while wills, which were re-

corded public documents that relied on the process of descent, were predictable because of the law of consanguinity. Such predictability and general public knowledge were considered a requisite in every transfer and in the new acquisition of property, and thus restraints on devises made sense to the public.

14. Samuel Richardson, *Clarissa*, L:115.

15. Ibid., L:53; L:190.

16. Ibid., L:53.

17. Habakkuk, "Marriage Settlements in the Eighteenth Century," 28.

18. Ibid., 21.

19. Samuel Richardson, *Clarissa*, L:52.

20. Ibid., L:188.

21. Ibid., L:53.

22. Habakkuk, "Marriage Settlements in the Eighteenth Century," 28.

23. Ibid., 22.

24. According to Randolph Trumbach, the uses to which a wife's fortune were put by these settlements were prescribed as either for investment in land for the husband's family, provision of portions for that family's younger children, or payment of that family's debts. Sometimes the portion went to the father-in-law, and sometimes it was shared by him and his son. If no explicit use were declared, the wife's portion went to the husband. See Trumbach, *Rise of the Egalitarian Family*, 81–82.

25. Samuel Richardson, *Clarissa*, L:77.

26. Bonfield, *Marriage Settlements*, 103.

27. Schwarz, "Clarissa and the Law," 433.

28. Cox, *Hatred Pursued Beyond the Grave*, 70.

29. In *Born to Rebel*, Sulloway says that inheritance "is a form of parental investment . . . [the] propensity for parents to invest wisely in offspring, which tends to result in their maximizing their inclusive fitness. Culture determines how this goal is fulfilled." Since throughout "human evolution, older siblings have typically possessed greater reproductive prospects than their younger siblings . . . parental investment [in] firstborns are like 'bluechip' securities" (65). See Sulloway, *Born to Rebel*, 62–67; see also Regt, "Inheritance and Relationships between Family Members," 157–59.

30. See Okin, "Patriarchy and Married Women's Property in England," 129–30, 138. According to Okin, the only way that a woman without adequate provision in a marriage settlement could subsequently gain any financial independence was by claiming what was called "her equity to a settlement," which required a husband who brought suit regarding his wife's portion to "act equitably" by settling some part of it on her as her separate estate. Prior to 1801, however, a wife could get into court only if her husband sued for his settlement of her portion, thus making it impossible for a woman to establish her independence, unless either her parents' marriage settlement stipulated that she keep part of her portion, or, upon her husband's suit for her portion, the court awarded her "equity to a settlement." Okin correctly argues that "very little effective change in the economic dependence of wives had occurred before 1800." See Staves, *Married Women's Separate Property in England*, for an analysis of the different ways courts handled separate maintenance contracts 1675 to 1833.

31. Boscolo, Cecchin, Hoffman, and Penn, *Milan Systematic Family Therapy*, 49; see also Samuel Richardson, *Clarissa*, L:80.

32. Schwarz, "Eighteenth-Century Abduction Law and *Clarissa*," 270–71.

33. Samuel Richardson, *Clarissa*, L:182.

34. Ibid., L:53.

35. Ibid., L:584.

36. Ibid., L:20.

37. Ibid.

38. Habakkuk, "Marriage Settlements in the Eighteenth Century," 16.

39. Wilson, *State of England*, 24; see also Habakkuk, "Marriage Settlements in the Eighteenth Century," 19.

40. See "Of Marriage."

41. Samuel Richardson, *Clarissa*, L:77.

42. Kingston, *Woman Warrior*, 43.

43. Qtd. in Bonfield, *Marriage Settlements*, 16.

44. Habakkuk, "Marriage Settlements in the Eighteenth Century," 101–2.

45. Samuel Richardson, *Clarissa*, L:41.

46. Ibid., L:212.

47. Ibid., L:80.

48. Ibid., L:1374.

49. Ibid., L:80.

50. Ibid., L:84.

51. Ibid., L:138.

52. Ibid., L:98.

53. Ibid., L:77.

54. In *Clarissa on the Continent*, Beebee contends that the legal details of the Solmes offer "remain somewhat unclear and preposterous," but claims this "lack of clarity only reinforces the mythic patriarchal image of James, Solmes, Mr. Harlowe, and Uncle Antony freely sharing land among themselves because they are male" (105). In fact, the legal details of the Solmes offer would not have been unclear to Richardson's "authorial audience"; see Rabinowitz, *Before Reading*. Richardson's readers probably understood this property transaction in a way comparable to how knowledgeable people today understand an "offer to purchase" which has numerous conditions that need to be satisfied before the sale is complete. While James Jr.'s plan has many contingencies incorporated into it before coming to fruition, Richardson's authorial audience probably would not have considered the plan preposterous.

55. Samuel Richardson, *Clarissa*, L:150.

56. Ibid., L:81.

57. Ibid., L:101.

58. Ibid., L:81.

59. Ibid., L:256.

60. Ibid., L:81.

61. Ibid., L:4; L:255, 50:60.

62. Ibid., L:405.

63. Ibid., L:408.

64. Ibid., L:782.

65. Ibid., L:474.

66. Ibid., L:256.

67. Ibid., L:239.

68. Ibid., L:96.

69. Ibid., L:1346.

70. Ibid., L:206.

71. Ibid., L:55.

72. Ibid., L:122.

73. Ibid., L:1322.

74. Qtd. in Habakkuk, "Marriage Settlements in the Eighteenth Century," 25.

75. Samuel Richardson, *Clarissa*, L:125.

76. Ibid., L:44.

77. Ibid., L:150.

78. Ibid., L:312.

79. Ibid., L:77.

80. See Palazzoli, Cirillo, Selvini, and Sorrentino, *Family Games*, 158.

81. Samuel Richardson, *Clarissa*, L:148–49.

82. Ibid., L:150.

83. Ibid., L:225–26.

84. Ibid., L:226.

85. Ironically, while Clarissa could not change these ironclad eighteenth-century property rules, she likely could have prevailed had she prosecuted Lovelace for abduction, primarily because the courts were insistent on not allowing a propertied female to be stolen from her father since then the father's estate would have been diminished. See Schwarz, "Eighteenth-Century Abduction Law and *Clarissa*," 274–82. Conversely, Clarissa would probably have lost if she had brought a rape charge, primarily because a high percentage of rape trials ended in acquittal; unlike abduction trials which were really about a father's estate, a rape trial often did not involve propertied issues and therefore were not a high priority for the court. See 282–98. The bottom line for legal matters in the eighteenth century concerned primarily whose estate was at stake and what court protection was needed for such financial matters.

Circular Ties: A Family Systems Reading of A. S. Byatt's *The Game*

Steven Snyder

Since the publication of the Booker Prize-winning *POSSESSION* in 1990, A. S. BYATT'S earliest novels, short stories, and criticism have begun to receive increased and well-merited scholarly attention, with many critics keying upon her inclination to suffuse the framework of her traditionally "realistic" novels with a serious self-reflexiveness about the artistic imagination. Indeed, Byatt's earliest works—*The Shadow of the Sun* (1964) and *The Game* (1967)—are rich with mythical and literary allusions and rehearse questions about the imagination's effect upon reality. In *The Shadow of the Sun,* for example, she told the story of an intelligent young woman caught between the literary imaginations of a Coleridgean writer/father and his chief academic critic, a situation which Byatt says reflected her struggle to come to terms with the two sides of her own imaginative nature.[1] In an introduction for the 1991 reissue of *Shadow,* she wrote, "the novel was about the paradox of Leavis preaching Lawrence when if the two had met they would have hated each other. It was about the secondary imagination feeding off, and taming, the primary."[2] This theme of contrasting imaginations was continued and in some ways reversed in Byatt's second novel, *The Game,* a story of sibling rivalry in which the primary artistic imagination of one sister supposedly feeds off and ultimately destroys the other, a literary scholar.

To some extent, too, popular reviewers of Byatt's early novels argued that her larger philosophical questions about the imagination overburdened the traditional realistic frameworks in which she had chosen to work. *The Game* is typical in this respect. Upon its release, Malcom Bradbury pointed out that its "literariness" made the novel "lumpish,"[3] while other reviewers called it overly reflective,[4] or laden with a design and artifice that made its characters too slight to carry its "philosophical load."[5]

By contrast, it is the "philosophical load" that has attracted the bulk of the academic critical attention.

Jane Campbell, for instance, insists that *The Game* is "more than a study of sibling rivalry or obsessive love."[6] She argues that its central action involves characters who try and fail to understand one another, thereby suggesting that "reality . . . cannot be contained within linguistic form."[7] And Giuliana Giobbi sees *The Game* as an intertextual postmodernist rewriting of earlier "female stories," one linking Byatt's fictional sisters to Jane Austen's Marianne and Elinor in *Sense and Sensibility*. Giobbi argues that the "conflicts and doubts, hinted at in the carefully structured forerunners of the female novel, are revealed and put under scrutiny" in *The Game*.[8]

Forging intertextual links is also the concern of Joanne V. Creighton, who sees a parallel between the sisters in *The Game* and Byatt's relationship with her real-life sister, Margaret Drabble.[9] Despite Byatt's statements that her work is not autobiographical, Creighton points to parallels between *The Game* and Drabble's *The Waterfall*. And by way of feminist/revisionist Freudian psychoanalysis, she suggests the two novels are "about the distinctive dynamics of fusion and differentiation within the female identity and especially within the female artist."[10] These dynamics, she argues, are marked in *The Game* and *The Waterfall* and rehearse the "oedipal and preoedipal conflicts which are at the core of female identity."[11]

In this sense, the various responses to *The Game* echo something of the split in imagination that Byatt was addressing, with popular reviewers arguing that the novel's philosophical concerns overburden its mimetic truthfulness, and academics leaping into its self-reflexiveness about the creative imagination. I want to suggest, however, that *The Game* is not so split, that its traditional realistic framework is neither slighted, as some have contended, nor hampered by an overly self-reflexive concern for the artistic imagination. The two halves, in fact, can be seen as complementary. To explore this issue, I will examine the way that Byatt's characters in *The Game* faithfully reflect a systems-based psychology familiar to many contemporary family therapists. Moreover, I will argue that a systems-based reading of the mimetic plot actually parallels and informs the novel's larger concern with the nature of representation. Because my argument is two-fold, I will first attend to the mimetic depictions of the characters and then deal with the novel in its philosophical dimensions, tying the two together in conclusion.

FAMILY SYSTEMS AND THE CHARACTERS IN *THE GAME*

Any family systems reading should necessarily do two things. First, it should involve close attention to a mimetically represented family or group of characters; and, second, it should direct our attention away from any simplified protagonist/antagonist notions of causality in plot action. Indeed, a good family systems reading can lead us toward an understanding of a novel that emphasizes the systemic nature of the characters' behavior without undermining their individuality or moral culpability. *The Game* cries out for such a reading, because Cassandra and Julia's behavioral patterns, which account for the main action of the novel, reflect the very idea of a rule-governed system, an idea reinforced by the title itself. From a family systems perspective, however, the title can be somewhat misleading, for a game implies a contest with winners and losers, an idea antithetical to systems analysis. Of course, some reviewers and critics have viewed Julia as *The Game's* winner.[12] She is, after all, still alive at the novel's close and envisioning a new life free from the toxicity of her relationship to Cassandra. But such a view overlooks the way Cassandra and Julia simultaneously seek to preserve and alter the homeostatic balance of their relationship, a balance that was set in early childhood and maintained throughout their lives.

To illustrate this, it will be helpful to review what the text reveals about the Julia and Cassandra's childhood, a task made easier by the wealth of information about the Corbetts' family history. Julia and Cassandra's parents, Jonathan and Elizabeth, were likely married in the early to mid-1920s and set up residence in the small Northumberland village of Benstone, living in "the last in a line of increasingly large grey stone houses fronting the street directly."[13] After three generations in Benstone, the family was maintaining a modest level of bourgeois comfort in a home capacious enough to house servants, a nursemaid, war refugees and the occasional traveling Quaker Friend.

Despite the busy, active nature of this household, the emotional climate was cool. Feelings were carefully suppressed and only displayed during services at the Meeting House.[14] Moreover, Jonathan Corbett rarely kissed his daughters, and he and his wife turned over the bulk of parenting responsibility to the servants: Elsie, the cook, who had been with the family since before or immediately after Cassandra's birth, and Inge, who came as a teenager.[15] It was Elsie and Inge who did the "scolding and the loving."[16] Indeed, an unwillingness to provide any basic guidance and nurture is the most distinctive aspect of the Corbetts' parenting style. In accordance with their Quaker beliefs, they "laid down no laws, exerted no pressure, expected nothing," thus allowing the children to make their own decisions. Both Julia and Cassandra were unhappy with this unwillingness to parent. As Cassandra says of her father, "I was not *ever* sure of him."[17]

Nevertheless, both daughters profess admiration for their father, yet say little about their feelings for their mother. Upon returning to Benstone at the time of Jonathan Corbett's illness, only Julia's husband Thor asks how Elizabeth is coping with her husband's illness; and it is Thor again who first greets Elizabeth.[18] Later, too, after Jonathan Corbett's death, only Thor helps the just-widowed Elizabeth "unfailingly," while Julia and Cassandra distract themselves with board games. Indeed, Cassandra's description of her mother emphasizes the imagery of a hardened emotional shell. "Her strength was a shell's strength," Cassandra muses. "That was the trouble; it provided a shell's simple invulnerability. A layer of hardened scales."[19]

Byatt, then, offers us a depiction of a family in which a rigid boundary exists between the executive subsystem (the parents) and the sibling subsystem, with no guidance and very little affection flowing from parent to child. A central concept of family systems-based psychology is that parents play a vital role in their children's integration into the family, as well as their eventual differentiation into separate selves.[20] In this instance, however, the sisters' affiliation and the subsequent differentiation were frustrated by Jonathan and Elizabeth Corbett's aloof parenting. Consequently, for any model of family affiliation, Julia and Cassandra were thrown back upon themselves. The result, in the language of family systems, was the creation of a tightly knit dyad, a sibling subsystem in which Julia and Cassandra were left alone to negotiate necessary developmental stages of their identity formation.

Unfortunately, dyads are inherently unstable, and often the more uncomfortable person in such a system will make a move to achieve the optimum level of closeness or distance.[21] What is important to note here is that both members of the dyad feel a desire to be a part of their family and apart from it, although the shifting intensity of their needs may foster tensions that hamper the creation of mutually agreed upon ego boundaries. In the case of Julia and Cassandra, who lacked any clear parental model for forming such boundaries, there was no way to be meaningfully affiliated and soundly differentiated from each other. It may be helpful here to think of family boundaries as a continuum, with one end representing "enmeshment" (overly diffuse boundaries), and the other "disengagement" (overly rigid boundaries).[22] Clearly, Cassandra and Julia lean toward the enmeshed end of the continuum. As in their childhood Game, the boundary between their identities became a kind of "no man's land," and their behavior toward one another can be seen as a series of desperate and overcorrecting attempts to "right" the perceived imbalance of closeness and distance.

In this light, Cassandra's childhood attempts to run-away were both a dramatic attempt to achieve differentiation from her family *and* to force her father to fulfill his parental responsibility, a strategy that failed on both counts. Time and again it was the Reverend Merton who had to stand in for the absent father and fetch Cassandra home. Reflecting on these incidents years later, she muses, "I meant to go. I must have meant to go. It may have been a failure, but it was not simply a gesture—it was an instinct of flight, powerful and unquestioned, bred of no particular complaint." But when Merton suggested to a teenage Cassandra that she try running to him instead, she revealed her desire for a stronger sense of paternal love, noting that Merton's "abstract good-will" was not personal enough. "It would have been nice if he had cared."[23]

Julia's desire for differentiation is perhaps less pronounced, but nonetheless present. Her instinct for flight manifested itself in childhood dreams of an escape to the city where she "imagined herself one of a furred and scented London crowd about to go on to some dance in a night club, vaguely wicked, vaguely risky."[24] And throughout her life she fears a complete enmeshment with her sister, at one point confessing to Ivan that she "was always scared stiff of waking up and finding that [she] was nothing but a thought in Cassandra's mind."[25] At the same time, though, Julia desperately seeks to connect with her sister. Upon seeing Cassandra for the first time after their father's death, she questions her own feelings: "I always think I need to make contact somehow; make her see I exist, make her *care*. I want her to take me into account."[26]

Like her sister, Julia's behavior is replete with the conflicting desires of affiliation and differentiation. She both accepts and rebels against Cassandra's regulations for their interaction, playing the Brontëan game of their childhood in which Cassandra made the rules that governed their play; but guiltily breaking the rules that forbade her entry into Cassandra's bedroom and private journal.[27] She also chased after her sister during Cassandra's childhood attempts to run away, crying, "Let me come too, Cassandra, let me come too, it isn't *fair*."[28] Julia, of course, is hurt by Cassandra's distance: "she would always . . . approach hopefully and far too early, be snubbed, and not only snubbed, but mind."[29]

And here, despite the invasive breaches of privacy, one can sympathize with Julia. After all, what other family affiliation did she have as a child? In essence, Cassandra is Julia's only meaningful connection to her family of origin. Certainly her attempts to draw near are clumsy and insensitive, but they are motivated out of a very real developmental need for closeness. At the same time, though, Cassandra is ill-equipped to function as a surrogate mother and father. Forced by her own parent's abdication of responsibility to become Julia's emotional parent, she risks losing her own identity. From Julia's perspective, however, Cassandra's repeated withdrawals appear as acts of aggression. She tells Simon, for instance, that her sister would turn her childhood behavior into overly dramatized betrayals: "And then she saw to it I was guilty of real crimes, that what I'd done I couldn't change or undo. She made me—take things—and then left me in possession."[30]

Of course, Cassandra's physical escape from the family is finally achieved when she goes to Oxford, but perhaps escape is the wrong word, for the attempt to put her family behind her is certainly short-lived. Julia, left at home, can only understand her sister's departure as yet another abandonment, and she soon invades Cassandra's life again by triangulating Simon Moffit into the dyad. It would be easy to cast Julia in the role of villain at this point, but such a view overlooks the sisters' problematic interdependence. After Cassandra's departure for Oxford, Julia tried to function without her sister. She "tried independence and wrote another story, which was rejected by the magazine," but "she could not keep up the Game alone, and had little else to do; she suffered a wild and aimless despair." At Oxford, Cassandra also experienced a "paralyzing, irrational, overwhelming fear," which she had felt only one other time in her life: when she was briefly separated from her sister for a few terms at private school. This terror, however, had diminished when Julia eventually joined her at the school.[31] In short, neither sister is capable of healthy differentiation perhaps because neither has yet experienced a solid base of familial affiliation out of which to grow into a separate identity.

Consequently, Julia, alone at Benstone, must use the only means at hand to draw her sister back into the unfinished family business. By forming an inappropriate relationship with Simon, she reheats the emotional intensity of her relationship with Cassandra, seeking simultaneously to draw closer to an understanding of her sister and to force a differentiating conflict. It is telling that her first meeting with Simon takes place while she was posting a letter to Cassandra, and that much of their subsequent conversation concerns her sister's personality. Moreover, just as Julia had come running to announce the publication of the appropriated childhood story, she immediately tells Cassandra upon her return to Benstone that she has been seeing Simon. On both occasions Julia attempts to force her sister into a constructive fight, one in which they can finally deal with their submerged tensions. Unfortunately, Cassandra fails to rise to occasions; instead, she characteristically "punished Julia by silence" after learning of the story's publication.[32] And she repeats this pattern when she learns of the affair with Simon, icily cutting off both Julia and Simon and never again speaking to them "more than was in politeness required of her."[33]

The adult lives both women pursue after this break also reflect their divergent strategies for dealing with their childhood predicament. Cassandra continues to withdraw from human connection, isolating herself in academia and cultivating "her walled-garden skills at the expense of any others she might have had."[34] Julia, on the other hand, replicates her family of origin with marriage to Thor, attempting to finally get it right, and transferring her problems into her new family. The transgenerational repetition of family patterns has been well researched, and thus it is not surprising to see Julie's daughter Deborah, who is essentially cut off from a close connection with her mother, reaching out to Cassandra at the time of Jonathan Corbett's death.[35] In effect, Deborah is reenacting Cassandra's childhood attempts to run away and Julia's triangulation with Simon. By instinctively pulling a third party into her family drama, Deborah seeks to reheat the emotional intensity with her mother, and, at the same time, open an avenue of escape. In some respects, she's more successful, for near the end of the novel, when Deborah tells her mother she is running away to Oxford, she manages to force a confrontation with her absentee parent, one that at last allows

Julia to at least look at her daughter "with a kind of animal affection."[36]

Jonathan Corbett's death, of course, brings the adult Julia and Cassandra together once again, and it triggers the return to their unresolved childhood tensions. Elizabeth Corbett, at the very moment her mothering is needed, characteristically abandons her daughters and goes to bed.[37] Cassandra characteristically retreats to the garden, and Julia, hungry for connection, follows her, desperately stating her longing: "I need company, Cassandra . . . nobody's left us anything to do. Come in now, *please*. We could play cards, or something. Like we used to do, remember?"[38] And the childhood game begins anew, both literally and metaphorically. Thus Julia's appropriation of her sister's life in *A Sense of Glory* becomes yet another failed attempt to attain the optimum level of closeness and distance. Indeed, Julia maintains a double-consciousness about the book, telling herself when she first conceives of writing the novel that "it would be a way of coming to grips with Cassandra, but also of detaching us. It would be a way of seeing her as a separate individual. Knowledge, after all, was love. A lighting up of one another."[39]

And after her father's death, Cassandra also attempts to redress her familial tensions. She opens a little to her sister and even begins to gain perspective on her own problem with emotional disengagement, agreeing to Julia's request for a visit to Oxford and admitting to herself that Julia's presence was "not formidable, was even likable."[40] Again, we see the women simultaneously searching for some livable balance between their conflicting needs of affiliation and differentiation, but this time with a greater awareness of their past failures. Cassandra writes in her journal, "When we were children, we were not quite separate. We shared a common vision, we created a common myth. And this, maybe, contained and resolved our difficulties."[41] Cassandra's newfound awareness, in the language of family systems therapy, is the therapeutic moment, the moment when individuals have begun to grasp an understanding of their predicament and are faced with the risk of morphogenetic change.[42]

Indeed, the publication of *A Sense of Glory*, Julia's effort "to come to grips" and to "detach," presents Cassandra with just such a moment. She can either confront her sister with constructive anger, or fall back upon the accustomed pattern of withdrawal. Clearly, Cassandra has a choice. Simon lays out the alternative to withdrawal, telling her, "You've got to fight. You've got to stay in the open. Read this book. . . . And then if you feel angry, write and tell Julia so—give her a chance to reply, but attack her face to face. . . . I think she'd be glad of that. There's sympathy and understanding in this book."[43] Cassandra, however, decides not to take the risk of morphogenetic change, choosing instead to escape what she perceives as "this grotesque shadow, our joint creature."[44] Julia also believes she can achieve separation after Cassandra's death, but her possession of her sister's journal suggests this may not be the case; and the novel prophetically closes with Cassandra's accusatory words bumping and sliding in the boot of Julia's car.

In this way, a family systems reading of *The Game* undermines any easy attempt to cite a single instance of culpability for Cassandra's suicide. The sisters' behavior, in fact, comes to form a self-sealing circle, one in which their actions simultaneously attempt to create change and destroy the possibility for change. Indeed, the novel diffuses the idea of a single causal agency without effacing the moral imperative for each character to understand and take responsibility for her own behavior. In the end, we cannot blame Julia for Cassandra's suicide—although she bears some responsibility as well—any more than we can blame Cassandra for failing to acknowledge, though she should have at least seen, her sister's need for closeness. The two actions are part of a systemic whole, one comprehensible in an understanding of the Corbett family's entire dynamic. To assign blame is to miss the special tragedy of the novel.

CASSANDRA AND JULIA AS SYMBOLS OF THE IMAGINATION

In the opening two chapters of *The Game,* Byatt sets up the novel's philosophical concerns with the artistic imagination and its relationship to reality. For *The Game*'s second epigraph, she has chosen a passage from Coleridge:

> The principle of the imagination resembles the emblem of the serpent, by which the ancients typified wisdom of the universe, with undulating folds, forever varying and forever flowing into itself—circular, and without beginning or end.

Coleridge refers here to an Ouroboros, or a self-consuming serpent, a symbol used by several ancient cultures to represent the universe's endless cyclical forces of creation and destruction. In an echo of Kant, the emphasis is changed from nature, the *ding an sich,* to the human imagination, which also seems to forever fold back into itself in endless cycles of creation and destruction. To comprehend the Ouroboros, Coleridge seems to suggest, is to gain perspective on the imagination's ability to endlessly shape and be shaped by reality. And it is just such a perspective that the characters in *The Game* seek. In fact, how they imagine the snake in the novel's opening two chapters corresponds to the way their imaginations understand reality.

Julia, of course, detests snakes. For her they are "dangerous and ugly, and we are *meant* to be repelled by them."[45] Watching a televised snake's hideousness immediately leads her to the notion that surface appearances betoken inner qualities:

> Whatever one ought think, she told herself, snakes are not beautiful creatures; they were mutilated and ugly; their faces were evil. As a man could be ugly and one could define him, and no one would dispute it, so could a beast. . . . This thought, of course, lead her back to the idea that an ugly man must be bad and dangerous, and this, given qualifications for *beauxlaids,* for those whose beautiful thoughts moulded and transfigured their horrid features, Julia was prepared to believe.[46]

For Julia, surface is reality. What impresses her most about Simon's broadcast is not its high-flown literary allusions or scientific speculations; rather, it is the "smooth rapidity of the camera work." But as the camera begins to select out discontiguous, abstract patterns within the jungle, her eye becomes "bewildered." And these patterns—"a phenomenon the camera can catch but the eye cannot"—leave her feeling alienated.[47] The imposition of patterns on nature, of course, is the first step toward abstraction, a move Julia instinctively resists.

Yet Julia is also a realistic novelist who is increasingly frustrated with her over-reliance on surface reality. She writes to Cassandra immediately after her father's death, confessing, "I'm completely bogged in my next book. I seem to have just come to a stop, I don't know why. I feel I've got to change everything, my subject matter, everything. I've got to dig deeper and spread wider. I want to write something with a few symbols and a Message."[48] *A Sense of Glory* emerges from this artistic block and becomes her failed attempt to change the way she imagines reality. She muses before commencing the book that modern novels "concerned themselves too exclusively with limitations. A novel," she speculates, "ought, ideally, to balance in a perpetual juggling trick the sense of the real limitation against a real awareness of possibility."[49]

Cassandra also seeks to balance her perspective on reality. Unlike Julia, her imagination has always moved too quickly from surface to symbol, thereby transmuting real objects into transcendent ideals of a higher reality. In chapter two we learn that

> She had elaborated, and believed, a network of symbols, which made the outer world into a dazzling but comprehensible constellation of physical facts whose spiritual interrelations could be grasped and woven by the untiring intellect. . . . Somewhere, under the network, the truth shone.[50]

This characteristic movement of her mind—from reality to art, and from art to symbolism, and finally to a transcendent theology—forms an ideological arc that echoes her youthful insistence on the historical reality of Christ, which changed into an interest in Romance, and finally into a search for the transcendent in ritual.[51] And as the novel opens, Cassandra's journal, which once recorded a world of Romantic stories of "moorland rapes and battles," has become a catalog of the daily dross, a way of transforming the corporeal aspects of her life into the patterns and ideas she finds more psychologically manageable.[52]

For Cassandra, then, the snake can only symbolize the brute reality of the natural world, a world insensate to higher truths. Carnality is precisely what her imagination must transcend. Writing to her imaginatively evoked version of Simon, she describes the serpent as a symbol of "our horror of finding ourselves necessarily embodied." It is "Eros," "bodily lust," and "debasing bodily functions." The soul, however, the true self, is symbolized by the butterfly; and, as she states the problem, "we cannot combine butterfly and serpent without corrupting the butterfly."[53]

Nevertheless, like her sister, Cassandra has become increasingly frustrated by the imaginative shackles she has forged, noting with "distress" the way her obsessively arranged possessions seem to exist solely for the purpose of feeding her journal, a habit which lends her life an alarming "weightless and meaningless" quality.[54] And Cassandra's journal writing, which attempts to reverse the traditional ontology of objects feeding the imagination, is increasingly haunted by fears of solipsism. For her, imaginative isolation, like its philosophical sibling—an imaginative overreliance on surface reality—has become untenable.

In contrast, the introduction of Simon's character is rich with irony. Indeed, Simon, the advocate of grasping reality with a "detached" eye, of "seeing everything for itself," is first glimpsed through the medium of television.[55] Moreover, his broadcast script is laced with double meanings that foreclose the possibility that any of the characters can wholly escape their blinders and see reality without human imagination and the necessity for human relationships. Simon's function in the novel's larger debate is to illustrate the failure of the empiricist's view to account for imagination and a moral imperative in human affairs.

Setting out the aim of his Amazon project, he inveighs against Romanticism by referencing Coleridge's idea that nature exists only through the imagination. "I would hope to approach these forests more neutrally," he says. "We are to observe unchecked, unchannelled growth, and destruction. I believe we can learn from this."[56] And learn he will, for his unwitting annunciation of his mission ironically forecasts the novel's subsequent development. For Simon, the snake must be approached without emotion, a human attribute that he *thinks* "we cannot afford in any area of life." Instead, he hopes "to make snakes familiar. Familiar."[57] The repetition of the word "familiar" here calls attention to its double function as both adjective and noun. In the former sense, Simon argues familiarity with the reality of nature is "one of the highest human qualities."[58] He says,

> Coming close to anything—mortality amongst mortals—changes our attitude to it, changes it, in our minds. Familiarity doesn't make things less mysterious—it does make them less vague. You might say we learn real fear instead of mystical fear.[59]

But as Simon becomes familiar with the Amazon, and after Miller's death (when he has in actuality come close to "mortality amongst mortals"), familiarity takes on a new sense, the sense of the mystical or talismanic symbol. Consequently, when his nontelevised presence enters the novel, the Amazon has become for him a human nightmare, a mystical image of mortality that he can neither fully comprehend nor escape, but which, as he ironically predicted, has changed his own attitude. Thus, Simon has, albeit unwillingly, drawn a step closer to accepting his inescapable symbol-making imagination.

He had wanted to see reality pure by isolating himself in nature, by denying his humanity, but Miller sought him out, and teased thoughts from him, thoughts he had been trying "to live with dumbly."[60] Slowly, a human connection formed. Simon tells Cassandra that he first thought Miller a fool: "But after a bit," he says, "you saw you could really rely on knowing where you were with him. I mean, if he liked you, he liked you, that was all there was to it." As a result of this human connection, Simon fails to see Miller's death with a naturalist's detachment, confessing to Cassandra that he played a game of seeing through Miller's eyes, "but it got to be not a game."[61] And as the novel closes, he, like Julia and Cassandra, faces the need to readjust his understanding of reality to account for his own imagination and other's humanity.

Thus, even in the novel's opening we see the principle characters in an argument about the nature of representation, one whose conflicting positions have reached and realized their limitations and are now groping back for some saner middle ground or balance. And here the search for a new imaginative balance parallels the psychological search for a healthier homeostatic balance. In this way, too, *The Game*'s philosophical debate about the imagination and reality anchors and accentuates its mimetic plot; for just as the characters fumble back toward a more healthy and moral accord, Byatt implies that the arguments over representation might profitably do the same.

The particular tragedy of the novel, of course, is that an accord on either level fails to take place. *A Sense of Glory*, Julia's clumsy attempt both to establish and sever her connection with Cassandra, overreaches. By transforming her sister into a symbol, Julia fails to see her as a dynamic, growing human being, one capable of morphogenetic change. Similarly, Cassandra, who for the first time in her life stands on the verge of squarely facing "the tyranny of objects," cannot overcome Julia's symbolization of her, mistakenly assuming that, like one of her possessions, her reality will be unalterably transformed by her sister's artistic imagination.

A central question becomes the inevitability of this failure: are unhealthy family relationships doomed to forever repeat the patterns set in childhood? Are imaginative attempts to balance imagination and reality equally fruitless? Campbell argues that the sisters' failure to understand each other betokens the failure of any linguistic representation to fully comprehend reality, a view that would seem to ally Byatt with the postmodernist idea that language is forever failed representation.[62] But such a reading underestimates the characters' real possibility for change, a possibility which is fundamental to our ability to sympathize with them. Indeed, it is difficult to view their failure as a tragedy if it is nothing more than the fictional grinding out of the dry post-modernist thesis that reality is ultimately unknowable.

The authorial fallacy not withstanding, Byatt's own critical statements might lead us to suspect such a reading of *The Game*. In the introduction to her collection of critical essays, *Passions of the Mind*, she writes,

> The problems of the "real" in fiction, and the adequacy of words to describe it, have preoccupied me for the last twenty years. If I have defended realism, or what I call "self-conscious realism," it is not because I believe it has any privileged relationship to truth, social or psychological, but because it leaves space for the thinking minds as well as bodies.[63]

She also acknowledges the influence of Iris Murdoch, and especially Murdoch's 1961 essay "Against Dryness," in which Murdoch makes a case that the mimetic "density" of fictional characters can open a space for moral reflection in a post-Christian world. Murdoch writes,

> The twentieth-century novel is usually either crystalline or journalistic; that is, it is either a small quasi-allegorical object portraying the human condition and not containing "characters" in the nineteenth-century sense, or else it is a large shapeless quasi-documentary object, the degenerate descendant of the nineteenth-century novel, telling, with pale conventional characters, some straight forward story enlivened with empirical facts.[64]

Murdoch further suggests that against these tendencies in fiction, writers "must pit the destructive power of the now so unfashionable naturalistic idea of character."[65] And here it is not too difficult to see the characters of Cassandra and Julia standing in for Murdoch's notions of the crystalline and journalistic impulses in the artistic imagination; nor is it difficult to see *The Game* as a depiction of these dense fictional characters struggling against their twentieth-century imaginations—struggling ultimately to see through them in order to locate a moral ground on which they can become more fully and effectively human.

From this perspective, close attention to the psychological faithfulness with which Byatt portrays her characters informs the novel's larger debate over artistic representation. She both acknowledges and fears the artistic object as an autotelic purity divorced from meaningful relationship to reality. At the same time, though, she is ever mindful that an over-reliance on mimeticism is an illusion, one that can overreach and distort reality with fatal consequences. Yet against this centuries-old representational stand-off, she pits the possibility and moral imperative for human change and growth in her densely mimetic characters. Similarly, a family systems understanding of *The Game* allows us to see beyond the issue of moral blame without effacing the need for people to grow in understanding of themselves and the undulating, circular ties they are forever forming with one another.

NOTES

1. Byatt, Introduction *Shadow of the Sun*, viii–ix.
2. Ibid., x.
3. Bradbury, "On from Murdoch," 74.
4. Flannery, Review of *The Game*.
5. "Child's Play."
6. Campbell, "Hunger of the Imagination," 150.
7. Ibid., 154.
8. Giobbi, "Sisters Beware of Sisters," 241.
9. Creighton, "Sisterly Symbiosis," 16.
10. Ibid., 19.
11. Ibid., 17.
12. Ibid., 24.
13. Byatt, *Game*, 38.
14. Ibid., 44.
15. Ibid., 84.
16. Ibid., 43.
17. Ibid., 49.
18. Ibid., 34, 40.
19. Ibid., 35.
20. See Bowen, *Family Therapy in Clinical Practice*, 306; Boszormenyi-Nagy and Framo, *Intensive Family Therapy*, 78; Minuchin, *Families and Family Therapy*, 57.
21. Bowen, *Family Therapy in Clinical Practice*, 307.
22. Minuchin, *Families and Family Therapy*, 54.
23. Byatt, *Game*, 36–37.
24. Ibid., 33.
25. Ibid., 104.
26. Ibid., 53–54.
27. Ibid.
28. Ibid., 36.
29. Ibid., 85.
30. Ibid., 232–33.
31. Ibid., 85.
32. Ibid.
33. Ibid., 112.

34. Ibid., 20.
35. See Michael E. Kerr and Murray Bowen, *Family Evaluations.*
36. *Byatt, Game*, 273.
37. Ibid., 51.
38. Ibid., 53–54.
39. Ibid., 148.
40. Ibid., 124.
41. Ibid., 276.
42. Napier and Whitaker, *Family Crucible*, 181–82.
43. Byatt, *Game*, 269.
44. Ibid., 277.
45. Ibid., 13.
46. Ibid.
47. Ibid., 11–12.
48. Ibid., 128–29.
49. Ibid., 163.
50. Ibid., 19–20.
51. Ibid., 20.
52. Ibid., 26.
53. Ibid., 27–28.
54. Ibid., 26.
55. Ibid., 24.
56. Ibid., 11.
57. Ibid., 14.
58. Ibid., 24.
59. Ibid., 23.
60. Ibid., 238.
61. Ibid., 240–41.
62. Campbcll, "Hunger of the Imagination," 154.
63. Byatt, *Passions of the Mind*, xv.
64. Ibid., xv, 18.
65. Ibid., 20.

Family Systems Therapy and Narrative in Toni Morrison's *The Bluest Eye*

Jerome Bump

ONE ASPECT OF *THE BLUEST EYE* THAT EVEN WHITE, MALE MIDDLE-class readers like myself can identify is its family dynamics. This assertion no doubt surprises those who believe that black families are more dysfunctional than white families, and that writers like Toni Morrison are making the problem worse. Such beliefs can prevent reader identification with the characters in the story. When we challenge these beliefs, we will find that the modern definition of a functional family is moving in the direction already taken by the black family, toward a structure of relations transcending blood kin which can include gays and lesbians.

Having dispelled one of the myths that may block some readers from identifying with the family dynamics of the novel, we can focus on the central emotional responses of engaged readers to the novel. In the process we will discover that family systems therapy is particularly qualified to help us understand the "Family Romance" that has become so popular in accounts of *The Bluest Eye* and in novels of the last two centuries.[1] By expanding the concept to that of the "Family Dance," as it is often called in family systems therapy, and focusing on what I will call the reader's "orphan feeling," we can define family dynamics that are more specific and yet more applicable to a wider variety of literary works. Tracing the orphan feeling in fiction is also a contribution to "affective" literary criticism and to emotional literacy.

Family systems therapy also sheds light on more traditional "intellectual" issues, such as the problem of narrativity in the novel. We will see how breaking the novel into parts that have to be reassembled by the reader mimics the dysfunctional communication of a disturbed family; how family dynamics provide a center of rationality, a predictable logic which carries the reader to the end of the story; and how "the narratological morphogenesis" is therapeutic. Finally, we will see that we don't merely identify with Pecola: because of the narrative technique we are implicated in what happened to her.

Our primary identification, however, is with Claudia. She is, I would argue, the protoreader for all readers, white as well as black, who have suffered from judging, and have been judged by, appearance; from misogyny or misandry; from prejudices of the middle class; and from pained or dysfunctional family life. For white readers also, it seems to me, her appeal is as much identification as it is sympathy for an oppressed minority.

This is not what most critics believe. Take, for example, this interpretation of the initial "Dick and Jane" epigraphs of the novel: "Each chapter is prefaced by fragments of the frenzied prose in order to continually remind the reader of the undeniable contrast between this pervasive white, middle class myth and the tragic dissolution of the novel's central character, Pecola Breedlove and her family, who are incapable of attaining this dream myth."[2] In fact, as we shall see, it is not only the Breedloves who are incapable of attaining the "dream" but the vast majority of families and thus readers, white as well as black, of all classes. Hence, almost all readers wanted at one time or another an optimal family. With clarity about the qualities of the family life for which most readers yearn, family systems therapy is particularly qualified to help us understand this desire, which is closely identified with the origin of the novel.

Janet Beizer defines "family romance" as "the 'attempt to rewrite origins, to replace the unsatisfactory fragments of a . . . past by a totalizing fiction' that recuperates loss and fulfills desire."[3] According to many critics of canonical literature, this fantasy, together with that of the Oedipus complex, is the origin of all storytelling.[4] Indeed, "the image of the orphan, the foundling or bastard, may well be identified with the genre" of the novel itself.[5] Protagonists such as Robinson Crusoe, Moll Flanders, Pamela, Clarissa, Jane Eyre, Oliver Twist, Daniel Deronda, Lucy Snowe, Jude Fawley, and Henry Esmond are said to be motivated by what Lukács calls "transcendental homelessness."[6] Yet scholars of African American literature often resist this term. Deborah McDowell points out that the "family romance" "is deromanticized in writings by the greater majority of black women."[7] Dana Heller argues that "Marianne Hirsch's treatment of family romance" reveals "the unmistakable cultural bias towards Freudian principles, implicit in which is a notion of family structure already in place, and a notion of origin as ultimately knowable. However, the modern European definition of family

plots has little relevance to a people displaced from their home-
land, denied their claims to origin, separated from one another,
forbidden their language, and refused participation in the dominant discursive economy."[8]

One of the goals of this essay is to replace the term "family
romance" with "family dance" to make more visible the extensive family dynamics of a wider variety of literary works. Family
systems therapy provides the best platform for this redefinition,
first of all, because it resists "the unmistakable cultural bias
towards Freudian principles" in the term "Family Romance."
Second, it is about the dynamics or "dance" of whole families, not
just fathers, mothers, or an individual child. Third, it is based on
extensive practice of family therapy and empirical studies, not
speculation about dreams and fantasies. Fourth, it is not limited
to intellectual abstractions such as the aforementioned "transcendental homelessness." It focuses on the emotions which
drive and, in my argument, define the family dance.

From the perspective of family systems therapy, the motivation for narrative is no longer defined as primarily a potentially
dysfunctional nostalgia for an ideal family that never was (that
easily becomes denial, compensation, totalizing fiction, or mere
wish fulfillment) but rather a practical, reasonable desire to live
in a more functional family, a desire that motivates some fictional
narrators and protagonists to achieve that goal. In other words,
besides obsession with the past, the concept of the family dance
makes us more aware of therapeutic possibilities in the present
and of a more practical hope for the future.

Family systems therapy supplements abstractions ascribed to
the origin of the novel such as "transcendental homelessness"
with a fuller sense of the emotion that these fictions embody, and
enables us to identify it outside the canon as well as in. When
Morrison begins her story with "Here is the family," she strikes
this keynote of the genre of the novel, echoing, among others, the
opening of *Anna Karenina* and *Great Expectations*.[9] Hence we
are not surprised that the second theme Morrison introduces in
her afterword (after that of judging by appearance) is that of the
family: "I chose a unique situation, not a representative one. The
extremity of Pecola's case stemmed largely from a crippled and
crippling family—unlike the average black family and unlike the
narrator's. But singular as Pecola's life was, I believed some aspects of her woundability were lodged in all young girls."[10] The
woundability is not limited to female readers. Much of the pain
that Pecola has experienced can be attributed to what has be-

come known as "patriarchy,"[11] but as the role of the son in the Breedlove family suggests, because most male as well as female readers have experienced some family dysfunction, readers of both sexes can to some extent relate to "the social and domestic aggression that could cause a child to literally fall apart."[12]

Admittedly, some readers may resist identification with the characters on the grounds that the domestic aggression experienced by black families, especially this "crippled and crippling family," is not comparable to that with which white readers are familiar.[13] Are black families really more dysfunctional? Some say yes, citing Senator Moynihan's 1965 report, *The Negro Family: The Case for National Action*.[14] Moreover, there is an "ongoing controversy surrounding a small but outstanding group of black female writers and critics' accusations that these writers are fracturing the image of an already besieged black American nuclear family. The complaint, which has been registered in the news media and academic journals, suggests that these writers—Toni Morrison among them—have betrayed the black family by failing to shoulder responsibility for restoring it to an image of wholeness and unity."[15] The usual defense is to focus on the black family's "oppressive circumstances" of racism, classism, and sexism.[16] Valid as this argument is, it oversimplifies the variety and achievements of black families. Even fictional black families are stereotyped.[17] Research on actual black families has defined more complex patterns and dispelled the myth of the black family as "a tangle of pathology." Moreover, family therapists support the claim that "white society finds it difficult enough to have traditional, nuclear, stable families itself."[18] Functional "families are rarely seen in clinical practice"—many mental health professionals even doubt their existence—yet "they are not rare in research volunteer samples, although whether they represent 5 percent or 25 percent of the general population remains to be determined."[19]

Of course, it is difficult to generalize about ethnic groups, and there would be no need to do so if the myths about black families did not encourage some readers to resist identification with the characters in *The Bluest Eye*.[20] Our goal here is simply to challenge that myth. In a classic medical study, the psychiatrists who made the statement above carefully researched black families, concluding that 22 percent were "optimal"; 33 percent were "competent but pained"; 38 percent were "dysfunctional"; and only 5 percent were "severely dysfunctional."[21] In their subsequent study of white families, only eight of forty couples, or 20 percent, by contrast, met the optimal criteria.[22]

More importantly, their standards of family success—an open rather than closed system characterized by love with detachment; equality between parents; successful individuation of children; honest, clear communication; flexible boundaries; and emotional expressiveness—suggest that what is most important is not how many people belong to the family (nuclear or not) but how they relate to one another. In other words, a family of choice can be and often is healthier than a family of blood.

Thus, the modern definition of a functional family is moving in the direction already taken, of necessity, by the black family:

> Under the yoke of slavery, permeable and unstable kinship structures were often necessary so that parents could entrust their children to someone else if they were sold or separated. Often, as a result, children were parented more by a community of caretakers than by their biological parents, and in this sense 'family' came to mean a structure of relations capable of transcending blood kin to form an extended family including neighbors and friends.[23]

The African American family includes "fictive kin": "unrelated individuals who often provide more family support services than blood kin. Many informally adopted children, for example, were reared by surrogate parents who were not their biological parents."[24] "At issue is not the structure but the functioning of the family"; in this tradition, gays and lesbians can belong and make significant contributions to healthy families.[25]

Exemplifying this expanded kinship structure, the McTeers take in Pecola. How would they be rated on the family scale? "The warmth, security, and sense of belonging which Claudia and Freida share with their parents" has earned them the label of the "happy McTeer family."[26] But, as in real life, such stereotypes are simplistic. Many readers can identify with the dysfunctional as well as the functional aspects of their family life. For example, many are familiar with the verbal abuse phase of the family dance:[27] Claudia tells us that "my mother's fussing soliloquies always irritated and depressed us. They were interminable, insulting, and . . . extremely painful in their thrust. She would go on like that for hours, connecting one offense to another."[28] "If we cut or bruise ourselves [adults] ask us are we crazy. When we catch colds, they shake their heads in disgust at our lack of consideration. . . . Our illness is treated with contempt."[29] When

Claudia gets sick she feels guilty and "no one speaks to me or asks how I feel."[30] When she throws up, "My mother's voice drones on. She is not talking to me. She is talking to the puke, but she is calling it my name: Claudia. . . . My mother's anger humiliates me; her words chafe my cheeks, and I am crying. I do not know that she is not angry at me, but at my sickness. I believe she despises my weakness for letting the sickness 'take holt.' "[31] Yet many readers can also identify with Claudia when she remembers another phase of the family dance, the love: "in the night, when my coughing was dry and tough, feet padded into the room, hands repinned the flannel, readjusted the quilt, and rested a moment on my forehead. So when I think of autumn, I think of somebody with hands who does not want me to die."[32] The better label for the McTeers might be "competent but pained" family.

"Dysfunctional" families are the reverse of "optimal" families. "Children growing up in these families are at risk for significant psychopathology. Often one child is scapegoated, and it is clear that his or her behavior diverts attention from the parental conflict"; the children may suffer "severe neuroses or reactive psychotic episodes."[33] In one pattern of the "dysfunctional" family there is a "chronic, unresolvable parental conflict. The parents appear to be at war."[34] This certainly sounds like Cholly and Pauline's family, the Breedloves, but in some respects they are even more unfortunate.

In "severely dysfunctional families" there are "often several family members with clearly manifest, severe, chronic psychopathology. . . . In these families severe parental communication deviance provides a training ground for the development of thought disturbances in vulnerable children . . . either a severe borderline disturbance or a schizophrenic syndrome of chronic duration."[35] Both Cholly and Pecola increasingly manifest severe psychopathology in the novel until Cholly rapes her and Pecola's final monologue reveals what would probably be called "a schizophrenic syndrome."

Thus, Pecola's family is "unlike the average black family and unlike the narrator's," but it is important to remember that her "woundability" is different in degree rather than in kind from that of many of her readers, white as well as black, who tend to be from dysfunctional or competent but pained families. In other words, many of Morrison's readers of all ethnicities can identify to some extent with the family dance of The Bluest Eye.

Those whose extended families have been affected by alcoholism (around forty million Americans) can relate even to the Breedloves. Claudia observes that Pecola's "father's always drunk"; in fact, Pauline loses her job because Cholly came there drunk asking her for money.[36] However, alcoholism is only one phase of the dance of dependency:

> Nothing, nothing, interested him now. Not himself, not other people. Only in drink was there some break, some floodlight, and when that closed, there was oblivion. But the aspect of married life that dumbfounded him and rendered him totally dysfunctional was the appearance of children. Having no idea of how to raise children, and having never watched any parent raise himself, he could not even comprehend what such a relationship should be. . . . So it was on a Saturday afternoon, in the thin light of spring, he staggered home reeling drunk and saw his daughter in the kitchen. . . . The clear statement of her misery was an accusation. He wanted to break her neck—but tenderly.[37]

How could Cholly proceed to rape his own daughter? In a sense he acts out the aggression of all the domestic and social systems that caused a child to "literally fall apart."[38] His destructiveness is a symptom of the dissolution, the "falling apart" of his whole family system. "Recover or repeat" is the primary refrain of the family dance, but of course very few families are in therapy and most simply repeat. Hence, there is a strong sense of family karma or fate. In the case of severely dysfunctional families like the Breedloves that are spiraling out of control, the choice is to recover, or to die. Throughout the description of the Breedloves there is that sense of an implacable "exterior fatality" we know so well from the cursed family systems in the great Greek domestic tragedies. The only way to prevent the end of the family system in *The Oresteia*, for example, is for a god to intervene. In one reading of *Wuthering Heights* only the intervention of a servant prevents the death of the whole family system.[39] No one intervenes to save the Breedloves: they face the ineluctable fatality of Psalm 109: "May the crimes of his fathers be held against him and his mother's sin never be effaced; May Yahweh bear these constantly in mind to wipe their memory off the earth."[40]

Family systems therapy helps us understand how even readers from normal families can relate to this sense of mysterious and powerful movements in the family dance that recur in the lives of individuals or generations. For Murray Bowen, the emotionally determined functioning of the family members generates a family emotional "atmosphere" or "field"; that, in turn, influences the emotional functioning of each person. It is analogous to the gravitational field of the solar system, where each planet and the sun, by virtue of their mass, contribute gravity to the field and are, in turn, regulated by the field they help create. One cannot "see" gravity, nor can one "see" the emotional field. The presence of gravity and the emotional field can be inferred, however, by the predictable ways planets and people behave in reaction to one another.[41]

These emotional fields are transmitted, sometimes with increasing turbulence, from one generation to the next.

Morrison is almost as great as Dickens in communicating emotional fields by describing objects. Her description of the Breedloves' torn sofa, for example, reveals how their entire family system seem to generate depression: "And the joylessness stank, pervading everything. . . . Like a sore tooth that is not content to throb in isolation, but must diffuse its own pain to other parts of the body—making breathing difficult, vision limited, nerves unsettled, so a hated piece of furniture produces a fretful malaise that asserts itself throughout the house and limits the delights of things not related to it."[42]

The key emotional field, in family systems therapy, is that of the marital relationship. Pauline was attracted to Cholly because, as we shall see, "instead of ignoring her infirmity, pretending it was not there, he made it seem like something special and endearing."[43] They got married and "Cholly was kindness still, but began to resist her total dependence on him."[44] Soon her neediness and his drinking took over and they become a classic alcoholic family.[45] Many readers recognize, consciously or unconsciously, the characteristic family dance of dependence that has been labeled coalcoholism or codependence:[46]

Cholly, by his habitual drunkenness and orneriness, provided them both with the material they needed to make their lives tolerable . . . once when a drunken gesture catapulted Cholly into the red-hot stove, she screamed, "Get him, Jesus! Get him!" If Cholly had stopped drinking, she would never have forgiven Jesus. She needed Cholly's sins desperately. The lower he sank, the wilder and more irresponsible he became, the more splendid she and her task became. In the name of Jesus. Not less did Cholly need her. She was one of the few things abhorrent to him that he could touch and therefore hurt. He poured out on her the sum of all his inarticulate fury and aborted desires. Hating her, he could leave himself intact.[47]

Naturally, when these two turn to parenting, they simply repeat, without awareness, what happened to them as children. As
we have seen, "having no idea of how to raise children, and having never watched any parent raise himself, [Cholly] could not
even comprehend what such a relationship should be."[48] Polly's
response is more familiar: "sometimes I'd catch myself hollering
at them and beating them, and I'd feel sorry for them, but I
couldn't seem to stop."[49] Family systems therapy makes us
aware of how the unfinished business of previous generations,
buried in the psyche, strikes the individual without warning,
against her will, sweeping her up in an all too familiar phase of
the family dance.[50]

If readers who are parents can relate to this dance, readers
who grew up in alcoholic families can identify especially with the
Breedlove children. They recall the atmosphere—"even from
where Pecola lay, she could smell Cholly's whiskey"—and readers from all kinds of dysfunctional families can identify with Pecola's feelings when her parents fought: Pecola "struggled
between an overwhelming desire that one would kill the other,
and a profound wish that she herself would die."[51] This wish,
which dominates her personality (epitomized in her prayer to
God, "Please make me disappear") is typical of the Lost Child
role in the alcoholic family system.[52] Readers from dysfunctional
families can also relate to the response of the Breedloves' son:
"Sammy cursed for a while, or left the house, or threw himself
into the fray."[53] When he joined the dance, Sammy "suddenly
began to hit his father about the head with both fists, shouting
'You naked fuck!' over and over and over." When Pauline hit
Cholly with a stove lid, "Sammy screamed, 'Kill him! Kill him!'
Mrs. Breedlove looked at Sammy with surprise and told him to
do what his father had failed to do, go out and get some coal."[54]
Double binds like this in alcoholic families are familiar themes in
fiction, described well, for example, by D. H. Lawrence in *Sons
and Lovers* and Lionel Garcia in *Hardscrub*.

The *basso continuo* in this dance is the "orphan feeling." One
of Toni Morrison's greatest achievements, one of the ways her
novels are able "to make the particularity of the African American experience the basis for a representation of humanity *tout
court*," is that she, like many other celebrated writers, can give
voice to many feelings that are locked up in most of us, impris-
oned by our emotional illiteracy. Because emotional literacy is
essential to successful psychotherapy and many other aspects of

life,[55] this may well be one of literature's most important contribution to our culture.[56]

Sooner or later, family systems therapy focuses on one's deep feelings of abandonment, of the ultimate alienation, of being an orphan in the world. This emotion inspires the self-destructive dance that can whirl from one generation to the next until the family is no more: "When Cholly was four days old, his mother wrapped him in two blankets and one newspaper and placed him on a junk heap by the railroad . . . he wondered whether it would have been just as well to have died there."[57] Rejected in this way by his own mother, he searches for his father when he becomes a "father" himself: "Cholly knew it was wrong to run out on a pregnant girl, and recalled, with sympathy, that his father had done just that. Now he understood. He knew then what he must do—find his father."[58] But his father tells him, "get the fuck outta my face!"[59] Deserted once again by his family, "Cholly was truly free. Abandoned in a junk heap by his mother, rejected for a crap game by his father, there was nothing more to lose"; he "loses" even the taboo against raping his own daughter.[60]

Because readers are familiar, consciously or unconsciously, with transgenerational repetition (one of the primary laws of family systems), they are not surprised when Cholly practices what he has learned.[61] Claudia's mother complains, "Folks just dump they children off on you. . . . That old trifling Cholly been out of jail *two* whole days and ain't been here *yet* to see if his own child was 'live or dead. She could be *dead* for all he know. And that *mama* neither. What kind of something is that?"[62] Family systems therapy reveals that, though deep and often not fully recognized, this "something" (abandonment) is feared by even readers from "normal" families.

Abandonment may be the central emotion even in what readers simply accept as the happy "white, middle class myth" of the family introduced in first words of *The Bluest Eye*.[63] It is evidence of the universality of this feeling that even our mythical hero Jane, in the archetypal Dick and Jane story, is apparently abandoned emotionally by her family. Perhaps because they are preoccupied with the stereotypes and the phrase "They are very happy," critics have not noticed that no family members answer the question "Who will play with Jane?"[64] As with so many families devoted to keeping up appearances, there may be a different reality behind the "very happy" smiling faces. Even Jane may be an orphan within her family. The only one who will play with Jane is a "friend" from outside the family. And that is also how Pecola's story ends: finally the only one who will play with her is an imaginary "friend."

Why didn't Pecola's "Mother" play with her? Why did Pauline abandon her daughter? First of all, she believed her daughter was unusually "ugly." Secondly, "It was her good fortune to find a permanent job in the home of a well-to-do family whose members were affectionate, appreciative, and generous. . . . More and more she neglected her house, her children, her man."[65] Discovering a seemingly more healthy family, hers seemed even worse by comparison. This is one of the unfortunate initial side effects of family therapy. The client, formerly unaware of "functional" families, becomes even more depressed when he or she sees just how "dysfunctional" his or her own family is. In fact, Pauline's family was in a destructive spiral that would have taken resources far greater than hers to rescue.

Pauline's kind of neglect is more common than Cholly's treatment of his daughter, but if both parents' abandonment of their family seems far from the dance that most readers know, even those from "optimal" families can identify with the feeling of being abandoned by God. When Pecola asks the child molester, Soaphead Church, for blue eyes, he prays, "Lord, how could you leave a lass so long so lone that she could find her way to me? How could you?"[66] That question inevitably echoes in the minds of all the readers who have had to face the death, disease, or serious injury of a friend or family member. Indeed, this feeling of abandonment by God is often described as a chief feature of modern civilization and a defining attribute of the novel.[67] Ultimately, abandonment is a central emotion of the human condition. As the protagonist's mother dies in Bret Lott's *Jewel* (1991), she whispers, "Your momma and daddy leave you at some point, and then you are on your own. Everyone ends up an orphan."[68]

In addition to illuminating the orphan feeling embodied in *The Bluest Eye*, family systems therapy encourages us to rise above the perspective of individual characters to that of the whole family and thus the level of the narrative; from this perspective it sheds light on more traditional literary problems such as the lack in this novel of a "center of rationality . . . foreseeable logic or any predictability in situations . . . [a] narrativity [that] is unavailing or invalid against an exterior fatality."[69] As we have seen, the law of transgenerational repetition provides a "logic" which carries the reader to the destruction at the end of the story, a "family plot" that is "exterior" in the sense that it is driven by previous generations.[70]

Yet family systems therapy also reveals how and why *The Bluest Eye* succeeds. First of all, much of family systems therapy focuses on making clients conscious of faulty family communication.[71] By successfully mimicking the chaos and "severe communication deviance" of a disturbed family, Morrison's narrative technique helps to prevent the reader from escaping and denying the reality of life in such a family. One reader suggested that "the breakdown of order in the language of the story suggests the breakdown of order in Pecola's mind."[72] Indeed it does, but that may put the cart before the horse. The disintegration of order in the language in the opening parodies of the white family myth mimics the breakdown of order in the family. From the point of view of family systems therapy, Pecola's madness is but an extrapolation of the systemic madness. Her language falls apart because her family falls apart. If her family had been able to consult a family therapist, she (and/or Cholly) would have been seen as "the identified patient" who presents the symptoms of the family's malaise.[73] Readers have noticed that Pecola has no voice in the story, no section of the novel for herself, but that is not unusual in such families.[74] The communication is experiential: the identified symptom bearer often acts out rather than verbally articulates the sickness in the family. Pecola's final breakdown is the result of the inevitable logic of the family dynamics embodied in the story: the system's madness generates the individual's and to some extent the reader's: Morrison's "addition of the element of insanity compromises consensus reality, and the reader is never allowed 'to integrate the data and make it harmonious.' "[75]

The novel begins "Quiet as it's kept." According to Morrison, "the words are conspiratorial. 'Shh, don't tell anyone else,' and 'no one is allowed to know this.' It is a secret between us and a secret that is being kept from us. . . . The intimacy I was aiming for, the intimacy between the reader and the page, could start up immediately because the secret is being shared. . . . I did not want the reader to have time to wonder, . . . 'What defense do I need, what distance maintain?' "[76] The primary narration, Claudia's, draws us further in because it "gives the reader pause about whether the voice of children can be trusted at all or is more trustworthy than an adult's. The reader is thereby protected from a confrontation too soon with the painful details, while simultaneously provoked into a desire to know them."[77]

Eventually "to read the book . . . is to ache for remedy."[78] The mere fact that the story is being told by a survivor suggests that some remedy is possible: "What Claudia's telling of the story shows, but does not say, is that the internalization of destructive standards can be avoided . . . we see this growth of mind in Claudia. We may experience some growth of our own if we read carefully and well."[79] For readers the narration itself is also one remedy. Kenneth Womack has shown how E. M. Forster employed "narrative therapy" in *Howards End* to challenge his nation to overcome class consciousness. His summary of White and Epston's *Narrative Means to Therapeutic Ends* is as applicable to *The Bluest Eye* as it is to *Howards End*: narratives "assist clients (or readers) in simultaneously identifying with and separating from the dilemmas that plague their lived experiences. . . . The telling and retelling of story furnishes readers with the capacity for . . . effecting a kind of narratological morphogenesis, or the transformation of their lives through the therapeutic interpretation of their textual experiences."[80] Following the fate of the characters, "as readers we become, intellectually, at least, their therapists—and, in a sense, our own."[81]

Claudia is able to keep her sanity partly because, like Jane Eyre, she has a tendency to get angry at the other and defend herself rather than to turn inward and sink into depression, and partly because as an adult third person narrator she tells the story of their childhood "simultaneously identifying with and separating from the dilemmas" they faced. She is more successful in this regard than, say, Lockwood, the protoreader in *Wuthering Heights* who, though a stranger, is coopted into the family dynamics.[82] Claudia is one of a long tradition of narrators who escape family disintegration that can be traced back at least to Helen in Anne Brontë's *Tenant of Wildfell Hall*. Helen is the only person who breaks out of the cycle of abuse and addiction in that novel because she too adopts a form of the talking cure. In her journal, eventually read by others, she unburdens herself of the family secrets, one of the primary therapies in family systems as in other therapies.[83] Unburdening herself in a similar fashion, becoming the narrator of her own life, Claudia escapes (and shows us how to escape) Pecola's fate. Yet she makes sure that memory of Pecola is *not* wiped off the face of the earth, ensuring that the lowly Breedloves assume a place in our collective unconscious as important as that of the great house of Atreus.[84]

According to the family dynamics of the novel, Claudia was able to do this primarily because she came from a healthier family than Pecola and thus she and her sister had more self-esteem. They had a mother who "monitored" them and modeled "resilience," teaching them to fight back when attacked.[85] In Pecola's case, it was her own father who raped her. But when Frieda is molested by their boarder (Mr. Henry), her father and mother attack him and drive him away.[86] When faced with the same accusation of ugliness that devastated Pecola, Frieda and Claudia "could not comprehend this unworthiness."[87] In Pecola's case, her mother simply accepted the damaging accusation. Pauline's experience at the movies made her a protoreader of the master narrative: "She was never able, after her education in the movies, to look at a face and not assign it some category in the scale of absolute beauty, and the scale was one she absorbed in full from the silver screen."[88]

Whether a family resists or reinforces the master narrative is crucial to a child's self-esteem. "In preparation for expected encounters with racism," for example, some black parents "felt that it was necessary to develop high self-esteem and self-confidence in their children."[89] Research has shown that "the more passive race-neutral stance may be an insufficient buffer."[90] In a similar predicament, Pauline's family of origin could have faced the problem of others' reactions to her club foot as well as the color of her skin and given her explicit assurance of their support, perhaps tapping into a story assuring her that she is a child of the universe or of God, or into other alternative narratives opposed to judging by appearance.[91] Instead, as they apparently got used to seeing her club foot, it became easier just to ignore it, thus contributing to the denial that sets Pauline up for the stares and remarks of others. "Restricted, as a child, to this cocoon of her family's spinning," Pauline thinks her club foot is "why she never felt at home anywhere, or that she belonged anyplace. Her general feeling of separateness and unworthiness she blamed on her foot."[92]

One day, leaning idly on a fence she heard a boy whistling: "she listened carefully to the music and let it pull her lips into a smile. . . . she felt something tickling her foot. She laughed aloud and turned to see. The whistler was bending down tickling her broken foot and kissing her leg. . . . He talked with her about her foot and asked, when they walked through the town or in the fields, if she were tired. Instead of ignoring her infirmity, pretending it was not there, he made it seem like something special and endearing. For the first time, Pauline felt that her bad foot was an asset."[93]

This, of course, is the kind of alternative narrative most of us need to fight the *"Thing"* that makes others "beautiful, and not us."[94] They get married and, as we have seen, her neediness and his alcoholism take over and destroy their family. When she has children of her own she does not provide them an alternative narrative like the one Cholly gave her; she reverts to the example of her family of origin, accepts the master narrative without questions, and spins a cocoon around their perceived ugliness:

> The Breedloves did not live in a storefront because they were having temporary difficulty adjusting to the cutbacks at the plant. They lived there because they were poor and black, and they stayed there because they believed they were ugly. . . . their ugliness was unique. No one could have convinced them that they were not relentlessly and aggressively ugly. . . . You looked at them and wondered why they were so ugly; you looked closely and could not find the source. Then you realized that it came from conviction, their conviction. It was as though some mysterious all-knowing master had given each one a cloak of ugliness to wear, and they had accepted it without question. The master had said, "You are ugly people." They had looked about themselves and saw nothing to contradict the statement: saw, in fact, support for it leaning at them from every billboard, every movie, every glance. "Yes" they had said, "You are right." And they took the ugliness in their hands, threw it as a mantle over them, and went about the world with it.[95]

The narrator tells us that Pecola had her own beauty, but her obsession with blue eyes prevented her from ever discovering that.[96] Because of the narrative technique we know we are implicated in what happened to Pecola. As the details of the story are revealed, the problem is transferred "to the presumably adult reader" and the family dance is identified as "a social disruption with tragic individual consequences in which the reader, as part of the population of the text, is implicated."[97] We know we are included in the "our" spoken by the protoreader, Claudia, at the end: "All of our waste which we dumped on her and which she absorbed."[99] We know that we too have made scapegoats of those whose appearance did not meet "our" standards of the "beautiful."

NOTES

I would like to thank John V. Knapp for his help with this essay.

    1. The term originated with Freud's "Der Familienroman Der Neurotiker" (1908). At first Freud associated these familial fantasies particularly with paranoiacs, but he soon realized they were part of normal maturation in which all

children seek liberation from the authority of parents. According to Freud, the Family Romance begins when parents focus their love on their new child and the child in turn identifies with and idealizes them. Eventually, often with the arrival of a sibling, the child perceives that he no longer receives all their love. (It is of course almost always a "he" in Freud's writing.) He begins to doubt the special attributes ascribed to them and may find solace in thinking that he is an adopted or stepchild, a foundling or bastard whose real parents have higher social standing. When he matures sexually, the story, for Freud, modulates into that of Oedipus.

2. Bjork, *The Novels of Toni Morrison,* 32; see also Tyrell, "Storytelling and Moral Agency," 14.

3. Beizer, *Family Plots,* 7.

4. Robert, *Origins of the Novel,* 22, 31; Beizer, *Family Plots,* 7; *Novel as Family Romance,* ix; and Hirsch, *Mother/Daughter Plot,* 9, 11.

5. Van Boheemen, *Novel as Family Romance,* 31.

6. Lukács, *Theory of the Novel,* 41; see also Van Boheemen, *Novel as Family Romance,* 45–46.

7. McDowell, "Reading Family Matters," 78.

8. Heller, "Reconstructing Kin," 213–14.

9. Bump, "Family Dynamics of the Reception of Art," 346–47.

10. Morrison, *Bluest Eye,* 210.

11. Mori, *Toni Morrison and Womanist Discourse,* 57–69.

12. Morrison, *Bluest Eye,* 210.

13. Puri, *Towards a New Womanhood,* 33.

14. Stewart, "Moynihan's 'Tangle of Pathology,'" 239; Rainwater and Yancey, *Moynihan Report,* 6, 152–53; Kelley, *Yo' Mama's DisFunktional!,* 3; Spaights, "Therapeutic Implications of Working with the Black Family," 183; Frazier, *Negro Family in the United States;* and Deutsch and Brown, "Social Influences in Negro-White Intellectual Differences." For thirty years, more balanced views of the African-American family, acknowledging its strengths, have dominated: see Hines and Boyd-Franklin, "African American Families," 66–67; Billingsley, *Climbing Jacob's Ladder;* Hill, *Strengths of African American Families;* Lewis and Looney, *Long Struggle;* McAdoo, *Black Families;* and Staples, *Black Family.*

15. Heller, "Reconstructing Kin," 213; McDowell, "Reading Family Matters," 84–86.

16. Stewart, "Moynihan's 'Tangle of Pathology,'" 250–51; Heller, "Reconstructing Kin," 213–14.

17. Puri, *Towards a New Womanhood,* 53.

18. Stewart, "Moynihan's 'Tangle of Pathology,'" 250.

19. Lewis and Looney, *Long Struggle,* 14.

20. Ariel, *Culturally Competent Family Therapy,* 6; Hardy, "Theoretical Myth of Sameness," 22.

21. Lewis and Looney, *Long Struggle,* 33.

22. Lewis, *Birth of the Family.* "Willie and Greenblatt (1978) provided research results which suggest that the middle-class Black family appears more egalitarian than any other family type and that rigid role differentiation for husbands and wives occurs more frequently in middle-class white families than middle-class Black families." See Spaights, "Therapeutic Implications of Working with the Black Family," 187.

23. Heller, "Reconstructing Kin," 217. See Hines and Boyd-Franklin, "African

American Families," 68, 71; Rivers and Scanzoni, "Social Families Among African Americans," 334; and Hill, *Strengths of African American Families.* Hill cites Wilhelmina Manns's study of influential "significant others" in black families: "64 percent of the persons who were cited as influential 'significant others' were nonrelatives" (29). See Manns, "Supportive Roles of Significant Others in African American Families," 207–12. In fact, the open rather than closed family system may well be the norm: "idealization of nuclear family privacy was a fairly recent historical alternative to a system in which servants, boarders, lodgers, or visiting distant kin moved more freely in and out of the household." See Coontz, "Historical Perspectives on Family Studies," 284.

24. Hill, *Strengths of African American Families,* 129.

25. Ibid., 71.

26. Puri, *Towards a New Womanhood,* 53; see also Heinze, *Dilemma of "Double-Consciousness,"* 74–76.

27. One version of family systems therapy that I have tried to advance in literary criticism is that based on treatment of addictions. In this kind of therapy there is a strong emphasis on admitting and tracing the effects of child abuse. See Bump, "Family Dynamics of the Reception of Art," 332; see also Bump, "D. H. Lawrence and Family Systems Theory," 66. For more on wives who try to control their families with their anger and verbal abuse see 69. In addition to verbal abuse, *The Bluest Eye* shows the effect of physical, sexual, and religious abuse. In their extensive analysis of abuse in African American families Toinette M. Eugene and James M. Poling subsume verbal abuse under emotional abuse. See Eugene and Poling, *Balm for Gilead.*

28. Morrison, *Bluest Eye,* 24.

29. Ibid., 10.

30. Ibid., 11.

31. Ibid., 11–12.

32. Ibid., 12.

33. Lewis and Looney, *Long Struggle,* 22.

34. Ibid., 23.

35. Ibid., 24–25.

36. Morrison, *Bluest Eye,* 101, 120.

37. Ibid., 160–61.

38. Ibid., 210.

39. Cohen, *Daughter's Dilemma,* 109.

40. See Psalm 109:14.

41. Kerr and Bowen, *Family Evaluation,* 54–55.

42. Morrison, *Bluest Eye,* 36–37.

43. Ibid., 115–16.

44. Ibid., 118.

45. There are many myths about such families. For example, is Pauline's "total dependence" on Cholly the cause of his drinking problems? It is a trigger but not the cause according to the disease model of alcoholism subscribed to by most addiction specialists. True alcoholism, which is what Cholly's appears to be, is a disease itself that is chronic, progressive, and fatal. Even if Pauline had not been totally dependent on him, presumably Cholly's drinking would have become a problem. "It is best to think of family violence and alcohol and drug abuse as overlapping but distinct problems which must both be treated in order to change either of them." See Eugene and Poling, *Balm for Gilead,* 151; see also Larry W. Bennett, "Substance Abuse and Domestic Assault of

Women," 760–69. It would be valuable, in my opinion, to explore in more depth the relationship between *The Bluest Eye* and the branch of family systems therapy that is based on the treatment of chemical dependence. See Bump, "Family Dynamics of the Reception of Art," 330–32; see also Fierz, "Polanski Misses," 106.

46. On the role of codependence and enmeshment in family systems, what Morrison called "anaconda love," see Gary Storhoff, "Anaconda Love," 291, 298–99, 305–6; see also Bump, "Family Dynamics of the Reception of Art," 331, 339–40, 345; and Bump, "D. H. Lawrence and Family Systems Theory," 63–74, especially 69–70 on the war of the sexes after marriage. Storhoff's account of the relationship of Ruth and Macon in Morrison's *Song of Solomon* (298–99) also fits that of Cholly and Polly in many ways.

47. Morrison, *Bluest Eye*, 42.

48. Ibid., 160.

49. Ibid., 124.

50. Bump, "Family Dynamics of the Reception of Art," 337–38.

51. Morrison, *Bluest Eye*, 40, 43.

52. Ibid., 45.

53. Ibid., 43.

54. Ibid., 44.

55. Gates, Jr., Introduction, xi.

56. Bump, "Teaching Emotional Literacy," 315–18; see also Goleman, *Emotional Intelligence.* For the importance of emotional literacy in family systems therapy, see John V. Knapp's description of Nathan Ackerman and Carl Whitaker in "Family Systems Psychotherapy," 234–35; see also Bump, "D. H. Lawrence and Family Systems Theory," 65, 71. Admittedly, "few literary critics, apart from feminists, reader-response critics, and composition theorists, have recognized the affective components of knowledge," but just as "effective teaching is . . . affective teaching," effective literary criticism is affective literary criticism. See Berman, *Diaries to an English Professor,* 226; Bump, "Left vs. Right Side of the Brain;" Weinstein and Fantini, *Toward Humanistic Education.* Aristotle recognized this long ago in his theory of tragedy and some critics try to maintain the tradition. See Bleich, *Readings and Feelings;* and Phelan, "Toward a Rhetorical Reader-Response Criticism," 241.

57. Morrison, *Bluest Eye*, 133–34.

58. Ibid., 151.

59. Ibid., 156.

60. Ibid., 160.

61. For explanations and illustrations of transgenerational repetition and what D. H. Lawrence called the "fatal chain of continuity." See Lawrence, *Complete Short Stories,* 545; Knapp, "Family Systems Psychotheraphy," 228, 231–32; Knapp, *Striking at the Joints,* 61–62, 69–71, 94–96; Spector, "Anne Tyler's *Dinner at the Homesick Restaurant*," 311, 320; Bump, "D. H. Lawrence and Family Systems Theory," 69–70; Bump, "Family Dynamics of the Reception of Art," 336–39, 342–43, 346–47; and the Old Testament: "Yahweh . . . lets nothing go unchecked, punishing the father's fault in the sons and the grandsons to the third and fourth generations." See Exodus 34:6–7; see also Numbers 14:18 and Deuteronomy 5:9.

62. Morrison, *Bluest Eye*, 25.

63. Bjork, *Novels of Toni Morrison*, 32.

64. Morrison, *Bluest Eye*, 3.

65. Ibid., 127.

66. Ibid., 180.

67. See Lukács, *Theory of the Novel*; see also Miller, *Disappearance of God.*

68. Lott, *Jewel*, 29.

69. Harding and Martin, *World of Difference*, 153.

70. Bump, "Family Dynamics of the Reception of Art," 335–38.

71. See Bateson, *Steps to an Ecology of Mind*; Haley, *Problem-Solving Therapy*; Erickson, *Healing in Hypnosis*; and Watzlawick, *Language of Change.*

72. Kubitschek, *Toni Morrison*, 32.

73. Believing that the "cross-sexual, cross-generational relationships of father and daughter functioned as the core of the nuclear family" (22), Cohen focuses in *The Daughter's Dilemma* on the sick daughter's role in the fictional family as the bearer of the family's symptoms. She traces the ways in which psychosomatic illness performs a regulating function, maintaining the closed family system.

74. Page, *Dangerous Freedom*, 54.

75. Heinze, *Dilemma of "Double-Consciousness,"* 153; Hume, *Fantasy and Mimesis*, 139. By the standards of poststructuralism, according to Hume, the fragmentations of the multiple narrations are actually positive in the total picture (55). However, Morrison's novels, "in their thematic messages about art, register strong disapproval of postmodern 'games.'" See Rainwater and Yancey, *Moynihan Report and the Politics of Controversy*, 96; ultimately, "Morrison derives her indeterminacies not from French postmodernism nor from the new, oddly dematerialized forms of Marxism but from the center of African American culture." See Hilfer, "Critical Indeterminacies in Toni Morrison's Fiction," 93.

76. Morrison, *Bluest Eye*, 212–13.

77. Ibid., 213.

78. Dee, "Black Family in Search for Identity," 319; McKay, *Critical Essays on Toni Morrison*, 20.

79. Tyrell, "Storytelling and Moral Agency," 17, 20.

80. Womack, "'Only Connecting' with the Family," 257.

81. Spector, "Anne Tyler's *Dinner at the Homesick Restaurant*," 312.

82. See Bump, "Family Dynamics of the Reception of Art," 341–42.

83. See Evan Imber-Black, *Secrets in Families and Family Therapy*, 73–75.

84. See Psalm 109:14.

85. See Eugene and Poling, *Balm for Gilead*, 44. See Victor A. Christopherson, "Implications for Strengthening Family Life."

86. Morrison, *Bluest Eye*, 98–101.

87. Ibid., 74.

88. Ibid., 122.

89. Peters, "Historical Note," 178; see also Richardson, "Racism and Child-Rearing."

90. Tatum, "Out There Stranded?," 230.

91. "For Zion was saying, 'Yahweh has abandoned me, the Lord has forgotten me.' Does a woman forget her baby at the breast, or fail to cherish the son of her womb? Yet even if these forget, I will never forget you." Isaiah 49:14–15; cf. Ps 27:10; John 14:18: "I will not leave you orphans."

92. Morrison, *Bluest Eye*, 111.

93. Ibid., 115–16.

94. Ibid., 74.
95. Ibid., 38–39.
96. Ibid., 46–47.
97. Ibid., 214.
98. Ibid., 205.

Forging a Family Discourse in Marilene Felinto's *The Women of Tijucopapo*: Or, Unraveling the Intricacies of Miscommunication

Sara E. Cooper

In *THE WOMEN OF TIJUCOPAPO* (*AS MULHERES DE TIJUCOPAPO*; 1982), Marilene Felinto forges a unique mix of magical realism and the regional novel to explore the social, political, and familial role of the poor woman of color in Brazil. In terms of agenda, themes, and autobiographical elements, Felinto's first novel can be compared to works by American writers Toni Morrison and Alice Walker.[1] Her fragmentary and mythic writing style, rich in culturally charged symbolism, also approximates that of Morrison or Dorothy Allison in its emphasis on the psychological and emotional. As noted by Márcia Cavendish Wanderly, the novel's mythic and magical qualities are the media through which Felinto explores a recuperation of origin that promises to mitigate the protagonist's anguish and fractured social identity—a fragmentation attributable to both the personal and political environment.[2] Although Felinto's novel is firmly situated in the sociopolitical and cultural setting of Brazil, frequent smatterings of English and references to American popular culture provide a bridge of commonality that opens *The Women of Tijucopapo* to a larger audience. In fact, much of the fascination of Felinto's work stems from her ability to bridge myriad sociopolitical and cultural differences and portray the difficulties of the Brazilian woman of color as universal, or mythic. Such is the novel's narrator and protagonist, Rísia, who seemingly haphazardly leads the reader to an understanding of her precarious position in her family, society, and national mythology. The objective of this study is to trace the articulation of Rísia's evolving place in the family and social system, a journey which is marked by her attempts at developing an alternative family discourse.

171

In Felinto's urgent and personal criticism of political and social injustice, she joins the ranks of illustrious Latin American writers such as Carlos Fuentes, Claribel Alegría, Elena Poniatowska, Lygia Fagundes Telles, Helena Parente Cunha, and Lucía Guerra, to name but a few.[3] More particularly, Felinto's implied social agenda and innovative writing style reflect the radical literary and political movement of Brazilian women writers of the post-1964 generations, which "starts as an almost self-depreciative and plaintive discourse and little by little is transformed into audacious and rebellious."[4] Critical response to *The Women of Tijucopapo* has included pointed references to the narrator's language as passionate, primordial and brutal. In a feminist reading grounded in Cixous's theory of *l'écriture féminine*, Alice A. Brittin and Kimberle Schumock López suggest that "Marilene creates a new language and a new self out of the matter of the swamp, processed through her body."[5] This reference to the definition of the word "tijuco," meaning "morass, slough, mud, mire, ooze, bog, marsh, swamp" (*Novo Michaelis Dictionary*) fittingly underlines the protagonist's penchant for the scatological and base, and for a language that some would not hesitate to call sordid, or even filthy. Cavendish Wanderly speaks of Rísia's "frightening linguistic aggression," while a review of the French translation calls the novel a "livre d'une rare violence verbale."[6] When questioned about her writing, Felinto's reply is both defensive and illuminating: "Intellectually, I have changed social rank. But, in a certain way, I remain marginal. I am always between both, without attempting to find a balance. Writing is not a normal activity. As for me, it is assigned to me by an evil god."[7] As usual, the humor in her voice underlies a serious concern. In essence, Felinto seems to ascribe her style to a lived liminality, be it of her mixed class identity or the intrusion of the spirit world into the terrestrial sphere. Hanging onto the edge of a social or personal space unerringly unearths a level of violence only prompted by the need to survive.

The violence of Rísia's narration is only one element of her journey away from her past and toward a new sense of self and family. Cavendish Wanderly recognizes that Rísia's search for alternative origins rests partly within a "doubly deprived" childhood: the hardship engendered by both her class and her sex. In essence, she is attempting to rescue not only herself, but also all women from the atrocious weakness that she perceives in her mother, a "ghost of cowardice and speechlessness" that humiliates and haunts her.[8] Although Sáenz de Tejada's work principally limits itself to an exploration of race and gender in Felinto's novel, she does agree that Rísia's pilgrimage is related to her family system. She explains, "This desire to find alternative spaces, away from the duality that she sees around her, is transformed into one of her incentives to travel, since she already wishes to escape the roles that are expected of her as a woman in her family."[9] Elsewhere Sáenz de Tejada adds that Rísia, although "tormented by the family and socioeconomic relations in her past . . . finds hope of liberty and recognition as an AfroBrazilian" at the end of her journey.[10]

Despite frequent mentions of the protagonist's role in a torturous family system and recurrent references to the striking language of the novel, extant criticism as of yet has not delved into Rísia's role in the family or how her family interactions are connected to her narrative structure and voice. Notwithstanding, one of the most outstanding elements in *The Women of Tijucopapo* is the protagonist's strange and mangled communication: with her family, her lover, her friends, and even the reader. The point of origination of the babble/Babel marking Rísia's narration seems to be her family's intricate system of miscommunication. The less clarity or transparency, the more muddied the water, the more Rísia's voice recuperates a remembered dialogue and the rules that govern it. In this way, the novel is a recreation of the family interaction (verbal and nonverbal), as jumbled and inconsistent as it might have been to her as a child. In this narrative, Rísia seems intent upon remembering, writing, and eventually communicating her family experience despite the fact that her task seems elusive, excruciating and almost insurmountable. It becomes ever clearer that on her journey, what Rísia is searching for is a new paradigm of family that allows her a place and a voice. The narrator/protagonist's interweaving of the elements of journey, family, memory, speech, and language are an attempt to assemble a comprehensible history and sense of self. Paramount to this study, her semantic and syntactical transgressions seem to empower her to imagine an alternative family system and attempt to create a productive family discourse. She imagines and models a new sort of language that violently transgresses the limits and boundaries set by her family and Brazilian society.

In most critical approximations to Felinto's novel, these transgressions are interpreted as a definitive sign of the protagonist's progress and even victory. Sáenz de Tejada sees the writing of *The Women of Tijucopapo* as a successful act of resistance.[11]

The protagonist is marching with the community of Amazons back to São Paulo to demand her own rights and the rights of her fellows, and thus she seems to have entered the reality and the tangibility of a social movement. In this act of resistance, she has undeniably broken with the passive image of her family's generations of women.[12] Cavendish Wanderly's analysis agrees that Rísia is triumphantly able to "travel through, conquer, devastate, and subjugate new spaces and assume roles new to women."[13] Nonetheless, there are many clues that indicate that Rísia has not truly escaped either the legacy of her own family and social system or the sophisticated system of fantasy and denial that she has always employed to maintain her internal exile. Instead, it seems more likely that her family system has not prepared her to face the world that surrounds her, and here when she is the closest to surpassing the dysfunction, she is ironically kept from having any idea of her failure. As is true in many instances, in this case the journey is much more significant, powerful, and successful than the destination. In the final analysis, Rísia's final dream-like entrance to an idealized community family of Amazonian women contains a variety of problematic elements that force the reader to question the clarity of her vision and the possibility of her moving beyond the confines of language, family, and society that bind her.

What remains is a questioning of the very basis of communication and our ability to escape the patterns that are instilled with the learning of language and interpersonal dynamics in the family system. A family systems reading provides fresh insight into these aspects of the novel, allowing a detailed analysis of the interpersonal dynamic and patterns of communication that frame the protagonist's experience and narrative voice.[14] Through a close reading of the text, it will be possible to trace the movement that the protagonist makes away from her origins and toward an alternative system of family and language, without obscuring the complexity of the process or imposing a mistaken finality on the end.

(MIS)COMMUNICATION IN AND OUT OF THE FAMILY SYSTEM

Sáenz de Tejada calls *The Women of Tijucopapo* "an existential and psychological journey in which Rísia is searching for her origins and her own voice."[15] At the same time it is an epistolary monologue that the protagonist, Rísia, addresses to her mother, in which she recalls scenes of family dysfunction: poverty, neglect, abuse, silence, and contradictory communication. Rísia is a poor young Afro-Brazilian woman who in many ways is struggling to escape from her family and socioeconomic origins, yet her vision of an alternative life takes her back to the place where she grew up—the arid, sparsely populated, and economically depressed Northeast. Irene Matthews, the English-language translator of *The Women of Tijucopapo*, comments that the novel is "in part the story of a series of returns, a series of dates that fix childhood in a calendar of spasmodic, traumatic, remembrances—of taste, and smell, and noise, and, often, of delicious fearfulness. . . . Ruling over all of the experiences are the terrors of silent Sundays, of emotional desertion by grandmother, by parents, by and sisters, by Nema, by Jonas, by the world."[16] The family preoccupation necessarily will color this literary journey.

Virginia Satir, family systems theoretician and psychiatric social worker, has done extensive study and writing on the communication patterns of family. Among her conclusions is the conviction that in order to understand the family system one must observe carefully the way a family communicates, on verbal and nonverbal levels, and how much they complicate, sabotage, and undermine communication as a way to maintain the family system *as is*. When a family employs a consistent pattern of contradictory or incoherent communication, while propagating the unspoken rule that no one may question or even openly recognize the communicative disparity, frequently at least one child will compensate by creating a fragmentary and coded form of expression.[17] In Satir's discussion of family communication patterns, she underlines how ingrained they are and how difficult they are to surmount.

The emphasis on communication in Felinto's novel is established at the outset, when words and meaning are shown to be problematic and alienating.[18] Over and over Rísia repeats that she would prefer to write in English, or something like English, even though her stated audience (her mother) does not speak the language. The construction of a queered and incomprehensible space between languages is characteristic of Felinto's work in general, according to João Camillo Penna, who argues that the novelist's agenda is actually to represent "a violence of unfamiliarity," which happens through the breaking down of language.[19] The novel begins by Rísia saying that she will translate her letter before she sends it, because, "I want what I may say to sound like English, another language that I know how to speak, a foreign language. Saying 'Good-bye, mother!' 'Good-bye, father!' 'Good-bye, everyone' sometimes strikes me as much more suitable than 'Adeus mae! pai! vocês!' "[20] Rísia says that she wants to communicate these things to her family, yet she cannot foresee speaking directly to her parents, or telling them the truth without disguising it somehow, or making it unintelligible. She explains, "Mother, you shitface. It's a little just so's you won't understand that I sing John Lennon. I want people to not understand. I'm going to talk in English."[21]

It is as if direct communication is too dangerous to be tolerated in her family, because it would inevitably disrupt the family's unstated, but nonetheless real, rules of conduct. In addition to the fairly standard injunction of children being seen and not heard, the family rules of communication include various prohibitions that protect the family reputation and anchor the family stability. Her father has apparent freedom of action and self-expression, while the women of the family must walk a fine line of language, being careful to not contradict the family myths. At the same time, a clear generational distinction means that it is both accepted and expected that Rísia's parents will verbally assault her, showing her what she must do by linguistically modeling what she mustn't do. Ironically, the narrator gives almost no voice to her father's discourse, privileging her mother's and siblings' passive-aggressive remarks, a phenomenon that will be discussed in further detail below. If speaking in English adheres to the family rules prohibiting her from direct confrontation, it is also a linguistic strategy that highlights her difference from her mother, father, and siblings. Perhaps this is what she means by "suitable," that the use of English is more in keeping with her present and future, whereas her native Portuguese is too firmly associated with her past. She can only express her individuality and verbalize her intention to maintain a separate being if she turns to a language that she has learned in adulthood. English, after all, does not have the same taint of memory, and her control of the language is a visible and audible sign that she is not who she was before. It firmly sets her apart from her past, but at the same time it separates her from herself, which she sees as a positive move. Rísia explains, "English . . . separates me from all that closeness of sending a letter from me in the language of my own people, in my own language. I don't want them to know about me like that, so closely. English gives me distance."[22] Even though she is writing and/or speaking to the people who have had the most emotional impact on her, her parents, her lover, and her best friend from childhood, she needs the distance of not showing herself completely. The narrator seems to be struck with the sonoric quality of language more than she is with the pragmatic linking of phonemes to units of meaning; the lyricism, the inherent musicality of language is less threatening than the meaning contained within the words as specific content. Rísia later says, "It would come out easier in English; places and the names of houses and people *sound more resonant in English,* just like in the movies."[23]

Rísia indicates that her interest in English as a form of communication or noncommunication has not just appeared, but rather it has progressed from earlier difficulties. In one passage the protagonist directly links stammering, a condition in which it is difficult to get words out, with her childhood and family experience. She says that she began to stammer after a confrontation between her mother and her father's lover, and then again when her mother tells the family about his affair with their aunt Ilsa.[24] Her inability to respond verbally to these family crises is tolerated, and perhaps encouraged, in the family system. In order for the family to remain intact, despite the inescapable presence of infidelity—a highly charged symbol of the family's emotional and physical deprivation as well as a dilemma in its own right—there is no room for multiple voices. Rather, the family voice has to represent the entire family ego, for all intents and purposes stripping away the boundaries between members. Murray Bowen's term "undifferentiated family ego mass" captures the contradictory sense of claustrophobia and comfort engendered by the family situation: as a child Rísia is stifled, yet assured of relative safety if she doesn't break the family rules.[25] A lifetime of keeping her thoughts and feelings inside has perfected her ability to avoid telling what she knows. Rísia states, "Now I don't stammer any longer, now I just get completely dumb or I talk directly in a foreign language. Or I leave straight away. But not being able to talk, being a stammerer, is a real incision, it's the very sign of a rupture, it's the greatest fright of all. Being a stammerer, then, made me shut up a lot. I became truly dumb." Although the protagonist obviously feels isolated and alienated in her home, her behavior is helping maintain the family system. Her silence and self-criticism around that silence (she explains, "every stammering individual is also a feeble spindleshanks") perpetuate her role in the family.[26]

A question central to this study is whether and how Rísia might be able to transcend the emotional pain and emptiness that characterize her home life and reflect her family role. Rísia is a silent witness and a scapegoat whenever necessary and, until she leaves for Tijucopapo and narrates this story, she can't even begin to break free. She needs both an impetus to leave and the hope that such a leaving might effect some change in her own life, if not in her family of origin. When her husband Jonas dies, it is the last straw; this last abandonment, after so much neglect and abandonment as a child, leaves her totally speechless and unable to function. Rísia yearns for her freedom, saying, "I'm here because I could no longer use the telephone. Because I couldn't talk any more. Because mine is a case of the loss of love. I was, once and for all, shattered into pieces."[27] Her rupture from the boundaries set by the family rules ironically deprives her of a sense of refuge, even though she reverts to the same behavior that was sanctioned inside the family system. The involuntary muteness she experiences is made all the more excruciating because she is psychologically in pieces, in contrast to her earlier experience of solidarity through speechlessness within the undifferentiated family ego mass. Her silence may sound the same (in its nonentity) to an outsider, but for her, it is a newly unregulated and therefore terrifying territory. She is a lost and lonely fragment, an unformed thought, an incomplete sentence.

Rísia's concept of communication reflects her confusion about trust, truth, and belief. She says that in her letter "maybe in English," she wants to recount something pure, "a life without betrayals. So that people won't believe it. I like to see people disbelieving what I alone believe in."[28] While she is criticizing a society in which all purity is automatically disbelieved, she is indirectly saying that this is also her belief system. Whereas she wants desperately to differentiate herself from this untrusting and untrustworthy society, it is next to impossible. She has learned that she can't speak the truth, so she must lie or evade the truth, and therefore even her speaking of the truth will be received as a lie. The inherent contradictions in her assumptions reflect the rationalizations of a double bind, a systemic dynamic present in her family. Bateson, et.al., describe the double bind as the perception of consistently conveyed contradictory messages, from persons believed to be crucial to the listener's survival, accompanied by the injunction not to question or escape the messages' contradictions. The result of chronic double-binding is that the "victim" will at some point cease to distinguish between the logical levels of the messages, will lose the ability to correctly interpret even clear messages from outside sources, and will in fact resort to radical "solutions" to the confusion and stress such as hallucinations and catatonia.[29] Rísia's family system has trained her by example to lie and to distrust every utterance, implicitly promising her love and safety in return. Telling the truth about her feelings or perceptions would shatter the system and any semblance of protection, and therefore is not a viable option. Paradoxically, the consequences of deceit and distrust include neglect and abuse, and one might imagine direct punishment in some cases. Despite the risk of punishment, the family rules of conduct will include an obligatory adherence to the avoidance of truth.

In her narration as well as in her life, Rísia relies on many techniques to distance and protect herself, often sabotaging communication by putting forth false or contradictory information. The concept of lying emerges more fully in chapter 5. Rísia says, "In São Paulo it was very difficult and so, among other things, I used to lie. I got to the point of actually lying. I would lie without rhyme or reason. I lied out of pure pleasure. I would say that I'd gone to the movies yesterday even though I hadn't, if I wanted to. Among other things, too, everything frightened me more than it should have done. I wish to God I could confess my anguish. Not knowing how was an anguish."[30] This passage is significant in that its slightly varied repetition actually expresses the anguish that Rísia says she feels, and at the same time it mirrors the babbling she says she does. The irony lies in that her steady stream of words implies communication, and this passage does effectively communicate a sense of her anguish, but the basis for the very discussion is false communication, or lies. In another section she says, "What I am is just a big liar. Once, at the end of a day, I threw myself onto my bed and said to myself: 'Well, today was a day full of big lies, wouldn't you agree?'"[31]

The narrator continues to emphasize her untruthful nature throughout the text, yet she often includes justifications or explanations for her need to avoid the truth. For instance, she says, "I lied frequently. At times I lied a lot. That was something else. But my lies are states of dreaming. Dreaming I always dreamed."[32] Whether Rísia is speaking metaphorically or simply, clearly or confusedly, she seems to remain conscious of certain cultural and family rules that one must follow in terms of language. What Rísia has learned about communication is that there are things one may and may not say, just as there are things one should say in certain circumstances. Prescribed communication includes the formal niceties that one must observe, saying the right thing rather than telling the truth. For instance, when people inquire how she is, she replies, "'As well as can be expected,' I used to reckon the reply should be."[33] By the same token, particularly in matters affecting family, she believes that all truths that might be painful should be hidden, by her and by others. In thinking back on her childhood, Rísia chides her mother, "And why (why didn't you just shut your mouth, mama?) why do I need to know that you were betrayed right at home by auntie?"[34]

Rísia's confusion around truth and reality manifests in a series of contradictory messages (again, reminiscent of the double-bind), like "I cried like never before. I cried like never before many times."[35] "People, boy, are hellfire. From the deepest pits of hell. People shatter me, that's all I know. But I love people." "I'm dying but not dying. . . . So be it—I'm dying but not quite dead."[36] "I don't know how to start things. I only know how to end things. But it's very difficult to get to the end, too. . . . It would be easy if I weren't exactly in the middle."[37] The dichotomies, mind changes, and subtle rephrasing mean that the text exists in a particularly ambiguous space. The narrator isn't sure of her own beliefs or experience, and thus she often corrects or contradicts herself. Yet despite the fact that Rísia says outright that she is confused and unsure of herself, this perplexity seems to be so ingrained that she isn't always aware that she is contradicting herself. Even more than that, the way she describes reality suggests that her worldview includes an inability to express what she does see or feel. She does not feel very competent to communicate, and at times appeals to the reader for help. "I don't know if that leads . . . (leads?) Is 'leads' what I want to say? 'Leads to somewhere?' But who cares?"[38]

As noted by Kimberle Schumock López, the novel "has no center, structured beginning, nor narrative closure. Marilene rejects linear narrative, relying instead on fragmentation, repetition and flashback to portray a more complex and organic creative consciousness."[39] In general terms, the text is a pastiche of images from different periods of Rísia's life and her emotional reactions to and philosophical ruminations about the remembered events. Although the temporal shifts are fairly easy to follow, the narrator employs another temporal and linguistic game that is considerably more difficult to penetrate. In speaking of Jonas's death, Rísia says, "When you died I'm going to write an elegy. If I believe it I can't get up. When you died I'm going to look, in all my old photographs, for my smiles. Will I never laugh again? When you died I weep my salt tears."[40] The switching of verb tenses within the same sentence, a technique that is repeated over and over, provides an intense challenge to the reader's perception of time and perspective. Rísia moves in and out of the present, past, and future in a nonsensical and contradictory juxtaposition of speculations. While this allows the patient reader a glance at the confusion accompanying the grief process, one should not assume that this is the only contributing factor in the narrative time play. Rísia is grieving, but she also is communicating with herself and others in the way she knows. In essence, she perceives as too risky any straightforward access to memory or history, and her experience of the present and the future time frames is equally fragmentary and perplexing. In Rísia's words, "Time. Time. Time. It's time itself that I can't stand. I can't bear time. Time is just one of two things: either it doesn't pass, or it passes by too fast. Will you make me a timetable, a frame, a clock, an alarm so I can move inside time? Because I'm not going to stand a time that's all fragmented, massive, monstrous, fearful, death."[41] Ironically, in the text, the narrator creates the exact vision of time that frightens and bothers her the most. Is this done in order to express her distress, or because she can't help but communicate in this way? The only thing that is clear beyond a doubt is that her altered and uncertain sense of time further underlines the disjointedness of her story.

Rísia's relationship with language and communication is often shown to be painful and difficult; perhaps it is for this reason that she chooses communication media that allow an avoidance of face-to-face contact. Two of these media that have an enormous impact on the novel are the letter and the telephone, which by virtue of their distance lend a feeling of safety to the interactions. In particular, the epistolary form—a private and uninterrupted narrative directed to one person—may seem to offer new hope of Rísia's being heard by her family. From the very first, Rísia's narrative is a dress rehearsal for a letter to her mother: a letter that should be written in English to provide even more distance (and safety) between herself and the recipient. The letter will tell her mother good-bye and remind her why it is necessary for Rísia to leave, to go back to Tijucopapo. It is a letter with harsh and blaming words, with wistful and melancholy words, and with words that are as difficult to hear as they are to say. It will stir up feelings and cause a rift, or at least put words to the rift that has been growing between Rísia and her family even as the ties that bind them together grow and stretch, trying to hold her in the system. It is a letter like a knife, with which she hopes to slice through the lies and the hidden truths and the silence. It is a letter that pounds again and again with its monotonous and repetitious prose to break up the static and solid mass of dysfunction. It is without a doubt a trouble-making letter. At the same time, it is by no means a direct or straightforward approach to establish communication with her family. Rather, Rísia wishes to talk to her family without having to listen to them, a mirror image of what she's learned all her life. It is likely that she is tired of listening, after being silent all of her life, and it is equally probable that she doesn't have any faith in her actual ability to speak in a face-to-face situation.

Speaking (especially to family) is equated with pain, as when Rísia and her mother meet her father's other woman, and her mother begins to call Analice names. She opens her mouth and lets loose with a torrent of words, "You shameless hussy, you whore, you tart, you devil . . . And mama had an attack and fell half-fainting at my side."[42] The fact that her mother has an attack directly after speaking the truth, after expressing her pain and anger, makes clear the reason that people in this family don't communicate. It is physically painful. Indeed, Rísia's family background has prepared her for a life of silence and isolation. When she explains why she left São Paulo for Tijucopapo she says, "I left because I almost lose my speech in the big city. Because my house, on Sundays, was completely crazy. It was a day of silence. Everyone would be at home, on their day off. And it was exactly the day on which dumbness was intensified. On Sundays, the people in my house never spoke to each other. Completely crazy."[43] Later she returns to this issue, saying, "I left home because on Sunday days people would glance at each other trying to guess what it was that they didn't want to say out loud."[44] While Rísia can perceive the insanity of a family that doesn't communicate, she is helpless to initiate any changes.

Rísia also is torn by her own need to speak, her fear of speaking, the pain of speaking, and the sense of frustration and futility that sometimes accompanies communication. She acknowledges that she talks all the time, saying, "I'm such a prattler, I rattle on with God and the devil himself about me myself."[45] Nevertheless, this is incredibly hard for her, the incessant and almost incoherent chatter, and she laments, "Oh, if I only had it in me not to talk about anything. I wish I could shut up for days at a time. Oh, if I were at least able to talk in a foreign language. Oh, if only I could only grunt. Oh, if I could only be an animal."[46] As the narrator goes on to fantasize about being a whinnying mare who would forget her pain and loss, she speaks of the physical energy that manifests to communicate the animal's feelings. Rísia is searching for a new mode of communication that will better serve her in her attempts to speak to and about her family. In a way she is trying to forge a new family discourse out of the silence, grunts, foreign language, lies, confusion, whinnies, and bursts of movement that she has experienced or can imagine.

Her journey to Tijucopapo is more than anything else a journey toward a new "family" language, an exploration of the words and images that are spinning around in her head. She desperately needs to learn who she is and where she belongs, and she can't do this without figuring out how to ask the right questions and tell herself the right answers. She must break away from the strictures that her family system has imposed, and the first element that must change is language, so that she may speak her truth and challenge the rules that have kept her miserable and compliant despite her wish to rebel. The new family discourse would include grunts and whinnies; it would be a language that escapes the simplistic equation of "words = communication." Communication would be more guttural and instinctive, and at the same time it would be easier and richer. Yet even now, on her way toward a new language and a new family history, she can't get her words out. She says, "I'm going to introduce people to the women of . . . , before I lose the track. Before I lose the track: the women of. Colored in red in many shades. I will."[47] Trying to create a new manner of expression is a project that still eludes her, as she says, "I traveled five hundred thousand miles trying to be the mare, which I'm still trying to be and still, right till now, not succeeding at."[48]

CHANGE: IMAGINING AN ALTERNATIVE FAMILY DISCOURSE

In the latter part of the narrative, it becomes obvious that Rísia has been moving away from her original family system for some time. She has gained an awareness of her own patterns and the dysfunction in her family, and she has begun to make friends with whom she can speak, tell the truth, and receive the emotional sustenance that was never available in her family. She says, "I had friends like water—clear and available for me to drink from."[49] They give her strength and support through their words, a discourse full of poetry and love. In the emotional drought of her life she thirstily immerses herself in their waters until she realizes that she must find her own words. This is made clear to her when she finds herself unable to call them, stuck in São Paulo without speech, "I could never again telephone my friends. It's months since I had so much as a conversation. When I had to choose my way of being, I opted for the one I knew best, the way of running away."[50]

Rísia realizes that she has been marked by her family system, and she is looking for a catharsis in Tijucopapo that will allow her to understand her memories and go on with her life. But even on Rísia's trip to Tijucopapo, she is stuck in a cycle of self-doubt and self-loathing. When she talks about her experiences and what effect they have had in her life, she often discounts the necessity and validity of the narration. For instance, when she talks about her difficulties with communication, specifically about her stammering, she then shrugs it off as something she shouldn't even address. She says:

> But I feel that I need to leave off talking nonsense, because getting stuck in remembering my stammering is nonsense and vile. Leaving off such nonsense, then, since every stammering individual is also a feeble spindleshanks, and I can't stand such weaklings like that, so leaving off all the nonsense, I shall speak, Nema, about what Sundays are like in São Paulo.[51]

In this manner Rísia momentarily tries to turn the narrative to a more acceptable topic, Sundays in São Paulo. This is consistent with the pattern of communication she learned as a child—one may not speak of the hidden truths, but rather one should focus conversation on social pleasantries. The fact that she simply can't continue with this topic, but gets sidetracked talking about the man she lost and the neighborhood bullies from childhood, shows that she is breaking away somewhat from the imposed silence and prescribed acceptable conversation. She has begun to fight the family and social system, even though she is still beset by the self-doubt and self-hatred she learned as a child.

Rísia is fleeing from the family and society that she knows, looking for a substitution in the women of Tijucopapo. Her understanding of them is a mixture of Brazilian myth and family legend, and it is implied that she believes that her mother was once one of the strong and rebellious women of Tijucopapo. She describes them in the following manner:

> Where these women came from, my heritage, women made of the substance of *tijuco*, thick-haired, dragging on their horses' manes,

straddling the beasts bareback, amazons. . . . The only thing that's known is that love makes them suffer.[52]

Rísia's fantasy that her mother was formerly one of the women of Tijucopapo is highly unlikely in reality, but it does afford her a degree of hope; if she is descended from a community of strong fighting women, then perhaps she can return to this identity and family. This is a complicated idealization, because these women also "suffered for love," as did Rísia's mother. Two key questions that emerge are why one suffers for love, and what it means about one's character. If Rísia perceives her mother as weak, and the Amazons as strong, then what is the relationship of suffering to weakness or strength? Is the question less about character or fortitude than about gender, since Rísia definitely does not mention her father or male lovers being in anguish? Does the narrator imply that she believes (as do many) that heartache is the bane and privilege of the feminine existence? Conceivably, then, the Amazons' harnessing of their suffering in service to their own ideals and objectives is the necessary lesson for the protagonist. In a manner of speaking Rísia is indeed attempting to rescue herself and all women from her mother's weakness (rather than from suffering), as suggested above by Cavendish Wanderly. She is actively searching for a new paradigm of how one may react to the inevitable injustices that accompany the unequal division of power in the contemporary family system.

A revolutionary language with the power to change life has to be believable, both for her and for her reader. As Rísia moves into the meat of the narrative, revealing more details of what she has been through, she protests that, "And this is not just another story. This is not all the fucking shit of just another story."[53] Nonetheless, in the narrator's attempt to imagine a new family and family discourse, she questions her own abilities to truly embrace a new way of thinking and talking. She worries that she would be an inadequate mother, for one because of her wish to compel her imagined son to be an engineer so that he would have control and not have to cry or be "a pansy." Then, in a brilliant moment of self-awareness, she decides that she would not follow the ingrained patterns of authoritative control and verbal abuse. She says that if she shouts at him, then she'll "cry and beg him to forgive me because I'm a bit crazy. And I'll own up to the mud I'm made of. And I'll tell him about Tijucopapo. And I'll contradict everything. I'll say that my way of conceiving things can't exist; nobody *is* an engineer. Nobody *is* anything. . . . The verb *to be* is something or other, some essence that doesn't go with the word *engineer*."[54] As Rísia forges a new discourse, she imbues it with the sense of contradiction and ambiguity that she knows to be inherent in language, as well as in families, where one can love and hate at the same time. At the same time, she makes it explicit, raw, and personal. She says that she would admit to her son who she is, where she is from, and what her limitations are. She would expose her own lies even as she made clear the intrinsic instability of words. She would question everything, like the necessity of men being strong and logical and in control, allowing him to question it all as well. She would even attack the structure of language, point out its weakness and inability to convey the true meaning of concepts or ideas.[55]

TIJUCOPAPO: IN CONCLUSION

The beginning of Rísia's catharsis, toward the end of the novel, coincides with the possible onset of sunstroke. She has almost arrived at Recife, when she says, "I'm sunstruck and labyrinthine. It's because I'm close to Recife and Recife muddles everything up for me. Recife is always dying from a delirium. From a fever of immeasurable degrees. Recife's delirium definitely doesn't come from peyote. It comes from sunstroke." She is overcome by the feelings and the sounds that surround her, and her language suggests that she is not completely in her mind or body. "When I came to, I was already in Pernambuco territory."[56] "Recife was on fire, hallucinated under its own sun."[57] The reader must determine whether the narrator's dream-like tale of seduction the day she enters Pernambuco is fantasy or not. The sex act that Rísia narrates is both personal and legendary; it is every man she has ever been with and more—one is tempted to question the reliability of the story based on the exaggerated detail alone. Moreover, the incorporation of every element that Rísia has dreamed on her journey is not entirely credible, leaving open the possibility that she is having another of her midday dreams of what she wishes to be true. Some of the narration even sounds like the mumbling of a somnambulist or the simple utterances of a child, a language distanced from self and others: "The man continued. The man and I ate bread. The man and I said good-bye to each other at the stable door. The man gave me a mare as a present."[58]

This passage marks the radical alteration of the novel, which is still narrated by Rísia, but now for the first time incorporates dialogue that is supposedly real rather than created in the narrator's mind as fantasy or projection. Is it realistic to give credence to this turn of events? The quotidian and unaffected quality of the dialogue, despite its fantastic content, makes it easy to slip into believing that it is true. If such is the case, then Rísia is starting a relationship that seems more honest, pure, and communicative than her family dynamic. The man confides in her, breaking her entrenched pattern of silence and alienation, and tells her that they won't lose touch, and that he won't abandon her, which is her greatest fear. Coincidentally, this relationship has occurred because of a chance meeting when Rísia has just decided that she wants to sleep with another man. Yet no matter how much the reader may wish for a happy ending (the happy ending that Rísia has talked about more than once), in the last part of the novel Rísia becomes less and less reliable in her accounts of what happens. Even Rísia doesn't know whether to believe herself, admitting, "I don't know if I believed it. I don't know if I believed that things happened in an interval of fantasies. Was I still suffering from sunstroke?"[59]

The revolution that Rísia had left São Paulo to start is happening here, in Tijucopapo, with "the smell of bombs and weapons exploding in the air," and she wonders "Who had stolen my plan?" She rides on, "scared to death, exposed to all sorts of danger."[60] Of course it's dangerous, this revolution, this destruction of her world, but how much of it has anything to do with literal grenades and gunshots? The revolution is a recreation of the stories she would tell her brothers and sisters when they were small, stories of "playful and fantastic" bandit monkeys [slang for policemen] fighting for justice and good. Now she is floating in a space of fantasy in which her dreams seem to become reality, but a caricature of reality based in her imagination. "So mama," she asks, "my lies aren't just a dream? My fantasies—will they come true one day, then? It's as if everything were taking place in an interval of fantasies and dreams."[61] In the next passage, Rísia falls into an abyss of consciousness, ostensibly because the militia have shot her mare out from under her, yet her mind is filled with the memory of a childhood fall, "the most undignified fall," which happened as she was preparing to wreak revenge upon her sister. Significantly, she remembers feeling "alone and unprotected" as a child, but when she wakes up in Tijucopapo, she is surrounded by "ten women my mothers. Ten faces of women my mothers. I had ten mothers. None of them was any use. I was so weak and unprotected that not even ten mothers would be any use. Nor ten hugs."[62] She drifts in and out of memory and fantasy, cursing her family, lamenting her past, feeling alone, and planning to keep on vomiting and lying to keep everyone away from her.

After this period of delirium, she awakens again to see the Amazonic Tijucopapo women around her bed, and she knows that she has seen them before, "in an illustration in a book, perhaps, back in school, a book with poems on seriemas," and that she has arrived.[63] But now instead of seeing them as women who are like her mother, she says that they are "women warriors. They were women who were not my mother. . . . Women in the defense of a just cause."[64] The people that she finds, the women of Tijucopapo, are both metaphorically and literally her new family as well as her old family. Her mother is from Tijucopapo, but had lost the sense of revolution, strength, and pride of the seventeenth-century Northeastern women who had "used kitchen utensils and basins of hot water to repulse an invading army of Dutch soldiers."[65] The women she finds are therefore of her own history, but have created (or recuperated) a utopian system not at all resembling the alienated and abusive patterns prevalent in contemporary society. After the nine months (and a whole life) of waiting, Rísia has found a community that she hopes can serve as a positive family system for her. They give her role models of strength and courage, self-defense, solidarity, tolerance, and clarity. They touch her tenderly rather than beat her. They come and find her rather than desert her.

Rísia needs to believe that she is really in Tijucopapo, and that Tijucopapo is what will save her from herself. She wants to invent a new family system based on affection, honesty, and communication, but has no experience or language on which to base such a creation. Her solution is to incorporate such legendary figures as the Tijucopapo women and the equally legendary bandit of the Northeast, Lampião.[66] Lampião, the name of the man who seduces her toward the end of her journey, is the universally known nickname of Virgilino Ferreira da Silva, famed for his violent rule of the Brazilian hinterland until his death in 1938.[67] What these historic figures have in common is their courageous nonconformity and determined revolutionary attitude—they provided a consistent and brutal challenge to the social system of Brazil in their day. In this manner they are adequate role models for Rísia, who does wish to produce change on a social level, but their example really doesn't offer her any help in terms of the family restructuring that she is trying to accomplish. First of all, it is never clear whether they are figments of Rísia's imagination or actual characters in the "fictional world" of the novel. However, this point might not be of great importance, since Rísia's inner turmoil finally must be resolved on an internal level. For these purposes, and in the ever-evolving tradition of the "talking cure," Rísia could conceivably make steps toward lifting her communicational barriers in an imagined family system. At first, Lampião seems to be the "perfect hero," because he and Rísia do manage to accomplish genuine verbal exchanges, and on his own accord he promises that they won't lose touch with each other. Given Rísia's history of being abandoned and the distrust that results, Lampião's verbal assurances are balm to her soul, even if she finds them hard to believe; when he speaks she only sees "a mouth moving."[68] His very choice of words might be seen as providing a calm and nonthreatening presence that doesn't overwhelm Rísia with unfamiliar emotionality. On the other hand, even in her fantasy, the women don't speak to her, and she perceives Lampião to be poetic but strangely difficult and bewildering to converse with. What initially promises to be a new system of family and interpersonal interaction becomes a disappointing repetition of the family of origin. The conversation between Rísia and Lampião, full of nonanswers, half-answers, and interruptions, is brutally painful to read.

> "So, we didn't lose touch with each other," the man began, coming closer to the bed.
> "No . . . and I wanted to thank you . . ."
> "How do you feel?" the man began again.
> "Inside some sort of solitude . . ."
> "Solitude speaks louder than anything. Solitude almost doesn't exist. You, for example, are pretty as a lake under the moonlight."
> "And you are a warrior who . . ."
> "Listen, have you seen Tijucopapo yet?" and he stretched his arm in the direction of the window. . . .
> "Do you understand the way I speak?"
> "You are as pretty as a lake under the moonlight . . ."
> "Do you understand the way I speak? Do you know what the word *thing* is?"
> "Solitude is what speaks the loudest. . . . Do you want to go with us down the BR [highway] that brings cars from São Paulo and takes cars to São Paulo? Our target is the Paulista Avenue . . ."[69]

It is as if the narrator is continuing with her monologue, merely being interrupted by an interlocutor who is interested mostly in himself. Rísia lands herself in a familiar dynamic in which the communicative patterns mirror those she learned as a child.

The final twist occurs when Rísia asks Lampião to write her letter to her mother as she dictates it. She is still unable to communicate directly with her family, insisting that, "I wanted some distance separating me from the words I spoke."[70] Despite the changes that Rísia has undergone in her nine-month rebirthing journey, she has not managed to escape the role of a fearful child in her family or achieve a level of comfort with straightforward communication in that setting. Indeed, reflecting upon her last quoted conversation with Lampião, it seems possible that the language skills that she has developed through the long journey's narration still have not prepared her to actually accomplish a basic communicative task with another human being. Not withstanding the lack of direct communication in this new relationship, Rísia is choosing to turn her life over to Lampião: she becomes his lover, she joins his revolution, she wants to have his baby, and she decides to ask him to transcribe her letter as she dictates it. The one element that has set her apart from her family system, the striking out on her own to find her self and tell her story, now suddenly is being sacrificed. She is finally preparing to write the letter to say good-bye to her family as she is entering another system with a similar role.

This is the final irony of *The Women of Tijucopapo*. After spending nine months in a journey to recuperate her voice and explore the terrain of her memory and the emotional baggage of her past, Rísia gives it all up at the end. She releases her narration to Lampião, who doesn't even hear her well in a simple conversation. If one interprets the novel in its entirety as Rísia's letter to her mother, and one believes that he has accepted to do the dictation, then one has to wonder how much of it has been changed by this dynamic. There are no real clues to a scribe having written the letter/novel, unless one assumes that the novel's fragmentation and incoherence are signs of a faulty communication and dictation rather than signs of the protagonist's emotional and psychological state. Nevertheless, one can't completely discount the idea. The story, problematic from the first because it relies completely on one character's perception of reality, now is complicated further by the possible addition of a second filter who was not even present during the events recounted here.

With a legendary conarrator, Rísia's story reaches toward a level of mythology that transcends a personal or individual family history. As such, it is particularly difficult for the reader to accept the complete lack of resolution at the close of the novel. So many elements are left unclear: Rísia's ability to leave her family behind her and define a new way of life and being, the relationship of the narration to the epistle that Rísia wants to write to her mother, and the reality of any or all of the events that are included in the narration. Where one would expect the happy ending that Rísia longs for, a comprehensible ending more in conjunction with a myth, all we are left with is the longing. Undoubtedly echoing the sentiments of the reader, the last words of the novel are, "I want to have a happy ending."[71] In the context of Rísia's story, ending with these words is probably the closest that she can get.

NOTES

1. In an interview with Edmílson Caminha in 1995, Felinto explains that she was overcome with nostalgia and longing when she moved to São Paulo from Recife as a young girl, and this served as a motivation to start writing, particularly scores of letters. The correlation to *The Women of Tijucopapo* is unmistakable. See Caminha, "Marilene Felinto," 186.

2. Cavendish Wanderly, "Quebec/Nordeste." Cavendish Wanderly articulates the novel's repeated references to the Brazilian period of post 1964 dictatorship and the "revolution" of working class people wearied by the censorship, oppression and government control that nevertheless did nothing to alleviate the predominant economic misery suffered throughout the Northeastern region of Brazil. Along with other critics, she also mentions the connections Felinto draws between this uprising and the more historically distant battle in which the real-life heroines of Tijucopapo, an area of Pernambuco, repulsed the Dutch invaders. See also Cavendish Wanderly's "Imagens da Mulher na Ficção Feminina pós-64."

3. Ferreira-Pinto, "Escritura," 82–83.

4. Cavendish Wanderly, "Imagens da Mulher na Ficção Feminina pós-64," 1.

5. Brittin and López, "Body Written," 52. Cavendish Wanderly, "Imagens da Mulher na Ficção Feminina pós-64," 4.

6. "Marilene Morose."

7. Ibid., 1. my translation.

8. Cavendish Wanderly, "Quebec/Nordeste," 4. Cavendish Wanderly, "Imagens da Mulher na Ficção Feminina pós-64," 3.

9. Sáenz de Tejada, "Raza y género en la narrativa femenina afro-brasileña," 280.

10. Sáenz de Tejada, "Representaciones de la negritud brasileña en *Mulher no Espelho y As Mulheres de Tijucopapo*," 46.

11. Sáenz de Tejada, "Raza y género en la narrativa femenina afro-brasileña," 271.

12. Ibid., 282.

13. Cavendish Wanderly, "Imagens da Mulher na Ficção Feminina pós-64," 4.

14. *The Women of Tijucopapo* is problematic as a FST narrative in that the first-person narrator doesn't want to allow the other voices of her family members to come through. "Directly observing" interaction between family members is impossible; because of this, the reader must always take into account the possible motives, agenda, and subjectivity of the character who is narrating. Likewise, the reader is forced to rely on the narrator's recreation of dialogue and speculation about communication that she would like to effect in order to comment upon the communicative patterns. Despite these limitations, the novel's intense focus on the family dysfunction and how this plays out in Rísia's adult life suggest that a family systems paradigm can be a useful tool in the novel's interpretation.

15. Sáenz de Tejada, "Raza y género en la narrativa femenina afro-brasileña," 279.

16. Irene Matthews, Afterword, 126.

17. A fragmentary and coded expression is one of the main indicators of what society has called schizophrenia. See Virginia Satir, *Conjoint Family Therapy*.

18. This is not to say that the text's language doesn't communicate to the reader. On the contrary, it is through an innovative and at times metaphoric use of language that the narrator establishes a strong link to the reader. For instance, the narrator likens her feelings to the rain, "damp and dripping. . . . I overflow myself and get sad. I almost drown under this rainlike feeling. It runs out of my wet hair and clings to my clothes and pastes them onto my body, and leaves me crouching and soaked and trembling on a corner crossway with no shelter" (29). This elaborate and evocative imagery clashes with the often childlike, repetitive, and fragmentary speech of the novel, and at the same time it emphasizes the importance of language for the text.

19. Penna, "Marilene Felinto e a Diferença," 213. Penna starts off his study with a linguistic analysis of a scene from "Horas Abertas," a short story from Felinto's collection entitled *Postcard* (1991). Hc shows how the protagonist, existing in a linguistic space between her native Portuguese and the Czechoslovakian novel she is reading, begins to lose the ability to distinguish the sounds and syllables heard around her as meaningful utterances (213–14).

20. Felinto, *Women of Tijucopapo*, 1.

21. Ibid., 52.

22. Ibid., 53.

23. Ibid., 2; emphasis added.

24. One can also see that there is a connection between her stammering and the family's poverty, because she talks about how poor her family was and how skinny she was. Nevertheless, her thinness also could be attributed to her need for excessive control and her tendency to self-abuse, which could manifest in anorexia nervosa. This is a common response to an abusive and out-of-control environment, and such a severe reaction would further emphasize Rísia's entrenched position within the family system.

25. Bowen, *Family Therapy in Clinical Practice*, 107.

26. Felinto, *Women of Tijucopapo*, 28.

27. Ibid., 47.

28. Ibid., 4.

29. Bateson, et al., "Toward a Theory of Schizophrenia," 251.

30. Felinto, *Women of Tijucopapo*, 13.

31. Ibid., 19.

32. Ibid., 86.

33. Ibid., 19.
34. Ibid., 21.
35. Ibid., 7.
36. Ibid., 25.
37. Ibid., 46.
38. Ibid., 17.
39. Brittin and López, "Body Written," 53.
40. Felinto, *Women of Tijucopapo*, 48.
41. Ibid., 51.
42. Ibid., 26.
43. Ibid., 44.
44. Ibid., 76.
45. Ibid., 52.
46. Ibid., 23.
47. Ibid., 45.
48. Ibid., 23.
49. Ibid., 88.
50. Ibid., 89.
51. Ibid., 28.
52. Ibid., 45.
53. Ibid., 62.
54. Ibid., 72.
55. Ibid., 72–73.
56. Ibid., 94.
57. Ibid., 95.
58. Ibid., 99.
59. Ibid.
60. Ibid., 100.
61. Ibid., 102.
62. Ibid., 109.
63. Ibid., 112.
64. Ibid., 113.
65. Matthews, Afterword, 127.
66. Felinto, *Women of Tijucopapo*, 102.
67. Matthews, Afterword, 121–22.
68. Felinto, *Women of Tijucopapo*, 99.
69. Ibid., 115.
70. Ibid., 116.
71. Ibid., 120.

Family Games and Imbroglio in *Hamlet*

John V. Knapp

> Need I repeat that the theatre critic's professional routine
> so discourages any association between real life and the
> stage, that he soon loses the natural habit of referring to the
> one to explain the other?
> —George Bernard Shaw, "Preface" to *Three Plays for Puritans*

I

Possibly EXCEPTING EITHER OF HOMER'S EPICS, *HAMLET* MAY BE THE
single most discussed work in all of western literature.[1] The
range of critical arguments about the play is astonishing in its
richness and variety, moving from explicitly allegorical readings
(Aguirre) to more "realistic" analyses (Heilbrun) to mythical
readings (Fergusson), with the most influential psychologically
oriented reading of it remaining Ernest Jones's Freudian-based
Hamlet and Oedipus (1949):

> [Hamlet's] long "repressed" desire to take his father's place in his
> mother's affection is stimulated to unconscious activity by the sight
> of someone [Claudius] usurping this place exactly as he himself had
> once longed to do. More, this someone was a member of the same
> family, so that the actual usurpation further resembled the imagi-
> nary one in being incestuous. . . . Hamlet's second guilty wish had
> thus been realized by his uncle, namely to procure the fulfillment of
> the first—the possession of the mother—by a personal deed, . . . by
> murder of the father.[2]

It is interesting to note how this too-familiar explanation,
merely one psychological view of Hamlet and his family, has
come to dominate so many late twentieth-century readings and
productions of the play.[3] The psychoanalytic perspective is so
pervasive that even as fine a reader of Shakespeare as Derek Jacobi is prompted to enact one of the more famous scenes in this

194

most famous work, Gertrude's closet scene, by having his Hamlet actually get on top of the character of the mother in her bed and "hump" her as he delivers his lines.[4] And, as I have argued elsewhere, actors and directors along with contemporary critics have drastically limited their understandings of imaginative literature generally, and Shakespeare's masterpiece in particular, by subscribing merely to a single psychological-clinical system, one now over one hundred years old.[5] In this essay, I will offer an alternative reading by reexamining, from the perspective of Family Systems Psychotherapy (FST),[7] questions of Gertrude's fidelity, the reader's understanding of sibling rivalry between King Hamlet and Claudius, and the triangulated interactions of the Hamlet family as each is clearly illuminated through the lens of a family systems paradigm.[6]

II

One realizes that in the minds of more traditional Renaissance scholars, for whom Freudian readings appear limited, one treads on uncertain ground, critically speaking, when one takes on any new mimetic stance rather than using the more traditional genre analyses, or historical recreations, or textual approaches.[7] Nonetheless, I agree with Bert O. States who believes that

> the business of a text is precisely to leave the page, not to be a text at all but an illusory reality, and an examination of character must inevitably deal with it as being, in one sense, "off the page [and] endowed with possible motives." Strictly speaking, the only way to keep characters *on* the page is to keep readers away from them.[8]

As I have argued elsewhere, criticism devoted to character study has focused much more on *intra*-characterological issues and rather less on the *inter*-personal interactions among them. As such, I will disagree with Harold Bloom's unequivocal "the question of *Hamlet* must *always* be Hamlet himself."[9] Not everyone thinks of Hamlet the way Bloom does. Park Honan, for example, argues for a different emphasis:

> [Shakespeare in writing *Hamlet*] is able to draw on the complicating pressure of Elizabethan domestic life. He appears to write from inside his own experience of a family's bonding, and the pathos arises from his hero's idealization of a prior normality. Shakespeare's parents were both alive when he wrote the play, and involved in its "unri-

valed imaginative power" is his ability to show, from within, the pressure of a family's emotional ties.[10]

In our zeal to look at the major character, Hamlet, we often forget that Hamlet is only one character construct, albeit the most important, aesthetically speaking, among several in the play. One could argue that Hamlet can't be well understood unless one *also* looks closely at Hamlet's human environment and intimate relationships within the play. Using family systems-oriented criticism, the critic now moves from focusing on a character's *intra*-psychic conflicts to a *systems* approach where the observer, at least temporarily, takes a "multipositional" view of the family in question, whether real or fictional. The family therapist Luigi Boscolo says: "all parts of a given system must, if the system is seen *systemically*, be given equal weight. . . . 'Neutral like Switzerland?' say outraged social activists [equating] neutrality with condoning atrocities. Actually, [we mean] multi-positional [rather] than non-positional. . . . Neutrality [is] . . . the effort to avoid *induction* by the family system."[11]

Of course, as literary humanists and critics, we cannot avoid ultimate moral judgments, but doing so wisely also requires us to avoid "induction" into any fictional family system. We remain skeptical of any given character's dominating claims on the "truth" of family life. Quick aside: the systems-alert reader speedily notices from this multipositional stance how much of what we know of Claudius comes out of the mouths of his bitterest foes and how seldom critics have ever seen fit to reexamine him within the total familial context.[12]

Hence, adapting our "neutral" FST stance, we examine all of the major characters as mimetic elements in a family system first, and *then* reassess the validity of what we think we know about them. Although generations of critics may have been unwittingly "inducted" into the Hamlet family system, we cannot understand Claudius, nor his family, nor Shakespeare's genius without looking closely at one of the Bard's least admired characters—and looking in from outside the existing family imbroglio.[13]

In this essay, I intend to consider some issues hitherto little discussed by critics of *Hamlet*—not as a means of demonstrating the "real truth" about the play—but as a complement to the extensive, elaborated, and at times excellent criticism already written about it. In the full light of the FST explanation, I intend to argue for a somewhat different view of *Hamlet* using a mixture of the recent insights afforded by the tools of FST and neo-Darwinian family studies;[14] I will also frankly speculate about issues for which there is less concrete textual evidence but more circumstantial and potential corroboration of the theoretical matters shaped by the critical tools of FST.[15]

III

For those with some basic understanding of family systems, I will begin my discussion of *Hamlet* by asking a number of questions about character motivation that are grounded directly in the text itself and then coordinate the FST psychological model with evidence from the play. Early in the play, Gertrude asks Hamlet a question that is either craftily disingenuous or breathtaking in its insensitivity:

> *Gert*: Thou know'st 'tis common, all that lives must die,
> Passing through nature to eternity.
> *Hamlet*: Ay, Madam, it is common.
> *Gert*: If it be,Why seems it so particular with thee?
>
> (I.ii.68–86)

Is this a *real* question in part of an ordinary conversational transaction? What is Gertrude meta-communicating to her son here? She knows full well his grief that answers *why* he seeks, metaphorically, "for [his] noble father in the dust," and says as much when a bit later Claudius asks her what is wrong with her son; Gertrude is aware, as Hamlet's mother, that his grieving process has been interrupted by her "o'er-hasty marriage" (II.ii.57) to his father's competitive brother.

Has she asked this kind of question before? By implication, she suggests that Hamlet's grieving is making her uncomfortable, and intimates that he should put aside his overwhelming sorrow in order to make *her* happy (cf. Culpeper, 248). Granting her sensitivity to his depression a bit later in the play (II.ii.56–57), some have argued that this is her way of assuaging or denying the possible guilt she feels over denying her own son his rightful place on the throne. As the feminist psychoanalytic critic, Lisa Jardine, points out, she "connive[s] in wronging her own blood-son (even if passively), . . . so that his filial duty towards his mother is now at odds with his obligations towards his father and himself (the legitimate line)." Jardine continues: "in so far as Gertrude is supposed to have behaved monstrously and unnaturally toward her first husband *and* her son, her guilt—in direct contrast to Claudius's—is culturally constructed so as to represent her as responsible without allowing her agency."[16] Jardine uses this view later to argue from a feminist perspective about the unfairness of pushing guilt on someone who has little or no agency with which to act. But, as I will argue shortly, this view of Gertrude is as one-sided as the earlier male assumptions about her being merely a weak vessel with no substantiality of her own.[17]

Her behavior ("o'er-hasty marriage") surprised Hamlet, his father, and many viewers inducted into their family belief system. Given Gertrude's oddly coldhearted question, one might usefully speculate about *her* grief or lack thereof, and hence about their family relationship *before* the king died. Some critics would argue that this type of question is no more capable of an answer than the famous one about the number of Lady Mac-Beth's children. I disagree. If for a moment we view the play through a lens that Northrop Frye might have called "low mimetic" and thus outside the more familiar sphere of Frye's Romance or high tragedy, we could argue that the question above would be more than appropriate had we explicit textual evidence.[18] Absent such direct evidence, one could still profitably speculate about such matters if one had tools such as FST and Sulloway's birth order effects research with which to pursue this line of inquiry.[19]

Thus, an FST-oriented reader might ask several questions about the Hamlet family's experience, before and after the king's death, and their family patterns of habitual response. For example, given her imperceptive question, why does the Queen want Hamlet to remain in Denmark and not return to Wittenberg (I.ii.118–19), especially since she is so sexually enchanted with Claudius? Would Hamlet's presence help or hinder her obviously erotic fascination with her new spouse? One could argue that, since it is obvious that she deeply loves her son (II.ii.168), she may still feel guilt over her son's loss of a father; perhaps irrationally, she hopes that Claudius could take on the role of father to him, as later in the play she scolds him: "Hamlet, thou has thy *father* much offended" (II.iv.8).

Does Gertrude merely want to reconstitute her family with a new spouse for herself and a new father for her son, thus placing herself, instead of old King Hamlet, at the forefront of her son's attention? In *Family Games: General Models of Psychotic Processes in the Family* (1989), Mara Selvini Palazzoli, et al. say that "*only* if 'an embroiled' relational organization has already taken over *before* the death of one of the parents," the surviving parent may easily behave in such a way as to provoke competitive strife . . . between the offspring and some member(s) of the extended family."[20] The authors call such an imbroglio set up by the surviving spouse a "war of succession."[21] It is often the "persistently suspended judgment on the part of the widowed parent on the matter of who was [emotionally] to succeed to the deceased" that set the scene for this undeclared war. Asking Hamlet to remain in Denmark, to the discomfort of both son and new spouse, makes Gertrude "the principle initiator of a series of confusing moves that tend to keep . . . her at the center of . . . her [child's] interest and concern."[22] Thus, simultaneously, Gertrude has obtained a new lover and aims for the primary focus of attention from her son. As Steven Ozment observes, not seeing the possibility that Gertrude is an active player constructing her own new life is an attitude that "sells contemporary women short when they are viewed as merely victims over centuries, and [ignores] the gains that always accompany losses in changing societies."[23]

Hamlet, of course, is having none of her fantasized exchange of fathers and so answers with what is to her a somewhat cryptic "Mother, you have *my* father much offended" (II.iv.9). Gertrude is not the first parent who wants her offspring's approval for a new marriage; thus, her earlier question (I.ii.68) appears less solicitous about her son's grief and more concerned with expunging the conflict she *feels* between Hamlet's grief and her own enchantment with her new husband. So, we ask the same question Hamlet asks? Why? Why would his loving mother betray, in Hamlet's eyes, his sorely missed father? What kind of a wife is she? What we know of the king's and queen's marriage comes almost exclusively from either King Hamlet or from Hamlet's own observations. Suppose that one hypothesizes that the family triangle may have begun long before the king's murder. The fact of Gertrude's "o'er hasty marriage" coupled with Hamlet's observation that the king loved his wife so much "That he might not beteem the winds of heaven / Visit her face too roughly" (I.ii.141–42) suggests that neither the son, nor the king, may have been fully aware of the familial tensions within the marriage chamber. Something *was* definitely rotten in the state of Denmark, and only after the king's death did that something become publically apparent. Although Hamlet agonizingly recalls that his father was devoted to her ("might not beteem," etc.) and then screams, "must I remember?" such spousal devotion may not have been reciprocated in quite the same way, a "fact" that Hamlet may (or may not) have known but could not, in any event, readily assimilate into his own thinking where he powerfully felt love for both parents.

Indeed, the youthful Hamlet, whom one might consider the male equivalent of being "green and in his salad days," is convinced that his mature mother cannot possibly still be interested in sex, since "at [her] age / The heyday in the blood is tame" (III.iv. 68–70).[24] He then turns his hatred upon Claudius, the "odd man out" in the triangle because Hamlet cannot accept the possibly differential love his parents bore for each other since both apparently still loved him. One is reminded, poignantly, of Shakespeare's idealized version of family love in sonnet 8 as the poet uses musical imagery to urge a single young man to marry:

> Mark how one string, sweet husband to another
> Strikes each in each by mutual ordering;
> Resembling sire, and child, and happy mother,
> Who all in one, one pleasing note do sing.[25]

If the Hamlet family didn't sing together in happy familial chorus, one could then speculate about the marital context Shakespeare might have imagined prior to the old king's death: was Gertrude no longer in love with King Hamlet and hence felt, upon his death, little of the loyalty due a husband from his wife (although King Hamlet still remained committed to her)? In discussing Gertrude's center of loyalty, both before King Hamlet's death and after, some critics have used Patrick Cruttwell's idea of a divided self. He argues that "Civil war—War inside the individual—is a favourite image, one that Shakespeare carries with him from the Sonnets themselves . . . to the plays which he wrote around the turn of the century, the plays which emerged from the crisis.[26]

Thus, one may note several examples of Gertrude's wifely conflicted and seemingly contradictory behavior during the play:

(A) she agrees with Hamlet not to tell Claudius of his plan (III.iv.181–96) during the closet scene and thus demonstrates, at first, loyalty to her son instead of to her new husband; she simply lies to Claudius immediately after the scene, telling him that Hamlet is as "mad as the sea and the wind when both contend / Which is the mightier." (IV.i.7)

(B) however, a little later, she defends Claudius against Laertes several times (IV.v.109–10, 122, 125), thus indicating an apparent ongoing, albeit contradictory, loyalty to Claudius.[27]

(C) both parents seem to love their son, yet, as I shall argue below, each is willing to use him to get what each wants—even at the cost of Hamlet's peace of mind.

To a critic using a family systems perspective, such spousal behavior would appear unlikely had the primary bonds among the original family not been conflicted before King Hamlet's death. Perhaps a pattern of triangulation (father and son allied against mother) may have been established earlier and, as with most families, one could assume that Gertrude was well aware of that male-oriented coalition. Resenting that the strongest familial bond existed between her husband and her son and that the king's connection to her was at once erotic yet more emotionally distant, she may wish to negotiate a new coalition, but this time with young Hamlet on *her* side vis-à-vis Claudius, instead of herself remaining the odd person out.

According to Hamlet, his parents' married life was charged with passion as he says of the king that she

> should hang on him
> As if increase of appetite had grown
> By what it fed on, and yet, within a month—
> Let me not think on't! Frailty, thy name is woman! (I.ii.143–46)

King Hamlet's own memory of the marriage was quite different from his son's. The king focused upon those qualities Gertrude gained in *social status* from having married him, as he says his "love was of that dignity / That it went hand in hand even with the vow / I made to her in marriage (I.v.48–49). Their marriage appeared to be based, at least according to old King Hamlet, on the vertical distance between spouses, almost as if Gertrude were his daughter, and the traditional verities of rank, rather than on young Hamlet's belief in their mutual passion. But is this spouse's view complete? Is old Hamlet, like Lear, confusing his royal status with emotional reciprocity?

The family historican, Ilana Ben-Amos, reminds us that although previous scholarship has assumed relationships between parent and *child* were governed by "strong norms . . . in early modern England," familiarly articulated "in terms of duties to rank, position in the family hierarchy, and to God," such characterizations of family life are not exhaustive. Indeed, "the force and implications of reciprocal exchange in family life have not been [hitherto] wholly recognized nor fully integrated into the [historical] literature."[28] Ben-Amos argues, through evidence from diaries, wills, and proceedings from the Old Bailey that family interactions during the early modern period were governed as much if not more so on "reciprocal exchange" and negotiated relationships.[29]

Early modern English writers recalling their childhoods and adolescence "perceived the help they offered to their parents not as a part of a divine scheme but as something the parents had earned or forfeited with their actions, behavior, and attitude."[30] In some cases, "parental death and the remarriage of a widowed parent caused friction and overt resentment." Indeed, "life histories resonate with allusion to family misfortune . . . [and one can find references to] aggression and ingratitude in a son whose father died and whose vengence was directed at his mother."[31] If assumptions of reciprocity between parent and child obtain, and among members of kin networks,[32] why not also between spouses? In sum, one can reasonably infer that King Hamlet's and his son's views of their previous family life were each based on rather different assumptions of an intimate home.

So whom do we believe regarding any characterization of the old Hamlet marriage: the son, whose love for both has made any belief incomprehensible that each did not love the other as strongly and as totally as he loved both his parents?; or the king, whose direct characterization of love for his wife appears more political and social than passionate—as suggested by their near-adult child? Or, should we believe Gertrude who, as they say, voted with her feet, marrying her brother-in-law just a few short weeks after the death of her first husband? Was King Hamlet a bit too formal and too much the warrior for his "seemingly virtuous Queen"?

If we see Gertrude as a strong woman unafraid to address her own interests, one might question how patiently Gertrude, the mimetic character, might have remained during all of those times in which the king was off challenging other kings of the world. According to the gravedigger, he defeated old Fortinbras, and was thereby gone, on the very day she gave birth to baby Hamlet (V.i.140–43). Had King Hamlet been more like an Othello, a warrior, and not recognized earlier her attraction to Claudius? Was the apparent ongoing rivalry between brothers before the murder, a rivalry ending with a parricide, anything she could have anticipated much less known about in her attraction to her husband's brother? Whatever answers have been suggested for these questions, it is clear that speculation about the genesis of the Gertrude/Claudius match is mimetically appropriate even absent detailed textual evidence. Reasoning about such matters requires an inferential logic that, coupled with subtle textual analysis of what *is* in the text, may ultimately prove productive.

To sum up Gertrude: we can infer that she felt strong enough emotions for Claudius to marry him a few short weeks ("not so much . . . two months . . . within a month . . . a little month" [I.ii.138–47]) after King Hamlet's death. She may not have known directly that Claudius killed King Hamlet but when her son plants the seeds of discord in her ear, she becomes torn in her loyalties. To believe Hamlet means giving up the romance she has just so recently found. To believe Claudius means ignoring or at least denying the wishes of the son she loves and knows so well. To do nothing results in the kind of vascilating decision-making that we see between III.iv.181 and IV.v.109. One could thus argue that her decision to drink the goblet at the end of act V was a conscious choice; perhaps at that moment, she realizes the stalemate she has tried mightily to deny for two acts: the existential impossibility of the split life she has had to lead since the closet scene. Hence, Gertrude finds in the moment that she can her "own quietus make," not with a bare bodkin but with a flagon of wine: "I will [drink], my Lord, I pray you pardon me" (V.ii.291).[33] In this sense, one tragic loss in *Hamlet* is the tragedy of Gertrude's irreconcilable familial loves and divided loyalties.

In systems analysis, one should not merely focus on one character's behavior without also examining those surrounding him/ her. Understanding characterological patterns proceeds by detailing the response and counterresponse found in every marriage. Thus, in order to help answer questions about Gertrude, we also need to understand what we know about her first husband, King Hamlet's personality. Clearly he is an "alpha male," confident enough in his own fighting abilities to wager everything, including his whole kingdom, against old Fortinbras (I.i.80–95).[34] As an older brother, his competition with his younger sibling, Claudius, was surely nothing new. Carolyn Heilbrun, citing Charlton Lewis's analysis of the Belleforest ur-plot, reminds us that Gertrude (using her current name) "was daughter of a King; to become King, it was necessary to marry her. The elder Hamlet, in marrying Gertrude, ousted Claudius from the throne. Shakespeare retained the shell of this in his play."[35] Thus, the intense rivalry between first and second-born sons over Gertrude could be said to have begun well before the opening of the play in front of us. As Frank Sulloway points out in his discussion of birth order effects: Firstborns, in spite of their veneer of self-confidence, were

> intense, anxious, on the defensive, and concerned about status. . . .
> First born boys . . . assert dominance in aggressive and punitive
> ways. . . . What is consistent about birth order is the *general gist of
> strategies*, not the specific behaviors employed to achieve these
> ends. . . . Social organisms seek access to valued resources in two
> basic ways—*domination* and *cooperation*. Status-enhancing behavior is a first born tendency . . . also a *male* tendency. Cooperation is
> a secondborn tendency, and . . . also a *female* tendency.[36]

Hence, from the vantage point of this neo-Darwinian family systemic perspective, we note the differences in old Hamlet's and Claudius's personalities *emerge* though their life-long competition for a family niche, the place from which to curry parental favor and later, as adults, to secure their own dominant position. Park Honan—speaking of *Julius Caesar* but applicable here—suggests that one could see the brothers' contrastive personalities as deliberate, a radical difference in characterization for Shakespeare: "the poet's intuitive method [is his] . . . inventing for each of his heroes a psychology allowing for subtle variations from the norm. For that he had no literary source."[37] In short, despite the absence of explicit textual evidence, one could reasonably infer that, since the brothers' rivalry was nothing new, both wife Gertrude and son Hamlet are merely the latest players to be inducted into the original "Brothers Elsinore" imbroglio. Apparently joining the family pattern, Gertrude has now allied herself with Claudius and is, in effect, using her son to complete her own happiness by asking him to changes teams in midgame, a switch he both bitterly resents and angrily refuses.

Of course, King Hamlet is equally guilty of using his son, but not for his own happiness; rather, he looks to Hamlet to avenge his anger at his brother, especially in the context of his former queen's suspected complicity in his murder. Thus, an important argument now takes the following shape: young Hamlet is the unwitting point in what is quite familiar to family therapists, a family triangle. *This* triangulation is radically different from the psychoanalytic "Oedipus" triangle because its dramatic effect on the son comes not from Hamlet's desire for his mother at the expense of his father, but rather because of his love for *both* parents.

Loving both, he is able to be used by both parents—King Hamlet *and* Gertrude—in order to help them continue old and apparently unresolvable conflicts that flourished before the king was murdered. This triangulation makes the contrast between Hamlet's feigned madness and any real loss of emotional control difficult, in certain places, to label accurately. Like so many children trapped between warring parents, Hamlet feels torn by his love for *both* and has thus been placed by them in an untenable situation.

Whichever way his allegiance turns, he risks alienating the other—a risk that, at first, seems easier for Hamlet to take against his mother since she is the one who has "wronged" his father by her "o'er hasty marriage." Nonetheless, his father, King Hamlet, is equally culpable in proposing an allegiance between his son and himself versus Hamlet's mother instead of coping with his wife himself and visiting her directly. Looking from this mimetic position, one wonders why this noted warrior never directly confronts his wife on his own but rather pushes his son to do his own proper work? Using a familiar family pattern, the Ghost is able to convince his son by some of the same guilt-rendering indirection as Hamlet's mother. Hamlet is overcome with pity and acts like any good son who feels an inner compulsion to obey his father's impassioned and heart-tearing request:

> *Ghost*:   My hour is almost come
>   When I to sulph'rous and tormenting flames
>   Must render myself up.
> *Hamlet*: Alas, poor ghost.
> *Ghost*:   Pity me not, but lend they serious hearing
>   To what I shall unfold.
> *Hamlet*: Speak, I am *bound* to hear. (I.v.3–7; emphasis
>   added)

Any reader curious as to why the ghost never visits his wife directly may turn to an experienced family systems specialist, Mara Selvini Palazzoli for illumination. To begin, Palazzoli suggests that

> what members of a family significantly exchange are mainly behaviors, not words, and these behaviors influence each other. All really momentous exchanges take place at an *analogical* level where, paradoxically, there is the greatest danger of misunderstanding, denial, and disproof.[38]

She reminds us that analogic behavior (both verbal and nonverbal) is often referred to by FST therapists with the language of games, and that one could usefully analyze familial behaviors through the therapeutic metaphor of the "family game." The concept of "game" in family systems is not a "rationally concocted scheme, coldly blueprinted in advance, by which cunning and duplicity are enlisted to get the better of one's own family." Rather, the "'embroiling' parent, or the parent who 'instigates,' does not [usually] have a clear idea of what he is doing. Only the occasional brief flash of insight lets him perceive, almost subliminally, that his conduct is blameworthy. This same line of reasoning holds for the patient's connivance."[39]

Hence, in *Hamlet*, readers initially assume that King Hamlet's unnatural death and the concomitant "betrayal" by his queen with his brother are elements of the same dastardly set of acts. By separating them into two different relationships—sibling rivalry and marital loyalty—the reader may be able to see old textual material in a slightly different context, allowing us to ask alternative questions. In any marital betrayal, for example, Palazzoli thinks it important to ask: "Who does the [identified patient or IP] feel has 'jilted' whom, for whom, and when?"[40] The IP, often the child or adolescent in the family, is often forced by the betrayed and angry spouse to take sides with the aggrieved against the betrayer.

When the betrayed spouse is the father—and the betrayer, the mother—the usual family and gender roles are often reversed:

> Our families with seriously disturbed patients are more likely, then, to be up against a two-fold factor of confusion. On the one hand, the father is a *passive* provoker, which contradicts the normally accepted gender role. He seduces the child and sets him up against the mother.[41]

Of course, being dead, King Hamlet is at somewhat a disadvantage in directly confronting his (former) spouse. Nonetheless, few scholars, critics, or directors have emphasized why the king's ghost speaks only his son and never directly his wife.[42] We know that the sources Shakespeare used did not include this directness in their plots (Saxo, Belleforest, Kyd, and so on), but since Shakespeare "was a reviser," according to Park Honan, that particular issue should not have posed such an enormous problem *per se*; hence, it remains that *through the son*, King Hamlet attempts to wean his "seeming virtuous queen" away from his major rival, his brother, but not through his own direct agency.[43]

Note, for example, the justified anger King Hamlet has toward what he perceives as his wife's betrayal, offering herself to his lifelong and, for him, unworthy antagonist, his own brother.

> [Claudius] won to his shameful lust
> The will of my most seem virtuous queen.
> O Hamlet, what a falling off was there
> From me, whose love was of that dignity
> That it went hand in hand even with the vow
> I made to her in marriage, and to decline
> Upon a wretch whose natural gifts were poor
> To those of mine! (I.v.45–52)

Not only is he angry with his own brother—as well as his wife—for possibly deceiving him *before* his death, he draws Hamlet into his apparent sibling rivalry by denigrating his brother's talents, including Claudius's (apparent) talent for seduction. His next line reflects in almost syllogistic form the bitterness he brings to bear on both brother and wife:

> But virtue, as it never will be moved,
> Though lewdness court it in the shape of heaven,
> So [lust], though to a radiant angel link'd,
> Will [sate] itself in a celestial bed
> And prey on garbage. (I.v.53–57)

Most of all, what a manipulative King Hamlet wants from his bereaved son is *surrogate* revenge:

> *King Ham.:* If thou didst ever thy dear father love—
> *Hamlet:*   O God!
> *King Ham.:* Revenge his foul and most unnatural murder.
>   (I.v.23–25)

Palazzoli enlarges on this parent/child coalition against the other parent, indicating that the real allegiance of one parent is not to the child but to the other spouse:

> when the moment of truth comes, the father will not "dare" to back up the child's rebellion against the mother. On the contrary, he will often take his wife's part and turn on the youngster, showing his disapproval [more on alliances during the discussion of the closet scene]. When this occurs, the adolescent's dismay and confusion are compounded by the fact that, in our type of [European] culture, it is

usually the father who wields sufficient sociocultural clout to put decisive pressure on his wife."[44]

This choice of agent (the child) to right a humiliating wrong is
odd in several ways, suggests Palazzoli, because the father

> will often be a man of considerable prestige in the outside world, re-
> spected and even revered: How can anyone imagine such a man act-
> ing like a doormat for a wife who is so obviously his inferior? Hence,
> [therapists note] . . . a majority of fathers who *fail* to conform to the
> stereotype of the strong, domineering male, and whose chosen strat-
> egy, in the spouse's stalemate, is an almost absurdly spineless and
> passive stance."[45]

Frank Sulloway's work gives the critic still another plausible reason for King Hamlet's passivity and Claudius's developing aggressiveness:

> Ample evidence demonstrates that *nature* and *nurture* represent a
> two-way street; [evolutionary biologists suggest that in] many spe-
> cies, environmental contexts trigger the release of hormones that
> regulate behavior. When a primate becomes an Alpha male, his tes-
> tosterone level rises. Give a low-ranking primate an injection of tes-
> tosterone and [it rises] to the top of the dominance hierarchy.
> [Displaced], the *previous* Alpha male suffers a reduction in his tes-
> tosterone level.[46]

Now, while it is clear that Renaissance physicians could hardly
check fatherly ghosts for adequate testosterone levels, Shakespeare had an intuitive sense for the diminution of self worth felt
by those recently brought down in public stature.[47] Hence, unable
to act himself, King Hamlet selects a likely familiar ally, his son,
to criticize Gertrude's recent (and to the king, unbelievable) behavior, especially because King Hamlet's own devotion to his
wife has not diminished. Thus, the displaced king delivers the
first of several contradictory messages to his son: Hamlet should
be furious and disgusted with his mother's behavior because of
the way she and his wretch of a brother have treated him, but
Hamlet shouldn't allow those emotions to cause hatred toward
her; let heaven (perhaps years down the road) and her own guilt
do that: "Taint not thy mind, nor let thy soul contrive / Against
thy mother aught. Leave her to heaven" (I.v.82–88).

After discussion of the Hamlet family architects, the parents,
we move to the next major character—from the family-of-ori-

gin—Claudius, the king's brother, who, as we have already noted, has been given rather bad press by the rest of the family. With a few exceptions, most of what we know about him comes from his rival brother, old King Hamlet, or the king's loyal son, Prince Hamlet. Although we have little textual evidence beyond what Hamlet tells us, we can still see some obvious differences between the brothers. King Hamlet was a warrior, who was so fierce that a mere glance seemingly could kill: "So frown'd he once when in angry parle / He smote the sledded Polacks on the ice" (I.i.63–64). He was also a confident gambler, who once risked his whole kingdom through "a seal'd compact / Well ratified by law and heraldy" in combat with old Fortinbras (I.i.86–87). Hamlet, of course, contrasts his father to Claudius, a "Hyperion to a satyr" (I.ii.140), or as the editor of the *Arden Shakespeare* suggests (following Belleforest) an "antithesis . . . between the sun-god with his majestic beauty, and a creature half man half beast [that] epitomizes in the two brothers the complex nature of man—like a god and like a beast—which will be a theme of Hamlet's later reflections."[48]

But is this description of the admitted fratricide, Claudius—generally taken as justified—the most critically productive way to see him? Perhaps there are alternatives. We have earlier employed the ideas of the evolutionary psychologist, Frank Sulloway, who usefully speaks of the sibling "niche" in human families:

> Among siblings, dramatic differences are commonplace. They arise because siblings cultivate distinct niches within the family. . . . The term *contrastive effects* has been used to describe these kinds of systematic sibling differences. Although the phenomenon is now well documented, the psychological mechanisms that underlie it are only beginning to be understood. . . . Within each family, the first two siblings manifested the greatest disparities . . . [gender] also played a part, with dissimilarities being greatest for same-sex pairs. . . . Siblings differed systematically in their identification with parents. If one sibling identified strongly with one parent, the adjacent sibling identified strongly with the other parent. Within each family, "split-parent" identifications were particularly pronounced for the first sibling pair.[49]

In short, the differences between King Hamlet and Claudius may well have begun as the perfectly ordinary differences in any family constellation, leaving aside for a moment Hamlet's judgments about the brothers' contrastive merits. The one-down younger sibling felt much injustice as the uncrowned brother. Sulloway says that

> Children are especially sensitive to injustices within their own families because the psychological mechanisms for detecting these inequities have evolved within this social context. This is why social class is a poor predictor of social radicalism. The motives for rebellion generally arise *within* families, not *between* them.[50]

Claudius's behavior was hardly unique in European history, as Park Honan suggests: "[Claudius's] regicide . . . was little more than an extension of medieval politics."[51] Further, Sulloway—after citing several examples in Europe during the decades immediately prior to the publication of *Hamlet*—announces that fratricide was the end result of some bitter Reformation antagonisms. From a Darwinian point of view, "fratricide is a tactic of last resort because it eliminates a substantial portion of the killer's genes from the population. Still, the occurrence of fratricide during high-stakes conflicts, or when valuable resources are particularly scarce [suggests that] . . . killing a sibling was merely an *extreme* manifestation of the most prevalent cause of social unrest: sibling strife."[52]

Familial guilt over his fratricide is readily understandable, therefore. So, what can we say to sum up Claudius since, as States has so eloquently put it, "sugaring o'er the devil with devotion's visage is a Renaissance commonplace"?[53] (1) Contrasted to King Hamlet, he is no warrior but more a diplomat. First, he has immediately sent to old Norway to try to diffuse the possibility that the recent change in Danish leadership might be taken as a sign of weakness. Their report to him "likes us well" (II.ii.80) and he is willing to consider allowing even the sharkish young Fortinbras to cross Danish soil; (2) Commonplace though it may be, Claudius suffers deeply from his sins. When Polonius merely gives Ophelia some commonplace advice, Claudius immediately translates it to himself: "O, 'tis too true! / How smart a lash that speech doth give my conscience!" (III.i.48–49); (3) He is attuned to nuances of human behavior, certainly in a way better than his brother who apparently could not or did not realize that his "seeming virtuous queen" could be so easily tempted into marrying his brother. He intuitively knows, for example, that Laertes will not harm him out of mistaken grief over his father's death (IV.v.122–25); (4) He is not, early on, bloodthirsty. After he and Polonius listen to Hamlet's anger at Ophelia and he believes there "will be some danger" for himself, he tells his councillor of his determination to send Hamlet to England where "Haply the seas, and countries different, / With variable objects, shall expel / This something-settled matter in his heart" (III.ii.170–72). All this occurs, of course, before the player-king scene and Hamlet's murder of Polonius; (5) Claudius is a kind of sophist orator, skillful in speaking with balanced sentences, polished tones, and is the master of the rhetorical figure, the oxymoron (I.ii.10–15); and (6) he is also a risk taker, but, in contrast to his brother, a gambler more out of desperation, less of confidence, willing to place his immortal soul in jeopardy for his place in the sun and his new queen. As he confesses his "rank offense" and weighs the alternatives in heaven's eyes, he sighs and hopes that "All *may* be well" (III.iii.36, 72; emphasis added).

Such behavior by a second-born is hardly surprising to Sulloway: "Laterborns are inclined to take risks, . . . a useful strategy in the quest to find an unoccupied niche, and it is a component of openness to experience."[54] One may contrast Sulloway's neo-Darwinian approach to the two brothers of Denmark with the psychoanalytic theory of Frances Schachter, who thinks that deidentification is a "defense" against sibling rivalry—an attempt to cope with the disruptive emotions arising from the Cain Complex.[55] Sulloway, on the other hand, eschewing "Cain complexes" and other familiar Freudian psycho-sexual explanations, says that "why siblings seek to be different is not defensive but offensive. Siblings are motivated to exploit unoccupied niches because they stand to gain something in the process: greater parental investment."[56]

So what happens with siblings if the niche is already occupied? Sulloway suggests that "contrastive effects are greatest for siblings adjacent in birth order" (as we think Claudius and King Hamlet were) and that in contrast to sisters who "assert their dominance through verbal means," brothers "typically avail themselves of physical aggression." Nonetheless, we must *not* assume a newer form of determinism here, as we witness with much of the early psychoanalytic commentary on *Hamlet*. Sulloway is clear that the

> choice between fratricide and sacrificing one's life for a sibling is dictated by *environmental contingencies*, and only secondarily by the repertoire of Darwinian strategies that have proved adaptive in the past. When it comes to Darwinism and human affairs, the story must be told as biography and social history, not as genetic determinism.[57]

Finally, we turn to Hamlet himself and Hamlet's feeling about his family. By the second act, it is clear that the angry and conflicted son is torn as much by his mother's "betrayal" as by his father's untimely demise. He fantasizes about his supposed formerly coherent family even in the context of planning revenge. One example: the reader recalls Hamlet's statement to the actors: "One speech in't I chiefly loved—t'was Aeneas's tale to Dido—and thereabout of it especially when he speaks of Priam's slaughter" (II.ii.442–44). In that scene, one of the more poignant elements in Virgil's lines is the queen's wrenching request of Priam: "Come to me, come to the altar; / It will protect us, or at least it will let us / Die all together."[58]

For Shakespeare, this closing of ranks of Priam's family to withstand the oncoming horror of "deadly Pyrrus" is reflected in Hamlet's own "chiefly loved" fantasy of an intact family, one where Hector's mother loves his father enough to die with him, and elderly father Priam loves Hector's mother enough to defend her to the death against Pyrrus's "villainous behavior."[59] By contrast, Hamlet's own recent family history has fallen short of this ideal, and so he turns those lines to his own rather bitter use to "catch the conscience of the King," his fratricidal uncle.

Another example of Hamlet's interactions with his "family" comes during the closet scene, when his father's ghost interrupts Hamlet's tirade against his mother as the faithful son (scathingly) contrasts Claudius to King Hamlet. One might ask why, at first ghostly appearance, Hamlet begs the "heavenly guards": "*save me* and hover o'er me with your wings" (III.iv.103). Save him from what? Save him from his father? Or save him from the double guilt he feels in berating his own mother and from the chastising he expects from his father? Indeed, Hamlet intuits the king's immediate purpose, and assumes in what could be acted in a defensive little-boy voice: "Do you not come your tardy son to chide, / That, laps'd in time and passion, lets go by / Th' important acting of your dread command? Oh say?" (III.iv.107–9). A knowledgeable family systems critic might suggest that Hamlet has seen this look before in his family. Does the father listen to his son's terror and see his offspring's own conflicted distress in angrily attacking Gertrude, his own mother? Neither parent appears to look at Hamlet *first* (recall Gertrude's earlier "thou hast thy *father* much offended"), but seeks initially, in each case, literally or metaphorically, the spouse; thus, King Hamlet's stern response to his frightened son is merely a repetition of his first visit. Any "comfort" is saved for his wife:

> Do not forget! This visitation
> Is but to whet thy almost blunted purpose.
> But look, amazement on thy mother sits,
> O, step between her and her fighting soul.
> Conceit in weakest bodies strongest works,
> Speak to her, Hamlet. (III.iv.110–14)

Ever attentive to his father, Hamlet turns to his mother, and asks, rather bruskly, "How is it with you, lady?" Indeed, like a good son, loyal to his father in the tug-of-war between parents but obviously still concerned with his own mother, Hamlet has vowed, just before the famous closet scene, to "Speak [daggers] to her, but use none. / My tongue and soul in this be hypocrites / How in my words somever she be shent, / To give them seals never my soul consent" (III.ii.374–75). The reason his "soul" will "never consent" is that for all his anger toward her, he still loves his mother, and contra Freud, loves her in the ordinary way an offspring loves a parent. Unfortunately, with his father's own anger and need for revenge flung in his face, Hamlet's emotional response to the first family reunion (so to speak) since his father's death is wrenchingly confused.

Hence, when she inquires after *him*, her own son, with a (momentary) genuine fear and concern, Hamlet answers by focusing *her* attention back to his father, having internalized his father's emotional needs again by commanding his mother to look "On him, on him! look you how pale he glares! / His form and cause conjoined, preaching to stones, / Would make them capable" (III.iv.125–27). Even as he speaks to his mother, begging her to attend to her (former) husband's appearance, Hamlet's guilt becomes intensified and he answers his father's "glare" by begging him, in the same half-line, not to make his son cry: "[to the King] Do not look upon me, / Lest with this piteous action you convert / My stern effects, then what I have to do / Will want true color— tears perchance for blood (III.iv.127–30). Poor Hamlet appears caught in a familial trap, and which ever way he turns, he winds up displeasing or frightening one parent to please the other—an intolerable situation for a son who loves both parents.

His love for both and resultant agony in trying to conceptualize them as separate people, a task forcefully undertaken in the context of divorce or death, is made even clearer a little later after Claudius tells Hamlet that it *is* good that Hamlet is bound for England "if thou knew'st our purposes" (IV.iii.46–49). Hamlet responds with a sarcastic reference to a "cherub that sees them," and to Claudius's unctuous puzzlement (and misguided attempt at correction) and says, "Farewell, dear mother." The following exchange points simultaneously to Hamlet's commonplace legal and Biblical definition of his parents, to his frantic unwillingness to think of them other than together, like Hector's mother and father, as the very ground of his familial being, and to his anger at his uncle and mother for presuming their current separateness. "*Hamlet*: Farewell, dear mother. / *King*: Thy loving father, Hamlet. / *Hamlet*: My *mother*: father and mother is man and wife, man and wife is one flesh—so, my *mother*" (IV.iii.50–53).

Gertrude refuses to acknowledge this dilemma in her son, and hence her earlier "Why seems it so particular with thee?" (I.ii.68). For her, the first marriage is already past and what is ahead is her primary concern. Thus, her emotional demands on her son as she begins the conversation by angrily assuming that Hamlet knows who his (new) "father" is and so asserting that Hamlet has "his father much offended." Once Polonius is killed, she is shocked, then confused, then rather quickly appears shamed by the comparison her son makes of the queen's two husbands. In demanding that she refuse Claudius's future sexual importunities, Hamlet pushes deeply into Gertrude's own internal conflicts, hitherto stoutly denied: possible guilt feelings about emotionally "abandoning" her former husband, strong maternal love for her son, and passionate erotic love for her new spouse.

Is she convinced enough, in the closet scene, to leave or to deny her current spouse in any loyalty conflict with her living son? Could she, on the other hand, ignore her son's near-plaintive entreaties and so remain loyal to her spouse? Indeed, one of the more energizing elements in the play is discovering Gertrude's most fundamental loyalties. Unable to reconcile them, Gertrude's death speaks to her inability, during the course of the play, to live daily with the ambiguity and divided loyalties she feels, and to Hamlet's loyalties to her as well as his father.

IV

What have the arguments and the evidence above told us that is interesting and worthy of our attention? To begin, it has been useful to consider the four major players—King Hamlet, his brother, Claudius, wife Gertrude, and son, Hamlet—as members of an extended family, subject both to the typical and to the unusual strains and shifting alliances common in families under stress. We could, of course, discuss some interesting dynamics with the Polonius family, but that will remain for another day. Second, we have reconsidered the perhaps less than ideal marriage of King Hamlet and Gertrude, finding that the wife's "o'er hasty marriage" to her husband's brother may be less puzzling if one considers the sources of information we have about the first marriage. Further, we have speculated that Gertrude's love for King Hamlet may have been different from the views of either father or son. In many marriages, the views of familial reality of the two bonded members of a triangulated coalition may well be quite different from the odd person out. If so, that might explain her "thrift" in saving the sweetmeats from her husband's funeral to "coldly furnish" (I.i.180) her "o'er hasty" wedding. Third, we have also noted the existential crisis Gertrude was pushed into during the closet scene, a crisis that may have seen its luminescent moment of clarity and inexorable solution during the few moments just before the queen hoisted the wine of death. Fourth, we have witnessed young Hamlet's being cast by each parent into his/her agent, either against the one spouse or for the other. As a triangulated offspring, Hamlet is emotionally torn between the two parents he loves and his so-called "feigned madness" may, at times, not be feigned at all. Fifth, we have noticed that readers' opinions of Claudius, as well as their views of the original Hamlet marriage, are all highly influenced by only two sources, the angry brother/husband and his grief-stricken loyal son. As such, the wise FST-oriented critic remains interested in rethinking that information, its context, and its sources, and then speculating on alternative possibilities. All of this reconsideration is made possible through the insights afforded by two new and related critical tools—family systems psychotherapy and neo-Darwinian evolutionary psychology.

NOTES

1. See Shakespeare, *Hamlet*, 81.

2. See Aguirre, "Life, Crown, and Queen;" Heilbrun, *Hamlet's Mother and Other Women*; Fergusson, *Idea of a Theatre*; Jones, *Hamlet and Oedipus*, 94.

3. Half a century ago, Fergusson said he objected to the Jones interpretation because it "reduce[d] the motivation of the play to the emotional drives of the Oedipus complex. This overworks the complex and takes us too far from the play itself" (*Idea of a Theatre*, 111).

4. Jacobi says that his choices to do this sort of thing (and others) comes "from the text" as he has "argued this with several weighty professors" that he

"make[s] a reasonable case." See Andrews, "Interview," 136. The weight he finds burdening his professors must have all been psychoanalytic since the text makes clear that the scene takes place in her "closet," an anteroom off the bedroom; as such, the closet is a place where a bed would be not likely be found. Furthermore, one weighty professor, Ralph Berry, calls stage business like Jacobi's (and some other late twentieth-century actors') "an unseemly wrestling scene." See Berry, "Hamlet's Doubles," *Shakespeare Quarterly* 37.2 (1986), 209.

5. See Knapp, *Striking at the Joints; Schoenbaum, Shakespeare's Lives,* 440–44; and Vickers, *Appropriating Shakespeare,* 281.

6. Many argue—with the currently fashionable bias against mimetic character—that it is somehow impermissible to view Hamlet and the other characters in the play as if they were "real" people, but, as Harold Bloom has countered, "this does not matter at all, since common readers and playgoers (and common believers) rightly continue to quest for personality." See Bloom, *Shakespeare,* 420. Of course, characters ultimately are *literary* constructs, but as constructs designed as representations of real people, they can be analyzed by using both textual evidence and inferential reasoning from such evidence.

7. States, *Hamlet and the Concept of Character,* 108; Livingston, *Models of Desire,* 28–29; Pechter, *What Was Shakespeare?,* 132.

8. States, *Hamlet and the Concept of Character,* 105.

9. Bloom, *Shakespeare,* 387.

10. Honan, *Shakespeare,* 283.

11. Boscolo, Cecchin, Hoffman, and Penn, *Milan Systemic Family Therapy,* 12; emphasis added.

12. Of course, to be fair, most critics have seen Claudius as primarily a "synthetic character," to use James Phelan's categorization scheme; that is, Claudius is often regarded somewhat less as a rounded mimetic figure and more as a plot function. Harold Bloom, for example, seems to suggest that Claudius's relative passivity after his fratricide makes him, relatively speaking, a nonactive player in the drama: "Claudius is all too content to have his nephew as heir; rotten as the state of Denmark is, Claudius has everything that he ever wanted, Gertrude and the throne." See Bloom, *Shakespeare,* 387.

13. In terms from cognitive psychology, one could say that readers of *Hamlet* have often been "side-participants," influenced by Freudian critics who are primarily addressing one another but are "overheard" by virtually all of the critical community and are thus so influenced by psychoanalytic terminology. See Gerrig, *Experiencing Narrative Worlds,* 105–6.

14. See Joseph Carroll, *Evolution and Literary History,* 346–47; Storey, *Mimesis and the Human Animal;* Sulloway, *Born to Rebel.*

15. Such speculation will, at times, also employ fragments of what little is known about the life of Shakespeare, the man. Richard P. Wheeler has discussed how the "nineteenth-century endeavor to find transcendence through merging the life and the works was replaced in the twentieth century by an insistence on separating the life from the works." See Wheeler, "Death in the Family," 129. FST-oriented criticism does not seek to "invent a biographical Shakespeare who led a life adequate to the transcendent status conferred on the wisdom of his art." Neither does FST-oriented criticism intend to "make the text . . . a timeless aesthetic artifact understood wholly on the basis of its formal design" nor to make *Hamlet* "an aggregate of historical data best understood apart from its formal structure." Like most Shakespearean criticism,

FST analysis is inclusive and rejects both ends of these "polarized extremes" (130).

16. Jardine, "'No Offense i' th' world'," 268.

17. Smith, "Heart Cleft in Twain," 207.

18. Frye, *Anatomy of Criticism*, 44.

19. Bert O. States points out a fundamental issue of character behavior regarding motivations not explicitly elaborated in the text, and the reader's/viewer's understanding of it: "If the probability of plot is that it will develop causally, the probability of character is that it will remain what it is. It will always be itself, or . . . what we expect it to be. It will rarely, if ever, surprise us. . . . [However,] I am prepared to believe that there are such things as character surprises in literature and drama, but one would have to inquire whether the surprise was a function of character-based or of genre-based expectations or of surprising developments in the plot. . . . In other words, part of the province of character in such a case would include an element of possible inconsistency." See States, *Hamlet and the Concept of Character*, 11, 13.

20. Palazzoli, Cirillo, Selvini, and Sorrentino, *Family Games*, 84.

21. Ibid., 84–86.

22. Ibid., 85.

23. Ozment, *Ancestors*, 38.

24. Overall, the play makes much more sense to this critic by thinking of Hamlet as a late adolescent. The grave-digger's recollection of Hamlet's age may be simply a character-creation mistake on Shakespeare's part, as many have believed, or a dating problem of editing and coordinating folios and quartos. One could also speculate and so distinguish the "day that . . . King Hamlet o'ercame Fortinbras" and the "very day that young Hamlet was born" with the possibility that though the Gravedigger had been "sexton here, man and boy thirty years," he did not immediately assume his gravedigging duties (V.i.140–43, 156) until after he (the boy) became a man, strong enough to wield a sexton's pickaxe.

25. Shakespeare, *Riverside Shakespeare*, 1751; see also Vendler, *Art of Shakespeare's Sonnets*, 78.

26. Cruttwell, *Shakespearean Moment*, 23–24.

27. Fergusson also noted both women's ambiguities: "Ophelia, like Gertrude, has great symbolic value in the economy of the play as a whole. Both women base their very beings upon their men; and both of them are attached at once to Hamlet and to Claudius's regime. Thus they are at once touching reminders of what might have been—the unity and health of the whole state—and victims of its actual illness and disunity" (*Idea of a Theatre*, 107). Nonetheless, as others have more recently argued (Phelan), reducing the vibrant mimetic qualities of a dramatic character to the schematic qualities associated with symbolic thematizing is a dangerous exercise usually accomplished only by reducing that character's richness and gritty texture to the contours of the particular theoretical model employed. Many feminist critics have justly taken umbrage at reducing the "very being" of Gertrude or Ophelia to their relationships to their men and have made distinctions between the Gertred of the First Quarto (Q1) and the Gertrude of the F texts. See Kehler, "First Quarto of *Hamlet*;" see also Showalter, "Representing Ophelia."

28. Ben-Amos, "Reciprocal Bonding," 292.

29. Ibid., 305.

30. Ibid., 303.

31. Ibid., 303–4.

32. Ibid., 307.

33. I owe much of the following discussion to an insightful conversation with the actor/director, Margaret A. Knapp.

34. Sulloway, *Born to Rebel*, 77.

35. Heilbrun, *Hamlet's Mother and Other Women*, 17; Charlton M. Lewis, *Genesis of Hamlet*, 36.

36. Sulloway, *Born to Rebel*, 76. Sulloway also cites Orville Brim, whose "list of *masculine* tendencies encompass traits such as leadership, self-confidence, assertiveness, competitiveness, and aggression. His list of *feminine* tendencies include such traits as affection, cooperation, and flexibility. . . . Firstborns of both sexes emerge as the 'alpha males' of their sibling system. . . . [In effect], birth order determines many traits that are stereotypically associated with gender" (76–77).

37. Honan, *Shakespeare*, 273.

38. Palazzoli, Cirillo, Selvini, and Sorrentino, *Family Games*, 69. Palazzoli is one of the more prominent members of the "Milan School" of FST—see the works cited below for a selective listing of her research—and in this area, she echoes the socioeducational writings of Gordon Wells. Using some of M. A. K. Halliday's work, Wells thinks of language as social action where "the exchange, rather than the individual utterance, [is] the basic unit of communication." See Wells, *Dialogic Inquiry*, 173. This exchange is often verbal and nonverbal (behavioral) simultaneously, a fact well known to all stage actors. See Noice and Noice, *Nature of Expertise in Professional Acting*, 25.

39. Palazzoli, Cirillo, Selvini, and Sorrentino, *Family Games*, 162.

40. Ibid., 72.

41. Ibid., 192.

42. Furness, *Shakespeare's Hamlet*, 298.

43. Honan, *Shakespeare*, 115, 275; Shakespeare, *Hamlet*, 82–122.

44. Palazzoli, Cirillo, Selvini, and Sorrentino, *Family Games*, 192.

45. Ibid., 192–93.

46. Sulloway, *Born to Rebel*, 88–89.

47. Honan, *Shakespeare*, 340.

48. Shakespeare, *Hamlet*, 438; see also Adelman, *Suffocating Mothers*, 263.

49. Sulloway, *Born to Rebel*, 96.

50. Ibid., 93.

51. Honan, *Shakespeare*, 283.

52. Ibid., 274.

53. States, *Hamlet and the Concept of Character*, 100.

54. Sulloway, *Born to Rebel*, 112.

55. Schachter, "Sibling Deidentification and Split-Parent Identification," 148.

56. Sulloway, *Born to Rebel*, 97.

57. Ibid., 355.

58. Virgil, *Aeneid*, 2:50.

59. Ibid., 2:50–51.

Part III
The World: Reading Family Systems Therapy *in extremis*

Crusading for the Family: Kurt Vonnegut's Ethics of Familial Community

Todd F. Davis

> We should return to extended families as quickly as we can,
> and be lonesome no more, lonesome no more.
> —Kurt Vonnegut, *Palm Sunday*

> When we talk about family, we are talking about the characters and themes that have woven together to form our identities. The family, which seems so concrete, is always an imaginal entity.
> —Thomas Moore, *Care of the Soul: A Guide for Cultivating Depth and Sacredness in Everyday Life*

I

FROM THE ONE TO THE MANY: POSTMODERN THOUGHT IN FAMILY SYSTEMS PSYCHOTHERAPY

MOVING AWAY FROM THE DELIMITING POSITION HARBORED IN MOST Freudian theory and practice, as well as the exclusionary focus on downstream causality embedded in much Lacanian analysis, family systems thinking appears to represent the more general shift in the social sciences toward certain postmodern ideas and paradigms that focus on multiplicity, layering, and local structures. With its emphasis upon relational modeling, family systems theory and practice stresses more than the solitary individual's journey toward psychic maturation, suggesting that such journeys be examined in terms of systems of power that ultimately reveal the symbiotic relationships which all humans take part in at every moment of their lives. Seeing the family complex as a highly nuanced, living organism, family systems dismisses the idea that power can be held—without the interaction of other family members—by a single (usually male) authority. Instead, family systems allows us to consider how power

221

functions are divided within familial structures, how they impact members of these systems, and how power is at all times interactive—moving and dynamic. Certainly, this form of psychotherapy helps to mark or identify the ebbs and flows of individual family members within the family structure while at the same time allowing for the examination of forces beyond the family that also influence and shape the structure any given family may take.

More recently, we have witnessed a turn toward the investigation of narrative and its central role in family systems psychotherapy. In *Tales and Transformations: Stories in Families and Family Therapy* (1994), Janine Roberts explores the ways in which current developments in family therapy focus on the role of narrative. "Linked to the so-called postmodern tradition in other disciplines," she writes, "narrative therapies emphasize construction of reality through language and consensus; a collaborative view of treatment; and an awareness of the different political, social, and cultural realities of and constraints on each of the participants."[1] The power of narrative in helping to establish, illuminate, and explain both healthy and unhealthy family systems appears undeniable. Of equal significance, however, is the fact that the very idea family systems holds a crucial position in the make-up of an individual, in his or her mental health, resides in the power of the narratives that shape us, in the ways we see our own lives as stories. In *The Stories We Are: An Essay on Self-Creation* (1995), William Lowell Randall explains that "in its plural form, *story* entices us with the sense of possibilities it conveys, the sense of options and alternatives. Not only might we be *a* story," he suggests, "but we might be *many* stories as well—of many kinds, on many levels, with many subplots and versions." The kinds of patterns that corporate and individual life manifest within a given family configuration gather their strength, their power, from the kinds of narratives that reside at the center of the family. Randall contends that the shift in family systems theory toward an emphasis on the stories that come together to make up any given family "points beyond the individual dimension of our existence to the communal one."[2]

As a writer of novels, short fiction, and essays, Kurt Vonnegut has crusaded for the better part of his career not only for the family—something most politicians and religious leaders have done to no avail—but for the possible forms the family might take as we move into the twenty-first century, the ideas that will shape those forms, and the centrality of story in this process. Because of Vonnegut's background in the social and hard sciences—he holds a master's degree from the University of Chicago in anthropology and studied chemistry and biology as an undergraduate at Cornell University—it seems only natural to look at his work through the different lenses of narrative therapy and family systems thought. The uneasy relationship between literary criticism and science that John V. Knapp describes in *Striking at the Joints: Contemporary Psychology and Literary Criticism* (1996) seems to be less an issue when examining Vonnegut's work, if only because Vonnegut himself dismisses the relative worth of dated Freudian theory in favor of more contemporary psychology.[3] I do not wish to represent Vonnegut's relationship to contemporary science as facile or benign, however. While he proudly recites the accomplishments of his brother Bernard Vonnegut, a research scientist who helped invent the method for seeding rain clouds and who was a professor of atmospheric sciences at the State University of New York at Albany for many years, Vonnegut also speaks plainly about how he lost faith in science when he saw its use in the destruction of Dresden, Germany, and later in the bombing of Hiroshima and Nagasaki. Vonnegut explains in an interview that after witnessing the awesome power of science in the service of humanity's hatred, he could no longer hope for some promised salvation in the technological advances of the scientific world:

> But for me it was terrible, after having believed so much in technology and having drawn so many pictures of dream automobiles and dream airplanes and dream human dwellings, to see the actual use of this technology in destroying a city and killing 135,000 people and then to see the even more sophisticated technology in the use of nuclear weapons on Japan. I was sickened by this use of the technology that I had such great hopes for. And so I came to fear it. You know, it's like being a devout Christian and then seeing some horrible massacres conducted by Christians after a victory. It was a spiritual horror of that sort which I still carry today."[4]

Vonnegut's association with science, then, consists of a healthy respect for the advances it potentially may offer combined with a very serious skepticism about how such advances will likely be used. Much of Vonnegut's fiction focuses on our culture's costly efforts to create technology—usually at the expense of human relationship—and its misuse in the hands of those who have been injured emotionally by familial neglect.

An early novel like *Cat's Cradle* (1963) presents a clear example of this narrative form, consisting of a man whose brilliance as a scientist is only matched by his remarkable inadequacy as a father. Unable or unwilling to give his children the love and support necessary for their development in a healthy family system, Dr. Felix Hoenikker presents each of them with a small piece of the deadliest compound ever created by science. As the novel moves forward we witness each child's search for love and acceptance in other family systems—all doomed to fail because members of these other systems merely masquerade as possible spouses, siblings, parents, or friends in order to gain access to the lethal compound, Ice-Nine. The final desecration and absolute destruction of the earth comes about when there are no longer families or communities that might help stave off the kind of despondency that leads to the release of the deadly compound into the environment. But Vonnegut's cautionary tale concerning the possible apocalyptic endings science may bring us is not his main theme. Rather, by using such narrative structures, Vonnegut hopes to cause his readers to take notice of their own lives, to examine the narratives that form the basis for their own thinking, and, finally, to look closely at the kinds of communities and family systems in which they live.

II
COMFORTING LIES: THE POWER OF NARRATIVE IN THE CONSTRUCTION OF FAMILY SYSTEMS

After the life-altering events of World War II—which Vonnegut chronicles in his most famous novel *Slaughterhouse-Five* (1969)—his search for some way to redeem his war experience led him to the University of Chicago where he studied anthropology under the tutelage of Dr. Robert Redfield. No longer grounded in the narrative of scientific progress, Vonnegut was drawn to ideas of cultural relativity. As he explains,

> A first-grader should understand that his culture isn't a rational invention; that all cultures function on faith rather than truth; that there are lots of alternatives to our own society. I didn't find that out for sure until I was in the graduate school of the University of Chicago. . . . It's a source of hope. It means we don't have to continue this way if we don't like it.[5]

And Vonnegut clearly does not want us to continue on the same cultural path he has observed for much of the second half of the twentieth century. Although Vonnegut believes that a great deal of the destruction and desecration of the planet and the life it supports results from advances in science and the technology it makes possible, he does not see it as the root source. Rather, time and again in speeches and in works of nonfiction like *Palm Sunday* (1981) and *Fates Worse Than Death* (1991), Vonnegut points to the increasingly dysfunctional systems in which contemporary families find themselves trapped. Vonnegut characterizes these systems or structures as "boxes," explaining in an interview that at present "each family is locked into its little box."[6] The result of such confinement, he suggests, is a lonesome, often self-destructive society. Similarly, in *Putting Difference to Work* (1991), Steve de Shazer explains that "for structural family therapists the dis-ease or dysfunction involves the structural and/or hierarchical misalignment of family relationships."[7] In many respects, then, Vonnegut plays the role of a structural family therapist when he attacks contemporary family configurations, offering alternative systems through the stories he tells.

Yet Vonnegut's advocacy for the removal of one system and its replacement with another should not be misconstrued as a turn toward modern essentialism, toward what Jean-François Lyotard in *The Postmodern Condition: A Report on Knowledge* (1979) depicts as the modern reliance on some grand narrative on which to base a claim for *the* truth. Vonnegut's crusade for the family in American culture clearly is not rooted in a dogmatic belief in a single essential truth that undergirds all reality; rather, Vonnegut appears to base his ideas on what can only be described as a postmodern leap of faith.[8] In a revelatory interview, he contends that everything we say "is a lie, because our brains are two-bit computers, and we can't get very high-grade truths out of them." Yet he does not despair. Vonnegut believes that "as far as improving the human condition goes, our minds are certainly up to that. That's what they were designed to do. And we do have the freedom to make up comforting lies. But we don't do enough of it."[9] According to Vonnegut, the stories we tell one another, the stories that serve as the basis for the structures or paradigms or systems we live in, should comfort others, make them more gentle, more kind, more caring. He argues "for the ordinariness of life, the familiarity of love" and hopes that these are the lies others will put their faith in, that such ideas will be at the center of the extended family systems he envisions.[10]

In *Families and Larger Systems: A Family Therapist's Guide through the Labyrinth* (1988), Evan Imber-Black contends that the nuclear family—a structure that has grown in frequency and importance during the second half of the twentieth century—often functions interdependently with a variety of other larger systems. Imber-Black's thesis confirms Vonnegut's own assertion that the nuclear family cannot and should not exclusively support any given family member's far-ranging needs. Imber-Black explains that "all families engage with larger systems"; healthy, differentiated families "are able to function in an interdependent manner with a variety of larger systems, utilizing information from these systems as material for their own growth and development."[11]

Vonnegut takes this idea to another level, however, in calling for the creation of some equivalent system. Prescriptive in the broadest, least invasive manner, Vonnegut crusades for the family not only by drawing attention to the ways we treat one another and the roles we play within our own nuclear systems, but also by advocating a paradigm shift to some form of the extended family. Vonnegut recognizes that we cannot return to an eighteenth- or nineteenth-century model of the extended family, most commonly associated with an agrarian economic structure. The market shift to industrialization and later to a postindustrialized economy perhaps explains best the patterns of migration that have radically transformed our nation over the last 150 years, destroying many communities in which several generations of a single family lived. Such communities, still evident in certain rural regions and among specific ethnic or religious groups—like the Mennonites and Amish, for example—quite often are composed of first, second, and third cousins, aunts and uncles, grandparents and great grandparents living in close proximity to one another, usually in the same county.

This model, as Vonnegut contends, offers a great deal to its members: the onus of raising a child no longer falls exclusively to the parents; love and support during times of grief or joy may be shared with more than a small handful of significant others; the impact of financial strife or medical catastrophe may be reduced by the larger number of people who can help confront and attempt to solve the situation. In such systems, many relatives partake and in turn fulfill similar roles. Vonnegut understands that such systems of blood relatives cannot be perpetuated under the patterns of the current economy—a fact that irks a writer and thinker like Wendell Berry who, surprisingly, shares many similarities in social thought and analysis with Vonnegut. Despite the obstacle of a postindustrialized market, however,

Vonnegut continues to make hopeful pleas for the establishment of some equivalent to the extended family in contemporary America.

III

SLAPSTICK: LABORING FOR LOVE, OR AT LEAST SOME COMMON DECENCY

During his studies with Dr. Redfield at the University of Chicago, Vonnegut was drawn to an examination of the folk society, its benefits as a "family" system, and the likelihood of developing such systems in the United States. Vonnegut describes the folk society as "a stable, isolated extended family" that creates community, or what he suggests humans need more than anything else—a sense of belonging.[12] "This is a lonesome society that's been fragmented by the factory system," Vonnegut explains. "People don't live in communities permanently anymore. But they should: Communities are very comforting to human beings. . . . Until recent times human beings usually had a permanent community of relatives," he observes. "They had dozens of homes to go to. So when a married couple had a fight, one or the other could go to a house three doors down and stay with a close relative until he was feeling tender again."[13] In Robert D. Putnam's provocative and controversial *Bowling Alone: The Collapse and Revival of American Community* (2000), Vonnegut's ideals are echoed and given more credence by Putnam's research as a political scientist at Harvard University. Drawing a clear map of the forces that have led to familial isolation in American culture, Putnam suggests that the marked drop in community organizations and volunteerism—the kinds of extended families which Vonnegut argues are viable in contemporary society—appears, in part, to be symptomatic of the kinds of structures or systems our families use to organize themselves.[14]

This shift in structures concerns Vonnegut because of his own experience growing up in Indianapolis, Indiana, where he lived among a large extended family that had resided in the midwestern city for more than half a century. As Richelle Gibson explains, "research into one's own family of origin is valuable in a unique way" for those working in family systems. "The process of research and investigation," she notes, "can place the therapist in touch with one's own personal history and how it has affected a person's growth into a distinctive personality . . . and furthers progress in individuation." She concludes that "in addition to investigation into the differentiation process, one's ethnicity can be found and reexperienced. Cultures from the past can be assimilated and rediscovered."[15]

While few critics have written about this aspect of Vonnegut's work, clearly he has made the kinds of efforts that Gibson advocates. His exploration of his family's history in Indianapolis, their position as artists and German Freethinkers, as well as owners of the Vonnegut Hardware, not only add an important dimension to Vonnegut's written work but to the narrative that shapes the structure of his own family system. Indeed, in *Palm Sunday*, Vonnegut thrills at his discovery of his great-grandfather's book, *Instruction on Morals*, and connects his own personal role in the Vonnegut family to the role played by his great-grandfather. In *Palm Sunday*, Vonnegut devotes much space to his family's history, looking back with a degree of nostalgia and sentimentality but also with a more objective, more critical eye for what truly may help people in terms of their emotional health. His flirtation with the past should not be misconstrued as indulgent; rather, as Gibson suggests, such work actually leads toward individuation.

In *Vonnegut in Fact: The Public Spokesmanship of Personal Fiction* (1998), Jerome Klinkowitz perceptively notes that "given the size and importance of his family in Indianapolis, their wealth and their attention paid to offspring (a communal support system including traditional family schools and a thriving family business with summer jobs for all), it is not surprising that Kurt would draw on their influence."[16] Indeed, given his childhood in a system that achieved a healthy homeostasis, yet one in which morphogenesis did indeed occur—most clearly in the shifts that took place in the Vonnegut home during the Great Depression—Vonnegut's longing for this utopian schema seems inevitable and natural. He openly admits that his vision for a return to extended families is utopian, explaining that "human beings will be happier—not when they cure cancer or get to Mars or eliminate racial prejudice or flush Lake Erie—but when they find ways to inhabit primitive communities. That's my utopia," he adds. "That's what I want for me."[17]

Despite Vonnegut's confession that the reincarnation of primitive folk societies likely exists only in utopian fantasies, he does make pointed use of this paradigm to suggest other ways of looking at family issues in contemporary America. As Russell Blackford and Peter Reed contend, while Vonnegut undercuts or critiques the idea that the creation of artificial extended families, like those we witness in *Slapstick* (1976), might actually succeed, he nevertheless remains committed to looking for possible alternatives to the present isolation and loneliness he observes most people mired in.[18] The gravity of *Slapstick*'s audacious, even absurd, narrative certainly runs closer to Vonnegut's own life than some critics may wish to grant.[19] As Vonnegut confesses in the novel's prologue, "This is the closest I will ever come to writing an autobiography."[20] At the center of Vonnegut's autobiography rests his relationship to his deceased sister Alice. He reveals that in many respects Alice was his muse. "I never told her so, but she was the person I had written for," Vonnegut states. "She was the secret of whatever artistic unity I had ever achieved. She was the secret of my technique."[21] Not only did Alice offer much of the inspiration for Vonnegut's literary craft, upon her death she provided him with an extended family through adoption. In an ironic twist, two days before Alice's death by cancer, her husband, James Carmalt Adams, died in a commuter train crash, leaving three sons between the ages of eight and fourteen and a one year old baby. Vonnegut and his first wife, Jane Cox Vonnegut, adopted Alice's three sons and raised them with their own children.

Out of the wreckage of the deaths of his sister and brother-in-law, in the midst of his newly formed family, Vonnegut attempts to make some sense, some order, from what can only be characterized as absurd and without order. In *Slapstick*, he examines his relationship to his sister, as well as the demise of his ancestral family in Indianapolis who had begun to disperse by the 1950s. At the close of the novel's prologue, Vonnegut tells us that the book "is about desolated cities and spiritual cannibalism and incest and loneliness and lovelessness and death, and so on. It depicts myself and my beautiful sister as monsters."[22] Of course, the only monstrous thing about the two siblings in the novel are their physical characteristics. Born dizygotic twins, Wilbur and Eliza Swain have six fingers and six toes, supernumerary nipples, massive brow-ridges, sloping foreheads and steamshovel jaws. But together they possess remarkable intellect and, later in their lives, a desire to see their utopian scheme for reorganizing America into thousands of artificial extended families put into practice.

As has been his habit since the revelatory preface to *Mother Night*, Vonnegut speaks directly to the reader in the prologue to *Slapstick* about his motivation for writing the novel and its eventual production. The transparency of such moments characterizes Vonnegut's continued efforts to move beyond the boundaries established by traditional fiction. As a postmodernist, he is at all times conscious of the artificial nature of his enterprise, but, as a person who desires to improve the human condition—or in this case, as a practicing family systems therapist of sorts—Vonnegut wishes to serve as a healthy, productive cell in the body politic, laboring to include the reader in the composition of the fictional moment. Vonnegut's use of metafiction establishes a kind of extended reading family by bringing disparate and far-ranging individuals into the act of story-making, a social benefit that undoubtedly pleases this self-proclaimed humanist.

Because of his love for his sister, a condition he would rather call "common decency," Vonnegut is driven to look for some means to fill the void left by her death. In *Love's Knowledge* (1990), Martha C. Nussbaum claims that there is ethical value to emotions, especially love, and the view of rationality that suggests emotions in some way mar productive thought is erroneous. She concludes that emotions are frequently more reliable and less deceptively seductive than intellectual calculations. Nussbaum suggests, moreover, that because "emotions have this cognitive dimension in their very structure, it is very natural to view them as intelligent parts of our ethical agency, responsive to the workings of deliberation and essential to its completion."[23]

In this way, we might characterize *Slapstick* as Vonnegut's ethical response to life's inane workings, to the crumbling structures of the family in America. In the hands of another author, such facts might very well lead to a story of despair or rage. Instead, Vonnegut presents us with a work dedicated to the memory of Laurel and Hardy, film comedians from the early twentieth century whose slapstick humor established a golden rule for the young Vonnegut during the Great Depression: in spite of our all-too-often cruel and humorless world, we must "bargain in good faith with (our) destinies."[24] His sister's destiny, her cruel and protracted bout with cancer, roils just beneath the surface of his story. But, as he recounts in the novel's beginning, Alice did, indeed, bargain in good faith with her destiny, and, toward the end of her life, when death was imminent, she described her demise in painfully humorous terms as "Soap Opera!" and "Slapstick."[25] In a review of the novel, John Updike claims, "Vonnegut's abashed and constant sorrow breaks through to touch the reader," but it does so more because of the immediate family he has known and lost than because of the extended family he dreams we all might have.[26] *Slapstick* proffers a means for combating loneliness. Vonnegut knows that he is not the only one to feel loss, and out of his compassion, his desire to treat others with common decency, he dreams of extended families where no one would suffer the loneliness that our society ignores as it feeds an economic machine that by its very nature fragments families.

As mentioned earlier, while at first it may seem odd to compare Vonnegut's ideas concerning family and community with those of farmer and man of letters Wendell Berry, it becomes increasingly clear that their moral and social agendas are surprisingly similar. In 1964, Berry made the decision to leave New York University, where he held a teaching position, in order to return to his ancestral home in Kentucky. Since that time he has reclaimed his place on the family farm, living in a family system comprised of an extended family of relatives and community members. Working his land by hand with a team of horses, Berry has also written over forty books of fiction, poetry, and nonfiction that argue for a return to local communities like those Vonnegut crusades for. In several of his essays, Berry contends that the most destructive element in our culture is the machinery of an economy that insists on transience. Like Vonnegut, Berry protests the increasing mechanization of our culture and its subsequent disregard for the physical and spiritual well being of the land and those it sustains. As Berry explains, few people have recognized "the connection between the 'modernization' of agricultural techniques and the disintegration of the culture and the communities of farming—and the consequent disintegration of the structures of urban life. What we have called agricultural progress has, in fact, involved the forcible displacement of millions of people."[27] Such displacement is the nature of our times. We are a nation of moving vans and subdivisions, of new homes built quickly from prefabricated parts by construction workers who often don't even live in the same state. Transience seems to be our inheritance. In order to find professional success that offers some small semblance of financial security, we are forced to leave behind our familial and cultural roots, to move at a moment's notice as we are awarded the next promotion.

In an interview, Vonnegut's own comments echo Berry's concerns. "Well I'm used to the rootlessness that goes with my profession," Vonnegut confesses. "But I would like people to be able to stay in one community for a lifetime, to travel away from it to see the world, but always to come home again. . . . Until recent times, you know, human beings usually had a permanent community of relatives."[28] While Berry attempts to reform this problem by crusading for a return to diversified agricultural practices, Vonnegut looks to an anthropologically designed social plan. Because of the extent to which America has become dependent upon the economic structures of factory production and its place politically and economically in the world market, Vonnegut sees no possibilities for a return to the life experienced by most Americans at the turn of the twentieth century. Instead, he proposes a plan that might be implemented as easily as the distribution of social security numbers. It is a plan based on the structure of Redfield's folk society, but designed to accommodate the patterns of life we find at the end of our century.[29]

Vonnegut's plan, outlined in the novel's fictional account of Swain's life, involves the creation of extended families by the government. Before Wilbur is forcibly removed from his twin sister, Eliza, the two grotesquely deformed but brilliant children envision a world without loneliness. By literally putting their heads together—"Eliza and I were perhaps ten thousand times as smart when we put our heads together as when we were far apart"—they produce some of the most important scientific and social advances the world has ever known.[30] Eventually, the Chinese, under the direction of Eliza, come to retrieve the writings of the two Swain children, but Eliza and Wilbur's plan to create extended families remains safely intact with Wilbur. After graduating from Harvard, Wilbur runs for and is elected the president of the United States. His campaign slogan, "Lonesome No More," refers to his promise to give everyone in the United States an extended family. Extended families are created randomly by replacing the middle name of every citizen with a series of names like Daffodil or Raspberry; those people with corresponding middle names immediately become a relative of some sort. What Wilbur and Vonnegut hope to solve with the proliferation of relatives is our lack of community. With extended families in place, whenever people move or find themselves in a strange place on their travels or need some kind of help, the family is there. Of course, Vonnegut does acknowledge that some family members are more generous than others, but he concludes that with enough family members there is always some relative who fits the bill.[31]

Wilbur's plan fails, however. In the course of the novel, the world as we know it goes, quite simply, to hell. America no longer exists as a democratic nation, and in its place kingdoms proliferate; because of tampering by scientists, the gravity on Earth fluctuates, destroying all manmade structures and making flight impossible; the Green Death and the Albanian Flu decimate the population, and Manhattan, where Swain resides, becomes an isolated island of ruins. None of these catastrophes, however, results from the leadership of Swain; rather, they are the residual products of those grand narratives against which Vonnegut has fought since his career began. Indeed, the only light in this post-apocalyptic landscape radiates from the relationships provided by the extended families that Wilbur helps establish just before the fall of the American government. In the end, only love, or common decency, remains as a means for hope.[32]

To the surprise of many critics, love and common decency are, indeed, the myths on which Vonnegut constructs the narrative of *Slapstick*. He remains, if nothing else, a fictional activist of sorts. Although some may consider such activism a weakness in the creation of art, Vonnegut nonetheless seeks to address our current state of family affairs. He works diligently to offer comforting narratives, to shake us from our resignation so that we may see alternative paradigms for our own family systems. Without becoming dogmatic or preachy—slapstick humor seldom allows for piety—Vonnegut pushes us to consider ways in which we may improve the world. Out of his own personal loss, he bargains in good faith, and like Laurel and Hardy, to whom the novel is dedicated, the grotesque, situational comedy of *Slapstick* not only leads to laughter but to the realization that a life led without the love and compassion, the common decency we might find in healthy family systems, is surely no life at all.

NOTES

1. Roberts, *Tales and Transformations*, 24.
2. Randall, *Stories We Are*, 10.
3. It should be noted that despite Vonnegut's own experience with and relationship to scientific study, some literary critics insist on using Freudian paradigms to read his work. In *Sanity Plea*, for example, Lawrence R. Broer uses an exclusively Freudian paradigm to read Vonnegut's stories. Although Vonnegut's family has a history of mental illness—his mother suffered from depression and eventually committed suicide, while his son Mark, diagnosed as a schizophrenic, recovered and is now a pediatrician—he has never regarded the work of Freud or other psychiatrists as much more than fanciful ideas. "So when my mother went crazy," Vonnegut explains in a speech delivered to the American Psychiatric Association, "long before my son went crazy, long before I had a son, and finally killed herself, I blamed chemicals, and I still do, although she had a terrible childhood." In the same speech, however, in addition to his

comments about "bad chemicals," once again Vonnegut espouses the virtues of extended families in combating the general malaise and poor emotional health of so many Americans. Addressing the group of psychiatrists, he says, "All of you, I am sure, when writing a prescription for mildly depressed patients, people nowhere as sick as my mother or my son were, have had a thought on this order: 'I am so sorry to have to put you on the outside of a pill. I would give anything if I could put you inside the big, warm life-support system of an extended family instead.'" See Vonnegut, *Fates Worse than Death*, 33–35.

4. Allen, *Conversations with Kurt Vonnegut*, 232.

5. Ibid., 104.

6. Vonnegut, *Wampeters, Foma, and Granfalloons*, 242.

7. de Shazer, *Putting Difference to Work*, 13.

8. See Davis, "Apocalyptic Grumbling" for a more detailed discussion of Vonnegut's postmodern conception of faith and humanism.

9. Allen, *Conversations with Kurt Vonnegut*, 77.

10. Ibid., 74.

11. Imber-Black, *Families and Larger Systems*, 14.

12. Allen, *Conversations with Kurt Vonnegut*, 194.

13. Ibid., 79–80.

14. See Putnam, *Bowling Alone*.

15. Gibson, "Discovering Your Roots," 53.

16. Klinkowitz, *Vonnegut in Fact*, 86.

17. Allen, *Conversations with Kurt Vonnegut*, 80.

18. See Blackford, "Definition of Love," Kurt Vonnegut's *Slapstick*." Perhaps his ability to move from cynicism and gloom to optimism and hope sets Vonnegut apart from other postmodern writers. Ever the realist, Vonnegut clearly understands the dire consequences of our actions and practices. On many occasions he has stated plainly that we will destroy the planet and each other within the next century if we do not change. Yet he cannot help but speak and write with a kind of blind hope in our potential goodness, in the power of grace and what he calls common decency. In *God Bless You, Dr. Kevorkian*, Vonnegut skips down the "blue tunnel" to the afterlife in order to interview both the famous and the infamous. During his interview with Eugene Victor Debs, "organizer and leader of the first successful strike against a major American industry, the railroads"—and a man who often appears in both Vonnegut's fiction and nonfiction—Vonnegut demonstrates his ability to straddle the divide between despair and faith. As he concludes the interview, Vonnegut reads a passage attributed to Debs, which also serves as the epigraph to Vonnegut's novel *Hocus Pocus:* "As long as there is a lower class, I am in it. As long as there is a criminal element, I am of it. As long as there is a soul in prison, I am not free" (38). The Vonnegut who speaks these words is the Vonnegut of hope, the Vonnegut who explains that "If it weren't for the message of mercy and pity in Jesus's Sermon on the Mount, I wouldn't want to be a human being. I would just as soon be a rattlesnake" (10). Yet when Debs asks Vonnegut how these words are received in America at present, Vonnegut does not mask the horrible truth of our present situation. Rather, he replies matter of factly, "People snicker and snort." And when Debs asks what the fastest growing industry in America is, Vonnegut states in the same manner that it is lamentably and ironically, "the building of prisons" (38).

19. By 1976, the honeymoon between Vonnegut and his critical audience was over. The attacks upon Vonnegut and his work that followed the release of *Slap-*

stick appeared to be nothing short of a witch hunt. The magic Vonnegut once worked in books like *Cat's Cradle* and *Slaughterhouse-Five* was now deemed by some critics as nothing more than a charlatan's tricks. As Vonnegut explains in an interview: "*Slapstick* may be a very bad book. I am perfectly willing to believe that. Everybody else writes lousy books, so why shouldn't I? What was unusual about the reviews was that they wanted people to admit now that I had never been any good. The reviewer for the Sunday *Times* actually asked critics who had praised me in the past to now admit in public how wrong they'd been." See Reed, "Lonesome Once More," 184.

20. Vonnegut, *Slapstick*, 1.
21. Ibid., 15.
22. Ibid., 18–19.
23. Nussbaum, *Love's Knowledge*, 40–41.
24. Vonnegut, *Slapstick*, 1.
25. Ibid., 11.
26. Updike, "All's Well in Skyscraper National Park," 43.
27. Wendell Berry, *Unsettling of America*, 41.
28. Allen, *Conversations with Kurt Vonnegut*, 79.
29. As discussed earlier, the anthropological theories of Redfield affect Vonnegut's thinking in dramatic ways. In *Palm Sunday*, Vonnegut explains that "when I went to the University of Chicago, and I heard the head of the Department of Anthropology, Robert Redfield, lecture on the folk society, which was essentially a stable, isolated extended family, he did not have to tell me how nice that could be" (116), and Vonnegut remains committed to the project of providing such structures or, at the very least, the idea of such structures to America. Vonnegut realizes, however, that these systems have their own potential flaws. In *Slapstick*, Eliza and Wilbur discuss the composition of extended families and the consequences of their composition. "[Fu Manchu] said that there was nothing new about artificial extended families in America," Wilbur narrates. "Physicians felt themselves related to other physicians, lawyers to lawyers, writers to writers, athletes to athletes, politicians to politicians, and so on. Eliza and I said these were bad sorts of extended families, however. They excluded children and old people and housewives, and losers of every description" (156–57). Vonnegut wants no part of systems of exclusion and clings tenaciously to his populist roots.
30. Vonnegut, *Slapstick*, 156.
31. When pressed about his ideas, Vonnegut explains that in an artificial extended family relatives would still act in much the same manner as they do today; the significant difference would be in the number of relatives: "If they asked for too much, he could tell them to go screw, just the way he would a blood relative. And there would be ads and articles in the family monthly about crooks or deadbeats in the family. The joy of it would be that nobody would feel alone and anybody who needed seven dollars until next Tuesday or a babysitter for an hour or a trip to the hospital could get it." See Allen, *Conversations with Kurt Vonnegut*, 79.
32. Vonnegut's continued advocacy for common decency, as opposed to love, involves his observation that the line between love and hate is too easily crossed. "I wish that people who are conventionally supposed to love each other," he remarks in the prologue to *Slapstick*, "would say to each other, when they fight, 'Please—a little less love, and a little more common decency'" (3). Such a notion is similar to Jerome Bump's description of "learning to love with detachment," a notion family systems therapy stresses in certain situations where a family member does harm to herself and/or to other family members. See Bump, "The Family Dynamics of the Reception of Art," 332.

Hollywood Exiles: Nathanael West's *The Day of the Locust* and Family Systems Therapy

James M. Decker

ALMOST INVARIABLY, READERS OF *THE DAY OF THE LOCUST* (1939) REC-
ognize that Nathanael West explodes Hollywood's self-projected
mythos as a "dream factory" by charting the exploits of a rather
pathetic band of marginal inhabitants. For seminal early critics
such as Randall Reid and James Light, West's characters exemplify the "fringe performers" who vacillate between "search and
frustration" and, ultimately, fail to benefit from the studio system.[1] In what Victor Comerchero characterizes as a "prose
Waste Land," West repeatedly lashes out against the commodi-
fication of human emotion that he encounters in Southern California.[2] Nevertheless, West pointedly refuses to mount a direct
attack on the underlying economic factors that support such a
phenomenon. Indeed, some of the most spiritually enervated
characters—such as Homer Simpson, Claude Estee, and Tod
Hackett—live in relative comfort.[3] While certainly cognizant of
Hollywood's inequitable distribution of wealth, West offers not
only a direct materialist critique but a more oblique psychological one as well.

One should remember that the riotous mob that dominates the
end of the novel mainly consists not of the economically impoverished but rather of the "tasteless, even horrible" middle-class
dreamers who "had come to California to die" but who "have
slaved and saved for nothing."[4] In essence, spiritual emptiness
functions as the primary target of West's grotesque rendering of
Hollywood's margins. In resisting the temptation to essentialize
the source of this malaise, West reveals his concern with systemic, rather than symptomatic, explanations of such manifestations as Homer's brutal attack of Adore Loomis, Tod's rape
fantasies, and Harry Greener's clownish antics. Family systems

theory—particularly as it applies to larger systems—provides readers of *The Day of the Locust* with a vital hermeneutic tool that echoes West's interest in cultural dysfunction.

As it applies to West's novel, family systems theory offers two particularly salient notions: social defenses and family scripts. As propounded by Yvonne M. Agazarian, the former concept refers to those conscious and unconscious strategies whereby an individual avoids interpersonal contact. Agazarian argues that while social defenses allow for a certain measure of escape, they may prove crippling to an individual who desires change: "Social defenses against communication enable people to moderate their interactions so that they have as much freedom as possible from the social anxieties and irritations that inevitably arise when one person tries to relate to another. Unfortunately, these social defenses are also the prison that prevents people from having authentic relationships when they want to."[5] Examples of social defenses include both aggression and masochism. As one will see below, such phenomena abound in *The Day of the Locust*, and the idea of social defense dovetails rather nicely with West's depictions of socially stunted characters such as Homer and Abe.

The latter concept, family scripts, helps explain the ritualistic nature of more social characters, such as Tod and Faye. John Byng-Hall defines family scripts as "a family's shared expectations of how family roles are to be performed within various contexts." In this conception, scripts do not necessarily canalize emotions or actions, for, as Byng-Hall notes, the "cast" may change.[6] Nevertheless, he observes that if individuals fail to "improvise" or "abandon the set script" they might get "typecast," a phenomenon that Agazarian refers to as "role-lock."[7] For the typecast or role-locked individual, actions may seem predetermined, already written. Role-locked individuals may experience a sense of entrapment, which may lead to bitterness or depression. In this way, family scripts share common ground with social defenses, for they both may foster a crippling homeostasis rather than differentiation or growth. Clearly, West, with his portrayal of the "cheated and betrayed" exiles who long for the planes to "crash once in a while so that they could watch the passengers being consumed in a 'holocaust of flame,'" presents his readers with a culture that lusts after change but retreats to inertia.[8]

Significantly, most of the characters in *The Day of the Locust* lack a basic family structure. West mentions nothing about the families of Homer, Tod, Abe Kusich, Earle Shoop, Miguel, or

Mary Dove. West further emphasizes the lack of primary family structure in the case of Harry and Faye Greener, for he mentions that Harry's wife—Faye's mother—abandoned the pair some time ago. Although they have no children, Claude and his wife constitute a family, as do the widowed Mrs. Loomis and her son, Adore. Only the Gingos, a displaced Eskimo clan that plays a very minor role in the novel, represent the nuclear family. Despite their dearth of visible family structures, West's characters find their actions quite colored by family history (both biological and surrogate). Developing ideas first expressed by Murray Bowen, Peter Titelman asserts that "extended family emotional systems" may result in an "unresolved attachment to [the individual's] family of origin."[9] Because one may trace conflicts and scripts backward from child to parent and from parent to grandparent, one may plainly see how issues from the past impinge on the present. In the case of West's menagerie of grotesques, physical displacement from family and familiar systems does not correspond with emotional distance, for self-imposed exile simply serves as a social defense and not as an effective strategy of differentiation.

Despite their fundamental inability to communicate with one another, West's characters apprehensively seek out companionship and build tentative relationships that rely on previous family scripts. In *The Day of the Locust*, such relationships tend toward the artificial, however, because the characters cannot terminate the social defenses that they undertook against their previous milieu. As a result, their emotional responses frequently seem inappropriate, muted, or eccentric. Jonathan Veitch astutely comments that "though social roles in *The Day of the Locust* do offer a kind of protection, they do so at the cost of a derealizing relation to the world . . . those subjects must succumb to the stereotypes, caricatures, and cartoons by which their identity is mediated."[10] In family systems terminology, the characters cannot improvise and, thus, they cannot grow. Of the many characters in *The Day of the Locust* that exemplify the principles of family scripts and social defenses, Abe Kusich and Harry Greener— relatively minor characters—and Homer Simpson, Faye Greener, and Tod Hackett—the principal figures in the book— offer the reader particularly vivid illustrations of the novel's concern with role-locks and miscommunication.

Abe, the diminutive gambler whom Tod stumbles on one day, typifies West's symbolic representation of the frustrated quest for meaning. Although he discovers Abe in a compromising position—inebriated and sleeping after being rejected by a prostitute—Tod quickly finds in Abe a fiercely loyal friend. Following a family script that places him in the role of benign curmudgeon, Abe constantly badgers Tod, yet he also supplies him with inside information about horse races, locates him an apartment, and looks after his welfare. At the San Bernardino Arms, moreover, Abe flits about like a concerned parent solving problems and offering advice, and he makes sure that Harry is not alone and consoles Faye by attending her father's funeral. As West paints him, Abe seems quite social, yet the character frequently behaves in a manner designed more to repel people than communicate with them, and Abe's combative loquacity masks an underlying sense of alienation. West explains the ostensible paradox of Abe's alternation between sentiment and hostility in the following passage: "when [Tod] got to know him better, he discovered that Abe's pugnacity was often a joke. When he used it on his friends, they played with him like one does with a growling puppy, staving off his mad rushes and then baiting him to rush again."[11] West's emphasis on repetition supports the interpretation that Abe and his friends follow a script or ritual, and the incongruity between Abe's behavior and his emotions suggests that the character employs the social defense of aggression to mask his essential vulnerability. Agazarian claims that "primary aggression experienced without conflict is simply an experience of potential energy" borne of frustration, and Abe certainly evinces such a quality.[12] Because friends such as Tod and Harry cast themselves in the opposite role—that of the teaser—they, too, follow the family scripts, those "already written story lines" that John Mince suggests live within everyone.[13] Only in rare moments—such as in the culminating scene of the cockfight—can Abe share his emotions in a relatively honest way.

Abe's reactions at the cockfight intimate the small man's true anguish and suggest his tragic inability to relate in a fully differentiated way with people. Abe—who must resort to prostitutes for the intimacy he craves but cannot articulate—establishes an emotional bond with Big Red, a gamecock that possesses admirable spirit but that lacks the physical ability to engage the likes of Juju, Miguel's beautiful champion bird. Indeed, Robert Emmet Long describes Abe's attachment to the bird as "a kinship of the disabled in a remorsely cruel world."[14] Overmatched, supine, and bleeding, Big Red nonetheless continues to fight, a fact that touches Abe—albeit not enough to terminate the competition—

and, momentarily, causes him to drop his gruff script and improvise:

> A large bubble of blood rose where the beak had been. The Red didn't retreat an inch, but made a great effort to get into the air once more. . . . Juju went up with him and got well above, then drove both gaffs into the red's breast. . . . Abe, moaning softly, smoothed its feathers and licked its eyes clean, then took its whole head in his mouth.[15]

Despite the brutality of the match, or perhaps because the primitive and violent actions lead to brief revelations of candor, Abe displays a tenderness with the bird unparalleled with his other actions in the book. Vincenzo DiNicola notes that "the axiom in systems theory [is] that it is impossible not to communicate in an interpersonal situation—even a mute response speaks volumes."[16] Abe's behavior in the above passage, largely silent or subverbal, expresses not mere empathy but instead the gentle, melancholy sympathy of one who has undergone similar experiences. By identifying Abe with Big Red, West captures the dwarf's emotional core and exposes his tough pose as a phenomenon as false as the bloated rubber horse at the bottom of Claude's swimming pool or the faux Egyptian temples housing Hollywood's elite. In literally swallowing the bird's blood, Abe, moaning, senses the futility of the fight, the delusion that he might succeed.

Nevertheless, Reid points out that "to discover the falseness of an illusion is not . . . to be delivered from it" and that "insight may only lead to frustration," and Abe's epiphany fails to lead to the change in behavior that Titelman refers to as "de-triangling" the "unemotional nonparticipation" of dysfunctional situations.[17] Immediately after the cockfight, and despite Big Red's death, Abe reverts to his usual script when faced with a conflict, but the role-lock proves ineffective. After the match, the spectators—including Tod, Faye, Earle, Miguel, and Claude—commence drinking and throw an impromptu party. Typically, the males hover about the seventeen-year-old Faye and seek to dance with her. Abe, too, desires Faye—who previously rebuffed Tod because he offered her "neither money nor looks"—even though he must compete with the likes of Earle and Miguel.[18] Despite the odds against him, Abe, adopting his typical script, challenges Earle: "he stood with his fists clenched and his chin stuck out. . . . He caught Earle by the seat of his trousers. 'Le'me dance.'"

Earle, whom West previously characterizes as someone who displays no emotion but then violently lashes out with no warning, dismisses Abe, who, like the outclassed Big Red, promptly kicks Earle. Abe, of course, has no chance against the lanky cowboy, but he squeezes Earle's testicles just as earlier he had done to those of the bird. Miguel, aiding Earle, then proceeds to knock Abe unconscious, but "he came to quickly, and began to curse," but the other men ignore him.[19] Ultimately, Tod forces him to go home, frustrated and angry.

Clearly, West intends the parallels between the gamecock and Abe to demonstrate the latter's lack of power and his concomitant use of rage as a social defense. Byng-Hall argues that "a child who does not develop a script which is shared with his peers behaves in an increasingly egocentric manner and becomes isolated."[20] Abe conforms to such a pattern, and his inability to communicate his desire to Faye herself, compels him to attack Earle. The social situation calls for a group solution, but Abe, unable to find an appropriate script or to improvise, abandons his typical verbal jabs and acts out. Agazarian explains that "when the energy in frustration is too much to contain, it tends to explode or implode."[21] Abe, a symbol of impotence measured against the gargantuan nature of Hollywood studio power, clearly opts for the former alternative.

Another fairly minor character, Harry Greener, ultimately takes the latter route of implosion. From the outset of the novel, Harry, a grizzled veteran of the pre-Hollywood stage, finds himself an outcast from a system that no longer values his talent for broad slapstick and versatile buffoonery. Once a proud member of a successful vaudeville act, Harry now lacks a saleable entertainment commodity and must live a subsistence existence by hawking "miracle solvent," a dubious polish. Employing many of the same conventions that characterized his act, Harry seems constantly on stage, even when faced with the mundane task of selling polish: "he began to practice a variety of laughs, all of them theatrical, like a musician tuning up before a concert."[22] Harry's artificial demeanor masks his inner emptiness and substitutes histrionics for true emotion, and Comerchero asserts that the old man "is incapable of genuine feeling."[23]

Adrift without his former occupation, Harry unconsciously seeks to recover his lost script by enacting it within his own family, which consists only of his teenage daughter, Faye. Employing comic antics as a buffer for his true feelings, Harry interacts with his daughter not in terms of a father-child relationship but in

terms of performance. Always on stage, Harry quite literally
uses a script when talking with Faye:

> "Speak to me, Daddy" she begged.
> She was baiting him without being aware of it.
> "What the hell is this," he snarled, "a Tom show?" . . .
> He laughed with his eyes closed and the sweat pouring down his
> brow. Faye knew only one way to stop him . . . she began to sing. . . .
> Homer was amazed. He felt that the scene he was witnessing had
> been rehearsed. He was right.[24]

In the above scene, Harry suffers a physical crisis, but the paralyzing homeostasis experienced by the family does not permit it
to respond in a way that matches the changing circumstances.
Role-locked as a clown, Harry continues to perform as in a gar-
ish melodrama, verbally jousting with his daughter rather than
looking to her for support or empathy. By clinging to his script,
Harry ignores Joan D. Atwood's notion of "reciprocal accommodation," in which subjects "make frequent attempts to disclose
their own subjective reality" and fails to communicate the depth
of his pain to Faye.[25] In turn, Faye responds not with an authentic
emotional reaction, but with the "ham sorrow" necessitated by
the family script.[26] As Faye announces to Homer, "the theater is
in [the family's] blood," and it seems clear that counterfeit emotions predominate in the Greener household.[27]

A master at improvisation, Harry nevertheless remains in a
role-lock with his daughter. Promiscuous and irreverent, Faye
rarely takes her father seriously and reacts to his jests in a habitual, prefabricated manner. Irving Malin notes Harry's "passive"
attitude in reference to her precocious sexual escapades, and it
seems clear that the lack of control that pervades his professional life applies equally to his family.[28] Long notes that one may
view both Harry and Faye as "overprojected and without personal identity," but this may ignore the family dynamic and the
effect their individual script has on their ability to avoid homeostasis.[29] Accustomed to playing a part and now deprived of an audience, Harry loses his sense of proportion and collapses the
boundaries between his personal and private life. Consequently,
he finds in Faye both audience and partner and—presumably—
slowly integrates her into his "act." While both characters do
lack personal stability, they each adhere to a fairly predictable
routine in their relations with one another, one that obfuscates
any profound sense of anguish or loss. The "overprojection" that

Long observes may stem from the blurring of the "boundary between reality and irreality" that Agazarian suggests separates
the quotidian aspects of life from fantasy.[30] Because Harry—and,
by extension, Faye—conflates his family script with his illusion-
based occupation, he would cast his personal identity not in the
more traditional terms that Long finds lacking but in those of his
"characters" or "bits." Flitting from one role to the next, Harry
nonetheless maintains a constant identity, that of the vaudeville
player. Drained by his attack, for instance, Harry hides his frailty
from Faye by "doing an exaggerated Negro shuffle."[31]

Ironically, the very role that prevents Harry from establishing
a healthy parental relationship with Faye results in the creation
of a surrogate family. Significantly, when Harry becomes ill, it is
this family, not Faye, who takes charge of his care: "Tod went to
see [Harry] almost every night. There were usually other guests.
Sometimes Abe Kusich, sometimes Anna and Annabelle Lee . . .
more often the Gingos, a family of performing Eskimos from
Point Barrow, Alaska."[32] These visitors provide Harry both with
the emotional sustenance that Faye fails to offer and with an audience. While Faye certainly attempts to nurse her father, she
cannot improvise well enough to cope. Upon hearing Harry's
strained breathing, "which [Faye] had taken for the death rattle," for example, she rushes to find Tod rather than attempting
to help her father.[33] Harry's serious condition falls outside of the
parameters established by the family script, and, unlike the surrogate family, Faye cannot adapt. When Harry dies, his pseudo-
family fills six rows at his funeral and seems to respond more
sincerely to the death than does Faye. The Gingos, for example,
view the body without hesitation and with devotion, while Faye
sobs theatrically and manages only "a quick peek" at the
corpse.[34] Mrs. Johnson, moreover assumes the role of funeral director that, more traditionally, Faye should have assumed.

In effect, Harry withers away, implodes because his reliance
on Faye as a "partner" appears threatened by his daughter's
growing independence and career aspirations. Harry's illness,
while all too real, represents a tangible emblem of his lack of differentiation. Increasingly, Harry's functional life requires Faye
to enact her part in the family script, but her ability or desire to
perform according to cue dissipates proportionately. For example, left alone by Faye—who "went to the pictures with that
Simpson guy"—Harry, longing for a vehicle to express his desire,
sheepishly recounts a scene from his life for Tod, who takes on
the role of caregiver.[35] Mechanically, Harry starts to recite his

part in "Enter Two Gents," only to stop short with a "second-act curtain groan so phony that Tod had to hide a smile."[36] Notably, this scene illustrates how Harry fuses his physical pain with his psychic wounds, for it underscores how the boundaries between fact and fiction evaporate within the old actor's world.[37] In avoiding his professional obsolescence, Harry adopts an implosive social defense doomed to fail.

Faye, of course, at first remains confined to Harry's orbit, and even after his death she continues to enact many of the lines in her original family script. In her relationships with men, Faye tends not to interact on a intimate level, but instead plays a part. The consummate actress, Faye seems to lack an emotional core, but her responses to Harry—and, in particular, to his death—suggest that her polymorphous nature stems not from an absence of identity, but from the presence of a role-lock. The child of an actor, Faye assumes the coping method of her father, whose paradigm calls for constant metamorphosis, disguise. In one revealing scene, Faye even masks her age: "Although she was seventeen, she was dressed like a child of twelve in a white cotton dress with a blue sailor collar." Furthermore, "her odd mannerisms and artificial voice puzzled [Homer]."[38] Like a young child, Faye plays make believe, only her charade substitutes for her reality. Protean, Faye alters her superficial characteristics at will, just as she flips through her "very thick pack" of hackneyed movie plots.[39] Veitch comments that such "ready-mades" blot out autonomy and "overwhelm subjectivity itself," and Faye's scripts certainly supply her with a prefabricated set of responses.[40] Caught in a cycle that triangulates any prospective lover with an unseen, mythical audience, Faye, paradoxically, struggles with a crippling homeostasis even as she cavorts from one role to the next. Such superficial transformations allow Faye to avoid the true human contact that could hurt her, for she gives nothing of herself that eschews the script.

Following Harry's death, Faye discovers herself both without her partner and without the funds to bury her father. Nevertheless, her defense mechanism allows her to act the part of a prostitute (despite Tod's offer to defray the funeral expenses) and earn enough money to pay for the burial:

> Suddenly she turned, lipstick in air, and spoke to Mary.
> "Can you get me into Mrs. Jenning's?"
> "What for?" Tod demanded. "I'll get the money."
> Both girls ignored him.

"Sure," said Mary, "you ought to done that long ago. It's a soft touch."

Faye laughed.

"I was saving it."

The change that had come over both of them startled Tod. They had both become very tough.[41]

Clearly, what attracts Faye to Mrs. Jenning's—an upscale brothel that Tod visits with Claude, a successful screen writer—is not the financial autonomy that it would provide, but the role that it allows her to act: the distraught but impoverished daughter who will sacrifice her morality to bury her beloved father properly. Tod's generous promise may offer a pragmatic solution to her dilemma, but it seems—to Faye—rather prosaic in contrast to the engaging part of the call girl. Because her sense of self cleaves so doggedly to her ability to simulate emotion, Faye fails even to register Tod's mundane gesture. As West characterizes her, Faye seems well-suited to working for Mrs. Jennings—whose prostitutes weave elaborate fantasies for an affluent clientele—because of both her detachment and her ability to create an illusion. Unfazed by her experiences, Faye ultimately drops the role as readily as she dismisses her would-be suitors.

Faye's relationship with Homer is emblematic of the actress's adherence to a family script even after that family no longer physically exists. In Homer, Faye locates not simply a source of money—for many men would provide her with financial security—but an echo of her previous family system, and at one point she even refers to him as "Daddy."[42] The much older Homer, moreover, overlooks Faye's carnal exploits just as Harry once did. Unlike Harry, however, Homer can provide Faye with a much more stable financial life. Once the "straight woman" to Harry's manic vaudevillian burlesque, Faye, as the nominal head of the family, now establishes herself as the lead player. Homer, with his quiet eccentricities and naïve sense of trust, provides her with an admirable foil. For Faye, Homer represents a figure of ridicule, a straight man:

His servility was like that of a cringing, clumsy dog. . . . His generosity was even more irritating. It was so helpless and unselfish that it made her feel mean and cruel no matter how hard she tried to be kind. And it was so bulky that she was unable to ignore it.[43]

Like her father before her, Faye reacts instinctively and exploits the comic possibilities of Homer's inept behavior. Denying her own beneficent impulses, Faye follows her script and treats Homer like a buffoon whom she must kick.

As with Homer, Tod offers the perceptive reader an important clue as to Faye's emotional health. Despite her relatively young age, Faye carries on numerous sexual relationships, such as those with Miguel and Earle.[44] Nevertheless, while these men may possess her body, they cannot penetrate her mind; she is numb to all but the rote physical demands of the various parts she plays. Tod, however, represents a figure quite alien to the typical men in Faye's life, and Faye seems to fear intimate contact with him because he might force her to drop her accustomed role. Although Faye recognizes that Tod is an earnest, fairly successful young studio artist, she does not allow him to approach her sexually: "she refused his friendship, or, rather, insisted on keeping it impersonal."[45] While she claims that Tod possesses neither looks nor money, in reality Faye rebuffs Tod for quite a different reason; he peers through her various masks and recognizes her for an emotional fraud. In Faye, West creates a character who stirs up a whirlwind of faux emotional responses in order to erect a barricade to her true psychological condition.

Homer Simpson provides an even more extreme example of a character who employs social defenses to avoid anxiety. Prior to relocating to California, Homer religiously adhered to a script that saw him work for ten hours a day and sleep for twelve. Homer's difficulty in staying awake when not engaged in bookkeeping vividly illustrates his fear of personal interaction. Socially inept, Homer avoids human contact by withdrawing and imploding. Indeed, Jay Martin describes him (and, interestingly, Faye) as "automata."[46] An example of the lengths Homer takes to avoid interaction occurs when Tod—whom Homer has previously met at Faye's apartment—attempts to say hello: "[Tod] watched [Homer] for a few minutes, then called out a friendly greeting. Without replying, Homer ran away."[47] Such behavior shelters Homer from the pain and embarrassment that he might suffer at the hands of more aggressive individuals like Abe. Tod may approach Homer with friendly motives, but the bookkeeper's defense mechanisms compel him to abscond rather than to face the possibility of pain. Nevertheless, Homer's self-isolation fails to negate his basic human need for companionship.

In the one aberration of his pre-California script, Homer attempts some clumsy advances toward an alcoholic resident of the hotel in which he works. Charged with collecting rent from Romola Martin, a perpetually intoxicated woman who "looked like a little boy," Homer enters the room, discovers the inconsolable woman, and experiences an uncontrollable desire for her.[48] Martin, at first assuming that Homer wants money, dismisses him, but when Homer "dropped [his] wallet in her lap" she asserts that she "could kiss [him] for being so nice." This response both entices and confuses Homer and leads him to an unaccustomed act of passion: "He caught her in his arms and hugged her. His suddenness frightened her and she tried to pull away, but he held on and began awkwardly to caress her. He was completely unconscious."[49] Homer's actions indicate that although he desires love and intimacy—however unconsciously—he lacks the appropriate script to achieve them. Notice that even when faced with a responsive Martin, Homer cannot properly adjust his level of intimacy, and he merely swings from one extreme to another. He cannot improvise, and his plan to treat love as a commodity—one more entry in his ledger of debits and credits—fails miserably.

In California, Homer's secondary social defense—work—does not exist, and, thus, Homer must devise a new routine to take its place. Before he meets Harry and Faye Greener, Homer's activity largely consists of sitting in a chair watching a lizard stalk a fly. Without the comfortable security of his work schedule, moreover, Homer fears sinking into a deep sleep from which he could not awake: "it was so hard for him to wake again. When he fell asleep, he was always afraid that he would never get up."[50] Left to himself, Homer, scared to face his own desire, tends to collapse emotionally. After Harry and Faye enter his circumscribed life, however, Homer finds himself once again attracted to an emotionally scarred woman. As he does with Romola Martin, Homer lacks the script to interact with the chameleon-like Faye. Faye makes sport of Homer and ultimately exploits him by moving into his house after Harry's death. Ironically, although Homer intuitively craves the young starlet, Faye compels him to allow Miguel and Earle—his "rivals" for Faye's affection—to live in his garage.[51] Such masochism, according to Agazarian, constitutes a common social defense.[52]

Homer thus substitutes masochism for work, a process best highlighted in the aforementioned party scene when Faye and Miguel consummate their lust. As Faye surges toward orgasm, she disturbs Homer with her moaning. Homer, though, reacts not with jealousy, disgust, or disappointment, but by diffidently attempting to assist his "sick" guest: "A little later she moaned again so he got out of bed, thinking she might want the hot water

bottle or some aspirin and a drink of water or something." Upon
receiving no response to his knocking, Homer enters Faye's
room and discovers her in the arms of Miguel, "both of them
naked."[53] Rather than acting, Homer stands paralyzed and hu-
miliated until Earle bursts into the room to confront his rival, Miguel. Regardless of his affection for Faye, Homer cannot deviate
from his subservient interaction with his housemate. By suffering in silence, Homer avoids articulating his feelings and expressing genuine emotion.

Ultimately, however, Homer cannot adjust to his new defense,
and he attempts to return to Wayneville. Tragically, his decision
to revert to the figurative womb of the Midwest—West refers to
"uterine flight" in an earlier passage—coincides with the novel's
climactic riot scene.[54] Mechanically walking toward the bus stop,
Homer gets caught in the current of the mob. Although he escapes, he crosses the path of little Adore, who tries to trick him
by dragging a wallet on a string. When a visibly numb Homer—
probably in delayed response to Faye's "betrayal" of his affection—refuses to pay attention, Adore forces him into
acknowledgement by hurling a rock at his face. Shaken from his
daze, "Homer landed on [Adore's] back with both feet, then
jumped again."[55] Despite Tod's intervention, Homer continues to
pummel the boy until the infuriated crowd rips him from the boy.
As Agazarian points out, unexpressed energy may either cause
implosion or explosion, and while hitherto Homer acts in accordance with the former paradigm, the naked violence of Adore's
conduct sparks him into an uncontrollable rage.[56] After habitually
avoiding conflict and emotional pain, Homer reacts quickly—if
automatically—to the physical discomfort caused by Adore's
rock. In essence, Homer expends his pent-up emotional energy
concerning Faye on a more tangible object, Adore.[57] Because he
fails to recognize the dangerous social context in which his actions occur—as well as the legal transgression he commits—
Homer unwittingly offers himself as a sacrifice to the bloodlust
of the mob. Interestingly, Homer cannot verbally defend himself
from the crowd—"Homer [rose] above the mass for a moment
. . . his jaw hanging as though he wanted to scream but
couldn't"—and reverts ineffectively to his pattern of implosion.[58]
In Homer, West offers a prime example of the crippling effects of
homeostasis on an individual's emotional autonomy.

In the character of Tod Hackett, however, West creates both
the observer and the observed. Tod, an ostensibly average artist
with pretensions to greatness, watches the denizens of California

with the eye of a clinical psychologist. Garnering material for his proposed opus, *The Burning of California*, Tod posits a series of sociological observations on the dubious character of the people he meets. Thrust into a foreign—and morally sordid—social setting, the "culturally uprooted" Tod seems lured by the depravity and decay that he encounters.[59] Slowly, Tod transforms from a detached "scientist" into an active participant in the marginal Hollywood culture. Consequently, Tod suffers a nervous breakdown when his pedigreed script cannot meet the demands of his new life.

Tod, displaced from his previous existence on the East coast, displays many of the same characteristics he observes in his new acquaintances. Immediately upon moving into the San Bernadino Arms, Tod slides into the existing social schema with ease, "listen[ing] to Harry's stories by the hour," sparring with Abe, and flirting with Faye.[60] Similar to almost every character in *The Day of the Locust*, however, Tod struggles with an overwhelming sense of loneliness, manifested in a tendency to drink to excess. Tod lacks both family ties and intimate friends, and his socialization confines itself to interacting with acquaintances such as Claude. Consequently, one may interpret Tod's attempt to seduce Faye as motivated less from sexual impulses as from an urge to establish a family-like contact. Indeed, as observed above, Faye treats Tod less like a formal suitor than as a brother. Tod responds to this makeshift family system by looking after the general welfare of his friends, such as when he visits the invalid Harry "almost every night" or attempts to hail a taxi for Homer.[61] Nevertheless, Tod's drunken desire for increased intimacy with Faye leads him to fantasize about—and attempt to realize— raping the seventeen-year old: "If he caught her now, she wouldn't escape. . . . Already he could feel how it would be when he pulled her to the ground."[62] For Tod, Faye's elusiveness represents a personal affront, a rejection of his overture of emotional warmth. Because he avoids self-analysis and opts for the cognitive haze offered by alcohol, however, Tod allows his vulnerability to mutate into dark aggression. Although he fails in his pursuit, Tod nonetheless demonstrates a potentially explosive defense mechanism quite at odds with his typically placid surface demeanor.

In a parallel situation—the party at Homer's house—Tod behaves much more in line with his standard defense of repression. A symbolic cuckold, Tod gazes impotently at Faye as she dances and flirts with Miguel and Earle. Rather than persuade her to dance with him, however, Tod seeks his typical escape and "pour[s] himself a quarter tumblerful, toss[es] it off, then pour[s] another drink."[63] In turning to alcohol, Tod enables himself to resist or combat his feelings of inadequacy and emptiness. Unlike Abe—who approaches, albeit unsuccessfully, Faye to request a dance—Tod mentally withdraws. Even when Faye stands before him in her lingerie, Tod cannot express his desire beyond an inarticulate "gasp."[64] Although intelligent and relatively glib—especially within the "family" system represented by Hollywood's outcasts—Tod finds it exceedingly difficult to communicate his true feelings with Faye, and even himself. As Malin observes, "Tod cannot see himself as actor with Faye," and Reid comments that Tod "cannot create any alternative" to the script in which more "primitive" individuals such as Miguel and Earle operate.[65] Tod's rigid script fails to allow him the "ability to separate [his] instinctually driven emotional reaction from [his] thoughtfully considered goal-directed functioning" that Titelman describes as characterizing a differentiated individual.[66] Tod cannot reauthor—in Atwood's terms—his script in a way appropriate to his desire.[67]

The stress of caring for his nominal family ultimately proves too much for Tod, and he cannot face the reality of Homer's explosion and brutal death. Injured and disoriented after Homer's violent outburst, Tod recognizes the prophecy of his *The Burning of California* montage, yet the reality of the riot confuses him nonetheless. Unlike the "poor devils" in his painting who revel in the savagery of the conflagration, Tod cannot detach himself from his underlying need for meaningful human contact.[68] The transient, malicious emotions of the mob contradict Tod's family script and disturb his sensibilities.[69] His typical altruistic ethos preempted by the scale of the insurgent throng's cruelty, Tod finds himself without a legitimate course of action, and, when rescued by a police officer, he mentally collapses. The emotionally fatigued Tod fails to distinguish between reality and fantasy and mimics the police siren in a delirious ejaculation. His family script ineffective and his defense mechanisms rendered useless, Tod emits a plaintive howl representative of his emotional hollowness.

Throughout his novel, West carefully avoids ascribing blame to characters such as Tod and Homer. Instead, he forges an atmosphere of helplessness and dashed dreams. John Mince would argue that West's strategy is the correct one, for he claims that "scripts reside within clients, yet have not been caused or promoted by the clients, their parents, or their children." He posits, moreover, that since scripts find their origins in the hazy realm of the ancient past, "all causal assignments are a waste of time and a mistaken epistemology."[70] Clearly, West recognizes the futility of ferreting out a root cause of his characters' symptoms, for the dysfunction in *The Day of the Locust* seems so pervasive that it constitutes the norm. Only through the proactive mode of therapy could such characters retool and "reauthor" their approach to human interaction and modify their family scripts to include a viable method of improvisation. In this way, characters would achieve differentiation by overcoming the paralyzing effects of ritual behavior with the more emotionally honest method of interaction offered by goal-directed improvisation.

NOTES

1. Reid, *Fiction of Nathanael West*, 120; Light, *Nathanael West*, 171.
2. Comerchero, *Nathanael West*, 121.
3. West's character, Homer Simpson, of course, later provided the name for the oafish father on the popular animated television series, *The Simpsons*.
4. West, *Day of the Locust* 61, 60, 178.
5. Agazarian, *Systems-Centered Therapy for Groups*, 119–20.
6. Byng-Hall, *Rewriting Family Scripts*, 4.
7. Ibid., 7, 4; Agazarian, *Systems-Centered Therapy for Groups*, 223.
8. West, *Day of the Locust*, 178.
9. Titelman, "Overview of the Bowen Theoretical-Therapeutic System," 9, 13.
10. Veitch, *American Superrealism*, 117.
11. West, *Day of the Locust*, 67.
12. Agazarian, *Systems-Centered Therapy for Groups*, 204.
13. Mince, "Scriptas Life-Form," 39.
14. Long, *Nathanael West*, 119.
15. West, *Day of the Locust*, 155.
16. DiNicola, *Stranger in the Family*, 188.
17. Reid, *Fiction of Nathanael West*, 135. Titelman, "Overview of the Bowen Theoretical-Therapeutic System," 39.
18. West, *Day of the Locust*, 67.
19. Ibid., 164.
20. Byng-Hall, *Rewriting Family Scripts*, 26–27.
21. Agazarian, *Systems-Centered Therapy for Groups*, 204.
22. West, *Day of the Locust*, 91.
23. Comerchero, *Nathanael West*, 139.
24. West, *Day of the Locust*, 95–96.
25. Atwood, "Social Construction Theory and Therapy Assumptions," 7.
26. West, *Day of the Locust*, 95.
27. Ibid., 98.
28. Malin, *Nathanael West's Novels*, 98.

29. Long, *Nathanael West*, 122.

30. Agazarian, *Systems-Centered Therapy for Groups*, 27.

31. West, *Day of the Locust*, 99.

32. Ibid., 103.

33. Ibid., 105.

34. Ibid., 129.

35. Ibid., 118.

36. Ibid., 119.

37. Atwood, "Social Construction Theory and Therapy Assumptions," 7.

38. West, *Day of the Locust*, 94.

39. Ibid., 105.

40. Veitch, *American Superrealism*, 114.

41. West, *Day of the Locust*, 124.

42. Ibid., 169.

43. Ibid., 143.

44. Faye tells Mary Dove that she "was saving it [her virginity]," but West undercuts her assertion throughout the text (*Day of the Locust*, 124).

45. Ibid., 67.

46. Jay Martin, *Nathanael West*, 333.

47. West, *Day of the Locust*, 79.

48. Homer's extreme behavior may reflect an inability to comprehend his sexual identity. As many critics have observed—including Reid and Comerchero—West explicitly alludes to Sherwood Anderson's Wing Biddlebaum via references to Homer's uncontrollable hands. Readers will remember that Anderson's character received persecution for his ostensibly homosexual overtures toward a young boy. Martin, who wears a "man's black silk dressing gown" and who wore "close-cropped hair" may startle Homer out of his mental trance because of her ambiguous gender identity. Such a theory would seem to explain why Homer suddenly manifests sexual longing.

49. West, *Day of the Locust*, 85.

50. Ibid., 82.

51. Typically, the term "starlet" referred to a beautiful young actress who had not yet achieved significant studio success and who, allegedly, would exchange sexual favors for screen time.

52. Agazarian, *Systems-Centered Therapy for Groups*, 120.

53. West, *Day of the Locust*, 170.

54. Ibid., 171.

55. Ibid., 181.

56. Agazarian, *Systems-Centered Therapy for Groups*, 204.

57. In *Nathanael West*, Long speculates that Homer's action represents a "symbolic rape of Faye" (138), but Agazarian's paradigm would suggest that his explosive defense mechanism stems from a more complex set of causes involving his family system.

58. West, *Day of the Locust*, 181.

59. Long, *Nathanael West*, 128.

60. West, *Day of the Locust*, 76.

61. Ibid., 103.

62. Ibid., 117.

63. Ibid., 163.

64. Ibid., 165.

65. Malin, *Nathanael West's Novels*, 98. Reid, *Fiction of Nathanael West*, 155.

66. Titelman, "Overview of the Bowen Theoretical-Therapeutic System," 14.

67. Atwood, "Social Construction Theory and Therapy Assumptions," 6.

68. West, *Day of the Locust*, 184.

69. In *The Writing of Nathanael West*, Alistair Wisker's postulation that the mob's "boredom becomes resentment which can only be satisfied by violence" (103) seems to parallel Agazarian's notion of explosive social defenses. Here, however, the defense proves a collective one and points to an extended family system.

70. Mince, "Script as Life-Form," 52.

Are Happy Families All Alike?: The Strange Case of Dr. Petruchio and Ms. Katherine

Marco Malaspina

"Happy families are all alike; every unhappy family is
unhappy in its own way."
—Leo Tolstoy, *Anna Karenina*

ALONG WITH *THE MERCHANT OF VENICE, THE TAMING OF THE SHREW*
is the real "problem play" of our own age. Staging the process of
subjugation of a woman to her husband, this once unproblematic
comedy nowadays appears to clash with some of our strongest
ideals about sexual discrimination. As ethically concerned readers and spectators, we find it difficult to think that Shakespeare
could have written this play with the primary purpose of making
us laugh at someone whom we would call a victim. It is then
hardly surprising that many contemporary critics have tried to
read *The Taming of the Shrew* from perspectives that could
allow us to enjoy it without feeling miserable or abused.

One possibility focuses on ironic reading. In effect, postwar
feminism has been more and more appealing to the play's apparent irony in order to lay open its deeply subversive discourse.[1]
Thus, we have readings emphasizing that Katherine's story is a
second-level fiction—that is, a story-within-a-story—and that
"Shakespeare tames the taming by making us see it through the
drunken, cozened eyes of a Cristopher Sly."[2] According to Karen
Newman,

> the foregrounded female protagonist of the action and her powerful
> annexation of traditionally male discoursive domains distances us
> from that system by exposing and displaying its contradictions. Rep-
> resentation undermines the ideology about women that the play
> presents and produces, both in the induction and in the Kate/Pe-
> truchio plot: Sly disappears as lord, but Kate keeps talking.[3]

Besides these so-called "revisionist" readings, feminist scholars, agreeing with Lynda Boose about the necessity to theorize
"a history that includes women," had also inquired into and
given impressive accounts of the difficult condition of women in
the Renaissance.[4] From this perspective, the performance of a
play as *The Taming of the Shrew* could be interpreted as an implicit denunciation. As Boose herself puts it, "ironically enough,
if *The Taming of the Shrew* presents a problem to male viewers,
the problem lies in its representation of a male authority so successful that it nearly destabilizes the very discourse it so bla-
tantly confirms."[5] In order to make this denunciation more
explicit, these scholars, adopting what one might call a new-his-
toricist methodology, provide us with accurate lists of the punishment tools that were used in the Renaissance to "tame" actual
shrews, or with historical documents of brutal practices such as
the skimmington.[6]

I

Though often persuaded by the sophisticated interpretations
and, especially, by the impressive historical knowledge of the
readings cited above, I would like to propose a different way of
looking at *The Taming of the Shrew*, moving the focus from
Katherine alone to Katherine as embedded within her family system. In fact, most of the essays I have mentioned seem to con-
centrate mainly upon two aspects of the play: its double level of
fictionality and what Boose calls "Kate's self-deposition"—that
is, the final scene—while Katherine's life within her family-of-origin is often relegated to the background. Since one of the most
valuable achievements of Shakespearean feminist criticism has
been the emphasis it has put on family, this omission seems to
me a curious phenomenon.[7] Probably, the lack of interest in
Katherine's family-of-origin could be explained by what Carol
Neely calls the "search for positive models," a search with "certain dangers: the heroines tend to be viewed in a partial vacuum,
unnaturally isolated from the rest of the play."[8] An approach
based on family systems therapy, focusing on interactions as
much as on individuals, may offer a valid antidote to the "unnatural vacuum" mentioned by Neely. Furthermore, as my discussion of Petruchio's behaviour using insights from Milton H.
Erickson's strategic therapy should explain, a family systems
reading may also cast a new light on the most outrageous aspect

of the play—that is to say, the "taming" of Katherine. Therefore, I propose that we assume the twice-detached position implied by the induction simply as an invitation to abstain from any immediate moral judgement on what is going to happen, and that we take our place besides Sly as if we were cotherapists, or students of family therapy, behind that exquisitely theatrical frame known as the one-way mirror.

As a matter of fact, what is going to happen has a certain clinical—and, maybe, cynical—interest: "what Shakespeare seems to have been doing in *Shrew*," Boose says, "is conscientiously modelling a series of humane but effective methods for behavioral modification."[9] The keyword here is "modification," as the title itself—*The Taming of the Shrew*—seems to point out: with its gerund, it is the only title in the Shakespearean canon that focuses our attention on a process, rather than on one or more characters, the outcome, or the genre. Which kind of modification? Though the "modification" may appear a behavioral one, it is not attained through a behavioristic approach, and it does not involve Katherine alone, but her whole family system.[10] Let us first observe the kind of family-of-origin to which she belongs.

II

Baptista enters with his two daughters. His first words are for the suitors of Bianca, the younger of the two:

> Gentlemen, importune me no farther,
> For how I firmly am resolved you know:
> That is, not to bestow my youngest daughter
> Before I have a husband for the elder. (I.i.48–51)

Notwithstanding its brevity, this passage provides us with a considerable amount of information. To start with an obvious consideration, we may note the historical gap between our society and Baptista's. First, in Baptista's world, fathers are supposed to have the right to "bestow"—or to detain—daughters when someone asks for their hand. Second, this right is acknowledged by suitors as well. Third, eldest daughters are to get married before youngest ones. When considering these banal differences of perspective, it is also important to define how widely they are shared: in fact, while we know that there had been a time in which the first two rules were almost universally valid, the third one is slightly more idiosyncratic.[11] Actually, as the subsequent dialogues will confirm, the insistence upon marrying Katherine first is dictated more by a personal wish of Baptista than by any inviolable social rule.

If this is really Baptista's wish, it seemed he is going to be disappointed: both suitors would rather die than marry Katherine, and she is, herself, quite displeased by her father's resolution:

> I pray you, sir, is it your will
> To make a stale of me amongst these mates? (I.i.57–58)

Behind our one-way mirror, we still have no clear idea of Katherine's position—we know only that she's "too rough" for Gremio and that her father will not allow her sister to get married before she does. Thus, instead of superimposing any interpretation to what she says, I propose to look carefully at her very first words and to make some preliminary hypotheses. At the structure of communication level, we can notice that Katherine's rhetorical question, though its content is related to Gremio and Hortensio, is directed to her father.[12] Should her hypothesis be correct, Baptista's will is to "make a stale of her among these mates." While "mates" is certainly referred to Gremio and Hortensio, what does she mean by "stale"?

Scholars usually assign it the meaning of "decoy-bird": thus, figuratively, either a person held out as bait to entrap someone, or a prostitute, or a laughing-stock. In this sense, Katherine would be the pigeon used by Baptista to entice the two suitors-hawks away from the more precious Bianca-bird. If this is the case, we may wonder *why* Baptista wants to keep Bianca away from her wooers and, moreover, how can he think to have any hope of success, since neither Gremio nor Hortensio are likely to be enticed by Katherine? There is, however, at least another possible hypothesis. In Shakespeare's time, "stale" also had the meaning of "stalemate."[13] Actually, Hortensio is not sure of the reason why Katherine has called him and Gremio "mates"—"'Mates,' maid? How mean you that?" (I.i.59). He supposes that she has wanted to mean "husbands." But Katherine could have intended another thing: as in a game of chess, Baptista, seeing that he is going to be checkmated—that is, to yield up his youngest daughter—is using Katherine to reach a stalemate, a deadlock situation in which neither player can win the game. Though this conjecture also fails to explain Baptista's aversion to the idea of surrendering Bianca, it accurately describes what is going on in the play, at least up to the end of the first act: A) Gremio and Hortensio—and Lucentio as well—want to marry Bianca; B) in order to do it they need Baptista's approval; C) Baptista won't agree until one of them accepts to marry Katherine; but D) none of them is going to do it.

With these two hypotheses—Katherine as a decoy or as a dead-locker—and the still open question about Baptista's motives in our shopping-cart, let us move on and meet Bianca, the younger sister:

> Baptista: Gentlemen, that I may soon make good
> What I have said—Bianca, get you in.
> And let it not displease thee, good Bianca,
> For I will love thee ne'er the less, my girl.
> Katherine: A pretty peat! It is best
> Put finger in the eye, an she knew why.
> Bianca: Sister, content you in my discontent.
> [To Baptista] Sir, to your pleasure humbly I
> subscribe.
> My books and instruments shall be my company,
> On them to look and practise by myself. (I.i.74–83)

Each of the characters of this little and vivid family picture seems eager to put on her or his own personal show: Baptista shows fondness for his youngest daughter, Katherine shows jealousy and resentment, and Bianca shows wisdom and deference to her father. Please note that I am using the verb *to show* instead of *to be* not because of skepticism over their emotions, but with a precise purpose: as the authors of *Paradox and Counterparadox* warn us, "the use of the verb *to be* condemns us to think according to the linear model," thus making us fail to keep in sight that family games are based as much on a shared set of rules as on the personality of each of the members.[14] In a similar way, if we accept to define Katherine as a woman who *is* rough—as she appears to be—maybe we will want to justify her, or laugh at her once she has been tamed, but we won't ask ourselves *why* she behaves this way, or better *what for*.[15]

What, then, are the *effects* of the above show? Baptista's display of fondness for Bianca literally obliges her humbly to subscribe his pleasure, that is, to get in and stay away from her wooers. On the other hand, it occasions Katherine's fit of jealousy. At first, this is directed against her sister only, but in the subsequent lines she will become slightly more explicit: "Why, and I trust I may go too, may I not? What, shall I be appointed hours, as though, belike, I knew not what to take and what to leave? Ha?" (I.i.102–4). To sum up, Baptista's words help to establish—or better to fortify—an intrafamilial alliance: Baptista and Bianca against Katherine.

The outline of this alliance becomes more evident with Katherine's reaction: by her assault, she confirms her sister in the role of victim, her father in the role of defender, and herself in what family therapists would call the "identified patient"—that is, the member who, in the family's opinion, needs to "get better." In effect, by the standards of Renaissance culture, her behavior is so socially unacceptable that, eventually, someone will have to intervene. Still, it is important to underline that her behavior is not congenital: it is part of a complex strategy, a strategy to which every member of her family contributes. I would also add that she does not appear particularly happy in her present situation. Actually, we could say that she is suffering. Although this fact appears obvious, many scholars seem to forget it when they come to analyze the end of the play.

Now, in order to check the effects of Bianca's sober reaction, we have to follow the triad inside their house. The second act begins with Bianca, her hands being tied and begging Katherine to let her free (II.i.1–7). It is a quite bizarre scene: are they just playing? Even if this were merely a game between children, we could not help noticing its symbolical implication: Bianca has her hands bound both literally and figuratively—that is, nobody can ask her hand—because of her bad-tempered sister. In fact, this misleading cause-effect explanation is a consequence of Baptista's indirect communication: as Bianca's wooers well know, it is Baptista who is keeping Bianca's hands bound, but since he never explicitly says so, it appears as if the kill-joy were Katherine.

This symbolical reading seems to be confirmed by Katherine's reaction, which immediately relates the odd opening scene to Bianca's wooers: "Of all thy suitors here I charge thee tell / Whom thou lov'st best. See thou dissemble not" (II.i.8–9). Anyway, whatever our hypothesis on the skirmish between Katherine and Bianca, it is not merely a game. As the subsequent lines reveal, what is at stake here are Katherine's deepest feelings:

> *Bianca:*   Believe me, sister, of all the men alive
> I never yet beheld that special face
> Which I could fancy more than any other.
> *Katherine:* Minion, thou liest. Is't not Hortensio?

> *Bianca:*   If you affect him, sister, here I swear
>   I'll plead for you myself but you shall have him.
> *Katherine:* O then, belike you fancy riches more.
>   You will have Gremio to keep you fair.
> *Bianca:*   Is it for him you do envy me so?
>   Nay, then, you jest, and now I well perceive
>   You have but jested with me all this while.
>   I prithee, sister Kate, untie my hands.
> *Katherine:* (*strikes her*) If that be jest, then all the rest was so.
>   (II.i.10–22)

If we ever had any doubt about it, this impressively mimetic sequence—which, adopting Watzlawick's terminology, we could call a "symmetrical escalation"—should utterly convince us that Katherine's roughness toward men is not a matter of caprice.[16] As Bianca has perfectly understood, Katherine envies her, and would gladly accept an exchange of roles. Yet Bianca has not guessed for the affection of whom Katherine envies her so badly; obviously, neither Hortensio nor Gremio, but someone whose love is definitely more essential:

> (*Enter Baptista*)
> *Baptista:* Why, how now, dame, whence grows this insolence?
>   Bianca, stand aside.—Poor girl, she weeps.—
>   Go ply thy needle, meddle not with her.
>   (*To Katherine*) For shame, thou hilding of a
>   devilish spirit,
>   Why dost thou wrong her that did ne'er wrong
>   thee?
>   When did she cross thee with a bitter word?
> *Katherine:* Her silence flouts me, and I'll be revenged.
> (*She flies after Bianca*)
> *Baptista:* What, in my sight? Bianca, get thee in.
> (*Exit Bianca*)
> *Katherine:* What, will you not suffer me? Nay, now I see
>   She is your treasure, she must have a husband.
>   I must dance barefoot on her wedding day,
>   And for your love to her lead apes in hell.
>   Talk not to me. I will go sit and weep
>   Till I can find occasion of revenge.
> (*Exit*)
> *Baptista:* Was ever gentleman thus grieved as I? (II.i.23–37)

Katherine could not have described her condition more explicitly: not only do suitors prefer Bianca, but also her father, the one whose love she most desperately needs. Moreover, in her fit of rage, she is even able to discern and verbalize how Bianca's conduct affects her: through her silence, that is through her exceedingly civil behavior. Bianca, the "poor girl" who know "so well her duty to her elders" and who has never wronged anybody, has thus the role that family therapists would define as a "passive provoker."[17]

At this point, though it would be extremely difficult to guess *what* will happen next, it is fairly easy to describe *how* it will happen among Baptista, Bianca, and Katherine.[18] Therefore, let's try to sum up our observations and hypotheses in a tentative frame. The Minola family is trapped in a homeostatic process, a stalemate in which every possible move seems to end in the same ineluctable loop. And, most important, every member of the family contributes to fuel the process. Baptista's program is clearly illustrated by Hortensio:

> He hath the jewel of my life in hold,
> His youngest daughter, beautiful Bianca,
> And her withholds from me and other more,
> Suitors to her and rivals in my love,
> Supposing it a thing impossible,
> For those defects I have before rehearsed,
> That ever Katherina will be wooed.
> Therefore this order hath Baptista ta'en:
> That none shall have access unto Bianca
> Till Katherine the curst have got a husband. (I.ii.117–26)

We may wonder why, though "supposing it a thing impossible," Baptista persists in imposing such a condition. In fact, if we compare his behavior to that of many other Shakespearean fathers of mono-parental families (Lear, Shylock, Brabantio, and Antiochus, for instance), his withholding of Bianca becomes less puzzling: lonely fathers, in Shakespeare at least, are not willing to give up their favorite—or only—daughter's affection. Even when they are wise enough to surrender, as in the case of Prospero or Simonides, they seem to find a kind of perverse pleasure in setting forth the most absurd obstacles and in subjugating bridegrooms to mortifying tests, however playful the intentions.[19] Incidentally, it may be worth observing that in Lear's family—structurally the most similar to Baptista's, since both have more than one daughter—Goneril and Regan, the eldest daughters, show dysfunctional behavior rather like Katherine's, not to mention the striking resemblance between Katherine's "she's your treasure" scene and Goneril's "He always loved our sister most" (I.i.290). In other words, Baptista seems to be caught in the double bind that afflicts most Shakespearean fathers: they want their favorite daughters' happiness, but they cannot accept the idea of letting them go. Katherine's behavior serves this paradoxical purpose remarkably well.

Bianca's position is hardly an enviable one: gratifying as it may sound, it also takes a lot of responsibility to be a favorite daughter. This position requires both moderation and strategy: she cannot disappoint her father—as Cordelia's story teaches us—but, at the same time, she cannot content herself for long with "music, instruments, and poetry." Her only chance is to learn very soon how to act slyly.[20] Thus, even her role of passive provoker is not to be interpreted as a sign of innate maliciousness, but as the part reserved for her by the Minola family's set of rules—at least as long as *The Taming of the Shrew* is to remain a comedy. We should not then be surprised by the amazing cunning of her "despair not" answer (III.i.40–43) to Lucentio's courtship.

Finally, there is Katherine, the IP or identified patient. Apparently, her personal deadlock is rather easy to explain. On the one hand, if she marries she has to leave, thus losing any hope of ever gaining her father's love. Furthermore, to go away would also mean to relinquish her control over Bianca and Baptista, who, once emancipated by her annoying presence, would eventually be able to "commune" (I.i.101) with one another unimpeded. On the other hand, behaving as she does, she knows perfectly well that she's not going to gain her father's favor anyway. In fact, the game is more complex: consciously or not, ill-tempered Katherine is indirectly useful to Baptista's secret strategy. From a systemic point of view, her symptom is not only functional to the homeostasis of the whole family, but also potentially rewarding for Katherine herself. Unable to obtain Baptista's love, she has at least become his secret accomplice by keeping Bianca away from potential husbands.

Obviously, this is too dangerous a game to go on for long. As Katherine is beginning to realize, sooner or later Bianca must have a husband, while she will be doomed "to lead apes in hell" all her life. And that won't be enough for Baptista to shift his inclinations. The therapists of the Milan School have given to the particular kind of secret alliance—or, better, coalition—like this one between Katherine and Baptista the name of "imbroglio," and have also illustrated how the process of disillusionment can often degenerate into psychosis.[21] Though neither schizophrenia nor anorexia are likely to lurk in the mind of a young Elizabethan woman, there are plenty of other mental and social "illnesses" among which to chose. Baptista has thus every reason to wonder whether "was ever gentleman thus grieved": as Katherine has promised, she will "go sit and weep" until she can find "occasion of revenge." And what better revenge than going on indefinitely as they are? Even Hamlet would not be able to conceive a more devastating requital.

III

A peculiar aspect of psychologically oriented criticism is that it avails itself of one part only of its system of reference—that is, the theoretical frame—while the therapeutic praxis must necessarily be left out: if *The Taming of a Shrew* were going to be a tragedy—a revenge tragedy, as Katherine seems to fancy—there would be no way to prevent it, exactly as no reading of *Othello*, however intelligent, can prevent the death of Desdemona. But *The Taming of the Shrew* is to be a comedy: how, then, to disentangle persuasively the dangerously enmeshed situation of the Minola family?

Most appropriately, the therapist is provided by Shakespeare himself through the entrance of Petruchio. In fact, Petruchio's taming of Katherine is usually interpreted more in terms of "education" than therapy: Katherine is "tamed" to married life in the way a hawk is "manned" to falconry.[22] This analogy, however offensive to our sensibilities, is clearly evident and fully exploited throughout most of the play, both at lexical and figurative levels. Still, it is an analogy that does not take in the initial condition of the two subjects: while a hawk, before being manned, is presumably freer and possibly happier than after, Katherine, as we have seen, starts from such a painful situation that her taming could even be read as a kind of "rescue."[23] From this point of view, the main core of the play—the *taming*—is the account of how Petruchio, a person outside the system, succeeds in cutting through the knots of the Minola family's game. What I am going to propose in the following pages is a comparison between the therapeutic traits of Petruchio's intervention and the equally bizarre techniques of one of the masters of strategic therapy, Milton H. Erickson.

"Strategic therapy," says Haley in *Uncommon Therapy: The*

Psychiatric Techniques of Milton H. Erickson, "is not a particular approach or theory but a name for those types of therapy where the therapist takes responsibility for directly influencing people."[24] Thus, while according to dynamic psychology, change is triggered mainly by the patient's understanding of herself or himself, a strategic therapist usually does not trust completely in self-exploration and insight. The case of Ruth, narrated by Erickson himself in Rosen's *My Voice Will Go with You,* is emblematic:

> At Worcester Hospital, the superintendent remarked one day, "I wish *somebody* could find some way of handling Ruth."
> I inquired about Ruth, a very pretty, petite twelve-year-old girl, very winning in her ways. You couldn't help liking her. She was so nice in her behavior. And all the nurses warned every new nurse who came to work there, "Keep away from Ruth. She'll tear your dress; break your arm or your foot!"
> The new nurses didn't believe that of sweet, winsome twelve-year-old Ruth. And Ruth would beg the new nurse, "Oh, would you please bring me an ice-cream cone and some candy from the store?"
> The nurse would do it and Ruth would accept the candy and thank the nurse very sweetly, and with a single karate chop break the nurse's arm, or rip her dress off, or kick her in the shins, or jump on her foot. Standard, routine behavior for Ruth. Ruth enjoyed it. She also liked to tear the plaster off the walls periodically.
> I told the superintendent I had an idea, and asked if I could handle the case. He listened to my ideas and said, "I think that will work, and I know just the nurse who'll be glad to help you."[25]

Erickson does not ask the superintendent why Ruth behaves the way she does. He has an idea, and wants to try it. Let us now consider Petruchio's first reaction to Hortensio's account of Katherine:

> Hortensio, peace. Thou know'st not gold's effect.
> Tell me her father's name and 'tis enough,
> For I will board her though she chide as loud
> As thunder when the clouds in autumn crack. (I.ii.92–95)

Here, too, there is no sign of interest in Katherine's reasons for being so rowdy. Petruchio wants a woman rich enough to be his wife: however rough she is, he is convinced that he will be able to handle the case. As Grumio rightly foresees, "he'll rail in his rope-tricks" (I.ii.110). "Rope-tricks" is a puzzling expression: it may be either Grumio's corruption of "rhetorics" or something concerned with jesting. Or both, I would suggest: Petruchio's strategy, like Erickson's, is based on the metaphorical as well as on the performative use of language—that is, based upon both words and action.

The first of their techniques has to do with timing. Strategic therapy, in order to be effective, should never last too long— usually five to ten sessions—and should be rather direct. "You want therapy, you want it fast, you're getting desperate," reports Erickson from his first meeting with a client. "Do you want me to give it to you in my way? Do you think you can take it? Because I can give it to you rapidly, thoroughly, effectively, but it will be a rather shocking experience."[26] Petruchio's preliminary interview with Baptista is likewise explicit:

> *Petruchio:* And you, good sir. Pray, have you not a daughter
> Called Katherina, fair and virtuous?
> *Baptista:* I have a daughter, sir, called Katherina.
> *Gremio:* You are too blunt. Go to it orderly.
> *Petruchio:* You wrong me, Signor Gremio. Give me leave. . . .
> Signor Baptista, my business asketh haste,
> And every day I cannot come to woo. (II.i.42–115)

From the very beginning, Petruchio makes clear that his courtship is going to be quite different from the traditional pattern. He won't "go to it orderly." If not an uncommon therapy, at the very least his intervention promises to be a fairly uncommon courtship. Therefore, when Baptista tries to oppose resistance (II.i.61–63), I would not hasten to interpret Petruchio's reply as merely dictated by the humbleness which the situation requires: if my previous hypotheses are correct, his "I see you do not mean to part with her" (II.i.64) could be more appropriate than Baptista pretends it to be.

Furthermore, once the terms of the marriage are already established, though apparently eager as he is to get rid of Katherina, Baptista goes on raising one more obstacle: "Ay, when the special thing is well obtain'd, / That is, her love, for that is all in all" (II.i.128–29). Now, isn't it amazing that in the most patriarchal of Shakespeare's plays we should find a father so willing at this point to respect his daughter's autonomy?[27] While positively struck by his praiseworthy show of sensibility, I cannot help wondering whether Baptista's care for Katherine's inclinations may also conceal an anxiety: should Katherine go away, Bianca will go off as well, thus leaving him completely alone. Anyway, Petruchio does not seems to share Baptista's perplexities—"For I am rough and woo not like a babe" (II.i.137)—and Baptista cannot but consent to Petruchio's desire to "have some chat with her" (II.i.162).

The first encounter between Katherine and Petruchio—nearly one hundred lines of uninterrupted and scintillating dialogue—stages what Petruchio had already anticipated: the meeting between "two raging fires" (II.i.132). Before pointing out some of its therapeutic features, it may be useful to get back to Ruth's case: what was Erickson's idea about how to handle her?

> One day I got a call. "Ruth is on a binge again." I went to the ward. Ruth had torn the plaster off the wall. *I* tore off the bed clothes. I helped her destroy the bed. I helped her break windows. I had spoken to the hospital engineer before going to the ward; it was cold weather. Then I suggested, "Ruth, let's pull that steam register away from the wall and twist off the pipe." And so I sat down on the floor and we tugged away. We broke the register off the pipe.
>
> I looked around the room and said, "There's nothing more we can do here. Let's go to another room."
>
> And Ruth said, "Are you sure you ought to do this, Dr. Erickson?"
>
> I said, "Sure, it's fun, isn't it? I think it is."
>
> As we walked down the corridor to another room there was a nurse standing in the corridor. As we came abreast of her, I stepped over and ripped her uniform and her slip off so she stood in her panties and bra.
>
> And Ruth said, "Dr. Erickson, you shouldn't do a thing like that." She rushed into the room and got the torn bedsheets, and wrapped them around the nurse.
>
> She was a good girl after that.[28]

We might wonder how to define this kind of intervention: therapy, taming, or what else? But what interests me here is a different question: how does it work? Maybe Petruchio would simply answer that "he kills her in her own humour" (IV.i.167). However, if we are looking for a slightly less concise rationalization of similar behavioral modifications, we may want to apply to Watzlawick: "If one person wants to influence another person's behavior, there are basically only two ways of doing it. The first consists of trying to make the other behave differently. This approach . . . fails with symptoms because the patient has no deliberate control over this behavior. The other approach consists in making him behave as he is already behaving."[29] This latter technique, widely used in family and strategic therapies, is known as "prescribing the symptom" and is the basic type of intervention in any treatment grounded on the therapeutic use of paradoxes. In opposition to what happens in a classic behavioral therapy, here the client, instead of being "punished" for retaining the symptomatic behavior and "rewarded" for abandoning it, is asked not to change. Thus, the prescription of the symptom, rather than breaking the link between behavior and reinforcement, undermines the very purpose of the symptomatic behavior: how to rebel against someone who is ordering us to rebel without incurring a paradox or making the symptom perfectly visible to all.

What happens in the first meeting between Katherine and Petruchio is, in some ways, a sort of paradoxical therapy. To begin with, the meeting itself compels Katherine to reframe drastically her own identity. For the first time on stage, Katherine cannot play any longer the role of obstacle between Bianca and her suitors: the object of desire, now, is precisely herself. Second, Petruchio does not adopt the jargon of courtly love. To her apparent disappointment, he calls her "Kate" (II.i.185) and joins eagerly in her high-spirited resort to obscene metaphorical chains (e.g., movable/joint-stool/asses/women," II.i.197–200) and puns (e.g., tale/tail, II.i.214–16). In this way, he not only establishes a difference between himself and other suitors, but also confirms her language—and her behavior—as appropriate.[30] Finally, proclaiming that he finds her "passing gentle" (II.i.236), "pleasant, gamesome, passing courteous / But slow in speech" (II.i.239–40), Petruchio indirectly prescribes Katherine her very symptom: that is, he invites her to be more shrewish. Actually, though his speech is usually interpreted as merely ironic, its performative effect becomes evident in Katherine's reaction: while it may be true that thus far "it is Kate who gets the best of her suitor,"[31] from this moment on she seems to be more and more bewildered.

Accustomed as she is to be ordered to be nice—by her father, by her sister, by Hortensio, and by Gremio—she does not know how to reply anymore. First, she tries to stop the now dangerous conversation ("Go, fool, and whom thou keep's command," II.i.251). Then, though covering it up through irony, she begins to feel a sort of admiration for this odd suitor of hers ("Where did you study all this goodly speech?" II.i.256). Eventually, even her father cannot help noticing that something has changed: "Why, how now, daughter Katherine? In your dumps?" inquires Baptista (II.i.277). Being in "one's own dumps" is "a dazed or puzzled state," and it implies "perplexity, amazement; absence of mind" (*OED*, def. 1–2). Indeed, not the sort of mood we would expect from the sharp-tongued Katherine.

Still, in order to break the stalemate, one further move is required. In effect, notwithstanding Petruchio's bravura, Katherine is far from being convinced: as Gremio echoes, "she says she'll see thee hang'd first" (II.i.293). At this point, any reasonable lover would probably give up. Enmeshed as she is in her family's never-ending game, any common-sense argument—as Hortensio's "No mates for you / Unless you were of gentler, milder mould" (I.i.59–60), for instance—would prove pathetically ineffectual. But Petruchio is no reasonable lover, as we have seen, and knows only too well how to disentangle such a situation. Resorting to paradoxical communication, he checkmates in as little as two lines:

> 'Tis bargain'd 'twixt us twain, being alone
> That she shall still be curst in company. (II.i.297–98)

By this astonishing move, which family therapists would call "counterparadox," he actually engages Katherine in a new "game without end": should she deny the "bargain," she would do nothing but corroborate it.[32] Trivial as it may appear, the turning point of the comedy relies precisely on this pragmatic paradox. Katherine and her father, as well as everybody else, are left literally speechless—"I know not what to say," falters Baptista (II.i.311)—and the wedding can be eventually announced.

The wedding day is rich in suspense: the bridegroom is late, and nobody can be sure whether he is going to arrive or not. Being a situation of shared incertitude, it provides us with an excellent vantage point to observe how each of the characters reacts under stress. The most amazing effect of Petruchio's delay is that of allowing Baptista to be finally able to display his affection for Katherine:

> Go, girl, I cannot blame thee now to weep,
> For such an injury would vex a saint,
> Much more a shrew of thy impatient humour. (III.ii.27–29)

Never has he spoken so gently to his daughter before. When Petruchio eventually arrives, his only concern is for Katherine:

> But where is Kate? Where is my lovely bride? (III.ii.90)
> But where is Kate? I stay too long from her. (III.ii.108)

But what a fool am I to chat with you,
When I should bid good morrow to my bride,
And seal the title with a lovely kiss. (III.ii.119–21)

Can this be interpreted as a display of genuine love? I do not
know. Anyway, it at least serves to establish Katherine as the
focus of attention, and not as the shrew but as the loved one. To
sum up, the general effect of this odd ceremony is that everyone's assumptions are completely subverted: "Such a mad marriage never was before" (III.ii.180), remarks Gremio. The
resulting confusion could actually be seen as part of a therapeutic process, since it is exactly when things start to be as "never
were before" that people begin to challenge their most entrenched patterns and to develop new ones. As long as everyone
is puzzled, homeostatic processes are suspended, and change
can go on.

No sooner are they married than Petruchio goes through with
the most important step of his strategy, that is, delivering Katherine from her family. He takes this step with disconcerting brutality—at least by our standards. However, he is very careful to
direct his vehemence at everybody but Katherine. Though she
is the very one who openly opposes some resistance, Petruchio
imposes his will on the others, and he does so through a paradoxical injunction—incidentally, another strategy widely used in
family therapy. By saying "Touch her whoever dare!" (III.ii.231),
he is actually ordering them not to do what they have no intention of doing. Here, again, the main effect of his behavior is to set
off Katherine in everybody's eyes: not only has she got a husband, but a husband who is ready to fight for her.

What happens in the fourth act, when they move to Petruchio's
house in the country, is so rough and bizarre that to establish
any analogy between Petruchio's behavior and any kind of therapeutic treatment could seem quite a hazardous step. Harold
Bloom, for example, though calling it "cure," prudently softens
its meaning by the inverted commas and the adjective "phantas-
magoric."[33] Nonetheless, if we think again at the case of Ruth,
the similarities between Erickson's and Petruchio's strategies
become conspicuous. For instance, the way in which Petruchio
exploits his servants' complicity is exactly the way in which Erickson and the nurse work together: they resort to the symptomatic behavior of their "patients," amplifying it to the extent that
both Ruth and Katherine cannot help taking up an oppositional
stance—that is, the "normal" behavior. Indeed, Ruth's "Dr. Er-

ickson, you shouldn't do a thing like that" seems to echo Katherine's "Patience, I pray you, 'twas a fault unwilling" (VI.i.143). Even the apparently inhuman tactic of reducing to starvation is not utterly alien to contemporary psychotherapy. Haley reports a case in which the mother of a severely disturbed eight-year-old child, following the detailed instructions that Erickson had given her, had been sitting her full weight upon her son for over six hours, reading a book:

> With the chapter finally finished, the mother got up and so did Joe. He timidly asked for something to eat. His mother explained in laborious detail that it was too late for lunch, that breakfast was always eaten before lunch, and that it was too late to serve breakfast. . . . Unfortunately, he had missed his breakfast, therefore he had to miss his lunch. Now he would have to miss his dinner, but fortunately he could begin a new day the next morning.[34]

Petruchio too is careful not to establish any explicit link between his will and Katherine's starvation—as well as all the other deprivations she must endure. His "way to kill a wife with kindness" (IV.i.195) is thus a way to inaugurate a complementary relationship with Katherine, while preventing the symmetrical escalation which would otherwise be triggered by "her mad and headstrong humour" (IV.i.196). From an ethical point of view, this is obviously unacceptable: why should be Katherine the one who must resign to the one-down position? However, Petruchio's paradoxical strategy has at least a relational advantage: it authorizes Katherine to delude herself that the struggle she is losing is not against her husband, but against an external enemy—be it misfortune, fate, or an absurd set of rules. In other words, it lets Katherine undergo submission preserving what little dignity her uneven society allows women. Besides, she also begins to derive some benefit from the public display of her one-down position: even Hortensio is now willing to be on her side ("Signor Petruchio, fie! You are to blame / Come, Mistress Kate, I'll bear you company," IV.iii.48–49).

The last intervention is probably also the most puzzling:

> *Petruchio:* Good Lord, how bright and goodly shines the moon!
> *Katherine:* The moon? The sun! It is not moonlight now.
> *Petruchio:* I say it is the moon that shines so bright.
> *Katherine:* I know it is the sun that shines so bright.
> *Petruchio:* Now, by my mother's son, and that's myself
> It shall be moon, or star, or what I list
> Or e're I journey to your father's house. (IV.v.2–8)

Why force Katherine into naming the "moon" the sun? This really smacks of obnoxious conditioning and could actually make her go mad. Yet it happens in an extremely delicate circumstance: on their way to Baptista's house, that is, when the "new" Katherine is going to be brought back to her old environment for the first time, while her relation with Petruchio is still highly precarious. Now, as Saussure teaches us, the fact that our nearest star is called "sun"—or, assuming they are supposed to be Italians, "*sole*"—is rather arbitrary. More exactly, it is one of the social conventions of that society for which Petruchio, wearing "unreverent robes" (III.ii.110), has shown no regard even during his wedding—that very same society which, as Boose has brilliantly illustrated, would have had no hesitation in strapping Katherine into a "cucking-stool" and "carting" her through the town.[35] Against these social conventions, Petruchio wants to establish his own conventions and wants his wife to share them, so that they may arrive at Baptista's house not as two individuals but as a close couple. At the same time, Katherine's seeming acceptance of her husband's vagaries is not an index of subalternity, but the sign that she has eventually found out how to deal with him. In fact, their paradoxical dialogue culminates with the sun being called "sun"—not "moon":

> *Katherine:* Forward, I pray, since we have come so far,
> And be it moon, or sun, or what you please.
> And if you please to call it a rush-candle,
> Henceforth I vow it shall be so for me.
> *Petruchio:* I say it is the moon.
> *Katherine:* I know it is the moon.
> *Petruchio:* Nay then you lie, it is the blessed sun.
> *Katherine:* Then, God be blessed, it is the blessed sun.
> (IV.v.12–18)

It is important to underline that, though the sun is once again the "sun," their quarrel has by no means been useless: it has actually provided a new kind of sun. It is neither Petruchio's, Katherine's, nor the society's sun anymore—it is their new-born family's sun. It is exactly through the processes of negotiating meanings that newly married couples become families—and, possibly, happy families, each one in its own way. Petruchio has satisfied himself that he has the power to decide over everything. At the same time, Katherine has discovered that "making him behave as he is already behaving" is an effective way to make him decide what she actually wants. This is the reason why I am equally unsatis-fied by readings that proclaim either Petruchio or Katherine the "winner" of the contention: their negotiation is not a zero-sum game, since its outcome is a success for both competitors. If we really have to find a winner, it appears to be their married life:

> *Katherine:* Husband, let's follow to see the end of this ado.
> *Petruchio:* First kiss me, Kate, and we will.
> *Katherine:* What, in the midst of the street?
> *Petruchio:* What, art thou ashamed of me?
> *Katherine:* No, sir, God forbid; but ashamed to kiss.
> *Petruchio:* Why, then, let's home again. Come, sirrah, let's away.
> *Katherine:* Nay, I will give *thee* a kiss. Now pray thee, love, stay.
> *Petruchio:* Is not this well? Come, my sweet Kate.
> Better once than never, for never too late.
> (V.i.130–38)

Now, even without considering that Katherine has decided to shift back to the "thee" form—which she had quit after the wed-ding—how can we not agree with Bloom when he affirms that "there is no more charming a scene of married love in all Shake-speare"?[36]

The therapy session is now approaching its term. Just before abandoning our place behind the one-way mirror, we are offered a last interaction: the controversial scene of "Kate's self-deposi-tion"—her often quoted "place your hands below your husband's foot" (V.ii.178). Is her attitude comparable to "the operation was a success, but the patient died," as an old joke reported by Wat-zlawick goes, and as both historically oriented feminist criticism and "non-revisionists" seem to imply?[37] Or should we interpret her final words ironically, as "revisionists" suggest? In my opin-ion, neither of the two. Though Katherine has never been as alive as now, irony is not the appropriate trope here. Her words are neither true nor false: they are strategic. That is, their meaning is not to be found at the level of content—what they *say*—but at the level of relation—what they *do*. They eventually allow Kath-erine to take revenge on her father: she is now the favorite daughter—"For she is chang'd, as she had never been" (V.ii.117)—but she is not desperate for his love anymore. From a systemic point of view, this outcome is neither the result of a sa-distic "behavioral modification," nor of Katherine's subtlety.[38] What has changed is not only *within* Katherine, but also *without*:

in her new family system, being a shrew does not serve any purpose—it is not a functional "symptom" anymore. Incidentally, we may notice how—in a play as in real life—change in one family member necessitates changes in other members. Bianca, far from pretending to be the "insipid" sister that Bloom insists she is, is released from the responsibility of being the favourite daughter and eventually able to assert openly her own rights.[39] And now that he is not "thus grieved" anymore, even Baptista, whose primal concerns were money and Bianca, seems more than happy to pay his twenty thousands crowns, and to grow old alone.

NOTES

1. See Bretzius, *Shakespeare in Theory*, 57.
2. See Dusinberre, *Shakespeare and the Nature of Women*, 106. Fineman, "Fratricide and Cuckoldry," 84.
3. Karen Newman, *Fashioning Femininity and English Renaissance Drama*, 42.
4. Boose, "Family in Shakespeare Studies," 735.
5. Boose, "Scolding Brides and Bridling Scolds," 179.
6. A "skimmington" refers to a skimming ladel used to thrash scolding wives or unfaithful husbands. Karen Newman, *Fashioning Femininity and English Renaissance Drama*, 35.
7. See Kahn, "Providential Tempest and the Shakespearean Family," see also Boose, "Father and Bride in Shakespeare."
8. Qtd. in Vickers, *Appropriating Shakespeare*, 327.
9. Boose, "Scolding Brides and Bridling Scolds," 198.
10. For a book-length study on Skinner's behaviorism applied to the reading of Shakespeare, see Murray, *Shakespeare's Imagined Persons*.
11. See Houlbrooke, *English Family Life;* see also Ingram, *Church Courts, Sex, and Marriage in England*, 134–40.
12. On the structure of communication level, see Watzlawick, Bavelas, and Jackson, *Pragmatics of Human Communication*, section 3.3.
13. See *O.E.D.*, "stale," def. 6, and the note on the Arden edition of the play. See Morris, Introduction, 174–75.
14. Palazzoli, Boscolo, Cecchin, and Prata, *Paradox and Counterparadox*, 27.
15. Watzlawick, Bavelas, and Jackson, *Pragmatics of Human Communication*, 45.
16. Ibid., 107–8.
17. "The 'active provoker' can usually be identified quite readily, whereas labeling the 'passive' one is more difficult, since he or she may easily be mistaken for a victim cowering in the tiny corner of the board to which his opponent's pawns have apparently confined him/her. Only when we look closely at this 'passive' player's unruffled, steady moving to and fro in his narrow little space, repeating his one move over and over again, do we discover his special way of

provoking." See Palazzoli, Cirillo, Selvini, and Sorrentino, *Family Games*, 164–65.

18. Watzlawick, Bavelas, and Jackson, *Pragmatics of Human Communication*, 185.

19. Boose, "Father and Bride in Shakespeare," 340.

20. On sister dyads and parental favor, see Sulloway's theory on birth order in *Born To Rebel*. According to Sulloway, the rebellious niche is usually occupied by laterborns. But "among sister dyads, some firstborns are distinctly non conforming, whereas some laterborns are distinctly conforming. These findings are restricted to pairs of sisters in two-child sibships" (149). This anomaly, well exemplified by the Minolas daughters, is related to the interactions between gender and family niches (firstborn position being also a "masculine" position). Furthermore, "absence of parental favor causes most offspring to adopt laterborn strategies" (355), as it appears to happen in the case of Katherine. Bianca, though naturally "born to rebel" (as she will eventually show, once out of the family), is thus allowed only a sly rebellion.

21. According to the systemic vocabulary, a coalition is an alliance which involves the crossing of a generational boundary, and is usually regarded as a potentially dysfunctional pattern. See Salvador Minuchin, *Families and Family Therapy*. For imbroglio, see Palazzoli, Cirillo, Selvini, and Sorrentino, *Family Games*, chapter 5.

22. Morris, Introduction, 125.

23. Bloom, *Shakespeare*, 29.

24. Haley, *Uncommon Therapy*, 17.

25. See Rosen, *My Voice Will Go with You*, 229–30.

26. Haley, *Uncommon Therapy*, 91.

27. See Boose, "Father and the Bride": "However true it was that the couple's willing consent was necessary for valid matrimony and however vociferously the official conduct books urged parents to consider the compatibility of the match, fathers like Cymbeline, Egeus, and Baptista feel perfectly free to disregard these requirements" (326).

28. See Haley, *Uncommon Therapy*, 230–31.

29. Watzlawick, Bavelas, and Jackson, *Pragmatics of Human Communication*, 237.

30. In a therapeutic context, communicating in the patient's language without becoming pathetic requires an extraordinary ability, yet sometimes it may turn out to be *the* crucial ability. For an astonishing example of Erickson's exploitation of this ability, see Haley, *Uncommon Therapy*, 120–21.

31. Karen Newman, *Fashioning Femininity and English Renaissance Drama*, 43.

32. Watzlawick, Bavelas, and Jackson, *Pragmatics of Human Communication*, 232–33.

33. Bloom, *Shakespeare*, 31.

34. Haley, *Uncommon Therapy*, 215–16.

35. Boose, "Scolding Brides and Bridling Scolds," 185–86.

36. Katherine's choice between the archaic and the modern form of the personal pronoun is very effective. Before the wedding, she addresses Petruchio both as "you" and, when she is extremely angry, as "thou/thee" (e.g., "Where did you study all this goodly speech" *vs.* "Go, fool, and whom thou keep'st command). After the wedding, she addresses him only as "you" (e.g., "Patience, I pray you" (IV.i.142); "I pray you, husband" (IV.i.154); "I dare assure you, sir"

(IV.iii.186). Once in Padua, she shifts back to the "thee" form, at least when they are alone. Now, since the "th-" form usually implied either rudeness or intimacy, especially when used in opposition to the "you" form, one could read Katherine's double shift as a sign of her evolving attitude toward Petruchio: contempt, submission, and complicity. See Joan Mulholland, " 'Thou' and 'You' in Shakespeare." Bloom, *Shakespeare*, 32.

37. Watzlawick, Bavelas, and Jackson, *Pragmatics of Human Communication*, 135.

38. Boose, "Scolding Brides and Bridling Scolds," 198. Bloom, *Shakespeare*, 33.

39. Ibid., 29.

Transgenerational Subsystems in Flannery O'Connor's Short Fiction

Denis Jonnes

WHILE GENERALLY AGREED THAT FAMILIES CONSTITUTE A PRINCIPAL focus of Flannery O'Connor's fiction, recent critics representing a range of approaches—feminist, gender studies, new historicist—remain sharply at odds in efforts to characterize an overall interactive pattern, or the significance and power ascribed particular positions, roles, or relational axes within the family. Louise Westling, for instance, notes that "most families in O'Connor's fiction are mother-dominated," but nevertheless asserts, in part with an eye to O'Connor's cultural conservatism and broader eschatological, Christian vision, that "O'Connor's ultimate identification is with paternal authority," her stories "repeatedly moving toward some sort of violent chastisement of the mother's authority by agents of an absent patriarch."[1] In a diametrically opposed reading, Claire Kahane views O'Connor's protagonists as protofeminists who "transgress (woman's) conventionally passive role, actively penetrating forbidden spaces, testing the potentials of an identity and a sexuality outside the father's law."[2] Even as O'Connor's heroines "engage in a continual repudiation of their womanhood . . . their flight invariably proves to be circular, bringing them face to face with the body of the mother."[3] While the mother, in Kahane's account, is "typically dead or absent," she remains a "spectral" figure presiding over a realm "where boundaries break down, where life and death become confused and identities unclear."[4]

Disagreement of this sort has prompted a more recent group of critics to posit gender-ambivalence, gender-contradiction, and gender-elision as effects of a deliberately intended authorial strategy. Gender-focussed readings acknowledge the familial dimensions of O'Connor's fiction, but point up her grimly sardonic, sometimes openly hostile treatment of courtship, marriage, and the heterosexual couple, and a general preference for characters who are celibate or widowed, as preempting ratification of conventional sex-marriage-family roles. Observing that O'Connor's fiction "affirms women who are able to take on positive masculine attributes," Marshall Gentry suggests that her work is marked to equal degree by an ever-more pronounced "feminization of men."[5] In "moving toward androgyny and hermaphroditism," her work culminates in the ideal of a transgendered subject and by implication relational configurations of an altogether different order from those associated with "family."[6]

Thus, while gender-based reading is essentially correct in underscoring a process Richard Giannone refers to as "gender displacement" (in the sense that O'Connor privileges neither maternal/feminine nor paternal/masculine poles), exclusive preoccupation with gender fails to account for how, in O'Connor's psychologically complex plots, characters re-embrace familial roles they initially seek to disavow.[7] In the discussion which follows, I will be applying Mara Selvini Palazzoli's approach to family systems, as well as recent historicist accounts of American postwar culture, to suggest (1) that O'Connor's apparent revalorizing of family consistently subordinates issues of gender to a transgenerational system in which transactions are determined more by age, generational status, and parent/child dyads than gender opposition and hierarchy; (2) that the interactive patterns which dominate her work represent an attempt to come to grips with a broader set of sociocultural forces associated with the anxieties and a new unsettling sense of collective vulnerability which arose with the outbreak of the cold war.

The development of family systems therapy in the course of the 1950s and 1960s reflected crucial advances in how family and its members were conceptualized.[8] The transactional basis of family systems therapy presupposes a "relational" concept of identity and self, but as all members of the family (whatever their age or gender status) are perceived as "players," it also ascribes greater margins of power and freedom to each member for initiating moves, counter-moves, or acts of distancing. As Palazzoli observes, the goal of family systems therapy remains that of enabling "the patient the dignity of carrying out voluntary, comprehensible actions." But in making such assertions, Palazzoli also argues the prior necessity of "assuming individual competence": "We never consider the patient's behavior compulsory, uncontrollable, or incomprehensible."[9] In contrast to psychoanalytic approaches which assign predetermined, essentially static "roles" to parental figures (with which the child must identify or disidentify if independence and maturity are to be attained), family systems therapy regards all family members as equal participants within a fluid, dynamic system, which may take either growth-promoting or pathogenic forms.

My interest in family systems theory here, however, is directed more at the ways in which Palazzoli has drawn attention to larger cultural and historical factors contributing to the rise of particular transactional patterns or culturally distinctive dysfunction. Commenting, for instance, on "hysteria in the sex-phobic bourgeoisie during the nineteenth century," Palazzoli asserts that "the sociocultural level determines the special way psychotic malaise will manifest itself during a certain period of history."[10] Similarly, speaking of anorexia nervosa, Palazzoli stresses that this is a syndrome "peculiar to the affluent society" and can be understood only in the context of a "Western cultural model.[11] Palazzoli identifies two broad trends within this model of special relevance to an account of the family dynamics at work in O'Connor: (1) "the shift in the position the child holds in the family, from relatively peripheral to one of paramount importance"; (2) "the ever-lengthening period of the offspring's life spent dependent on the parents, due to longer periods of higher education and difficulty in finding a job," a situation resulting in "the parents continuing for a longer period to feel responsible for their offspring."[12] Thus, while Palazzoli speaks of "the blurring of generational dividing lines (as) a constant in families with severe patients"—a remark again of immediate relevance to the interactive pattern characteristic of O'Connor's work—she notes that "the universally pathogenic phenomenon of blurred intergenerational boundaries" arises in part as a response to the particular stresses with which the modern family in advanced industrial cultures must cope.[13] But in drawing a link between intrafamilial transactions and sociocultural context, Palazzoli's work also begins to suggest a conceptual basis for grasping what I would see as the culturally distinctive solutions O'Connor envisioned for the predicaments associated with "prolonged adolescence," new forms of dependency and the "blurring of generational boundaries."[14]

If the interactive pattern characteristic of O'Connor's families accords with general, long-term sociocultural trends, it also incorporates responses to a more specific set of sociocultural variables. Reflecting the Eisenhower-era domestic revival with its reaffirmation of the middle-class nuclear family—and the kinds of boundaries built into the closed family unit—O'Connor's families are also characterized by a profound vulnerability and the frequency with which families or family members are marked as targets of sudden, lethal, and indiscriminately inflicted violence. In referring to "the personal and political terrors" of her fiction, Patricia Yaeger suggests that the all-encompassing, inescapable sense of threat which pervades O'Connor's work reflects an experience of national, collective trauma associated with the Second World War and, in the aftermath of Hiroshima and the Holocaust, the outbreak of the cold war and the ever more real threat of nuclear armageddon.[15] George Kennan, a principal architect of American cold war policy, was to note in describing the cultural environment of early cold war America and the nation's unprecedented strategic vulnerability: "A country which in 1900 had no thought that its prosperity and way of life could be in any way threatened by the outside world had arrived by 1950 at a point where it seemed to be able to think of little else but this danger."[16] In stressing how the violence which is such a distinctive feature of her fiction mirrors anxieties about what she herself was to characterize as "the terrible world we are coming to," Jon Bacon has argued that O'Connor reenacts and critiques a larger postwar narrative in which the United States, identified with "bucolic images of moral virtue" and an ideologically promulgated domesticity, increasingly perceived itself, with the intensification of the nuclear arms race and development of long-range delivery systems, as the target of attack.[17] Bacon notes that "the sense of imminent doom pervading her fiction" derived not only from O'Connor's personal situation ("her awareness that lupus would kill her at any time"), but more resonantly from "her knowledge that a vast number of Americans and a vast area of U.S. territory could be destroyed at a moment of international crisis."[18] Explicit in drawing connections between her position as writer, her "regionalism," and the outbreak of the cold war arms race, O'Connor herself was to observe that "So far as I am concerned as a novelist, a bomb on Hiroshima affects my judgment of life in rural Georgia."[19]

In making the point that "the human family is an organization geared to life and survival in every sense, both of the individual and of the species," Palazzoli lends support to accounts by cultural historians of how "in the cold war it was the vision of the sheltered, secure family" on which "Americans set their sights."[20] In underscoring how "family," "domesticity," and the "home" became dominant postwar values, Elaine Tyler May comments that "within (the home) the potentially dangerous social forces of the new age might be tamed, where they could contribute to the secure and fulfilling life to which postwar women and men aspire."[21] But as Tom Engelhardt has suggested in *The End of Victory Culture: Cold War America and the Disillusioning of a Generation* (1995), the development of nuclear weaponry and the inexorability with which technology itself dictated decision-making (culminating in the strategy of Mutual Assured Destruction [MAD] which made vulnerable civilian populations into a pillar of deterrence) had a corrosive effect on the authority of political and social institutions entrusted with the defense of the nation and the survival of its way of life—effects visible, I would suggest, in the succession of ineffectual, problematic parent figures which dominate O'Connor's fiction and the peculiarly skewed families over which they preside. If O'Connor's narratives reproduce an "ideology of domestic containment" which sought, as Robert J. Corber has argued, to "represent the Oedipal structure of the middle-class nuclear family as natural," they also reflect a new postwar skepticism toward those in whom authority was vested and their capability for ensuring a stable, secure social life.[22] In what Bacon characterizes as O'Connor's "divided" and "dysfunctional" families, "domestic existence" becomes "insufferable" and "the typical relation between parent and child" is "one of spite and resentment."[23] But the inference Bacon draws—that O'Connor's critique yields to an eschatological vision transcending immediate issues of family and personal life—nevertheless overlooks how O'Connor's narratives, even when seemingly most dismissive of conventional domestic arrangements, remain rooted in a transactional matrix defined by family and kinship ties. The consistency with which the "question" of the family is foregrounded suggests the social and institutional parameters of O'Connor's fiction remain relatively fixed, but the transactions that characterize her plots also point to a fundamental reconfiguring of the family whereby transgenerational subsystems are given priority over conjugal or intragenerational axes within the family.

In her preoccupation with the transgenerational, O'Connor moves across terrain in which psychoanalytically influenced criticism has felt most at home, but her modellings of family nevertheless suggest we might usefully discard the "oedipal" family metaphor and apply the more conceptually flexible language and insights of family systems theory. In the first instance, however much O'Connor's preoccupation with "family" accords with a larger postwar cultural dynamic—and all that this would imply in terms of the redomesticizing of women, new "permissiveness" toward children, and the "pastoralism" of burgeoning postwar suburbs—O'Connor's families clearly display features which distinguish them from the postwar *Father Knows Best* idealization of domestic life. Headed by a single widowed parent, or parent surrogate—more often a mother ("The Life You Save May Be Your Own," "Good Country People," "Everything That Rises," "Comforts of Home," "Greenleaf," "Enduring Chill"), but also fathers ("The Lame Shall Enter First," "Judgement Day"), or, as in "The Artificial Nigger" or "A View of the Woods," grandfathers who take over or arrogate to themselves parental responsibility—O'Connor's families are invariably truncated versions of the dual-parent, nuclear ideal. While often conforming to an absent-father pattern (and hence reflective of the de- or anti-masculinizing process feminist and gender critics see at work in O'Connor's texts), the isolation of the parent effectively dramatizes the question of a parent's capacities for meeting his/her responsibilities qua parent. The nominal authority of the prototypical O'Connor parent is emphasized by the social position he/she occupies—white, middle-class, property-owning, economically independent—and the responsibility he/she wields for still-dependent son(s) or daughter(s). In this sense, her fiction can be said to invoke 1950s-style expectations concerning nurturing/disciplining roles and the kind of social and moral authority vested in parents.[24] But at the same time, the demands placed on the single parent and his/her isolation help to account for the peculiar tensions and ambivalences encountered, especially in her late fiction—both the feelings of protectiveness which children display toward parental figures but also the resistance they put up in efforts to overcome dependency.

In tracing out what I would see as an underlying continuum of concerns—the fragility of O'Connor's subnuclear, single-parent, transgenerationally centered families as they confront a world of duplicity, criminal aggression, and ultimately irrational, inchoate violence—I would nevertheless see O'Connor's families as something more than simply "passive objects of historical change."[25] Family members engage in a variety of strategies in an effort to achieve equilibrium, cohesion, and a sense of personal identity. In considering O'Connor's evolving treatment of familial dysfunction, intergenerational conflict and the crisis of parental authority, I would point to four variants of the family dynamic—centered on shifting perceptions of the parental figure in his/her relation to the child—which informs O'Connor's fiction.

Given its complex intertextuality—the repetititon and reworking of themes and motifs from story to story—and the use of a third-person narratorial voice which is constantly shifting in its "allegiances" (what Carol Shloss calls the "narrator's chameleon voice"), classification of O'Connor's work into distinct "phases" or "periods" is necessarily suggestive and provisional.[26] Nevertheless, in following Palazzoli's view that familial dysfunction results from fundamental disruption on the level of the parental (and that familial equilibrium can be regained only once the parental function has been restored), I would suggest that O'Connor's positioning of the parent provides a useful starting point for discussion of interactive patterns in her fiction.[27] With the caveats that must attach to any schematization of such a complex body of work, the variants sketched out here can be seen to evolve in terms of how "threat" is identified and the capability for response, *in particular on the part of the parent*, ascribed the family or its members:

(1) *The Etiolated Parent*: The family as target of assault from violent, implacable forces external to itself, and parental figures shown as simply lacking the resources with which to cope. In the direst scenarios, the parent is powerless to prevent the annihilation of its members.

(2) *The Collusive Parent*: A second, more comic group of narratives centering on parental figures who are ascribed authority and power, but actively collaborate with outsiders in ways which bring about the disruption of the families over which they preside.

(3) *The Extended Parent*: A third, more radical variant of the pattern, here involving parents who are confident of themselves in their positions as parents and reach out beyond the boundaries of the family in an effort to extend their parenting capabilities to other-than-family members. In establishing alliances with these outsiders they neglect their own offspring, thereby instigating a sequence of transactions that typically culminate in catastrophe.

(4) *The De/Re-authorized Parent*: If the prototypical O'Connor family is headed by an almost invariably problematic parental figure, the parent in the fourth variant confronts a child who seeks to arrogate to him/herself the parental role, but who in the course of conflict precipitates a fundamental reconfiguring of the family involving renewed recognition of generational boundaries.

As the sequence of variants is meant to suggest, where in her earlier fiction dysfunction is more often precipitated by a figure or situation external to the family, in her late work sources of disruption are increasingly located within the family itself. As the individual family member in the later more internally focused narratives comes to a new recognition of his/her identity qua family member, he/she is also increasingly ascribed the power to act on the knowledge gained in the course of familial conflict. The ever more militant attitudes voiced by son/daughter figures in O'Connor's late work entail forms of opposition intended to discredit the generally well-meaning but tradition-centered, culturally and politically obtuse parent. In this sense, O'Connor's son/daughter figures come to speak with a knowledge and an authority (frequently endorsed by the narratorial voice itself) parents are perceived to lack, and thus initiate a process, similar to O'Connor's displacing of gender, of generational levelling. This is a process which can be characterized in terms of what John V. Knapp, following Palazzoli, refers to as "parentification," a reconfiguring which occurs when a child assumes or is assigned a parental role.[28] Here, we observe the adolescent or postadolescent child appropriating for him/herself the parental position by way of a counter-move to the perceived lapse or failure of the parent to understand where the best interests of the child or family (or even the parent) lie. But it is also ultimately in terms of historical dislocation, trauma, and vulnerability that I would see O'Connor's parent figures, particularly in the late, more rhetorically complex fiction, caught up in a transactional process that points to a new more open family system (indeed, in certain respects, like that envisaged by family systems therapy itself) in which individual family members, whatever their generational position, are ascribed greater responsibility for their actions.[29]

1. THE ETIOLATED PARENT

In "A Good Man Is Hard to Find," one of the earliest, most violent, and still most shocking of O'Connor's stories, a family—husband, wife, three young children and the husband's mother—bound for a Florida holiday survive an auto accident on a remote country road only to be set upon by an escaped felon and his two cohorts, who lead the members of the family off to the woods to be gunned down one by one. The accident occurs after the grandmother persuades her son to turn off the highway to visit a plantation she believes she has remembered from her childhood. Unaware of the danger the family faces, the grandmother, whose voice and actions dominate the story, banters amiably with the killer, but she can do nothing to alter the consequences—culminating with her own death—that ensue with grim inevitability once the accident has occurred. Indeed, as proves the case with many of O'Connor's older, female protagonists, the grandmother's sociability and good intentions only serve to hasten her and her son's family's demise.

"Greenleaf" incorporates configurations—a widowed mother with two grown sons—typical of O'Connor's "late period," but nevertheless identifies the sources of violence with figures and forces external to the family proper. Beginning with a relatively trivial incident—a stray bull belonging to the sons of Mr. Greenleaf, the mother's tenant farmer, has wandered onto her farm—the story records a succession of ever-more desperate attempts by Mrs. May, the widowed mother of two grown sons, to have the animal removed. Greenleaf's twin boys, who stand in caricatural contrast to Mrs. May's two sons, are Second World War veterans who have married French women and built up successful dairy farms with the help of GI Bill educations and VA loans. Beneficiaries of a rapidly changing class structure and a new, more egalitarian, postwar political order, they also embody something from which Mrs. May feels she and her sons have been excluded. While the story criticizes the mother's patrician disdain for her tenant and his Bible-reading, pentecostal wife and her failure to keep up with the new technologies Greenleaf's sons have installed and mastered ("a milking parlor built according to the latest specifications. . . . metal stanchions gleamed ferociously. . . . The milk ran in pipes from the machines to the milk house and was never carried in no bucket")—the central issue is that of the May family's cohesion: their readiness to stand together and meet the threats posed by what the Greenleafs and their symbolically charged bull represent—tests they utterly fail.[30] Unable to persuade her sons to help in her efforts to have the bull removed, the mother is increasingly isolated as the animal eats through her garden and roams freely across her property.

While the story reflects patterns typical of the later stories in which grown sons or daughters oppose ineffectual parents, the mother in this instance responds by virtually disowning her disaffected offspring: "you two should have belonged to Mrs. Greenleaf"—a statement that only further alienates the two young men, the younger son, caustically retorting to his brother, "that neither you nor me is her boy."[31] The two sons—the elder an in-

surance agent exploiting poor blacks; the younger an embittered
college instructor ("He didn't like anything. He drove twenty miles
to the university where he taught and twenty back, but he said he
hated the twenty mile drive, and he hated the second-rate university and he hated the morons who attended it")—become ever
more verbally aggressive.[32] In one heated exchange, the younger
son snaps at his mother: "I wouldn't milk a cow to save your soul
from hell."[33]

Despite efforts to reassert her authority and reestablish generational boundaries ("I am the only *adult* on this place,") she
is powerless to hinder the growing animosity between the two
siblings, who end up brawling—the younger son finally brought
to the floor where he lies powerless, "like a large bug on his back
with the edge of the over-turned table cutting him across the
middle and broken dishes scattered on top of him."[34] When the
two boys refuse the mother's final appeal for assistance, she suc-
cumbs to lacerating self-pity: "I'm the victim. I've always been
the victim."[35] Relegated to the margins of the property—and the
family—over which she putatively presides, she stands at the
end of the story alone in a field, seeming to welcome, in "freezing
unbelief," the sudden charge of the bull that kills her.

In tracking a process of spiralling, ever-more acute intrafamilial aggression—initially prompted by outsiders who embody everything the mother believes her family has been denied—the
narrative would seem to reinforce O'Connor's convictions about
"the terrible world we are coming to." Despite the story's domestic focus and deployment of characters identified in terms of position within or in proximity to family, the deeper-lying dynamic
(the indifference of the two sons to the mother's plight and her
failure to reaffirm herself in the parental role) suggests that, as
in "A Good Man Is Hard to Find," when confronted by an external threat for which there can be no effective countermeasure,
the family comes to function at only the most nominal of levels.
Whatever the façades of hospitality and civility older adult figures seek to keep up, they are brought low by "others" marked
by the absence of kinship ties to the protagonist, the aura of
threat accentuated in large part by their spatial or topographical
position vis-à-vis the family—either by their association with the
"foreign" (as in the case of the Greenleaf sons who have seen
military service in Europe and married French wives), or by the
distance they have traversed prior to their confrontration with
the family.

Such stories suggest families in O'Connor's fictional universe

are defined by their fundamental vulnerability and helplessness—something to which the postwar world had condemned
those born into it—but as O'Connor's fiction evolved in the 1950s
and early 1960s, it also depicts characters bringing into play
strategies—some successful, some not—in efforts to reaffirm
the possibility of sustaining family ties, restoring familial equilibrium and, indeed, upholding the possibility of surviving the
forces—political, social, technological—reshaping the postwar
world. Critics like Carter W. Martin and John F. Desmond have
characterized this effort in the same eschatological terms
O'Connor herself used to describe her fiction and the beliefs
which underpinned it. Thus, for instance, Martin comments,
while "plausible and understandable on the naturalistic plane, . . .
the actions of her characters take their final meanings from a
plane above the natural."[36] But however the links between
O'Connor's storytelling practice and her Catholicism are finally
construed, the immediate, transactional basis of her fiction remains a matrix of courtship, marriage, family, and kinship. It is
in these terms her characters come to articulate what I would
see as a new, distinctive ideal of what goes into the making of
"family" and the conditions under which "family" might be con-
stituted and preserved. In part, this is exemplified in the form of
counter-example: stories where characters—whether parents or
children—enter into transactions that serve to weaken and undermine the family or the kind of support a family, under optimal
circumstances, might be called upon to offer, but which in so
doing begin to suggest the grounds for a counter-response.

2. The Collusive Parent

It is in this context that I would identify a second, more comic
group of narratives centering on parental figures who deploy essentially collaborative strategies in conjunction with outsiders in
efforts to "support" offspring—in ways, however, which bring
about the humiliation of children over whom they wield authority,
and thus only end up by reinforcing a sense of the family's isolation. In "The Life You Save May Be Your Own," Shiftlet, the one-
armed war vet and itinerant handyman, appears at the door of
the country home of a single mother (a farmwoman), and her
handicapped daughter. Initially suspicious ("'I don't know nothing about you'") of the "tramp," she is won over by his displays
of modesty and seeming wisdom ("'Maybe the best I can tell you

is, I'm a man, but listen lady . . . what is a man?'") and, on the more practical side, the repairs he makes to the farm (which, as Shiftlet emphasizes, "was because he had taken a personal interest in it").[37] Impressed by his abilities, she begins to view him a potential husband for her otherwise unpromising, deaf-mute daughter. Reticent at first ("I can't get married right now. . . . Everything you want to do takes money and I ain't got any"), Shiftlet is only persuaded to accept the mother's proposal ("you'd be getting a permanent house and a deep well and the most innocent girl in the world") when she throws in the offer of "the '28 or '29" Ford that he has repaired.[38] Having registered the marriage, Shiftlet and his new bride drive off on their honeymoon. When they stop for a meal at a diner, the young woman lays her head on the counter and falls sound asleep. Telling the counterman she is a hitchhiker and that he is "in a hurry to reach Tuscaloosa," he abandons his wife, driving off in the automobile which he "had always wanted but had never been able to afford."[39] The mother's unwitting role in abetting Shiftlet's con is made clear from the outset as she shamelessly touts her daughter's virtues: "she's the sweetest girl in the world. I wouldn't give her up for nothing on earth. She's smart too. She can sweep the floor, cook, wash, feed the chickens, and hoe. I wouldn't give her up for a casket of jewels."[40]

Manley Pointer, the Bible-selling huckster in "Good Country People," like Shiftlet, manages to ingratiate himself with Mrs. Hopewell, the mother of a young woman handicapped by the loss of a leg in a hunting accident ("literally blasted off at the age of ten"), the artificial leg she has worn since then, and "a weak heart" ("The doctors had told Mrs. Hopewell that with the best of care, Joy might see forty-five").[41] While the daughter has obtained a Ph.D. in philosophy and, in a display of independence, changed her name to Hulga, the mother feels she has only made herself into a social misfit ("The Ph.D. had certainly not brought her out any . . . every year she grew less like other people").[42] Initially hoping to put the salesman off, the mother relents when he informs her that, like her daughter, he has "this heart condition" and "may not live long."[43] Sympathizing with the near invalid and his "sincere and genuine" manner, she invites him into the home for dinner.[44] The salesman uses the occasion to approach the sullen Hulga who, unexpectedly, responds with interest and affection for someone who, like her, "may die."[45] Having decided, largely as a result of the mother's endorsement, that the salesman is forthright in his intentions, she agrees to meet him, where, after a perfunctory courtship, she is asked—as a sign of compliance with her own insistence that they be completely "honest"—to show and then to detach her artificial leg—which she does, only to watch helplessly as he places it in the bag in which he carries his Bibles and runs off. In both instances, maternal obtuseness leads inevitably to the humiliation of daughters incapable of fending for themselves. Here, O'Connor's grotesque, brutal parodies of courtship would seem to underscore something more than ambivalence about gender. While Shiftlet and Pointer are clearly unscrupulous males willing to say and do whatever they can to achieve their ends, their duplicity and the ease with which they gain entrance into the household and secure the parents' approval essentially serve as object lessons. Their actions would seem to justify the sort of suspiciousness of outsiders which the ideology of "domestic containment" fostered, but these characters also underscore how easily, once locked into the closed logic of "nuclearity" and shut off from the larger world, the family can become a target for those preying on it from without and seeking to exploit its members for their own ends.

3. The Extended Parent

A third, more radical variant of the pattern involves parents who, confident of themselves in their positions as parents, reach out beyond the boundaries of the family in an effort to offer their imagined parenting capabilities to other-than-family members. Here, it is the overzealous application of the parental impulse—the parent moving beyond the boundaries that separate family from external world—which places the family, either the parent figures or child or both at risk. The civic-minded widower-father in "The Lame Shall Enter First," absorbed in efforts to rehabilitate Rufus Johnson, a juvenile offender, and offer him a proper upbringing, fails to perceive the depth of his own ten-year old son's grief following the death of mother/wife. Indeed, it becomes clear that Rufus represents a kind of surrogate for the son, and perhaps an outlet through whom the father can avoid acknowledging the grief experienced by the son, whom the father dismisses as "selfish, unresponsive, greedy" and "showing no intellectual curiosity whatsoever."[46] While Rufus believes himself under "the power of Satan" ("when I die I'm going to hell"), the father is convinced that proper education will enable the young man, with his "I.Q. score of 140," to put his criminal past behind him and achieve a productive life. In his superpaternalism, the father encourages Rufus to open his eyes to the wider world of science and technology, convinced in this way Rufus will grow out of his "superstitious" belief in Satan:

> [The father] talked the kind of talk the boy would never have heard before. . . . He roamed from simple psychology . . . to astronomy and the space capsules that were whirling around the earth faster than the speed of sound and would soon encircle the stars. He wanted to give the boy something to reach for besides his neighbor's goods. He wanted him to *see* the universe, to see that the darkest parts of it could be penetrated."[47]

Providing the sort of encouragement he fails to offer his own son, the father tries to prod Rufus into awareness of what his intelligence offers him: "you can be anything in the world you want to be. You can be a scientist or an architect or an engineer or whatever you set your mind to, and whatever you set your mind to be, you can be the best of its kind."[48]

The uncannily smart but viciously defiant Rufus persists in his petty thievery only to provoke the father into both ever more combative efforts to gain the delinquent boy's trust and ever acuter neglect of his own child's needs. By rejecting the father and asserting his "independence" of adult authority, Rufus, however, wins the admiration of the young son, who shows himself more than willing to follow the charismatic teenager's increasingly authoritative advice. The father only perceives the error of his ways when he discovers his son, a target in Rufus's ruthless campaign to discredit the father's belief in good works ("To show up that big tin Jesus!"), has committed suicide.[49] Increasingly isolated and desperate for the care and attention only the mother had afforded him, the young boy hangs himself: the father discovers the young boy's body "just below the beam from which he had launched his flight into space."[50] In maleficent parody of the father's application of behaviorist—i.e., "scientific"—precept in his campaign to rehabilitate wayward youth, Rufus had assured the ten-year old the mother was awaiting him in "heaven" like an astronaut in orbit. Here, the extension of the parental impulse to a figure beyond the confines of the family precipitates catastrophe—the death of a child—for which the father pays finally by forfeiture of his paternal status.

In its initial set of moves, "The Comforts of Home," among the most grimly ironic of all O'Connor's short stories, resembles the opening of "The Lame Shall Enter First": a juvenile criminal—here a teenage girl jailed "on a bad check charge"—is introduced into the home by a well-meaning parent. But as the action unfolds and events are recorded from the vantage point of an older son who immediately sees the mother's error, it displays the transactional dynamic characteristic of O'Connor's late work, and can be better viewed as a transitional variant. In a situation characteristic of O'Connor's late fiction, it is Thomas, the celibate, thirty-five year old son, who, committed to the undisturbed domesticity he and his mother have shared since the father's death, appropriates for himself the parental role that the widowed mother has, in the son's view, irresponsibly relinquished when she takes custody of the "nympermaniac" teenager, Sarah Ham. The more the girl insinuates herself into the mother's favor, the greater the urgency of the son's attempts to protect the mother from the girl's increasingly provocative behavior. When his attempts to reason with the mother ("in a few days that girl will have left town, having got what she could out of you") are rebuffed ("suppose it were you?"), he finds himself thrown back onto his own resources.[51] Here, the intensity of his efforts to take countermeasures and reconstitute the tranquillity of a domestic life on which he has come to depend culminates in the mother's death and the son's arrest for her murder.

The nightmarish sequence of events with which the story climaxes underscores the abruptness with which in O'Connor's late stories, power, authority, mastery are secured, transferred, lost, displaced. Thomas's seeming overdependency on the mother and identification with the dead father in efforts to restore the status quo ante point to a classically oedipal scenario, as Frederick Asals, in a now standard reading, has suggested. In Asals's account the source of disruption is neither the mother nor the young girl, but the "repressed" son who recoils in terror at the prospect of an erotic encounter with his "anima" as represented by the teenage girl.[52] While the story can be seen to criticize the son for the domestic ideal he will do anything to defend ("home was to Thomas home, workshop, church, as personal as the shell of a turtle and as necessary"); and while it is equally clear the mother displays laudable intentions in her desire to assist the "disadvantaged" young girl, the claim that Sarah Ham represents a potential mate and thus an opportunity (here, encouraged by the mother) for Thomas to overcome his dependency, the girl's behavior (mockery of the mother, drunkenness, theft of the father's handgun) mark her, like Rufus Johnson or the Misfit, as one of O'Connor's incorrigibles.[53] While the girl is clearly identified in terms of the "sexuality" she flaunts (her nudity and general lasciviousness), her behavior toward the son suggests less the expression of desire or affection than a wish to ridicule anything that smacks of feeling or attachment. Thus, while, on the one level, the narrative seems to recognize and condemn Thomas for his lack of charity and small-mindedness, in its excoriating depiction of the girl, it endorses Thomas's criticism of the mother for failing to see what the girl is up to. Recognizing the protagonist's limitations, the narrative also accepts his modesty as a "virtue," given what are presented as the alternatives.

But if Thomas is disturbed by his mother's blindness to Sarah Ham's true motives (what in fact the narrative identifies as the absence of any real motive), what drives him finally to "rage" and sets in motion the sequence culminating in the mother's death, is the mother's repeated assertion of an essential equivalence between himself and the girl ("it might be you. . . . I would not send *you* back to jail, Thomas")—a response with which the narrative itself would seem to concur.[54] The differences between the thirty-five year old sedentary "county historian" and restless, criminally inclined young girl are glaring, and Thomas cannot believe his mother is so credulous. It is, of course, arguably this "blindness" which has permitted her to indulge her son for as long as she has. Her flaw, in this sense, is an undiscriminating "motherliness"—the fact that in "pursuing virtue with such a mindless intensity, everyone involved was made a fool of and virtue itself became ridiculous." But Thomas's increasing frustration with the mother also begins to point to a growing, more differentiated sense of self. If he briefly entertains the possibility of leaving his mother's home—a move that would constitute an unambiguous declaration of independence—Thomas nevertheless sees that Sarah Ham is ruthless enough to pose a threat to the mother's life. In a clear, seemingly justified instance of "parentification," Thomas decides to remain and to protect the mother he now perceives as "a defective child" from her own ill-advised decision: "She proceeded always from the tritest of considerations—it was the *nice thing to do*—."[55]

Given, however, his narrow range of real-life experience, Thomas shows himself helpless in his search for remedies. Never having known real independence, he feels himself compelled to reach back to the memory of the dead father ("It was at these times that Thomas truly mourned the death of his father"), a figure he "had not been able to endure in life," but who here promises the possibility of decisive action: "The old man would have had none of this foolishness. Untouched by useless compassion, he would have pulled the necessary strings . . . and the girl would have been packed off to the state penitentiary to serve her time."[56] The narrative, of course, suggests the son has been right to distance himself from the father—a violent, unscrupulous, domineering man—and clearly, too, the mother has felt comfortable in her relation with the son precisely because he is everything the father was not (when Thomas tells his mother the father "would have put his foot down," the mother visibly "stiffens," replying "You are not like him").[57] But as Sarah Ham, stepping up her efforts to intimidate Thomas and his mother, becomes increasingly violent, the father—a ghostly but ever more insistent presence ("his father took up a squatting position in his mind")—seems the only source of solutions.[58]

While the story suggests an interactive pattern in which a child becomes "involved in the parents' relational problems," it would be a mistake to see the son's action here as a matter of "siding" with a particular parent in the child's misconceived efforts to rectify or compensate for discord between mother and father.[59] The apparent alliance between father and son is, in this instance, simply a measure of the desperation the son feels as he seeks to come to grips with his own feelings of helplessness. In part because it violates his own perception of who he is and what he represents (in this sense he has differentiated himself from both mother and father), Thomas initially refuses the "father's" advice:

> Several ideas for getting rid of (Sarah) had entered his head but each of these had been suggestions whose moral tone indicated that they had come from a mind akin to his father's, and Thomas had rejected them. He could not get the girl locked up again until she did something illegal. The old man would have been able with no qualms at all to get her drunk and send her out on the highway in his car, meanwhile notifying the highway patrol of her presence on the road, but Thomas considered this below his moral stature.[60]

But as the mother's failure to see Sara Ham's behavior for the danger it represents places the parent in ever greater jeopardy, he becomes more and more compliant in following out the father's suggestions that he simply do whatever it takes to have the girl removed from the house.

Here, in effectively reconstituting the father, Thomas can be seen to appropriate the paternal role and place himself in a position of generational parity vis-à-vis the mother. Indeed, in what appears to be a process of "parentification," he confirms himself in his self-appointed role as the mother's guardian. At the same time, in rejecting his own initially more moderate approach to conflict, and simply aligning himself with the dead father, he would seem to reposition himself as son anxious to live up to parental expectations, thereby denying his own growing sense of who he is and what he stands for. If he deploys what Gary Storhoff has referred to as "a compensatory coping mechanism" in coming to grips with his earlier failures (a result, he feels, of his complacency and passivity), it would, nevertheless, be wrong to see this as a case of oedipal identification.[61] Just as the son's anger at the introduction of Sarah Ham into the home points less to a continuing attachment to the mother than a new emerging sense of self (given that the mother fails to distinguish between Thomas and the girl), so too recourse to the father is more a symptom of the son's failure to apply an independently conceived strategy appropriate to the occasion. Indeed, the readier he is to heed the father, the more uncontrollable his behavior becomes ("His expression was a turmoil of indecision and outrage. His pale blue eyes seemed to sweat in his roiling face"), the less his chances of finding a satisfactory solution.[62] When he seeks out the sheriff, a friend of the father, to report the theft of the father's gun by the girl, he is "barely coherent."[63] When he finds the revolver unexpectedly returned to his desk drawer, Thomas loses what is left of his moral bearings. In his efforts to incriminate the girl, he plants the weapon in her handbag. Detected in the act by the now infuriated girl, he makes a grab for the gun before she can use it. Completely under the influence of the father ("as if his arm were guided by his father"), Thomas impulsively takes aim and shoots at Sarah ("Fire! the old man yelled").[64] To his horror (and Sara's delight), he kills the mother as she throws herself forward in an effort to protect the girl.

On the one level, in committing a criminal act and bringing about the death of the mother, Thomas ironically confirms the mother's perception of the son and the delinquent girl as equals. But if there is no way in which Thomas here can be "exonerated," his actions spring from sources of a fundamentally different kind and order than the girl's. Whereas Sarah Ham is described from the outset as "born without the moral faculty— like somebody else would be born without a kidney or a leg" and thus incapable of distinguishing between right and wrong, his actions reflect his wish to act against what is identified within the story as a real threat.[65] Thus, however misconceived his identification with the father, his action is the consequence of a first step in the direction of independence and maturity. If he fails, it is because he has taken this step "too late," has remained too long in a state of dependency, and once emancipated lacks the experience and knowledge needed to cope with the unexpected and the unpredictable. The recourse to the father can be read, of course, as an act of "regression," but identification with the paternal here in no way signifies, oedipal fashion, a step toward "maturity." The father's advice is a recipe for disaster and, indeed, suggests in yet another way how O'Connor's parental figures work against the interests of their families. Power and authority reside neither in the mother, nor, as the oedipal paradigm customarily suggests, in the father, whose "actions" here only serve to hasten the family's demise. If the story points to an ultimate equivalence between mother and son—both victims, both "trapped" within a "family" that has offered only spurious shelter—it also intimates a new, more "realistic" appraisal of the parent on the part of the child.

4. THE DE/RE-AUTHORIZED PARENT

While Thomas acts on a dawning but imperfectly actualized sense of self, the dynamic at work in "The Comforts of Home" signals a decisive reorientation, characteristic of O'Connor's late work, around the problematics of emancipation and autonomy. Her "late" characters—Thomas, Asbury in "The Enduring Chill," Julian in "Everything That Rises Must Converge," Mary Grace in "Revelation"—are all ultimately at odds with parental figures and the parent confronts a child seeking to assert his/her independence. But, significantly, the more zealous these figures seem to be in affirming their autonomy, the more profoundly implicated they become in the families from which they try to distance themselves. The locking of the adolescent or postadolescent child into a dyadic unit from which there is no possibility of escape would seem, in terms of setting and narrative scope, to underscore the restrictiveness of O'Connor's families, a circumstance generally exacerbated by the education and experience the adolescent child has gained outside the home.

That O'Connor's later protagonists, whatever their actual age,

are routinely denied the independence, prerogatives and responsibilities associated with adulthood seems nevertheless equally
central to the kind of knowledge and insight they come to possess—the capacity for seeing through what her fiction identifies
as the complacency and smug façades of American postwar domesticity. Neither adolescents nor adults, they are positioned in
a kind of liminal space; their "freedom" from convention and
their status as 'outsiders' afford what they themselves feel to be
a broader perspective and more acute powers of discernment
and moral judgment. However restricted the authority they actually possess, they imagine themselves more knowledgeable and
thus better equipped to handle the world than parental figures
identified as agents of a "tradition" or values O'Connor's late
narratives recognize as marginal to postwar American social and
political life. These are narratives in which the "parentification"
impulse achieves a kind of culmination. Julian in "Everything
That Rises" speaks of his mother as "a child" ("her eyes were as
innocent and untouched by experience as they must have been
when she was ten") and acknowledges he has no choice but to
chaperone her on her bus-ride across town; Asbury in "The Enduring Chill" wants to "assist" his mother "in the process of
growing up."[66] Indeed, that these figures function as focalizers
initially suggests their appraisals of the parent are correct. In
"Everything That Rises Must Converge," the mother's nostalgic
fantasies of her own sheltered girlhood underscore her childish-
ness, and the narrative confirms the son's point of view insofar
as the mother remains oblivious to the effect her words and actions have on others—to the point finally of provoking the black
mother into physically striking back. But if the protagonists in
O'Connor's late fiction insist ever more demonstratively on their
independence from parents, these stories ever more emphatically suggest the difficulties placed in the young protagonist's
path. The more zealous their affirmations of autonomy, the more
inescapable family seems to become.

In "The Enduring Chill" "home" is signified as confining, carc-
eral, as that which must be escaped at all costs if Asbury, the
young aspiring writer is to "to liberate" his "imagination" and
achieve the independence ("We've got to think free if we want to
live free") he feels necessary to achieve his goal of being a
writer.[67] But the difficulties Asbury experiences—his "writer's
block" and the withering of his imagination (conditions amplified
in his anticipation of death and the "burial" symbolically inscribed in his name)—are linked ultimately with the fact of de-

parture and separation, with his rejection of home and his widowed mother. The Manhattan to which Asbury has made his escape and where he subsequently falls ill is evoked as a frozen wasteland: "Alone in his freezing flat, huddled under his two blankets and his overcoat and with three thicknesses of the *The New York Times* between, he had had a chill one night."[68] If the wintry city is metaphorical of sterility and failure ("his two lifeless novels, his half-dozen stationary plays, his prosy poems, his sketchy short stories"), his inertness is adduced here as a consequence of self-willed exile, narcissistic self-absorption, nullification of desire for anything or anyone but the self cut off from all familial or other social ties.[69] On the one level, the "message" of the story is clear: Asbury's ambitions are thwarted precisely to the extent "he had always relied on himself" and has made "self" into the subject of his art.[70] In his fatuous misquote of Yeats (he writes of his imagination "whirling off into the widening gyre") or equally incongruous invocation of Kafka, Asbury displays not insight but simply that he is, as the priest he has invited to the home for literary discussion tells him, "a lazy ignorant conceited youth."[71]

Given the kinds of oppositions and equivalences the story posits (home = survival and life; Manhattan = illness and death), Asbury in fact has no choice but to return—a moment experienced as one of galling defeat. In a phrase emphasizing the dimensions of trauma hovering in the background, the sister sardonically characterizes the brother's homecoming as "the artist arriving at the gas chamber."[72] More distressing than the return itself is the element of compulsion, i.e., that he has no choice but to relinquish the autonomy he has heroically struggled to secure in effecting his escape from "the slave's atmosphere of home."[73] Just as Asbury characterizes the mother as "child," homecoming implies return to a condition from which he has labored in vain to liberate himself and he initially welcomes the death ("He had failed his god, Art, but he had been a faithful servant and Art was sending him Death") he believes preferable to a life of continued dependency.[74]

But the fact that Asbury has no choice but to return is rendered here as the basis for a larger recognition, and a corrective to what the narrative presents as his mistaken notions about art and writing. Signifying the inescapability of the corporeal, the specificity and boundedness of being (or, that "being" is finally something other than the signification of being), the parent and the home she presides over here denote a dimension that the son has failed to acknowledge in his zeal to make a life for himself. The narrative suggests that only in the experience and knowledge of what is most familiar, immediate, most intimate (conditions identified with the mother whose "way had simply been the air he breathed"), do notions of "consciousness" or what consciousness might achieve, i.e., a work of art, begin to take on a meaning.[75] In the final lines of the story, Asbury continues to resist ("a last impossible protest escaped him"), but he is on the verge of genuine insight: "The old life in him was exhausted. He awaited the coming of new. . . . The fierce bird appeared all at once to be in motion . . . the last film of illusion was torn as if by a whirlwind from his eyes." The "the fierce bird"—the eagle-shaped water stain on the wall of his childhood bedroom—is an emblem of "the Holy Ghost" and all that this suggests in terms of revivifying power and regenerative force. More significant, however, are the associations with his boyhood ("The fierce bird which through the years of his childhood . . . had been poised over his head, waiting mysteriously"); the bird as something intimately identified with the space (the room, the house and, in the symbolic connections the story draws between "mother" and "Holy Ghost," the very "air" he breathes) in which he spent his childhood years and where, as the ending makes clear, he will live out the remainder of his life.[76] Whatever its larger eschatological import, the conclusion seems to affirm that only by recognizing and accepting—and not denying—generational boundaries is a productive life possible. To sever oneself from family, to rely solely on one's own psychological, intellectual and aesthetic resources, is to condemn oneself to artistically crippling isolation.

If O'Connor's late fiction stages a generationally marked conflict between parental figures and adolescent (or not-yet fully adult) son and daughter figures in which the older figure is inevitably found wanting, these struggles are never resolved in terms that unambiguoulsy endorse the younger protagonists, or confirm them in the parental role they appropriate for themselves. The initial reversal of positions (whereby the morally superior child comes to pass judgment on the parent) is typically subjected to a further twist, in which the younger protagonist's credibility, whatever advantage he or she has managed to secure, is voided, and the younger figure revealed to be as lacking in perspicacity and maturity as the "adult." This compels O'Connor's protagonists in turn to acknowledge their continued implication in a familial matrix—and generational hierarchies—they initially seek to escape or deny. If from one perspective, this might qualify O'Connor's transgenerational dyads as pathogenic and her protagonists as locked into patterns of overdependency in which there is little hope of change, O'Connor's late narratives also point to a new sort of insight in which renewed recognition by son/daughter figures of generational boundaries becomes a necessary step towards the achievement of genuine independence.[77]

In "Everything That Rises Must Converge," the protagonist, the son of a widowed mother, becomes, like Asbury, ever harsher in his criticisms of the parent. Initially directed at the most trivial ("the mother's hideous hat"), these embrace an ever broader array of behaviors: her bigotry ("She would not ride the buses by herself at night since they had been integrated"), misplaced pride in her patrician ancestry, and finally, like Thomas's mother, her failure to recognize who or what the son has become.[78] In the mother's confident assertions of self and identity ("I most certainly do know who I am"), rooted as they are in the questionable glories of the past—"Your great-grandfather had a plantation and two hundred slaves"—she displays hopelessly atavistic measures of selfworth and esteem.[79] But if Julian takes the trouble to rebut her assertions ("'There are no more slaves,' he said irritably"), he feels in fact his mother is simply making a fool of herself, and the conversations leave him weary and depressed—a situation which resembles the "sterile hopelessness and despair" Palazzoli describes patients experiencing when "parents are so heavily indicted" the patient feels himself equally worthless.[80] Living in nostalgic recreations of the past, the mother is blind to the actuality of the world around her: she "persists in thinking they did well to have an apartment in (what) had been a fashionable neighborhood forty years ago," whereas Julian sees the houses for what they are—"bulbous-colored monstrosities of a uniform ugliness. . . . Each house with a narrow collar of dirt around it in which sat, usually, a grubby child."[81] Convinced that he can "see her with absolute clarity," Julian perceives his mother living "according to the laws of her own fantasy world, outside of which he had never seen her set foot."[82]

In opposing the mother, Julian, like Asbury, feels he has managed to achieve whatever he has become independently of the parent: "in spite of growing up dominated by a small mind, he had ended up with a large one; in spite of all her foolish views, he was free of prejudice and unafraid to face facts . . . he had cut himself emotionally free of her and could see her with complete objectivity. He was not dominated by his mother."[83] As mother and son proceed on their fateful bus journey across town, the son's desires, however, are reframed and his own relation to "history" and "politics" shown to be as fantasmatic as the mother's. He, like the mother, "withdraws into the inner compartment of his mind where he spent most of his time . . . a kind of mental bubble in which he established himself when he could not bear to be a part of what was going on around him."[84] And like the mother, he too is incapable of seeing or understanding the effects of his actions on others, here in particular of how his abusive language ("Nobody in the damn bus cares who you *are*") so disturbs the mother that it endangers her already fragile health.[85] While he plays himself off ever more hyperbolically as the enlightened liberal—demonstratively sitting next to a black businessman on the bus; imagining himself married to a black woman—his espousal of liberal ideals is revealed as little more than a tactic in a covert conflict between a mother desperate to preserve an identity rooted in an irretrievable past and a resentful, ultimately overdependent son whose behavior is motivated as much as the mother's by the experience of loss and deprivation—of a home and an upbringing that the mother was incapable of providing him. In a manner typical of O'Connor's technique, the apparent banality of the plotting—departure from home, waiting for and boarding the bus, the crosstown trip, the deboarding and final climactic encounter over the coin the mother hands the black woman's young son—becomes the vehicle for a much fiercer struggle on the level of psyche and self: a battle ultimately waged over the sources of identity, the possibility of independence, and the meaning of family. If Julian's mother is depicted as a marginal figure shunted aside by "history," it is her image of herself as "Godhigh," as living embodiment of family, tradition, and the possibility of an integral, identifiable "self," which enables her to perceive her son as himself a figure of worth and potential. Whatever the actuality of the son's position—whether he will ever achieve anything he himself might value—the mother continues to affirm her faith in his abilities and "the future ahead of him."[86] Despite repeated provocation, she avoids open polemic and refuses to oppose or reprimand him. There is, in this sense, an element of the protective, self-effacing mother, a refusal to see the son as at fault, even when he is most openly abusive.

The moment of what appears to be the most acute divergence coincides with an epiphany-like revelation of a "familialist" imperative which the son, like Thomas in "The Comforts of Home" and Asbury in "The Enduring Chill," would seem to have violated in his blindness to the effects of his actions on the mother's already weakened condition. Abruptly confronting the prospect of the mother's death, Julian grasps the depth of his attachment and his own role in hastening her demise. The son's speech here oscillates between the anguished appeals of an abandoned child ("He dashed forward and fell at her side, crying, 'Mamma, Mamma!'") and the endearments of a spouse or lover ("Darling, sweetheart, wait!"), uttered as he comprehends the gravity of the mother's condition and the dimensions of affect he has denied within himself.[87] Perceiving the mother's near comatose state—a moment in which she too again reverts to her childhood (asking her old nursemaid to take her "home")—he is immobilized by the feelings of shame, guilt, and self-abasement that overwhelm him, and he cannot bring himself to leave her side. As in "A Good Man Is Hard to Find," "Greenleaf," "The Comforts of Home," the death of the parent is a moment of defeat and powerlessness, of familial dissolution, and of the body at its limits ("his feet moved numbly as if they carried him nowhere"). With its undercurrents of fantasmatic fusion ("The tide of darkness seemed to sweep him back to her"), it is a moment in which clearly, however, generational boundaries are breached and a peculiar equivalence affirmed.[88] The abrupt shifts of verbal register—the baroque, semantically dense language of O'Connor's epiphanies stands starkly at odds with the overall lucidity of her narratives—point to powerful, conflicting, inchoate forces that defy conventional modes of signification, but simultaneously to a powerful recognition of the lost object—a bonding, needless to say, that has meaning only in the course of an experience of loss.

The reaffirmation by son/daughter figures of their subordinate status in a generational hierarchy (we might speak here of a "reparentification" of the parent) points to a condition of continued deep-lying dependency. But the attempt by son/daughter figures to reestablish such dependency is itself belated, and needless to say, grounded in fantasy insofar as the parent in O'Connor's families never wields the power needed to satisfy such demands in the first place. If on the one hand, the hostility directed by child at the parent, and the kind of authority the parent is conventionally perceived to represent, would seem to accord with an essentially oedipal pattern of antiparental hostility—the child's sense of self and self-worth impelling the child to oppose the parent and assert his/her independence—O'Connor's transgenerational narratives reposition parent and child in ways that underscore both renewed recognition of generational boundaries and a fundamental parity—a move that can be read in "Everything That Rises Must Converge" as signalling a new kind of distance and objectivity, and in this sense the reascription of precisely the sort of autonomy the child has sought but been denied. The overdetermined deficiencies of the parental figure—parents incapable of making their way in the world; parents as targets of criticism by their own grown children—make clear from the outset that, whatever the child's demands for security and protection, the parent is incapable of providing them. If Julian is reimplicated qua son in the family he has sought to renounce, this occurs in relation to a parent who has herself been refigured as child. Thus, when, in his final traumatic appeal, Julian seems to recognize the mother qua mother, it only serves to underscore the contingencies—the isolation and vulnerability—that define *both* child and parent. Whatever the faults of O'Connor's postadolescent, not-yet adult sons and daughters, they are, in this respect, identified as possessors of a new kind of knowledge ("the world of guilt and sorrow") rooted in a transgenerational experience of trauma and loss.[89] Legatees of insight, they become in O'Connor's final stories the voice of a new, de-oedipalized domesticity—a family pattern that was to inform a broad range of American postwar fiction and drama, and in ever more forceful ways shaped the generational and familial politics of the postwar era.

NOTES

1. Westling, "Fathers and Daughters in Welty and O'Connor," 111.
2. Kahane, "Maternal Legacy," 242.
3. Ibid., 247.
4. Ibid., 243.
5. Gentry, "Gender Dialogue in O'Connor," 65–66.
6. Ibid., 62.
7. See Giannone, "Displacing Gender."
8. See Knapp, *Striking at the Joints*, Bump, "Family Dynamics of the Reception of Art;" and Palazzoli, Cirillo, Selvini, and Sorrentino, *Family Games.*
9. Palazzoli, Cirillo, Selvini, and Sorrentino, *Family Games*, 223.
10. Ibid., 193.
11. Ibid., 177–78.
12. Ibid., 178.
13. Ibid., 23.
14. Following Palazzoli, I am suggesting here that family patterns within the literature of particular periods often coalesce around specific configurations and sequences. Notable instances of such historically conditioned interactive patterns are what I have elsewhere called "the sentimental family paradigm"

(which achieves a kind of culmination in the Richardsonian novel) or "the failed marriage plot" central to high modernist poetry and narrative. See Jonnes, *Matrix of Narrative*, especially chapter 11, "Family Paradigm, Story Sequence."

15. Yaeger, "Woman Without Any Bones," 107.

16. Qtd. in Schaub, *American Fiction in the Cold War*, 126.

17. O'Connor, *Habit of Being*, 90. Bacon, *Flannery O'Connor and Cold War Culture*, 28.

18. Ibid., 30.

19. O'Connor, *Mystery and Manners*, 134.

20. Palazzoli, Cirillo, Selvini, and Sorrentino, *Family Games*, 272. See May, *Homeward Bound*, 15.

21. Ibid., 14.

22. Bacon, *Flannery O'Connor and Cold War Culture*, 48. Corber, *In the Name of National Security*, 7.

23. Bacon, *Flannery O'Connor and Cold War Culture*, 47.

24. In discussion of the cases her team of therapists most frequently encountered, Palazzoli notes that these almost invariably involved families where parents felt an intense emotional involvement in their children: "The great majority of the families (we treated) features parents who place their offspring at the center of their lives. These are parents whose very identity is essentially reflected in their children's successful development, which is the key to their personal fulfillment. They are closely tied to their children by such behavior patterns as overprotection, morbidly anxious attachment, overindulgence, etc." (Palazzoli, Cirillo, Selvini, and Sorrentino, *Family Games*, 59). Dysfunction in such instances usually centered on a "transgenerational coalition"—one parent becoming overinvolved with a child—usually at the expense of the other parent.

25. Coontz, "Historical Perspectives on Family Studies," 284.

26. Shloss, *Flannery O'Connor's Dark Comedies*, 69.

27. Palazzoli refers to children in "rigidly dysfunctional systems" who "seem to willingly assume the role of reformers, by indicting an oppressed parent, by tying down a potentially fugitive parent, or by trying to take the place of an unsatisfactory one" (45). The "prescription" that her team developed—which essentially involves isolating and reestablishing the autonomy of the parent or parental couple—was "mainly designed to deal with the universally pathogenic phenomenon of blurrred intergenerational boundaries" (Palazzoli, Cirillo, Selvini, and Sorrentino, *Family Games*, 23).

28. Knapp, "Family Systems Psychotherapy, Literary Character, and Literature," 226.

29. The families that Palazzoli describes display distinct affinities with the sorts of families and the transactional patterns encountered in O'Connor's fiction: in both instances, families are in some sense "over-nuclearized," the parent-child relation characterized by high degree of dependency and overinvolvement, children are hyper-critical, and indeed, in the most extreme cases, have recourse to pathological acts. O'Connor's narratives of familial interaction would diverge from the patterns described by Palazzoli in the degree to which the children's critique of the parent is generally born out on the level of the diegesis—although this is counterbalanced by the child's belated recognition of who or what the parent qua parent has meant to him/her. But it is also worth noting that in her efforts to restore the parental couple to their "rightful" place, Palazzoli also presupposes a strength and degree of autonomy on the part of children who have become over-dependent, over-manipulative, or sought to

supplant a parent. In this sense, just as her therapeutic approach assumes a certain rejuvenescence of the parental couple (the parents should "steal away from home like two adolescents" [Palazzoli, Cirillo, Selvini, and Sorrentino, *Family Games*, 54]), it also ascribes adult-like attributes to children who must learn to fend for themselves.

30. O'Connor, *Everything That Rises Must Converge*, 41.

31. Ibid., 36, 44.

32. Ibid., 34.

33. Ibid., 36.

34. Ibid., 36, 45.

35. Ibid., 44.

36. Carter W. Martin, *True Country*, 137.

37. O'Connor, *A Good Man Is Hard to Find and Other Stories*, 53, 54, 56, 57, 60.

38. Ibid., 62.

39. Ibid., 65.

40. Ibid., 58.

41. Ibid., 174, 175.

42. Ibid., 175–76.

43. Ibid., 180.

44. Ibid., 184.

45. Ibid., 186.

46. O'Connor, *Everything That Rises Must Converge*, 148, 163.

47. Ibid., 150, 164, 151.

48. Ibid., 177.

49. Ibid., 187.

50. Ibid., 190.

51. Ibid., 117.

52. See Asals, *Flannery O'Connor*, 110.

53. O'Connor, *Everything That Rises Must Converge*, 130.

54. Ibid., 118.

55. Ibid., 117, 118.

56. Ibid., 121.

57. Ibid., 127.

58. Ibid., 128.

59. Palazzoli, Cirillo, Selvini, and Sorrentino, *Family Games*, 224.

60. O'Connor, *Everything That Rises Must Converge*, 134.

61. Storhoff, "Family Systems in Louise Erdrich's *The Beet Queen*," 344.

62. O'Connor, *Everything That Rises Must Converge*, 135.

63. Ibid., 136.

64. Ibid., 141.

65. Ibid., 118.

66. Ibid., 4, 83.

67. Ibid., 91, 98.

68. Ibid., 83–84.

69. Ibid., 92.

70. Ibid., 109.

71. Ibid., 91, 107.

72. Ibid., 90.

73. Ibid., 91.

74. Ibid., 103.

75. Ibid., 92.

76. Ibid., 114.

77. One can also observe here an echo of Robert Kegan's idea of the fifth balance (the interindividual), where "sharing the self at the level of intimacy permits the emotions and impulses to live in the intersection of systems, to be re-solved between one self system and another" (106). Hence, genuine independence does not mean freedom *from*, in the context of the family, but freedom *with* the family. This kind of freedom, ideally, recognizes appropriate boundaries while still maintaining a level of intimacy. See Kegan, *Evolving Self.*

78. O'Connor, *Everything That Rises Must Converge*, 4, 3.

79. Ibid., 6.

80. Palazzoli, Cirillo, Selvini, and Sorrentino, *Family Games*, 225.

81. O'Connor, *Everything That Rises Must Converge*, 4.

82. Ibid., 11.

83. Ibid., 12.

84. Ibid., 11.

85. Ibid., 9.

86. Ibid., 11.

87. Ibid., 22.

88. Ibid., 23.

89. Ibid.

General Bibliography

Adelman, Janet. *Suffocating Mothers: Fantasies of Maternal Origin in Shake-speare*. New York: Routledge, 1992.

Agazarian, Yvonne M. *Systems-Centered Therapy for Groups*. New York: Guilford, 1997.

Aguirre, Manuel. "Life, Crown, and Queen: Gertrude and the Theme of Sovereignty." *RES*, NS 47.186 (1996): 163–74.

Akhtar, Salman. "The Syndrome of Identity Diffusion." *American Journal of Psychiatry* 141 (1984): 1381–85.

Allen, Katherine R., Rosemary Blieszner, and Karen A. Roberto. "Families in the Middle and Later Years: A Review and Critique of Research in the 1990s." *Journal of Marriage and the Family* 62 (2000): 911–26.

Allen, William Rodney. *Conversations with Kurt Vonnegut*. Jackson: University Press of Mississippi, 1988.

Almeida, David M. Elaine Wethington, and Amy L. Chandler. "Daily Transmission of Tensions Between Marital Dyads and Parent-Child Dyads." *Journal of Marriage and the Family* 61 (1999): 49–61.

Andrews, John F. "Interview: Derek Jacobi on Shakespearean Acting." *Shakespeare Quarterly* 36.2 (1985): 134–40.

Archer, Sally. "A Feminist's Approach to Identity Research." In *Adolescent Identity Formation*, edited by Gerald R. Adams, Thomas P. Gullotta, and Raymond Montemayor, 25–49. Newbury Park, CA: Sage, 1992.

Ariel, Schlomo. *Culturally Competent Family Therapy: A General Model*. Westport, CT: Prager, 1999.

Aries, Phillippe. *Centuries of Childhood: A Social History of Family Life*. Trans. Robert Baldick. London: Cape, 1962.

Asals, Frederick. *Flannery O'Connor: The Imagination of Extremity*. Athens: University of Georgia Press, 1982.

Atwood, Joan D. "Social Construction Theory and Therapy Assumptions." In *Family Scripts*, edited by Joan D. Atwood, 1–33. Washington, DC: Accelerated Development, 1996.

Baber, Kristine, and Katherine Allen. *Women and Families: Feminist Reconstructions*. New York: Guilford, 1992.

Bacon, Francis. *The Works of Francis Bacon*. Ed. James Spedding, Robert Leslie Ellis, and Douglas Denon Heath. London: Longmans, 1857.

Bacon, Jon. *Flannery O'Connor and Cold War Culture*. New York: Cambridge University Press, 1993.

Baker, J. H. *An Introduction to English Legal History*. 3rd ed. London: Butterworths, 1990.

Barbauld, Anna Laetitia. *The Correspondence of Samuel Richardson*. 6 vols. London: Richard Phillips, 1804.

Barnard, Charles P., and Ramon Garrido Corrales. *The Theory and Technique of Family Therapy*. Springfield, IL: Thomas, 1979.

Barthes, Roland. *S/Z*. New York: Hill and Wang, 1974.

Barton, John. *Playing Shakespeare*. London: Methuen, 1984.

Bateson, Gregory. *Mind and Nature*. New York: Bantam, 1979.

———. *Steps to an Ecology of Mind*. New York: Ballantine, 1972.

Bateson, Gregory, et al. "Toward a Theory of Schizophrenia." *Behavioral Science* 1 (1956): 251–64.

Baumeister, Roy F. *Identity: Cultural Change and the Struggle for Self*. New York: Oxford University Press, 1986.

Bee, Helen. *The Journey of Adulthood*. 4th ed. Englewood Cliffs, NJ: Prentice Hall, 2000.

Beebee, Thomas O. *Clarissa on the Continent*. University Park, PA: Penn State University Press, 1990.

Beizer, Janet. *Family Plots: Balzac's Narrative Generations*. New Haven: Yale University Press, 1986.

Ben-Amos, Ilana Krausman. "Gifts and Favors: Informal Support in Early Modern England." *Journal of Modern History* 72 (2000): 295–338.

———. "Reciprocal Bonding: Parents and Their Offspring in Early Modern England." *Journal of Family History* 25.3 (2000): 291–312.

Bennett, Larry W. "Substance Abuse and Domestic Assault of Women." *Social Work* 40.6 (1995): 760–69.

Berg, Insoo Kim, and Ajakai Jaya. "Different and Same: Family Therapy with Asian-American Families." *Journal of Marital and Family Therapy* 19.1 (1993): 31–38.

Berger, Kathleen Stassen. *The Developing Person Through the Lifespan*. 5th ed. New York: Worth Publishers, 2001.

Berman, Jeffrey. *Diaries to an English Professor: Pain and Growth in the Classroom*. Amherst: University of Massachusetts Press, 1994.

Berry, Ralph. "Hamlet's Doubles." *Shakespeare Quarterly* 37.2 (1986): 204–12.

Berry, Wendell. *The Unsettling of America: Culture and Agriculture*. San Francisco: Sierra Club, 1977.

Berzoff, Joan. "From Separation to Connection: Shifts in Understanding Women's Development." *Affilia* 4 (1989): 45–58.

Billingsley, Andrew. *Climbing Jacob's Ladder: The Enduring Legacy of African-American Families*. New York: Simon and Schuster, 1992.

Bjork, Patrick Bryce. *The Novels of Toni Morrison: The Search for Self and Place within the Community*. New York: Peter Lang, 1992.

Blackford, Russell. "The Definition of Love: Kurt Vonnegut's *Slapstick*." In *The Critical Response to Kurt Vonnegut*, edited by Leonard Mustazza, 193–207. Westport, CT: Greenwood, 1994.

Blackstone, William. *Commentaries on the Laws of England*. 4 vols. Chicago: University of Chicago Press, 1979.

Bleich, David. *Readings and Feelings: An Introduction to Subjective Criticism*. Urbana, IL: NCTE, 1975.

Blincoe, Noel. "Is Gertrude an Adultress?" *ANQ* 10.4 (1997): 18–27.

Bloom, Harold. *Shakespeare: The Invention of the Human.* New York: Riverhead, 1998.

Bonetti, Kay. "An Interview with Maxine Hong Kingston." In *Conversations with Maxine Hong Kingston,* Skenazy and Martin, 33–46.

Bonfield, Lloyd. *Marriage Settlements, 1601–1740: The Adoption of Strict Settlement.* Cambridge: Cambridge University Press, 1983.

Boose, Lynda E. "The Family in Shakespeare Studies; or—Studies in the Family of Shakespeareans; or—The Politics of Politics." *Renaissance Quarterly* 40 (1987): 707–42.

———. "The Father and Bride in Shakespeare." *PMLA* 97.3 (1982): 325–47.

———. "Scolding Brides and Bridling Scolds: Taming the Woman's Unruly Member." *Shakespeare Quarterly* 42.2 (1991): 179–213.

Boscolo, Luigi, and Paolo Bertrando. "The Reflexive Loop of Past, Present, and Future in Systemic Therapy and Consultation." *Family Process* 31.2 (1992): 119–33.

Boscolo, Luigi, Gianfranco Cecchin, Lynn Hoffman, and Peggy Penn. *Milan Systemic Family Therapy: Conversations in Theory and Practice.* New York: Basic, 1987.

Boszormenyi-Nagy, Ivan, and James L. Framo. *Intensive Family Therapy: Theoretical and Practical Aspects.* New York: Harper and Row, 1965.

Bowen, Murray. *Family Therapy in Clinical Practice.* 3rd ed. Northvale, NJ: Jason Aronson, 1985.

Bradbury, Malcolm. "On from Murdoch." *Encounter* 31 (July 1968): 72–74.

Bretzius, Stephen. *Shakespeare in Theory: The Postmodern Academy and the Early Modern Theater.* Ann Arbor: University of Michigan Press, 1997.

Brittin, Alice A., and Kimberle Schumock López. "The Body Written: *L'écriture féminine* in Two Brazilian Novels: *A Hora da Estrela* and *As Mulheres de Tijucopapo.*" *Lucero* 1 (1990): 48–55.

Broer, Lawrence R. *Sanity Plea: Schizophrenia in the Novels of Kurt Vonnegut.* Tuscaloosa: University of Alabama Press, 1994.

Brontë, Charlotte. *Jane Eyre: Authoritative Text, Backgrounds, Criticism.* Ed. Richard J. Dunn. 2nd ed. New York: Norton, 1987.

Bump, Jerome. "D. H. Lawrence and Family Systems Theory." *Renascence* 44.1 (1991): 61–80.

———. "The Family Dynamics of the Reception of Art." *Style* 31.2 (1997): 328–50.

———. "Left vs. Right Side of the Brain: Hypermedia and the New Puritanism." *Currents in Electronic Literacy* 1.2 (1999). <www.cwrl.utexas.edu/currents/fall99/bump.html>.

———. "Teaching Emotional Literacy." In *Writing and Healing: Toward an Informed Practice,* edited by Charles M. Anderson and Marian M. MacCurdy, 313–35. Urbana, IL: NCTE, 2000.

Buss, Helen. "Memoir with an Attitude." *a/b: Auto/Biography Studies* 12.2 (1997): 203–24.

Byatt, A. S. *The Game.* New York: Vintage, 1992.

———. Introduction to *The Shadow of the Sun.* New York: Vintage, 1991.

————. *Passions of the Mind: Selected Writings.* New York: Vintage, 1993.

Byng-Hall, John. *Rewriting Family Scripts: Improvisations and Systems Change.* New York: Guilford, 1995.

Caminha, Edmílson. "Marilene Felinto: A Escritura Inconformada." In *Palavra de Escritor: Entrevistas com Carlos Drummond de Andrade*, by Edmílson Caminha, 181–88. 2nd ed. Brasília: Thesaurus, 1995.

Campbell, Jane. "The Hunger of the Imagination in A. S. Byatt's *The Game.*" *Critique* 29.3 (1998): 147–61.

Carroll, John. *Selected Letters of Samuel Richardson.* Oxford: Clarendon, 1964.

Carroll, Joseph. *Evolution and Literary History.* Columbia: University of Missouri Press, 1995.

Cavendish Wanderly, Márcia. "Imagens da Mulher na Ficção Feminina pós-64." In *Revista Mulheres e Literatura*, edited by Luiza Lobo. *Núcleo Interdisciplinar de Estudos da Mulher na Literatura.* <w3.openlink.com.br/mielm/cavendish.htm>.

————. "Quebec/Nordeste: esboço de análise comparativa entre os *romances Bonheur d'occasion*, de Gabriélle Roy, e *Mulheres de Tijucopapo*, de Marilene Felinto." In *Revista Mulheres e Literatura*, edited by Luiza Lobo. *Núcleo Interdisciplinar de Estudos da Mulher na Literatura.* <w3.openlink.com.br/mielm/cavendish.htm>.

Chan, Mimi, and Roy Harris. "Listen, Mom, I'm a Banana." In *Asian Voices in English*, edited by Mimi Chan and Roy Harris, 65–78. Hong Kong: Hong Kong University Press, 1991.

Chase, Richard. "The Brontës: A Centennial Observance." *Kenyon Review* 9 (1947): 487–506.

Cheung, King-Kok. "Don't Tell: Imposed Silences in *The Color Purple* and *The Woman Warrior.*" *PMLA* 103.2 (1988): 162–74.

————. "Self-Fulfilling Visions in *The Woman Warrior* and *Thousand Pieces of Gold.*" *Biography* 13.2 (1990): 143–53.

"Child's Play." *Times Literary Supplement* 19 January 1967: 41.

Chin, Frank. "The Most Popular Book in China." In *Maxine Hong Kingston's "The Woman Warrior,"* Wong, 23–28.

Christopherson, Victor A. "Implications for Strengthening Family Life: Rural Black Families." In *Building Family Strengths: Blueprints for Action*, edited by Nick Stinnett, Barbara Chesser, and John DeFrain, 67–73. Lincoln, PA: Lincoln University Press, 1979.

Churchman, C. West. *The Systems Approach.* New York: Delta, 1968.

Cohen, Paula Marantz. *The Daughter's Dilemma: Family Process and the Nineteenth-Century Domestic Novel.* Ann Arbor: University of Michigan Press, 1991.

Comerchero, Victor. *Nathanael West: The Ironic Prophet.* Seattle: University of Washington Press, 1964.

Coontz, Stephanie. "Historical Perspectives on Family Studies." *Journal of Marriage and the Family* 62 (2000): 283–97.

Corber, Robert J. *In the Name of National Security: Hitchcock, Homophobia, and the Political Construction of Gender in Postwar America.* Durham, NC: Duke University Press, 1993.

Court, Franklin. *Institutionalizing English Literature: The Culture and Politics of Literary Study, 1750–1900.* Stanford, CA: Stanford University Press, 1992.

Cox, Jane. *Hatred Pursued Beyond the Grave: Tales of Our Ancestors from the London Church Courts.* London: HMSO, 1993.

Creighton, Joanne V. "Sisterly Symbiosis: Margaret Drabble's *The Waterfall* and A. S. Byatt's *The Game.*" *Mosaic* 20.1 (1987): 15–29.

Cruttwell, Patrick. *The Shakespearean Moment.* New York: Vintage, 1960.

Dasenbrock, Reed Way. "Intelligibility and Meaningfulness in Multicultural Literature in English (Excerpts)." In *Maxine Hong Kingston's "The Woman Warrior,"* 159–69.

Davis, Todd F. "Apocalyptic Grumbling: Postmodern Humanism in the Work of Kurt Vonnegut." In *At Millennium's End: New Essays on the Work of Kurt Vonnegut*, edited by Kevin A. Boon, 149–65. Albany: State University of New York Press, 2001.

de Shazer, Steve. *Putting Difference to Work.* New York: Norton, 1991.

Decker, James M. "Choking on My Own Saliva: Henry Miller's Bourgeois Family Christmas in *Nexus.*" *Style* 31.2 (1997): 270–89.

Dee, Ruby. "Black Family in Search for Identity." *Freedomways* 11 (1971): 319.

Dell, O. F., and Harry Goolishian. "Order Through Fluctuation: An Evolutionary Epistemology for Human Systems." *Austrialian Journal of Family Therapy* 2 (1981): 175–84.

DeMarr, Mary Jean. *Barbara Kingsolver: A Critical Companion.* Westport, CT: Greenwood, 1999.

DeMause, Lloyd, ed. *The History of Childhood: The Untold Story of Child Abuse.* New York: Bedrick, 1988.

Demo, David H., and Martha J. Cox. "Families with Young Children: A Review of Research in the 1990s." *Journal of Marriage and the Family* 62 (2000): 876–95.

Desmond, John F. *Risen Sons: Flannery O'Connor's Vision of History.* Athens: University of Georgia Press, 1987.

Deutsch, M., and B. Brown. "Social Influences in Negro-White Intellectual Differences." *Social Issues* (1964): 27–36.

DiNicola, Vincenzo. *A Stranger in the Family: Culture, Families, and Therapy.* New York: Norton, 1997.

Durston, Christopher. *The Family in the English Revolution.* Oxford: Blackwell, 1989.

Dusinberre, Juliet. *Shakespeare and the Nature of Women.* 2nd ed. New York: St. Martin's Press, 1996.

Edelson, Marshall. *Language and Interpretation in Psychoanalysis.* 1975. Chicago: University of Chicago Press, 1984.

Elkaim, Mony. *If You Love Me, Don't Love Me: Constructions of Reality and Change in Family Therapy.* Trans. Hendon Chubb. New York: Basic, 1989.

Engelhardt, Tom. *The End of Victory Culture: Cold War America and the Disillusioning of a Generation.* Amherst: University of Massachusetts Press, 1998.

Erickson, Milton H. *Healing in Hypnosis.* New York: Irvington, 1983.

———. *My Voice Will Go With You: The Teaching Tales of Milton H. Erickson, M.D.* Ed. Sidney Rosen. New York: Norton, 1982.

Erikson, Erik H. *Childhood and Society.* 2nd ed. New York: Norton, 1963.

———. *Identity: Youth and Crisis.* New York: Norton, 1968.

Esterson, Allen. *Seductive Mirage: An Exploration of the Work of Sigmund Freud.* Chicago: Open Court, 1993.

Eugene, Toinette M., and James M. Poling. *Balm for Gilead: Pastoral Care for African American Families Experiencing Abuse.* Nashville: Abingdon, 1998.

Everett, Barbara. *Young Hamlet.* Oxford: Clarendon, 1989.

Felinto, Marilene. *As Mulheres de Tijucopapo.* Rio de Janeiro: Ed. Paz e Terra, 1982.

———. *The Women of Tijucopapo.* Trans. Irene Matthews. Lincoln: University of Nebraska Press, 1994.

Fergusson, Francis. *The Idea of a Theatre: A Study of Ten Plays.* 1949. Princeton: Princeton University Press, 1972.

Ferraro, Thomas J. *Ethnic Passages: Literary Immigrants in Twentieth-Century America.* Chicago: University of Chicago Press, 1993.

Ferreira-Pinto, Cristina. "Escritura, Auto-representação e Realidade Social no Romance Feminino Latino-Americano." *Revista de Crítica Literaria Latinoamericana* 45 (1997): 81–95.

Fierz, Charles L. "Polanski Misses: A Critical Essay Concerning Polanski's Reading of Hardy's *Tess.*" *Literature/Film Quarterly* 27.2 (1999): 103–9.

Fineman, Joel. "Fratricide and Cuckoldry: Shakespeare's Doubles." In *Representing Shakespeare,* Schwartz and Kahn, 70–109.

Finkelstein, Bonnie B. *Forster's Women: Eternal Differences.* New York: Columbia University Press, 1975.

Flannery, Joseph. Review of *The Game. Best Sellers* 28.1 (1968): 470W.

Fleischner, Jennifer. *A Reader's Guide to the Fiction of Barbara Kingsolver.* New York: HarperPerennial, 1994.

Fong, Bobby. "Maxine Hong Kingston's Autobiographical Strategy in *The Woman Warrior.*" *Biography* 12.2 (1989): 116–26.

Forster, E. M. *A Room with a View.* 1908. New York: Dover, 1995.

Fraiman, Susan. *Unbecoming Women: British Women Writers and the Novel of Development.* New York: Columbia University Press, 1993.

Framo, James L. "A Personal Retrospective of the Family Therapy Field: Then and Now." *Journal of Marital and Family Therapy* 22.3 (1996): 289–315.

Franz, Carol, and Abigail Stewart. *Women Creating Lives: Identities, Resilience, and Resistance.* Boulder, CO: Westview, 1994.

Frazier, E. F. *The Negro Family in the United States.* Chicago: University of Chicago Press, 1966.

Freud, Sigmund. *Introductory Lectures in Psychoanalysis.* Trans. and ed. James Strachey. New York: Norton, 1966.

———. *The Standard Edition of the Complete Psychological Works of Sigmund Freud.* Trans. James Strachey. Vol. 9. London: Hogarth, 1959.

Frye, Northrop. *Anatomy of Criticism: Four Essays.* New York: Atheneum, 1957.

Fullinwider-Bush, Nell, and Deborah B. Jacobvitz. "The Transition to Young Adulthood: Generational Boundary Dissolution and Female Identity Development." *Family Process* 32 (1993): 87–103.

Furness, Horace Howard. *Shakespeare's Hamlet: A New Variorum Edition.* Vol. 1. Philadelphia: J. B. Lippincott, 1905.

Furstenberg, Frank F. "The Sociology of Adolescence and Youth in the 1990s: A Critical Commentary." *Journal of Marriage and the Family* 62 (2000): 896–910.

Gallagher, Lowell. *"Mise en Abyme,* Narrative Subjectivity, and the Ethics of Mimesis in *Hamlet:* Gertrude Talks." *Genre* 28 (1995): 513–42.

Garcia, Lionel G. *Hardscrub.* Houston: Arte Publico, 1989.

Gates, Henry Louis, Jr. Introduction to *Toni Morrison: Critical Perspectives Past and Present,* edited by Henry Louis Gates, Jr., and Anthony Appiah, ix–xiii. New York: Amistad, 1993.

Gentry, Marshall Bruce. "Gender Dialogue in O'Connor." In *Flannery O'Connor,* Rath and Shaw, 57–72.

Gergen, Mary. "Finished at 40: Women's Development within the Patriarchy." *Psychology of Women Quarterly* 14 (1990): 471–93.

Gerrig, Richard J. *Experiencing Narrative Worlds: On the Psychological Activities of Reading.* New Haven: Yale University Press, 1993.

Giannone, Richard. "Displacing Gender: Flannery O'Connor's View from the Woods." In *Flannery O'Connor,* Shaw, 73–95.

Gibson, Richelle. "Discovering Your Roots: Extended Family History with Implications for the Systems Therapist." *Progress: Family Systems Research and Therapy* 3 (1994): 53–67.

Gilbert, Sandra M. "Plain Jane's Progress." In *Jane Eyre,* Beth Newman, 475–501.

Gilligan, Carol. *In a Different Voice.* Cambridge: Harvard University Press, 1982.

Gillis, John R. *A World of Their Own Making: A History of Myth and Ritual in Family Life.* Oxford: Oxford University Press, 1997.

Giobbi, Giuliana. "Sisters Beware of Sisters: Sisterhood as a Literary Motif in Jane Austen, A. S. Byatt, and I. Bossi Fredrigotti." *Journal of European Studies* 22 (1992): 240–58.

Goleman, Daniel. *Emotional Intelligence: Why It Can Matter More than IQ.* New York: Bantam, 1995.

Goodwin, Frederick K., and Kay Redfield Jamison. *Manic-Depressive Illness.* New York: Oxford University Press, 1990.

Gopnik, Alison, Andrew N. Meltzoff, and Patricia K. Kuhl. *The Scientist in the Crib: Minds, Brains, and How Children Learn.* New York: Morrow, 1999.

Gottlieb, Beatrice. *The Family in the Western World: From the Black Death to the Industrial Age.* Oxford: Oxford University Press, 1993.

Graff, Gerald. *Professing Literature: An Institutional History.* Chicago: University of Chicago Press, 1987.

Greene, Mott T. " 'Mom Always Liked You Best': Review of Frank Sulloway's *Born to Rebel.*" *Isis* 90 (1999): 332–38.

Gullestad, Marianne, and Martine Segalen, eds. *Family and Kinship in Europe.* London: Pinter, 1997.

Habakkuk, H. J. "Marriage Settlements in the Eighteenth Century." *Transactions of the Royal Historical Society,* 4th Ser., 32 (1950).

Haley, Jay. *Problem-Solving Therapy*. New York: Harper Colophon, 1976.

———. *Strategies of Psychotherapy*. New York: Grune and Stratton, 1963.

———. *Uncommon Therapy: The Psychiatric Techniques of Milton H. Erickson*. 1973. New York: Norton, 1986.

Hall, Elizabeth. "A Conversation with Erik Erikson." *Psychology Today* 17 (1983): 22–30.

Hapgood, Robert, ed. *Hamlet, Prince of Denmark: Shakespeare in Production*. Cambridge: Cambridge University Press, 1999.

Harding, Wendy, and Jacky Martin. *A World of Difference: An Inter-Cultural Study of Toni Morrison's Novels*. Westport, CT: Greenwood, 1994.

Hardy, Kenneth V. "The Theoretical Myth of Sameness." In *Minorities and Family Therapy*, edited by George W. Saba, Betty M. Karrer, and Kenneth V. Hardy, 17–34. New York: Haworth, 1990.

Heilbrun, Carolyn G. *Hamlet's Mother and Other Women*. New York: Columbia University Press, 1990.

Heinze, Denise. *The Dilemma of "Double-Consciousness": Toni Morrison's Novels*. Athens: University of Georgia Press, 1993.

Heller, Dana. "Reconstructing Kin: Family, History, and Narrative in Toni Morrison's *Beloved*." In *Race-ing Representation: Voice, History, Sexuality*, edited by Kostas Myrsiades, 213–30. Lanham, MD: Rowman and Littlefield, 1998.

Hilfer, Anthony C. "Critical Indeterminacies in Toni Morrison's Fiction." *Texas Studies in Language and Literature* 33.1 (1991): 91–95.

Hill, Robert B. *The Strengths of African American Families: Twenty-Five Years Later*. Lanham, MD: University Press of America, 1999.

Hines, Paulette Moore, and Nancy Boyd-Franklin. "African American Families." In *Ethnicity and Family Therapy*, edited by Monica McGoldrick, Joe Giordiano, and John Pearce, 66–84. New York: Guildford, 1996.

Hirsch, Marianne. *The Mother/Daughter Plot: Narrative, Psychoanalysis, Feminism*. Bloomington: Indiana University Press, 1989.

Hoffman, Lynn. *Foundations of Family Therapy: A Conceptual Framework for Systems Change*. New York: Basic, 1981.

Holaday, Woon-Ping Chin. "From Ezra Pound to Maxine Hong Kingston: A Bridging of Autobiography and Fiction." *Iowa Review* 10 (1979): 93–98.

Honan, Park. *Shakespeare: A Life*. New York: Oxford University Press, 1998.

Hong, George K. "Application of Cultural and Environmental Issues in Family Therapy with Immigrant Chinese Americans." *Journal of Strategic and Systemic Therapies* 8 (1989): 14–21.

Houlbrooke, Ralph A. *The English Family, 1450–1700*. London: Longman, 1984.

———, ed. *English Family Life, 1576–1716*. Oxford: Blackwell, 1988.

Hoy, Jody. "To Be Able to See the Tao." In *Conversations with Maxine Hong Kingston*, Skenazy and Martin, 47–66.

Hufton, Olwen. "Women, Work, and Family." In *A History of Women in the West*. Vol. 3. *Renaissance and Enlightenment Paradoxes*, edited by Natalie Zemon and Arlette Farge. Cambridge: Harvard University Press, 1993.

Hume, Kathryn. *Fantasy and Mimesis*. New York: Methuen, 1984.

Hunsaker, Steven. "Nation, Family, and Language in Victor Perera's *Rites* and

Maxine Hong Kingston's *The Woman Warrior*." *Biography* 20.4 (1997): 437–61.

Imber-Black, Evan. *Families and Larger Systems: A Family Therapist's Guide through the Labyrinth*. New York: Guilford, 1988.

———. *Secrets in Families and Family Therapy*. New York: Norton, 1993.

Ingram, Martin. *Church Courts, Sex, and Marriage in England, 1570–1640*. Cambridge: Cambridge University Press, 1987.

Jackson, Don D. "The Question of Family Homeostasis." *Psychiatric Quarterly Supplement* 31 (1957): 79–90.

Jardine, Lisa. "'No Offense i' th' world': *Hamlet* and Unlawful Marriage." In *Critical Essays on Shakespeare's Hamlet*, edited by David Scott Kastan, 258–73. New York: Prentice Hall, 1995.

———. *Reading Shakespeare Historically*. New York: Routledge, 1996.

———. *Still Harping on Daughters: Women and Drama in the Age of Shakespeare*. New York: Columbia University Press, 1989.

Jobling, Ian. "Personal Justice and Homicide in Scott's *Ivanhoe*: An Evolutionary Psychological Perspective." *Interdisciplinary Literary Studies* 2.2 (2001): 29–43.

Jones, Ernest. *Hamlet and Oedipus*. 1949. Garden City: Doubleday, 1954.

Jonnes, Denis. *The Matrix of Narrative: Family Systems and the Semiotics of Story*. Berlin: Mouton de Gruyter, 1990.

Josselson, Ruthellen. *Finding Herself: Pathways to Identity Development in Women*. San Francisco: Jossey-Bass, 1987.

———. *Revising Herself: The Story of Women's Identity from College to Midlife*. New York: Oxford University Press, 1996.

Kahane, Claire. "The Maternal Legacy: The Grotesque Tradition in Flannery O'Connor's Female Gothic." In *The Female Gothic*, edited by Juliann E. Fleenor, 242–56. Montreal: Eden, 1983.

Kahn, Coppélia. "The Providential Tempest and the Shakespearean Family." In *Representing Shakespeare*, Schwartz and Kahn, 217–43.

Kamps, Ivo. "Review. Shakespearean Criticism: 'It Is a Kind of History.'" *College English* 56.3 (1994): 331–47.

Kegan, Robert. *The Evolving Self: Problem and Process in Human Development*. Cambridge: Harvard University Press, 1982.

———. *In Over Our Heads: The Mental Demands of Modern Life*. Cambridge: Harvard University Press, 1994.

Kehler, Dorothea. "The First Quarto of *Hamlet*: Reforming the Widow Gertred." *Shakespeare Quarterly* 146.4 (1995): 398–413.

Kelley, Robin. *Yo' Mama's DisFunktional!: Fighting the Culture Wars in Urban America*. Boston: Beacon, 1997.

Kerr, Michael E. "Chronic Anxiety and Defining a Self." *Atlantic Monthly* (1988): 35–58.

Kerr, Michael E., and Murray Bowen. *Family Evaluation: The Role of the Family as an Emotional Unit that Governs Individual Behavior and Development*. New York: Norton, 1988.

Kerrigan, William. *Hamlet's Perfection*. Baltimore: Johns Hopkins University Press, 1996.

Kingsolver, Barbara. *Animal Dreams*. New York: HarperCollins, 1990.

Kingston, Maxine Hong. "Personal Statement." In *Approaches to Teaching Kingston's "The Woman Warrior,"* Lim, 23–25.

——. *The Woman Warrior: Memoirs of a Girlhood among Ghosts*. 1976. New York: Vintage, 1989.

Klinkowitz, Jerome. *Vonnegut in Fact: The Public Spokesmanship of Personal Fiction*. Columbia: University of South Carolina Press, 1998.

Knapp, John V. "Family Systems Psychotheraphy, Literary Character, and Literature: An Introduction." *Style* 31 (1997): 223–54.

——, ed. *Literary Character*. Lanham, MD: University Press of America, 1993.

——. "Situated Learning: Red-Eye Milton and the Loom of Learning." *Tomorrow's Professor* 236 (6 July 2000). Stanford University Learning Laboratory. <tomorrows-professor@lists.Stanford.edu>.

——. *Striking at the Joints: Contemporary Psychology and Literary Criticism*. Lanham, MD: University Press of America, 1996.

Knapp, John V., and Kenneth Womack, eds. "Family Systems Psychotherapy and Literature/Literary Criticism." *Style* 31.2 (1997).

Knights, L. C. *An Approach to Hamlet*. London: Chatto and Windus, 1961.

Kroger, Jane. *Identity Development: Adolescence through Adulthood*. Thousand Oaks, CA: Sage, 2000.

——. *Identity in Adolescence: The Balance between Self and Other*. 2nd ed. New York: Routledge, 1996.

Kubitschek, Missy Dehn. *Toni Morrison: A Critical Companion*. Westport, CT: Greenwood, 1998.

Lappas, Catherine. "The Way I Heard it Was . . .": Myth, Memory, and Autobiography in *Storyteller* and *The Woman Warrior*." *CEA Critic* 57.1 (1994): 57–67.

Larson, Reed, and David Almeida. "Emotional Transmission in the Daily Lives of Families: A New Paradigm for Studying Family Process." *Journal of Marriage and the Family* 61 (1999): 5–20.

Lawrence, D. H. *The Complete Short Stories*. New York: Viking, 1962.

Lee, Robert G. "*The Woman Warrior* as Intervention in Asian American Historiography." In *Approaches to Teaching Kingston's "The Woman Warrior,"* Lim, 52–63.

Lewis, Charlton M. *The Genesis of Hamlet*. New York: Henry Holt, 1907.

Lewis, Jerry M. *The Birth of the Family: An Empirical Study*. New York: Brunner/Mazel, 1989.

Lewis, Jerry M., and John G. Looney. *The Long Struggle: Well-Functioning Working-Class Black Families*. New York: Brunner/Mazel, 1983.

Li, David Liewei. "The Naming of a Chinese American 'I': Cross-Cultural Sign/ification in *The Woman Warrior*." *Criticism* 30 (1988): 497–515.

Lidoff, Joan. "Autobiography in a Different Voice." *a/b: Auto/Biography Studies* 3.3 (1987): 29–35.

Light, James F. *Nathanael West: An Interpretive Study*. 2nd ed. Evanston: Northwestern University Press, 1971.

Lim, Shirley Geok-lin, ed. *Approaches to Teaching Kingston's "The Woman Warrior*." New York: MLA, 1991.

Livingston, Paisley. *Models of Desire: Rene Girard and the Psychology of Mimesis*. Baltimore: Johns Hopkins University Press, 1992.

Loevinger, Jane. *Ego Development: Conceptions and Theories*. San Francisco: Jossey-Bass, 1976.

Long, Robert Emmet. *Nathanael West*. New York: Ungar, 1985.

Lott, Bret. *Jewel*. New York: Washington Square, 1991.

Lukacs, Georg. *The Theory of the Novel: A Historico-Philosophical Essay on the Forms of Great Epic Literature*. Trans. Anna Bostock. 1920. London: Merlin, 1971.

Lupton, Julia Reinhard, and Kenneth Reinhard. *After Oedipus: Shakespeare in Psychoanalysis*. Ithaca: Cornell University Press, 1993.

Lyotard, Jean-François. *The Postmodern Condition: A Report on Knowledge*. Trans. Geoff Bennington and Brian Massumi. Minneapolis: University of Minnesota Press, 1984.

Lytle, Jean L., Linda Bakken, and Charles Romig. "Adolescent Female Identity Development." *Sex Roles* 37 (1997): 175–85.

Mackey, Susan K. "Nurturance: A Neglected Dimension in Family Therapy with Adolescents." *Journal of Marital and Family Therapy* 22 (1996): 489–508.

Malin, Irving. *Nathanael West's Novels*. Carbondale: Southern Illinois University Press, 1972.

Manns, Wilhelmina. "Supportive Roles of Significant Others in African American Families." In *Black Families*, McAdoo, 198–213.

Marcia, James E. "Development and Validation of Ego Identity Status." *Journal of Personality and Social Psychology* 3 (1966): 551–58.

——. "The Ego Identity Status Approach to Ego Identity." In *Ego Identity: A Handbook for Psychosocial Research*, edited by James E. Marcia, Alan S. Waterman, Daniel R. Matteson, Sally L. Archer, and Jacob L. Orlofsky, 3–21. New York: Springer-Verlag, 1993.

——. "The Relational Roots of Identity." In *Discussions on Ego Identity*, edited by Jane Kroger, 101–20. Hillsdale, NJ: Lawrence Erlbaum, 1993.

"Marilene Morose." Review of *Les femmes de Tijucopapo*. Littétature Estrangère. Liberation.com. (19 March 1998). <liberation.com/livres/98 mars/980319felinto.html.>

Markstrom-Adams, Carol. "A Consideration of Intervening Factors in Adolescent Identity Formation." In *Adolescent Identity Formation*, edited by Gerald R. Adams, Thomas P. Gullota, and Raymond Montemayor, 173–92. Newbury Park, CA: Sage, 1992.

Martin, Carter W. *The True Country: Themes in the Fiction of Flannery O'Connor*. Nashville: Vanderbilt University Press, 1970.

Martin, Jay. *Nathanael West: The Art of His Life*. New York: Hayden, 1970.

Masson, Jeffery Moussaieff. *Final Analysis: The Making and Unmaking of a Psychoanalyst*. New York: HarperPerennial, 1991.

Matteson, David R. "Differences Within and Between Genders: A Challenge to the Theory." In *Ego Identity: A Handbook for Psychosocial Research*, edited by James E. Marcia, Alan S. Waterman, David R. Matteson, Sally L. Archer, and Jacob L. Orlofsky, 69–110. New York: Springer-Verlag, 1993.

Matthews, Irene. Afterword to *The Women of Tijucopapo*, by Marilene Felinto, 123–32. Lincoln: University of Nebraska Press, 1994.

May, Elaine Tyler. *Homeward Bound. American Families in the Cold War Era.* New York: HarperCollins, 1988.

Mayr, Ernst. *The Growth of Biological Thought.* Cambridge: Harvard University Press, 1982.

McAdams, Dan P. *Power, Intimacy, and the Life Story: Personological Inquiries into Identity.* New York: Guilford, 1988.

McAdoo, H. P., ed. *Black Families.* 3rd ed. Thousand Oaks, CA: Sage, 1997.

McDowell, Deborah E. "Reading Family Matters." In *Changing Our Words: Essays on Criticism, Theory and Writing by Black Women,* edited by Cheryl A. Wall, 389–415. New Brunswick: Rutgers University Press, 1989.

McGoldrick, Monica. "Women through the Family Life Cycle." In *Women in Families: A Framework for Family Therapy,* in Monica McGoldrick, Carol M. Anderson, and Froma Walsh, 200–226. New York: Norton, 1991.

McKay, Nellie Y. *Critical Essays on Toni Morrison.* Boston: G. K. Hall, 1988.

Miller, Elise. "Kingston's *The Woman Warrior*: The Object of Autobiographical Relations." In *Compromise Formations: Current Directions in Psychoanalytic Criticism,* edited by Vera J. Camden, 138–54. Kent, Ohio: Kent State University Press, 1989.

Miller, J. Hillis. *The Disappearance of God.* Cambridge: Harvard University Press, 1963.

Mince, John. "The Script as Life-Form: Parasites of Meaning." In *Family Scripts,* edited by Joan D. Atwood, 35–56. Washington, DC: Accelerated Development, 1996.

Minuchin, Salvador. *Families and Family Therapy.* Cambridge: Harvard University Press, 1974.

———. *Family Kaleidoscope.* Cambridge: Harvard University Press, 1984.

Minuchin, Salvador, and Michael P. Nichols. *Family Healing.* New York: Touchstone, 1993.

Minuchin, Salvador, Wai-Yung Lee, and George M. Simon. *Mastering Family Therapy: Journeys of Growth and Transformation.* New York: John Wiley, 1996.

Mitchell, Sally. *Daily Life In Victorian England.* Westport, CT: Greenwood, 1996.

Moore, G. E. *Principia Ethica.* 1902. Buffalo, NY: Prometheus, 1988.

Moore, Thomas. *Care of the Soul: A Guide for Cultivating Depth and Sacredness in Everyday Life.* New York: HarperCollins, 1992.

Mori, Aoi. *Toni Morrison and Womanist Discourse.* New York: Peter Lang, 1999.

Morris, Brian. Introduction to *The Arden Shakespeare: Taming of the Shrew,* by William Shakespeare. London: Methuen, 1981.

Morrison, Toni. *The Bluest Eye.* New York: Penguin, 1994.

Moynihan, Daniel Patrick. *The Negro Family: The Case for National Action.* Washington, DC: Office of Planning and Research, 1965.

Mulholland, Joan. "'Thou' and 'You' in Shakespeare: A Study in the Second-Person Pronoun." *English Studies* 48 (1967): 34–43.

Murray, Peter B. *Shakespeare's Imagined Persons.* Lanham, MD: Barnes and Noble, 1996.

Myers, Victoria. "The Significant Fictivity of Maxine Hong Kingston's *The Woman Warrior*." *Biography* 9.2 (1986): 112–25.

Napier, Augustus Y., and Carl Whitaker. *The Family Crucible*. 1978. New York: Harper Perennial, 1988.

Newman, Beth, ed. *Jane Eyre: Case Studies in Contemporary Criticism*, by Charlotte Brontë. New York: St. Martin's Press, 1996.

Newman, Karen. *Fashioning Femininity and English Renaissance Drama*. Chicago: University of Chicago Press, 1991.

Noice, Tony, and Helga Noice. *The Nature of Expertise in Professional Acting: A Cognitive View*. Mahwah, NJ: Lawrence Erlbaum, 1997.

Nussbaum, Martha C. *Love's Knowledge: Essays on Philosophy and Literature*. New York: Oxford University Press, 1990.

O'Brien, Ellen J. "Revision by Excision: Rewriting Gertrude." *Shakespeare Survey* 45 (1992): 27–35.

O'Connor, Flannery. *Everything That Rises Must Converge*. 1965. New York: Farrar, Straus, and Giroux, 1996.

———. *A Good Man Is Hard to Find and Other Stories*. 1955. New York: Harcourt Brace Jovanovich, 1976.

———. *The Habit of Being: Letters of Flannery O'Connor*. Ed. Sally Fitzgerald. New York: Random House, 1980.

———. *Mystery and Manners: Flannery O'Connor—Occasional Prose*. Ed. Sally Fitzgerald and Robert Fitzgerald. New York: Farrar, Straus, and Giroux, 1971.

O'Day, Rosemary. *The Family and Family Relationships, 1500–1900*. New York: St. Martin's Press, 1994.

"Of Marriage." *Grub Street Journal* 122 (4 May 1732).

Okin, Susan Moller. "Patriarchy and Married Women's Property in England: Questions on Some Current Views." *Eighteenth-Century Studies* 17 (1983–84): 129–38.

Outka, Paul. "Publish or Perish: Food, Hunger, and Self-Construction in Maxine Hong Kingston's *The Woman Warrior*." *Contemporary Literature* 38.3 (1997): 447–82.

Ozment, Steven. *Ancestors: The Loving Family in Old Europe*. Cambridge: Harvard University Press, 2001.

Page, Philip. *Dangerous Freedom: Fusion and Fragmentation in Toni Morrison's Novels* Jackson: University Press of Mississippi, 1995.

Palazzoli, Mara Selvini. *Work of Mara Selvini Palazzoli*. Ed. Matteo Selvini. Trans. Arnold J. Pomerans. London: Jason Aronson, 1988.

Palazzoli, Mara Selvini, Luigi Boscolo, Gianfranco Cecchin, and Giuliana Prata. *Paradox and Counterparadox: A New Model in the Therapy of the Family in Schizophrenic Transaction*. New York: Jason Aronson, 1978.

Palazzoli, Mara Selvini, Stefano Cirillo, Matteo Selvini, and Anna Maria Sorrentino. *Family Games: General Models of Psychotic Processes in the Family*. Trans. Veronica Kleiber. New York: Norton, 1989.

Patterson, Serena J., Ingrid Sochting, and James E. Marcia. "The Inner Space and Beyond: Women and Identity." In *Adolescent Identity Formation*, edited by Gerald R. Adams, Thomas P. Gullotta, and Raymond Montemayor, 9–24. Newbury Park, CA: Sage, 1992.

Paulsen, Frederich. *The German Universities: Their Character and Histori-cal Development*. London: Macmillan, 1895.

Paulson, Suzanne Morrow. *Flannery O'Connor: A Study of the Short Fiction*. Boston: Twayne, 1988.

Pechter, Edward. *What Was Shakespeare?: Renaissance Plays and Changing Critical Practice*. Ithaca: Cornell University Press, 1995.

Penna, João Camillo. "Marilene Felinto e a Diferença." *Revista de Crítica Li-teraria Latinoamericana* 41 (1995): 213–53.

Peters, Marie Ferguson. "Historical Note: Parenting Young Children in Black Families." In *Black Families*, McAdoo, 167–82.

Phelan, James. "Character, Progression, and the Mimetic-Didactic Distinc-tion." *Modern Philology* 84 (1987): 282–99.

———. *Reading People, Reading Plots: Character, Progression, and the Inter-pretation of Narrative*. Chicago: University of Chicago Press, 1989.

———. "Toward a Rhetorical Reader-Response Criticism: The Difficult, the Stubborn, and the Ending of *Beloved*." In *Toni Morrison: Critical And Theo-retical Approaches*, edited by Nancy J. Peterson, 225–44. Baltimore: Johns Hopkins University Press, 1997.

Piercy, Fred P., and Douglas H. Sprenkle. "Marriage and Family Therapy: A Decade Review." *J. of Marriage and the Family* 52 (1990): 1116–26.

Piercy, Fred P., Douglas H. Sprenkle, and Joseph L. Wetchler, eds. *Family Therapy Sourcebook*. 2nd ed. New York: Guilford, 1996.

Pilalis, Jennie, and Joy Anderton. "Feminism and Family Therapy—A Possible Meeting Point." *Journal of Family Therapy* 8 (1986): 99–114.

———. *Forgotton Children: Parent-Child Relations from 1500–1900*. Cam-bridge: Cambridge University Press, 1983.

Pollock, Linda. *A Lasting Relationship: Parents and Children over Three Cen-turies*. Hanover, NH: University Press of New England, 1987.

Powers, William T. *Behavior: The Control of Perception*. Chicago: Aldine, 1973.

Puri, Usha. *Towards a New Womanhood: A Study of Black Women Writers*. Jaipur, India: Printwell, 1989.

Putnam, Robert D. *Bowling Alone: The Collapse and Revival of American Community*. New York: Simon and Schuster, 2000.

Rabinowitz, Peter J. *Before Reading: Narrative Conventions and the Politics of Interpretation*. Ithaca: Cornell University Press, 1987.

Rahman, Tariq. "The Double-Plot in E. M. Forster's *A Room with a View*." *Ca-hiers Victoriens et Édouardiens* 33 (1991): 43–62.

Rainwater, Catherine. "Worthy Messengers: Narrative Voices in Toni Morris-on's Novels." *Texas Studies in Language and Literature* 33.1 (1991): 96–113.

Rainwater, Lee, and William L. Yancey, eds. *The Moynihan Report and the Pol-itics of Controversy*. Cambridge: MIT Press, 1967.

Randall, William Lowell. *The Stories We Are: An Essay on Self-Creation*. To-ronto: University of Toronto Press, 1995.

Rath, Sura P., and Mary Neff Shaw, eds. *Flannery O'Connor: New Perspec-tives*. Athens: University of Georgia Press, 1996.

Reed, Peter J. "Lonesome Once More: The Family Theme in Kurt Vonnegut's

Slapstick." In *The Vonnegut Chronicles: Interviews and Essays*, edited by Peter J. Reed and Marc Leeds, 113–22. Westport, CT: Greenwood, 1996.

Regt, Ali de. "Inheritance and Relationships between Family Members." In *Family and Kinship in Europe*, Gullestad and Segalen, 146–63.

Reid, Randall. *The Fiction of Nathanael West.* Chicago: University of Chicago Press, 1967.

Richardson, Barbara Blayton. "Racism and Child-Rearing: A Study of Black Mothers." Ph.D. diss., Claremont Graduate University, 1981.

Richardson, Samuel. *Clarissa, or The History of a Young Girl.* 1747–48. Ed. Angus Ross. London: Penguin, 1985.

Rivers, Rose Merry, and John Scanzoni. "Social Families Among African Americans: Policy Imperatives for Children." In *Black Families*, McAdoo, 338–48.

Robbins, Bruce. "Modernism and Literary Realism: A Response." In *Realism and Representation*, edited by George Levine, 225–31. Madison: University of Wisconsin Press, 1993.

Robert, Marthe. *Origins of the Novel.* 1972. Trans. Sacha Rabinovitch. Bloomington: Indiana University Press, 1980.

Roberts, Janine. *Tales and Transformations: Stories in Families and Family Therapy.* New York: Norton, 1994.

Rosen, Sidney, ed. *My Voice Will Go with You. The Teaching Tales of Milton H. Erickson, M.D.* New York: Norton, 1982.

Russell, John. *Hamlet and Narcissus.* Newark: University of Delaware Press, 1995.

Rychlak, Joseph F. "A Psychotherapist's Lessons from the Philosophy of Science." *American Psychologist* 55.10 (2000): 1126–32.

Ryff, Carol, and Susan Migdal. "Intimacy and Generativity: Self-Perceived Transitions." *Signs* 9 (1984): 470–81.

Sadoff, Diane F. "The Father, Castration, and Female Fantasy in *Jane Eyre.*" In *Jane Eyre*, Newman, 518–35.

Sáenz de Tejada, Cristina. "Raza y género en la narrativa femenina afro-brasileña." *Revista de Crítica Literaria Latinoamericana* 46 (1997): 269–85.

———. "Representaciones de la negritud brasileña en *Mulher no Espelho* y *As Mulheres de Tijucopapo.*" *Afro-Hispanic Review* 16 (1997): 45–52.

Salzinger, Kurt. "The Road from Vulnerability to Episode: A Behavioral Analysis." *Psycoloquy* 2.5 (1991).

Satir, Virginia. *Conjoint Family Therapy.* 1964. Palo Alto, CA: Science and Behavior Books, 1967.

———. *The New Peoplemaking.* Mountain View: Science and Behavior Books, 1988.

Schachter, Frances Fuchs. "Sibling Deidentification and Split-Parent Identification: A Family Tetrad." In *Sibling Relationships: Their Nature and Significance Across the Life-Span*, edited by Michael E. Lamb and Brian Sutton-Smith, 123–52. Hillsdale, NJ: Lawrence Erlbaum, 1982.

Schaub, Thomas Hill. *American Fiction in the Cold War.* Madison: University of Wisconsin Press, 1991.

Schoenbaum, Samuel. *Shakespeare's Lives.* Rev. ed. Oxford: Clarendon, 1991.

Schueller, Malini. "Questioning Race and Gender Definitions: Dialogic Subversions in *The Woman Warrior*." *Criticism* 31 (1989): 421–37.

Schwartz, Murray, and Coppélia Kahn, eds. *Representing Shakespeare: New Psychoanalytic Essays*. Baltimore: Johns Hopkins University Press, 1980.

Schwarz, Joan I. "Clarissa and the Law: Inheritance, Abduction, and Rape." Ph.D. diss., University of Wisconsin, Madison, 1993.

———. "Eighteenth-Century Abduction Law and *Clarissa*." In *Clarissa and Her Readers: New Essays for the Clarissa Project*, edited by Carol Houlihan Flynn and Edward Copeland, 269–308. New York: AMS, 1999.

Segalen, Martine. *Historical Anthropology of the Family*. Trans. J. C. Whitehouse and Sarah Matthews. Cambridge: Cambridge University Press, 1986.

Shakespeare, William. *The Arden Shakespeare: Hamlet*. 1982. Ed. Harold Jenkins. Surrey: Thomas Nelson, 1997.

———. *The Arden Shakespeare: Taming of the Shrew*. Ed. Brian Morris. London: Methuen, 1981.

———. *The Riverside Shakespeare*. Ed. G. Blakemore Evans. Boston: Houghton Mifflin, 1974.

Shaw, George Bernard. *Three Plays for Puritans*. New York: Brentanos, 1904.

Shloss, Carol. *Flannery O'Connor's Dark Comedies: The Limits of Inference*. Baton Rouge: Louisiana State University Press, 1980.

Showalter, Elaine. "Representing Ophelia: Women, Madness, and the Responsibilities of Feminist Criticism." In *Shakespeare and the Question of Theory*, edited by Patricia Parker and Geoffrey Hartman, 77–94. New York: Methuen, 1985.

Shuttleworth, Sally. *Charlotte Brontë and Victorian Psychology*. Cambridge: Cambridge University Press, 1996.

Simmons, Diane. *Maxine Hong Kingston*. New York: Twayne, 1999.

Simon, Fritz B., Helm Stierlin, and Lyman C. Wynne. *The Language of Family Therapy: A Systemic Vocabulary and Sourcebook*. New York: Family Process, 1985.

Skenazy, Paul. "Kingston at the University." In *Conversations with Maxine Hong Kingston*, Skenazy and Martin, 118–58.

Skenazy, Paul, and Tera Martin, eds. *Conversations with Maxine Hong Kingston*. Jackson: University Press of Mississippi, 1998.

Sluzki, Carlos E., and Eliseo Veron. "The Double Bind as a Universal Pathogenic Situation." In *Double Bind: The Foundation of the Communicational Approach to the Family*, edited by Carlos E. Sluski and Donald C. Ransom, 251–62. New York: Grune and Stratton, 1976.

Smith, Rebecca. "'A Heart Cleft in Twain': The Dilemma of Shakespeare's Gertrude." In *The Woman's Part: Feminist Criticism of Shakespeare*, edited by Carolyn Ruth Swift Lenz, Gayle Greene, and Carol Thomas Neely, 194–210. Urbana: University of Illinois Press, 1980.

Snarey, John. *How Fathers Care for the Next Generation*. Cambridge: Harvard University Press, 1993.

Spaights, Ernest. "The Therapeutic Implications of Working with the Black Family." *Journal of Instructional Psychology* 17.4 (1990): 183–89.

Spector, Judith Anne. "Anne Tyler's *Dinner at the Homesick Restaurant*: A Critical Feast." *Style* 31 (1997): 310–27.

Spring, Eileen. "Strict Settlement Law." In *Law, Economy, and Society, 1750–1914: Essays in the History of English Law*, edited by G. R. Rubin and David Sugarman, 168–91. Abingdon, UK: Professional Books, 1984.

Staples, Robert. *The Black Family: Essays and Studies*. 5th ed. New York: Van Nostrand Reinhold, 1994.

States, Bert O. *Hamlet and the Concept of Character*. Baltimore: Johns Hopkins University Press, 1992.

Staves, Susan. *Married Women's Separate Property in England, 1660–1833*. Cambridge: Harvard University Press, 1990.

———. "Separate Maintenance Contracts." *Eighteenth-Century Life* 11 (1987): 78–101.

Stern, Daniel N. *The Interpersonal World of the Infant: A View From Psychoanalysis and Developmental Psychology*. New York: Basic, 1985.

Stewart, Michelle Pagni. "Moynihan's 'Tangle of Pathology': Toni Morrison's Legacy of Motherhood." In *Family Matters in the British and American Novel*, edited by Andrea O'Reilly Herrera, Elizabeth Mahn Nollen, and Sheila Reitzel Foor, 237–54. Bowling Green, OH: Bowling Green State University Press, 1997.

Stone, Lawrence. *The Family, Sex, and Marriage in England, 1500–1800*. New York: Harper and Row, 1977.

Storey, Robert. *Mimesis and the Human Animal: On the Biogenetic Foundations of Literary Representation*. Evanston, IL: Northwestern University Press, 1996.

Storhoff, Gary. "'Anaconda Love': Parental Enmeshment in Toni Morrison's *Song of Solomon*." *Style* 31 (1997): 290–309.

———. "Family Systems in Louise Erdrich's *The Beet Queen*." *Critique* 39.4 (1998): 341–52.

———. "Faulkner's Family Crucible: Quentin's Dilemma." *Mississippi Quarterly* 51.3 (1998): 465–82.

Subotnick, Kenneth L., and Keith H. Nuechterlein. "Prodromal Signs and Symptoms of Schizophrenia Relapse." *Journal of Abnormal Behavior* 97.4 (1988): 405–12.

Sullivan, Zohreh T. "Forster's Symbolism: *A Room with a View*, Fourth Chapter." *Journal of Narrative Technique* 6 (1976): 217–23.

Sulloway, Frank J. *Born to Rebel: Birth Order, Family Dynamics, and Creative Lives*. New York: Vintage, 1997.

Tatum, Beverly Daniel. "Out There Stranded?: Black Families in White Communities." In *Black Families*, McAdoo, 214–33.

Temple, Sir William. *An Essay on Popular Discontents. Miscellanea. The Third Part*. 1701.

Thornton, E. M. *The Freudian Fallacy: An Alternative View of Freudian Theory*. New York: Dial, 1984.

Titelman, Peter. "Overview of the Bowen Theoretical-Therapeutic System." In *Clinical Applications of Bowen Family System Theory*, edited by Peter Titelman, 7–49. New York: Haworth, 1998.

Todd, Emmanuel. *The Making of Modern France: Politics, Ideology, and Culture*. Oxford: Blackwell, 1991.

Traub, Valerie. *Desire and Anxiety: Circulations of Sexuality in Shakespearean Drama*. New York: Routledge, 1992.

Trumbach, Randolph. *The Rise of the Egalitarian Family*. New York: Academic, 1978.

TuSmith, Bonnie. "Literary Tricksterism: Maxine Hong Kingston's *The Woman Warrior: Memoirs of a Girlhood among Ghosts*." In *Anxious Power: Reading, Writing, and Ambivalence in Narratives by Women*, edited by Carol J. Singley and Susan Elizabeth Sweeney, 279–94. Albany: State University of New York Press, 1993.

Tyrell, Lynne. "Storytelling and Moral Agency." In *Toni Morrison's Fiction: Contemporary Criticism*, edited by David Middleton, 3–26. New York: Garland, 1997.

Updike, John. "All's Well in Skyscraper National Park." In *Critical Essays on Kurt Vonnegut*, edited by Robert Merrill, 40–47. Boston: G. K. Hall, 1990.

Van Boheemen, Christine. *The Novel as Family Romance: Language, Gender, and Authority from Fielding to James Joyce*. Ithaca: Cornell University Press, 1987.

Vancouver, Jeffery B. "Living Systems Theory as a Paradigm for Organizational Behavior: Understanding Humans, Organizations, and Social Processes." *Behavioral Sciences* 41 (1996): 165–204.

VanSpanckeren, Kathryn. "The Asian Literary Background of *The Woman Warrior*." In *Approaches to Teaching Kingston's "The Woman Warrior*," Lim, 44–51.

Veitch, Jonathan. *American Superrealism: Nathanael West and the Politics of Representation in the 1930s*. Madison: University of Wisconsin Press, 1997.

Vendler, Helen. *The Art of Shakespeare's Sonnets*. Cambridge: Harvard University Press, 1997.

Vickers, Brian. *Appropriating Shakespeare: Contemporary Critical Quarrels*. New Haven: Yale University Press, 1993.

Virgil. *The Aeneid of Virgil*. Trans. Rolfe Humphries. New York: Charles Scribner's Sons, 1951.

Visher, Emily B., and John S. Visher. *Therapy with Stepfamilies*. New York: Brunner/Mazel, 1996.

von Bertalanffy, Ludwig. *General Systems Theory: Foundations, Development, and Application*. New York: George Braziller, 1968.

Vonnegut, Kurt. *Cat's Cradle*. New York: Dell, 1963.

———. *Fates Worse than Death*. New York: G. P. Putnam's Sons, 1991.

———. *God Bless You, Dr. Kevorkian*. New York: Seven Stories, 1999.

———. *Hocus Pocus*. New York: G. P. Putnam's Sons, 1990.

———. *Palm Sunday: An Autobiographical Collage*. New York: Delacorte, 1981.

———. *Slapstick, Or Lonesome No More*. New York: Delacorte/Seymour Lawrence, 1976.

———. *Slaughterhouse-Five*. New York: Dell, 1969.

———. *Wampeters, Foma, and Granfalloons*. New York: Delacorte/Seymour Lawrence, 1974.

Wang, Linda. "Marriage and Family Therapy with People from China." *Contemporary Family Therapy* 16.1 (1994): 25–37.

Wang, Wayne, dir. *Dim Sum: A Little Bit of Heart.* With Laureen Chew and Kim Chew. Pacific Arts Video, 1987.

Watzlawick, Paul. *The Language of Change.* New York: Basic, 1978.

Watzlawick, Paul, Janet Beavin Bavelas, and Don D. Jackson. *Pragmatics of Human Communication: A Study of Interactional Patterns, Pathologies, and Paradoxes.* New York: Norton, 1967.

Watzlawick, Paul, John Weakland, and Richard Fisch. *Change: Principles of Problem Formation and Problem Resolution.* New York: Norton, 1974.

Weinstein, Gerald, and Mario D. Fantini, eds. *Toward Humanistic Education: A Curriculum of Affect.* New York: Praeger, 1970.

Wells, Gordon. *Dialogic Inquiry: Towards a Sociocultural Practice and Theory of Education.* Cambridge: Cambridge University Press, 1999.

West, Nathanael. *The Day of the Locust.* 1939. New York: Norton, 1975.

Westling, Louise. "Fathers and Daughters in Welty and O'Connor." In *The Female Tradition in Southern Literature,* edited by Carol S. Manning, 110–24. Urbana: University of Illinois Press, 1993.

Wetchler, Joseph L., and Fred P. Piercy. "Transgenerational Family Therapies." In *Family Therapy Sourcebook,* Piercy, Sprenkle, and Wetchler, 25–49.

Wheeler, Richard P. "Death in the Family: The Loss of a Son and the Rise of Shakespearean Comedy." *Shakespeare Quarterly* 51.2 (2000): 127–53.

Whitaker, Carl A., and William M. Bumberry. *Dancing with the Family: A Symbolic-Experiential Approach.* New York: Brunner/Mazel, 1988.

Whitbourne, Susan K. *The Aging Individual: Physical and Psychological Perspectives.* New York: Springer-Verlag, 1996.

———. *The Me I Know: A Study of Adult Identity.* New York: Springer-Verlag, 1986.

White, Michael, and David Epston. *Narrative Means to Therapeutic Ends.* New York: Norton, 1990.

Whitt, Margaret Early. *Understanding Flannery O'Connor.* Columbia: University of South Carolina Press, 1995.

Willie, C. V., and S. L. Greenblatt. "Four 'Classic' Studies of Power Relationships in Black Families." *Journal of Marriage and the Family* 40 (1978): 691–94.

Wilson, Thomas Sir. *The State of England, Ann Dom. 1660.* Ed. F. J. Fisher. The Manuscripts among the State Papers in the Public Record Office. London: Offices of the Society, 1936.

Winnicott, D. W. *The Maturational Process and the Facilitating Environment.* New York: International Universities Press, 1965.

———. *Playing and Reality.* 1971. London: Routledge, 1991.

Wisker, Alistair. *The Writing of Nathanael West.* New York: St. Martin's, 1990.

Womack, Kenneth. "'Only Connecting' with the Family: Class, Culture, and Narrative Therapy in E. M. Forster's *Howards End.*" *Style* 31 (1997): 255–69.

———. "A Passage to Italy: Narrating the Family in Crisis in E. M. Forster's *Where Angels Fear to Tread.*" *Mosaic* 33.3 (2000): 129–44.

————. "Unmasking Another Villain in Conrad Aiken's Autobiographical Dream." *Biography* 19.2 (1996): 137–57.

Wong, Sau-ling Cynthia. "Autobiography as Guided Chinatown Tour?: Maxine Hong Kingston's *The Woman Warrior* and the Chinese-American Autobiographical Controversy." In *Multicultural Autobiography: American Lives*, edited by James Robert Payne, 248–79. Knoxville: University of Tennessee Press, 1992.

————. Introduction to *Maxine Hong Kingston's "The Woman Warrior,"* Wong, 3–14.

————, ed. *Maxine Hong Kingston's "The Woman Warrior": A Casebook.* New York: Oxford University Press, 1999.

————. *Reading Asian American Literature: From Necessity to Extravagance.* Princeton: Princeton University Press, 1993.

Woodward, Amanda L. "Infants Selectively Encode the Goal Object of an Actor's Reach." *Cognition* 69 (1998): 1–34.

Wyatt, Bryan N. "The Domestic Dynamics of Flannery O'Connor: *Everything That Rises Must Converge.*" *Twentieth-Century Literature* 38.1 (1992): 66–87.

Yaeger, Patricia Smith. "The Woman Without Any Bones: Anti-Angel Aggression in *Wise Blood*." In *New Essays on Wise Blood*, edited by Michael Kreyling, 91–116. New York: Cambridge University Press, 1995.

Zeldin, Theodore. *An Intimate History of Humanity.* London: Vintage, 1998.

Zomchik, John P. *Family and the Law in Eighteenth-Century Fiction: The Public Conscience in the Private Sphere.* Cambridge: Cambridge University Press, 1993.

Notes on Contributors

Rosemary D. Babcock is a doctoral candidate in the Department of English at Northern Illinois University. Her scholarly interests concern the cultural history of nineteenth-century British fiction.

Jerome Bump is Professor of English at the University of Texas at Austin. The former editor of *Texas Studies in Language and Literature*, he is the author of two volumes on Gerard Manley Hopkins, as well as numerous articles. He is currently working on a book on family systems and literary study.

Sara E. Cooper is Assistant Professor of Spanish at California State University, Chico, where she is a teacher-scholar focusing on feminist and queer analysis of contemporary Latin American women and their cultural production. Cooper is the author of a number of articles and translations regarding Latin American literature. Her current projects include a critical analysis of queer family in Latin American literature and the editing of two volumes—a multiauthored volume of critical essays on family systems in Hispanic literature and a collection of translated short stories by the Cuban writer Mirta Yañez.

Todd F. Davis is Associate Professor of English at Goshen College. The author of numerous articles and reviews in such journals as *Critique, Studies in Short Fiction, Style, Mississippi Quarterly*, and *Yeats/Eliot Review*, among other quarterlies, Davis is the author of *Ripe*, a book of poems, and the coeditor of *Mapping the Ethical Turn: A Reader in Ethics, Culture, and Literary Theory*.

James M. Decker is Associate Professor of English at Mount St. Clare College, and his research focuses on narrative space in various works of American literature. His articles have appeared in such journals as *Deus Loci, George Eliot-George Henry*

Lewes Studies, Paintbrush, and *PMPA.* He is currently revising a manuscript on Henry Miller's narrative form.

LEE ANN DE REUS is Assistant Professor of Human Development and Family Studies and Women's Studies at Penn State Altoona. She has published numerous articles and book chapters on such subjects as feminist pedagogy and women's adult development, including issues of identity and generativity. Her work was recently featured in *Competence and Character through Life,* edited by Anne Colby, Jacquelyn James, and Daniel Hart, as well as in *Generativity and Adult Development: How and Why We Care for the Next Generation,* edited by Dan P. McAdams and Ed de St. Aubin.

DENIS JONNES is Visiting Professor of English at Kyushu University in Fukuoka, Japan. His publications include *The Matrix of Narrative: Family Systems and the Semiotics of Story,* as well as various articles on narratology in such journals as the *Journal of Narrative Technique, Journal of Literary Semantics, Lessing Yearbook,* and *Colloquia Germanica.* He is currently at work on a volume entitled *Children of Empire: Generational Politics in American Postwar Literature,* which examines parent-child centered narrative in the texts of such writers as William Styron, Flannery O'Connor, Vladimir Nabokov, Jack Kerouac, Sylvia Plath, Arthur Miller, Tennessee Williams, and William Inge.

JOHN V. KNAPP is Professor of English at Northern Illinois University, where he has taught modern literature and teacher training since 1971. He is author of *Striking at the Joints: Contemporary Psychology and Literary Criticism* and many articles on British literature. He has recently completed a dissertation in Educational Psychology at the University of Wisconsin-Madison entitled "Red-Eye Milton and the Loom of Learning: English Professor Expertise."

MARCO MALASPINA is a doctoral candidate at the University of Pisa, Italy. He is the author of *LIZ: Manuale per lo studente,* a textbook of Italian literature for high school students. His dissertation applies family systems theory to Shakespeare's plays. He is the coeditor of *The Why of Literature.*

JOAN I. SCHWARZ is an attorney in Stoughton, Wisconsin, where she has her own practice specializing in employment discrimination and family law. She is also a lecturer in the Departments of Languages and Literatures and of Women's Studies at the University of Wisconsin-Whitewater, where she teaches interdisciplinary courses in law and literature, and gender and the law. Her essay, "Eighteenth-Century Abduction Law and *Clarissa*," recently appeared in *Clarissa and Her Readers: New Essays for the Clarissa Project*, edited by Carol Houlihan Flynn and Edward Copeland.

STEVEN SNYDER is Associate Professor of Humanities at Grand View College in Des Moines, Iowa, where he directs the Interdisciplinary Studies program and teaches in the LOGOS great books curriculum.

GARY STORHOFF is Associate Professor of English at the University of Connecticut at Stamford. In addition to his many publications on American and African-American literature, Storhoff has published articles using family systems therapy on works by William Faulkner and Louise Erdrich. He is currently writing a book on family systems theory and American literature.

KENNETH WOMACK is Associate Professor of English at Penn State Altoona. In addition to coauthoring *Recent Work in Critical Theory, 1989–1995: An Annotated Bibliography* and coediting three volumes on *British Book-Collectors and Bibliographers* in the *Dictionary of Literary Biography* series, Womack is the coeditor of *Mapping the Ethical Turn: A Reader in Ethics, Culture, and Literary Theory*. He is editor of *Interdisciplinary Literary Studies: A Journal of Criticism and Theory*, as well as coeditor of the internationally acclaimed *Year's Work in English Studies*.

Index